THE PASSING
OF TRADITIONAL SOCIETY

Modernizing The Middle East

By DANIEL LERNER

with the assistance of LUCILLE W. PEVSNER

and an introduction by DAVID RIESMAN

THE FREE PRESS OF GLENCOE
COLLIER-MACMILLAN LIMITED, LONDON

FIRST FREE PRESS PAPERBACK EDITION 1964

For information, address:
The Free Press of Glencoe
A Division of The Macmillan Company
The Crowell-Collier Publishing Company
60 Fifth Avenue, New York, N. Y., 10011

Collier-Macmillan Canada, Ltd., Toronto, Ontario

DESIGNED BY SIDNEY SOLOMON

Library of Congress Catalog Card Number: 58-6487

For My Mother

L O U E T T A   L E R N E R

Who Passed From Traditional Ways
To A Modern Style
With Dignity And Grace

This book is sponsored jointly by
The Center for International Studies, Massachusetts Institute of Technology,
AND
The Bureau of Applied Social Research, Columbia University.

The field studies were conducted by the Columbia Bureau, which produced the following country reports:

TURKEY — Daniel Lerner, George K. Schueller, Mary Stycos
LEBANON-SYRIA — William N. McPhee, Rolf B. Meyersohn
EGYPT — Patricia L. Kendall, Benjamin B. Ringer
JORDAN — Joseph M. Stycos
IRAN — Benjamin B. Ringer, David L. Sills

The book was prepared, with assistance from
Paul L. Berkman of the Columbia Bureau,
under the auspices of the M.I.T. Center.

Preface to the Paperback Edition

A DECADE of effort went into the studies from which this book was made. Another half-decade has passed since the book appeared. These fifteen years have witnessed the passing of traditional society from every continent. No area of the world has resisted the attractions, despite the increasingly evident risks, of modernization. The emerging nations have hastened to become new states and emulate the ways of modern societies.

Haste has made waste; risks have turned into losses. The "want: get ratio" has been upset—since people have learned to want for more than they can get. As a result, the "revolution of rising expectations" we celebrated so confidently fifteen years ago has, in many places, become a "revolution of rising frustrations." Modernization, it now appears, is harder than one supposed. Why is this so? Two difficulties are paramount.

One is a "technical" difficulty—or can be made to seem so. This is the problem of raising income fast and high enough so that poor people, while raising their own consumption to acceptable levels, will still have something left over to save. These savings—so runs the technical argument—will then go into investment that raises production levels, which in turn will again raise both consumption and saving levels. In this way there will be generated a self-sustaining cycle of growth to replace the vicious circle of poverty in which most traditional societies still live.

The trouble with this cogent technical solution is people. They don't do what, on any rational course of behavior, they should do. They want more consumption, but they don't worry about saving and think little about productive investment. Instead of limiting their families, so that each member can have a larger share to consume, they produce a population explosion. As a result every gain in real income is promptly swallowed up by the extra mouths to feed. This sort of behavior has led economists to focus their recent studies on "non-economic factors" and development planners to broaden their attention from technical assistance (as in Point IV) to "human resources" (as in AID). We now recognize that modernization can succeed only in the measure that it meets its second paramount difficulty—its "people problems."

This book's focus on modernization as people-problems thus is just as valid now, and even more timely than it was six years ago. Were I rewriting the book now, I would make changes to take account of events. I would sound less unqualifiedly optimistic about the republican stability of Turkey, for example, since the two recent military coups impose qualification. But the dogged insistence of the new regime on maintaining constitutional forms and improving democratic procedures reinforces the underlying confidence that Turkey remains our best hope for republican stability in the Middle East. I would be less concerned now by Nasser's use of external adventures to avoid the harder people-problems of internal participation; instead I would congratulate him on having followed our advice. But these changes concern the transitory flow of the daily news— and this book explicitly disclaimed the function of a current events reader.

The central perspective has been validated by events of the past six years. Few today will quarrel with the view of modernity as a "behavioral system" or with the proposition that modernization requires a systemic "transformation of lifeways" if growth is to be made self-sustaining. Nor do the specific relations posited for the systemic transformation seem contrived today, as they did to some readers six years ago.

Even the charge of "ethnocentrism" that was heard a few years back— when the "Ugly American" was in vogue—has been seen through as a superficial slogan. The people-problems of modernization do include an "ethnocentric predicament." But in this predicament the ethnocentricity of Americans aiding development programs abroad is only the minor term; the major term is the ethnocentricity of the developing peoples themselves. The last few years have shown us the cruelty of Indonesians in dealing with their own Eurasians, the hostility of most South Asians to their "Overseas Chinese," the depredations by East Africans against Indians, the merciless conflicts between Greeks and Turks, the ethnocentric "Egyptianization" that terrorized and penalized all minorities including the oldest Egyptian stock—the Christian Copts.

The ethnocentric predicament is confounded by failure to realize that modernization appears as Westernization by historical coincidence. Modernity is primarily a state of mind—expectation of progress, propensity to growth, readiness to adapt oneself to change. The nations of the North Atlantic area first developed the social processes—secularization, urbanization, industrialization, popular participation—by which this state of mind came to prevail. The "Western Model" is only historically Western; sociologically it is global. The recent history of the U.S.S.R. and Japan shows how effectively these processes can modernize societies that are geographically remote from the West. The data in this book (see "The System

We may smile at the images of America that turn up in these interviews: the "clean and rich life" seen by a Turkish grammar school graduate; the grocery store with "myriads of round boxes, clean and all the same dressed, like soldiers in a great parade"[6] which the grocer of Balgat, eager to visit America, had seen in a film; the no less eloquent vision of an agricultural engineer:

> Ever since I was a child I used to dream and think about people. I used to imagine all people equal, having nice homes. In my imagination I used to send their children to school and educate them. Now, as an adult, I know that America is that country I used to dream about.

The British in the Arab world have tended to prefer the Chief to the Grocer, and perhaps the Beduin to the agronomist. They have admired gentlemanly conduct more than the consumer or trader mentality, "courage cultures" more than "ingenuity cultures." Though there are plenty of Americans who share the values of T. E. Lawrence (or the metaphorically somewhat similar ones of D. H. Lawrence), these do not predominate in our view of the Middle East, and of course not in our teaching at Robert College or the American University of Beirut. Whatever our own misgivings about the "great parade" of cans at the supermarket, whatever our awareness that we do not live up to the dream of the Turkish agronomist, and that if we did, our life would still lack meaning, we cannot bring ourselves to begrudge others the literacies and comforts that no longer wholly assuage us. Just as only an arrogant and heartless rich man can say to the poor man, "Why do you want my job, with my troubles and taxes?," so very few Americans are likely to say to the Turks: "Don't be like us," and even fewer to say: "Don't be like us even in your own particularistic way."

Even so, there are a number of Americans who do feel this way about preliterate tribes they have lived among as anthropologists. They would hardly speak of "their" people, as Mr. Lerner speaks of the Traditionals in this volume, as "constricted"; rather, they may find themselves challenged in their deepest premises, whatever their professions of neutrality. Most anthropologists, I believe, have felt that admirable patterns of culture were perishing on the periphery of the advancing West, and it was a major wrench of perspective for Margaret Mead, on returning to the Manus after twenty-five years, not to be sad that they had opted for the American ideas of progress and democracy.[7] I have asked myself why so little of this feeling, familiar enough to sociologists, has found its way into Professor Lerner's account. And it occurred to me that it may be harder to love and admire illiterates than preliterates. The former live in a world which is in part modern and communicative. They have lost many of their most active and enterprising spirits to that world, only a few of whom have returned, as priests or doctors or agitators, to try to enlighten or alleviate—or exploit—their own. In *Fontemara* Ignazio Silone implies that the South Italian peasants whom he loves would be better off if not even literate enough for speech, for then their tyrants could only beat them, as they beat donkeys, but could not sway or deceive them. Robert Redfield, who has written sensitively on such matters, draws the distinction between peasants who live within the ambiance of others' literacy, gaining from it crumbs of a culture not their own, and preliterates in a truly isolated orbit (at least potentially so, as on relatively inaccessible islands or pueblos) who have built their own culture over time.

Then, too, quite apart from such theoretical distinctions, there may be strong temperamental disharmonies between some cultures and others, as between individuals who "should" like each other but just don't. I recall a young anthropologist telling me how, thoroughly steeped in cultural relativism, he had reacted only sympathetically to "his" tribe of Central American Indians until one day he found he couldn't stand the way they kicked dogs— all sorts of rites, and what Mr. Lerner would call constrictions, did not faze him, but cruelty to dogs made him squirm. In what I have said, I have already implied my own allergy to the oppression of women. Many of the Muslims described in this book will strike some Americans as harsh without grandeur, superior to women without gallantry. Charles Morris in *Paths of Life* indicates on largely ideological grounds the strong antitheses between Christian or Buddhist values and those of traditional Islam.[8]

But stronger perhaps than ideological and religious differences are the barriers imposed by the growing wealth of Americans in contrast to the increasing poverty of the overpopulated countries like Egypt. Even our empathic strata, of which anthropologists are among the avant-garde, have trouble understanding squalor where it is neither picturesque nor stable. And the very fact that non-Westerners have often incorporated many

Western aspirations makes them either tongue-tied or fanatical in seeking to expound their own values to us in terms we can grasp.[9] Thus, while Mr. Lerner may approve of those Middle East illiterates who appear to have moved away from tradition, it is possible that the forms of tradition in question are, for him and for many of us, simply among its less appealing versions.

But if that is so, it may work the other way, too, and make the crossing of the historic barriers harder still. Perhaps this has something to do with the fact that "the" Arabs were once a great civilization. The illiterate in his depression, and the modernizer in his impatience, live amid the ruins of greatness. How open and how empathic will Americans be, how magnanimous, if our turn comes to live amid the ruins of our modernity?

While Mr. Lerner shows that every encounter with another people is a confrontation with ourselves—a theme he develops in observing how listening to the radio may at once unsettle people and create feelings of identity among the newly unbound—his major tasks in this book are, on the one hand, to present portraits of the several countries (some of which are more "country-like" than others) and, on the other hand, to develop a typology of transition to illuminate both the portraits and the global movements of peoples they represent. I want to say a few words in conclusion about this typology. Most typologies in sociology are dualistic or dichotomous: folk-urban; *Gemeinschaft-Gesellschaft*; status-to-contract; cosmopolitan-local; sacred-secular; and so forth. Mr. Lerner's cast of characters puts the Moderns on the one side—they are cosmopolitan, urban, literate, usually well-off, and seldom devout—and the Traditionals on the other side—they are just the opposite. But in between he puts several categories of Transitionals: people who share some of the empathy and psychic mobility of the Moderns while lacking essential components of the Modern style, notably literacy. These Transitionals are the men in motion, variously proportioned in the different countries, who listen to American jazz in Beirut, to the trusted BBC even in Cairo, to the Voice of the Arabs and Radio Moscow in Damascus. Many of them don't live in a city—yet. But, already encouraged by the media into ecological window-shopping, they can imagine living in one—even in one outside their native land.

There are, however, evident technical problems about extrapolating from one-shot interviews into the careers of men in motion. Thus, while the questionnaire got certain biographical data and allowed one to see something of the interviewee's orientation at a specific point in time, yet "Transitional" is a dynamic category —here presented without triangulation. Undoubtedly, some who are categorized as "Transitional" are simply members for life of a class which is open at both ends—a middle class; they may even be a major source of their country's transition without having themselves greatly altered their outlook or their exposure to the media. ("Modern," of course, is no fixed destiny, but a relative term: by the time some "Transitionals" go "Modern," that constellation will have changed.)

Despite such ambiguities, inevitable in a first approximation, I believe that Mr. Lerner is justified in using a moving term on the basis of a snapshot interview—using a term, moreover, which applies both to the respondent's style of life and to his (highly correlated) responsiveness to mass communications. For the author's purposes are contemporary, not timeless, and they lead him to emphasize what is changing and likely to change rather than what, by high fortune or low, seems for the time being more fully stabilized and polarized. However an individual in the Transitional bracket might describe his own fate, we, the outsiders, view his destiny in terms of our preoccupations—which, nevertheless, are now also partially his—and we can, in terms of our own history, visualize potentials in his attitudes which he himself as yet lacks the insight to interpret. (How long a time will it be before he is sending researchers to America and putting us in categories beyond our own horizons?)

As I have said, the Transitional is defined as one who attends to the mass media, but cannot read. What will a society look like which is dominated by such "post-literate" types? What will religion be like when freed both from oral tradition and from a book? These futures are hard to conceive, for print still has prestige all over the world, partly because the elder statesmen were nurtured on it, and partly because it has been the Western and Christian road to advance (just as it has been the road among the Chinese civil servants). In the West, print was the first mass medium, slowly absorbed; the newer media have been cumulative, and they have upset old elites and old values only slowly. (Indeed, in the United States, the media do not so much displace each other as displace other things, such as work and conversation.) Eventually perhaps, or so I would hope, the newer media may provide tie-ins to print, so that people suckled on film and radio may be weaned on books. We must never forget the enthusiasm for knowledge, for understanding, of people just a step away from Tradition—the hunger for print of the Puritans, of the Russians in the 20's, of the Mexicans and the Filipinos today. A Syrian hairdresser expresses in this book his great unhappiness because

I am illiterate and so can understand nothing about life. Another thing that makes me unhappy is my inability to teach my only son, and I can't find the way how to do this.

A preliterate, of course, would not say that: he knows that he understands life, and that his son will be taught the one and only way. But on the evidence of this book and others in the same demesne, there are very few preliterates left, and the illiterates are no longer clear as to who they are, or as to "the way how." In this sense, we are becoming one world, even while nationalism and the search for technological prowess are supplying the false and facile answers and the new illiteracy of seeming understanding.

Perspectives

I.

The Grocer and The Chief: A Parable

THE VILLAGE of Balgat lies about eight kilometers out of Ankara, in the southerly direction. It does not show on the standard maps and it does not figure in the standard histories. I first heard of it in the autumn of 1950 and most Turks have not heard of it today. Yet the story of the Middle East today is encapsulated in the recent career of Balgat. Indeed the personal meaning of modernization in underdeveloped lands can be traced, in miniature, through the lives of two Balgati—The Grocer and The Chief.

My first exposure to Balgat came while leafing through several hundred interviews that had been recorded in Turkey during the spring of 1950. One group caught my eye because of the underlying tone of bitterness in the interviewer's summary of the village, his earnest sense of the hopelessness of place and people. These five interviews in Balgat were moving; even so, something in the perspective seemed awry. For one thing, the interviewer was more highly sensitized to what he saw than what he heard. The import of what had been said to him, and duly recorded in his reports, had somehow escaped his attention. I, having only the words to go by, was struck by the disjunction between the reported face and the recorded voice of Balgat. For another thing, the interviews had been made in the early spring and I was reading them in the late fall of 1950. Between these dates there had been a national election in which, as a stunning surprise to everybody including themselves, practically all qualified Turks had voted and the party in power—Atatürk's own *Halk* Party—been turned out of office. Nothing like this had ever happened before in Turkey, possibly because neither universal suffrage nor an opposition party had ever been tried before. The dazed experts could only say of this epochal deed that the Anatolian villagers had done it. Since it would be hard to imagine Anatolian villagers of more standard pattern than the Balgati whose collected opinions were spread before me, I had it on top authority that during the summer they had entered History. But it was not immediately obvious by what route.

What clues existed were in a few words spoken by the villagers. These words we collated with the words that had been spoken to the interviewers by hundreds of villagers and townspeople throughout the Middle East. As we tabulated and cross-tabulated, a hunch emerged of what in Balgat spoke for many men, many deeds. Comparing cases by class and country we gradually enlarged our miniature into a panorama. Our hypothesis, heavy now with vivid details and many meanings, took shape. Four years later an oversize manuscript on the modernizing Middle East was in hand. To see how close a fit to Middle East reality was given by our picture of it, I went out for a self-guided tour and final round of interviews in the spring of 1954. My odyssey terminated where my ideas originated: in Balgat, on the eve of a second national election. With Balgat, then, our account begins.

Balgat Perceived: 1950

The interviewer who recorded Balgat on the verge—his name was Tosun B.—had detected no gleam of the future during his sojourn there. "The village is a barren one," he wrote. "The main color is gray, so is the dust on the divan on which I am writing now." Tosun was a serious young scholar from Ankara and he loved the poor in his own fashion. He had sought out Balgat to find the deadening past rather than the brave new world. He found it:

I have seen quite a lot of villages in the barren mountainous East, but never such a colorless, shapeless dump. This was the reason I chose the village. It could have been half an hour to Ankara by car if it had a road, yet it is about two hours to the capital by car without almost any road and is just forgotten, forsaken, right under our noses.

Tosun also sought and found persons to match the place. Of the five villagers he interviewed, his heart went straight out to the village shepherd. What Tosun was looking for in this interview is clear from his *obiter dicta*:

It was hard to explain to the village Chief that I wanted to interview the poorest soul in the village. He, after long discussions, consented me to interview the shepherd, but did not permit him to step into the guest-room. He said it would be an insult to me, so we did the interview in someone else's room, I did not quite understand whose. The Chief did not want to leave me alone with the respondent, but I succeeded at the end. This opened the respondent's sealed mouth, for he probably felt that I, the superior even to his chief, rather be alone with him.

When the shepherd's sealed mouth had been opened, little came out. But Tosun was deeply stirred:

The respondent was literally in rags and in this cold weather he had no shoe, but the mud and dirt on his feet were as thick as any boot. He was small, but looked rugged and sad, very sad. He was proud of being chosen by me and though limited tried his best to answer the questions. Was so bashful that his blush was often evident under the thick layer of dirt on his face. He at times threw loud screams of laughter when there was nothing to laugh about. These he expected to be accepted as answers, for when I said "Well?" he was shocked, as if he had already answered the question.

His frustration over the shepherd was not the only deprivation Tosun attributed to the Chief, who "imposed himself on me all the time I was in the village, even tried to dictate to me, which I refused in a polite way. I couldn't have followed his directions as I would have ended up only interviewing his family." Tosun did succeed in talking privately with two Balgat farmers, but throughout these interviews he was still haunted by the shepherd and bedeviled by the Chief. Not until he came to interview the village Grocer did Tosun find another Balgati who aroused in him a comparable antipathy. Tosun's equal hostility to these very different men made me curious. It was trying to explain this that got me obsessed, sleeping and waking over the next four years, with the notion that the parable of modern Turkey was the story of The Grocer and The Chief.

Aside from resenting the containment strategy which the Chief was operating against him, Tosun gave few details about the man. He reported only the impression that "the *Muhtar* is an unpleasant old man. Looks mean and clever. He is the absolute dictator of this little village." Nor did Tosun elaborate his disapproval of the *Muhtar*'s opinions beyond the comment that "years have left him some sort of useless, mystic wisdom." As a young man of empirical temper, Tosun might be expected to respond with some diffidence to the wisdom of the ancients. But the main source of Tosun's hostility, it appeared, was that the Chief made him nervous. His notes concluded: "He found what I do curious, even probably suspected it. I am sure he will report it to the first official who comes to the village."

Against the Grocer, however, Tosun reversed his neural field. He quickly perceived that he made the Grocer nervous; and for this Tosun disliked *him*. His notes read:

The respondent is comparatively the most city-like dressed man in the village. He even wore some sort of a necktie. He is the village's only grocer, but he is not really a grocer, but so he is called, originally the food-stuffs in his shop are much less than the things to be worn, like the cheapest of materials and shoes and slippers, etc. His greatest stock is drinks and cigarettes which he sells most. He is a very unimpressive type, although physically he covers quite a space. He gives the impression of a fat shadow. Although he is on the same level with the other villagers, when there are a few of the villagers around, he seems to want to distinguish himself by keeping quiet, and as soon as they depart he starts to talk too much. This happened when we were about to start the interview. He most evidently wished to feel that he is closer to me than he is to them and was curiously careful with his accent all during the interview. In spite of his unique position, for he is the only unfarming person and the only merchant in the village, he does not seem to possess an important part of the village community. In spite of all his efforts, he is considered by the villagers even less than the least farmer. Although he presented to take the interview naturally, he was nervous and also was proud to be interviewed although he tried to hide it.

All of this pushed up a weighty question: Why did the Chief make Tosun nervous and why did Tosun make the Grocer nervous? These three men, representing such different throughtways and lifeways, were a test for each other. Looking for answers, I turned to the responses each had made to the 57 varieties of opinions called for by the standard questionnaire used in Tosun's interviews.

The Chief was a man of few words on many subjects. He dismissed most of the items on Tosun's schedule with a shrug or its audible equivalent. But he was also a man of many words on a few subjects—those having to do with the primary modes of human deportment. Only when the issues involved first principles of conduct did he consider the occasion appropriate for pronouncing judgment. Of the Chief it might be said, as Henry James said of

George Eliot's salon style, *"Elle n'aborde que les grandes thèmes."*

The Chief has so little trouble with first principles because he desires to be, and usually is, a vibrant soundbox through which echo the traditional Turkish virtues. His themes are obedience, courage, loyalty—the classic values of the Ottoman Imperium reincarnate in the Atatürk Republic. For the daily round of village life these are adequate doctrine; and as the Chief has been outside of his village only to fight in two wars he has never found his austere code wanting. This congruence of biography with ideology explains the Chief's confidence in his own moral judgment and his short definition of a man. When asked what he wished for his two grown sons, for example, the Chief replied promptly: "I hope they will fight as bravely as we fought and know how to die as my generation did."

From this parochial fund of traditional virtues, the Chief drew equally his opinions of great men, nations, issues. The larger dramas of international *politique* he judged solely in terms of the courage and loyalty of the actors, invoking, to acknowledge their magnitude, the traditional rhetoric of aphorism. Generations of Anatolian *Muhtars* resonated as he pronounced his opinion of the British:

I hear that they have turned friends with us. But always stick to the old wisdom: "A good enemy is better than a bad friend." You cannot *rely* on them. Who has heard of a son being friends with his father's murderers?

With his life in Balgat, as with the Orphic wisdom that supplies its rationale, the Chief is contented. At 63 his desires have been quieted and his ambitions achieved. To Tosun's question on contentment he replied with another question:

What could be asked more?. God has brought me to this mature age without much pain, has given me sons and daughters, has put me at the head of my village, and has given me strength of brain and body at this age. Thanks be to Him.

The Grocer is a very different style of man. Though born and bred in Balgat, he lives in a different world, an expansive world, populated more actively with imaginings and fantasies—hungering for whatever is different and unfamiliar. Where the Chief is contented, the Grocer is restless. To Tosun's probe, the Grocer replied staccato: "I have told you I want better things. I would have liked to have a bigger grocery shop in the city, have a nice house there, dress nice civilian clothes."

Where the Chief audits his life placidly, makes no comparisons, thanks God, the Grocer evaluates his history in a more complicated and other-involved fashion. He perceives his story as a drama of Self *versus* Village. He compares his virtue with others and finds them lacking: "I am not like the others here. They don't know any better. And when I tell them, they are angry and they say that I am ungrateful for what Allah has given me." The Grocer's struggle with Balgat was, in his script, no mere conflict of personalities. His was the lonely struggle of a single man to open the village mind. Clearly, from the readiness and consistency of his responses to most questions, he had brooded much over his role. He had a keen sense of the limits imposed by reality: "I am born a grocer and probably die that way. I have not the possibility in myself to get the things I want. They only bother me." But desire, once stirred, is not easily stilled.

Late in the interview, after each respondent had named the greatest problem facing the Turkish people, Tosun asked what he would do about this problem if he were the president of Turkey. Most responded by stolid silence—the traditional way of handling "projective questions" which require people to imagine themselves or things to be different from what they "really are." Some were shocked by the impropriety of the very question. "My God! How can you say such a thing?" gasped the shepherd. "How can I . . . I cannot . . . a poor villager . . . master of the whole world."[1]

The Chief, Balgat's virtuoso of the traditional style, made laconic reply to this question with another question: "I am hardly able to manage a village, how shall I manage Turkey?" When Tosun probed further ("What would you suggest for *your village* that you cannot handle yourself?"), the Chief said he would seek "help of money and seed for some of our farmers." When the Grocer's turn came, he did not wait for the question to be circumscribed in terms of local reference. As president of Turkey, he said: "I would make roads for the villagers to come to towns to see the world and would not let them stay in their holes all their life."

To get out of his hole the Grocer even declared himself ready —and in this he was quite alone in Balgat—to live outside of Turkey. This came out when Tosun asked another of his projective questions: "If you could not live in Turkey, where would you want to live?" The standard reply of the villagers was that they would not live, could not imagine living, anywhere else. The forced choice simply was ignored.

When Tosun persisted ("Suppose you *had* to leave Turkey?") he teased an extreme reaction out of some Balgati. The shepherd, like several other wholly routinized personalities, finally replied that he would rather kill himself. The constricted peasant can more easily imagine destroying the self than relocating it in an unknown, i.e. frightful, setting.

The Chief again responded with the clear and confident voice of traditional man. "'Nowhere," he said. "I was born here, grew old here, and hope God will permit me to die here." To Tosun's probe, the Chief replied firmly: "I wouldn't move a foot from here." Only the Grocer found no trouble in imagining himself outside of Turkey, living in a strange land. Indeed he seemed fully prepared, as a man does when he has already posed a question to himself many times. "America," said the Grocer, and, without waiting for Tosun to ask him why, stated his reason: "because I have heard that it is a nice country, and with possibilities to be rich even for the simplest persons."

Such opinions clearly marked off the Grocer, in the eyes of the villagers around him, as heterodox and probably infidel. The vivid sense of cash displayed by the Grocer was a grievous offense against Balgat ideas of tabu talk. In the code regulating the flow of symbols among Anatolian villagers, blood and sex are permissible objects of passion but money is not. To talk much of money is an impropriety. To reveal excessive *desire* for money is—Allah defend us!—an impiety.[2]

Balgati might forgive the Grocer his propensity to seek the strange rather than reverse the familiar, even his readiness to forsake Turkey for unknown places, had he decently clothed these impious desires in pious terms. But to abandon Balgat for the world's fleshpots, to forsake the ways of God to seek the ways of cash, this was insanity. The demented person who spoke thus was surely accursed and unclean.

The Grocer, with his "city-dressed" ways, his "eye at the higher places" and his visits to Ankara, provoked the Balgati to wrathful and indignant restatements of the old code. But occasional, and apparently trivial, items in the survey suggested that some Balgati were talking loud about the Grocer to keep their own inner voices from being overheard by the Chief—or even by themselves.

As we were interested in knowing who says what to whom in such a village as Balgat, Tosun had been instructed to ask each person whether others ever came to him for advice, and if so what they wanted advice about. Naturally, the Balgati whose advice was most sought was the Chief, who reported: "Yes, that is my main duty, to give advice. (Tosun: *What about?*) About all that I or you could imagine, even about their wives and how to handle them, and how to cure their sick cow." This conjunction of wives and cows, to illustrate all the Chief could imagine, runs the gamut only from A to B. These are the species that the villager has most to do with in his daily round of life, the recurrent source of his pains and pleasures and puzzlements. The oral literature abounds in examples of *Muhtar* (or his theological counterpart, the *Hoca*) as wise man dispensing judgment equally about women and cows.

Rather more surprising was Tosun's discovery that some Balgati went for advice also to the disreputable Grocer. What did they ask *his* advice about? "What to do when they go to Ankara, where to go and what to buy, how much to sell their things." The cash nexus, this suggested, was somehow coming to Balgat and with it, possibly, a new role for the Grocer as cosmopolitan specialist in how to avoid wooden nickels in the big city. Also, how to spend the real nickels one got. For the Grocer was a man of clear convictions on which coffee-houses played the best radio programs and which were the best movies to see in Ankara. While his opinions on these matters were heterodox as compared say, to the Chief's, they had an open field to work in. Most Balgati had never heard a radio or seen a movie and were not aware of what constituted orthodoxy with respect to them. Extremists had nonetheless decided that these things, being new, were obviously evil. Some of them considered the radio to be "the voice of The Devil coming from his deep hiding-place" and said they would smash any such "Devil's-box" on sight.

At the time of Tosun's visit, there was only one radio in Balgat, owned by no less a personage than the Chief. In the absence of any explicit orthodox prohibition on radio, the Chief, former soldier and great admirer of Atatürk, had followed his lead. Prosperous by village standards, being the large landowner of Balgat, he had bought a radio to please and instruct his sons. He had also devised an appropriate ceremonial for its use. Each evening a select group of Balgati foregathered in the Chief's guest room as he turned on the newscast from Ankara. They heard the newscast through in silence and, at its conclusion, the Chief turned the radio off and made his commentary. "We all listen very carefully," he told Tosun, "and I talk about it afterwards." Tosun, suspecting in this procedure a variant of the Chief's containment tactics, wanted to know whether there was any disagreement over his explanations. "No, no arguments," replied the Chief, "as I tell you I only talk and our opinions are the same more or less." Here was a new twist in the ancient role of knowledge as power. Sensing the potential challenge from radio, the Chief restricted the dangers of innovation by partial incorporation, thus retaining and strengthening his role as Balgat's official opinion leader.

Tosun inquired of the Grocer, an occasional attendant at the Chief's salon, how he liked this style of radio session. The grocer, a heretic perhaps but not a foolhardy one, made on this point the shortest statement in his entire interview: "The Chief is clever and he explains the news." Only obliquely, by asking what the Grocer liked best about radio, did Tosun get an answer that had the true resonance. Without challenging the Chief's preference for news of "wars and the danger of wars"—in fact an exclusive interest in the Korean War, to which a Turkish brigade had just been committed—the Grocer indicated that after all *he* had opportunities to listen in the coffee-houses of Ankara, where the audiences exhibited a more cosmopolitan range of interests. "It is nice to know what is happening in the other capitals of the world," said the Grocer. "We are stuck in this hole, we have to know what is going on outside our village."

The Grocer had his own aesthetic of the movies as well. Whereas the Chief had been to the movies several times, he viewed them mainly as a moral prophylactic: "There are fights, shooting. The people are brave. My sons are always impressed. Each time they see such a film they wish more and more their time for military service would come so that they would become soldiers too." For the Grocer, movies were more than a homily on familiar themes. They were his avenue to the wider world of his dreams. It was in a movie that he had first glimpsed what a *real* grocery store could be like—"with walls made of iron sheets, top to floor and side to side, and on them standing myriads of round boxes, clean and all the same dressed, like soldiers in a

great parade." This fleeting glimpse of what sounds like the
Campbell Soup section of an A & P supermarket had provided
the Grocer with an abiding image of how his fantasy world might
look. It was here, quite likely, that he had shaped the ambition
earlier confided to Tosun, "to have a bigger grocery shop in the
city." No pedantries intervened in the Grocer's full sensory relationship to the movies. No eye had he, like the Chief, for their
value as filial moral rearmament and call to duty. The Grocer's
judgments were formed in unabashedly hedonist categories. "The
Turkish ones," he said, "are gloomy, ordinary. I can guess at the
start of the film how it will end. . . . The American ones are exciting. You know it makes people ask what will happen next?"

Here, precisely, arose the local variant of a classic question.
In Balgat, the Chief carried the sword, but did the Grocer steer
the pen? When Balgati sought his advice on how to get around
Ankara, would they then go to movies that taught virtue or
those that taught excitement? True, few villagers had ever been
to Ankara. But things were changing in Turkey and many more
Balgati were sure to have a turn or two around the big city before they died. What would happen next in Balgat if more people
discovered the tingle of wondering what will happen next? Would
things continue along the way of the Chief or would they take
the way of the Grocer?

Balgat Revisited: 1954

I reached Ankara in April after a circuitous route through the
Middle East. The glories of Greece, Egypt, Lebanon, Syria, Persia
touched me only lightly, for some part of me was already in
Balgat. Even the Blue Mosque and St. Sophia seemed pallid,
and I left Istanbul three days ahead of schedule for Ankara. I
had saved this for last, and now here I was. I was half afraid
to look.

I called a transportation service and explained that I wanted
to go out the following day, a Sunday, to a village some eight
kilometers south that might be hard to reach. As I wanted to
spend the day, would the driver meet me at 8 A.M. and bring
along his lunch?

While waiting for the car, next morning, my reverie wandered
back through the several years since my first reading of the Balgat

interviews. Was I chasing a phantom? Tahir S. appeared. With solitude vanished anxiety; confidently we began to plan the day. Tahir had been a member of the original interview team, working in the Izmir area. As Tosun had joined the Turkish foreign service and was stationed in North Africa, where he was conducting an inquiry among the Berbers, I had arranged in advance for Tahir to revisit Balgat with me in his place. Over a cup of syrupy coffee, we reviewed the questions that had been asked in 1950, noted the various responses and silences, decided the order in which we would repeat the old questions and interpolate the new ones.

As the plan took shape, Zilla K. arrived. She had no connection with the original survey, but I wanted a female interviewer who could add some Balgat women to our gallery. I had "ordered" her, through a colleague at Ankara University, "by the numbers": thirtyish, semi-trained, alert, compliant with instructions, not sexy enough to impede our relations with the men of Balgat but chic enough to provoke the women. A glance and a word showed that Zilla filled the requisition. We brought her into the plan of operations. The hall porter came in to say our car was waiting. We got in and settled back for a rough haul. Twenty minutes later, as we were still debating the niceties of question-wording and reporting procedure, the driver said briskly: "There's Balgat."

We looked puzzled at each other until Tosun's words of 1950 recurred to us: "It could have been half an hour to Ankara if it had a road." Now it did have a road. What was more, a *bus* was coming down the road, heading toward us from the place our driver had called Balgat. As it passed, jammed full, none of the passengers waved or even so much as stuck out a tongue at us. Without these unfailing signs of villagers out on a rare chartered bus, to celebrate a great occasion of some sort, we could only make the wild guess that Balgat had acquired a regular bus service. And indeed, as we entered the village, there it was—a "bus station," freshly painted benches under a handsome new canopy. We got out and looked at the printed schedule of trips. "The bus leaves every hour, on the hour, to Ulus Station. Fare: 20 Kuruş." For about 4 cents, Balgati could now go, whenever they felt the whim, to Ulus in the heart of Ankara. The villagers were getting out of their holes at last. The Grocer, I thought, must be grinning over the fat canary he had swallowed.

We took a quick turn around the village, on our way to check in with the Chief. Things looked different from what Tosun's report had led us to expect. Overhead wires were stretched along the road, with branch lines extended over the houses of Balgat. The village had been electrified. Alongside the road deep ditches had been dug, in which the graceful curve of new water pipe was visible. Purified water was coming to Balgat. There were many more buildings than the 50-odd Tosun had counted, and most of them looked new. Two larger ones announced themselves as a school and a police station. An inscription on the latter revealed that Balgat was now under the jurisdiction of the Ankara district police. They had finally got rid of the *gendarmerie,* scavengers of the Anatolian village and historic blight on the peasant's existence. "These fellows are lucky," said Tahir drily. Feeling strange, we made our way along the erratic path through the old village, led and followed by a small horde of children, to the house of the Chief. Tahir knocked, an old woman with her head covered by a dark shawl appeared, the children scattered. We were led into the guest room.

The Chief looked as I had imagined. His cheeks a bit more sunken, perhaps, but the whole *présence* quite familiar. Tall, lean, hard, he walked erect and looked me straight in the eye. His own eyes were Anatolian black and did not waver as he stretched out a handful of long, bony fingers. "*Gün aydin, Bey Efendim,*" he said. "Good day, sir, you are welcome to my house." I noted in turn the kindness which opens a door to strangers and the Chief responded that we honored his house by our presence. This completed the preliminary round of *formules de politesse* and steaming little cups of Turkish coffee were brought in by the Chief's elder son. The son was rather a surprise—short, pudgy, gentle-eyed and soft spoken. He bowed his head, reddening slightly as he stammered, "*Lütfen*" (Please!) and offered the tray of demi-tasses to me. I wondered whether he had learned to fight bravely and die properly.

As the Chief set down his second cup of coffee, signifying that we could now turn to the business of our visit, I explained that I had come from America, where I taught in a university, with the hope of meeting him. There, in my own country, I had read about Balgat in some writing by a young man from Ankara who, four years ago, had talked at length with the Chief and other persons in his village. This writing had interested me very much and I had often wondered, as the years passed by, how things were going in the village of Balgat and among its people. When I had the opportunity to come to Turkey I immediately decided that I would visit Balgat and see the Chief if I could.

The Chief heard me through gravely, and when he spoke I knew I was in. He bypassed the set of formulas available to him —for rejecting or evading my implied request—and responded directly to the point. I was right to have come to see Balgat for myself. He remembered well the young man from Ankara (his description of Tosun in 1950 was concise and neutrally-toned). Much had changed in Balgat since that time. Indeed, Balgat was no longer a village. It had, only last month, been incorporated as a district of Greater Ankara. This was why they now had a new headquarters of Metropolitan police, and a bus service, and electricity, and a supply of pure water that would soon be in operation. Where there had been 50 houses there were now over 500, and even he, the Muhtar, did not know any more all the people living here.

Yes he had lived in Balgat all his life and never in all that time seen so much happen as had come to pass in these four years:

It all began with the election that year. The *Demokrat* men came to Balgat and asked us what was needed here and told us they would do it when they were elected. They were brave to go against the government party. We all voted for them, as the *Halk* men knew no more what to do about the prices then, and the new men did what they said. They brought us this road and moved out the *gendarmerie*. Times have been good with us here. We are all *Demokrat* party here in Balgat now.

The Chief spoke in a high, strong, calm voice, and the manner of his utterance was matter-of-fact. His black eyes remained clear as he gazed steadily at the airspace adjoining my left ear, and his features retained their shape. Only his hands were animated, though he invoked only the thumbs and the index fingers for punctuation. When he had completed his statement, he picked his nose thoughtfully for a moment and then laid the finger alongside the bridge. The tip of the long, bony finger reached into his eyesocket.

I explained then that the young lady had come with us to learn how such changes as the Chief mentioned were altering the daily round for village women. Might she talk with some of them while

Tahir Bey and I were meeting the men? The Chief promptly suggested that Zilla could speak with the females of his household. (Tosun's resentful remark that, had he followed the Chief's suggestions, "I would have ended up only interviewing his family" came back to me later that evening, when Zilla reported on her interviews with the Chief's wife and daughters-in-law. All three had identified Balgat's biggest problem as the new fashion of young men to approach girls shamelessly on the village outskirts—precisely what the Chief had told me in answer to the same question. Tosun had been wise.) But if the Chief still used his containment tactics with the women, in other directions he had taken a decidedly permissive turn. Tahir and I, he said, could walk about Balgat entirely as we wished and speak with whomsoever it pleased us to honor— even, he added with a smile in response to my jest, some non-*Demokrat* Party men, if we could find any. We chatted a bit longer and then, having agreed to return to the Chief's house, we set out for a stroll around Balgat. Our next goal was to find the Grocer.

After a couple of bends and turns, we came to a coffee-house. Here was something new and worth a detour. We stopped at the door and bade the proprietor *"Gün aydin!"* He promptly rushed forward with two chairs, suggested that we sit outdoors to benefit of the pleasant sunshine, and asked us how we would like our coffee. (There are five ways of specifying the degree of sweetening one likes in Turkish coffee.) Obviously, this was to be on the house, following the paradoxical Turkish custom of giving gratis to those who can best afford to pay. In a matter of minutes, the male population of Balgat was assembled around our two chairs, squatting, sitting on the ground, looking us over with open and friendly curiosity, peppering Tahir with questions about me.

When our turn came, the hierarchy of respondents was already clear from the axis along which their questions to us had been aligned. Top man was one of the two farmers Tosun had interviewed in 1950. He too was tall, lean, hard. He wore store-clothes with no patches and a sturdy pair of store-shoes. His eyes were Anatolian black and his facial set was much like the Chief's. But his body was more relaxed and his manner more cocky. He sat with his chair tilted back and kept his hands calmly dangling alongside. This seemed to excise punctuation from his discourse and he ambled along, in response to any question, with no apparent terminus in view. Interrupting him, even long enough to steer his

flow of words in another direction, was—the obvious deference
of the whole group toward him constrained us—not easy. His voice
was deep and harsh, with the curious suggestion of strangling in
the throat that Anatolian talk sometimes has. The content was
elusive and little of his discourse made concrete contact with my
notebook.

As I review my notes on that tour of monologue-with-choral-
murmurs, he appears to have certified the general impression that
many changes had occurred in Balgat. His inventory included, at
unwholesome length, all the by-now familiar items: road, bus,
electricity, water. In his recital these great events did not acquire
a negative charge, but they lost some of their luster. The tough
old farmer did not look shining at new styles of architecture, nor
did he look scowling, but simply looked. Under his gaze the new
roofs in Balgat were simply new roofs. The wonder that these new
roofs were *in Balgat* shone in other eyes and cadenced other voices.

These other voices were finally raised. Either the orator had
exhausted the prerogative of his position (he had certainly exhausted Tahir S., whose eyes were glazed and vacant) or the issue
was grave enough to sanction discourtesy toward a village elder.
The outburst came when the quondam farmer undertook to explain
why he was no longer a farmer. He had retired, over a year ago,
because there was none left in Balgat to do an honest day's work
for an honest day's lira. Or rather two lira (about 36 cents)—the
absurd rate, he said, to which the daily wage of farm laborers had
been driven by the competition of the voracious Ankara labor
market. Now, all the so-called able-bodied men of Balgat had
forsaken the natural work praised by Allah and swarmed off to
the Ankara factories where, for eight hours of so-called work,
they could get five lira a day. As for himself, he would have none
of this. Rather than pay men over two lira a day to do the work
of men, he had rented out his land to others and retired. He was
rich, his family would eat, and others might do as they wished.

The protests that rose did not aim to deny these facts, but simply
to justify them. Surprised, we asked whether it was indeed true
that there were no farm laborers left in Balgat any more. "How
many of you," we quickly rephrased the question, "work on farms
now?" Four hands were raised among the 29 present, and all of
these turned out to be small holders working their own land. (These
four were sitting together and, it later turned out, were the only

four members of the *Halk* Party among the group, the rest being
vigorous *Demokrat* men.)

Galvanized by the intelligence now suddenly put before us
(even Tahir S. had reawakened promptly upon discovering that
there were hardly any farmers left in Balgat), we started to fire
a battery of questions on our own. As this created a din of responding voices, Tahir S.—once again the American-trained interviewer
—restored order by asking each man around the circle to tell us,
in turn, what he was now working at and how long he had been
at it. This impromptu occupational census, begun on a leisurely
Sunday, was never quite completed. As it became clear that most
of the male population of Balgat was now in fact working in
the factories and construction gangs of Ankara—*for cash*—our own
impatience to move on to our next questions got the better of us.

How did they spend the cash they earned? Well, there were
now over 100 radio receivers in Balgat as compared to the lone
receiver Tosun had found four years earlier. There were also seven
refrigerators, four tractors, three trucks, and one Dodge sedan.
Most houses now had electric lights and that had to be paid for.
Also, since there was so little farming in Balgat now, much of
the food came from the outside (even milk!) and had to be
bought in the grocery stores, of which there were now seven in
Balgat. Why milk? Well, most of the animals had been sold off
during the last few years. What about the shepherd? Well, he
had moved to a village in the east a year or so ago, as there were
no longer any flocks for him to tend. How was the Grocer doing?
"*Which one?*" The original one, the great fat one that was here
four years ago? "O, that one, he's dead!"

Tahir S. later told me that my expression did not change
when the news came (always the American-trained interviewer!).
I asked a few more questions in a normal way—"What did he die
of?", "How long ago?"—and then let the questioning pass to Tahir.
I don't recall what answers came to my questions or to his. I
do recall suddenly feeling very weary and, as the talk went on,
slightly sick. The feeling got over to Tahir S. and soon we were
saying goodbye to the group, feeling relieved that the ritual for
leavetaking is less elaborate than for arriving. We promised to
return and said our thanks. "*Güle, güle,*" answered those who
remained. ("Smile, smile," signifying farewell.)

"What a lousy break," growled Tahir in a tone of reasonable

indignation as we started back toward the house of the Chief. He was speaking of the Grocer. I didn't know what to say by way of assent. I felt only a sense of large and diffuse regret, of which indignation was not a distinct component. "Tough," I agreed. As we came up to the Chief's house, I told Tahir we might as well return to Ankara. We had gathered quite a lot of information already and might better spend the afternoon putting it together. We could come back the next day to interview the Chief. The Chief agreed to this plan and invited me to be his guest for lunch next day. We collected Zilla K. and our driver and drove back to the city. Zilla did most of the talking, while Tahir and I listened passively. The driver said only, as I paid him, "I didn't need to bring along my lunch after all."

The Passing of Balgat

While dressing slowly, the next morning, I planned my strategy for lunch with the Chief. Had he learned anything from the Grocer? Clearly his larger clues to the shape of the future had come from Atatürk, whose use of strong measures for humane new goals had impressed him deeply as a young man. But surely he had also responded to the constant stimuli supplied by the Grocer, whose psychic antennae were endlessly *seeking* the new future here and now. The Chief, rather consciously reshaping his ways in the Atatürk image, had to be reckoned a major figure in the Anatolian transformation. But the restless sensibility of the Grocer also had its large, inadequately defined, place. Whereas the masterful Chief had been able to incorporate change mainly by rearranging the environment, the nervous Grocer had been obliged to operate through the more painful process of rearranging himself. Most villagers were closer to his situation than to the Chief's. The Grocer then was my problem and, as symbol of the characterological shift, my man. It was he who dramatized most poignantly the personal meaning of the big change now under way throughout the Middle East.

I recalled Tosun's unflattering sketch of him as an anxiety-ridden pusher, an "unfarming person" who "even wore some sort of necktie." What had located these details, what had made the Grocer a man I recognized, was Tosun's acid remark: "He most evidently wished to feel that he is closer to me than he is to [other villagers] and was curiously careful with his accent all during the interview." Tosun had seen this as vulgar social climbing, but there was something in this sentence that sounded to me like History. Maybe it was the 18th century field-hand of England who had left the manor to find a better life in London or Manchester. Maybe it was the 19th century French farm lad, wearied by his father's burdens of *taille* and *tithe,* who had gone off to San Francisco to hunt gold and, finding none, had then tried his hand as mason, mechanic, printer's devil; though none of these brought him fortune, he wrote home cheerfully (in a letter noted by the perspicacious Karl Marx) about this exciting new city where the chance to try his hand at anything made him feel "less of a mollusk and more of a man." Maybe it was the 20th century Polish peasant crossing continent and ocean to Detroit, looking for a "better 'ole" in the new land.

The Grocer of Balgat stood for some part of all these figures as he nervously edged his psyche toward Tosun, the young man from the big city. I'm like you, the Grocer might have been feeling, or I'd like to be like you and wish I could get the chance. It was harsh of Tosun, or perhaps only the anti-bourgeois impatience of an austere young scholar looking for the suffering poor in a dreary village, to cold-shoulder this fat and middle-aged man yearning to be comfortably rich in an interesting city. But the Grocer had his own sort of toughness. He had, after all, stood up to the other villagers and had insisted, even when they labeled him infidel, that they ought to get out of their holes. Though dead, he had won an important victory. For the others, despite their outraged virtues, *had* started to come around, once they began to get the feel of Ankara cash, for advice on *how* to get out of their holes. Had they also acquired, along with their new sense of cash, some feel for the style of life the Grocer had desired? That was what I wanted to find out in Balgat today.

I walked out of the hotel toward Ulus station, just around the corner. This time I was going to Balgat by bus, to see how the villagers traveled. We crowded into a shiny big bus from Germany that held three times as many passengers as there were seats. The bus was so new that the signs warning the passengers not to smoke or spit or talk to the driver (while the bus is moving) in German, French, and English had not yet been converted into Turkish. There was, in fact, a great deal of smoking and several animated conversations between the driver and various passengers occurred, in the intervals between which the driver chatted with a crony whom he had brought along for just this purpose.

In Balgat I reported directly to the Chief. He appeared, after a few minutes, steaming and mopping his large forehead. He had been pruning some trees and, in this warm weather, such work brought the sweat to his brow. This was about the only work he did any more, he explained, as he had sold or rented most of his land in the last few years, keeping for himself only the ground in which he had planted a small grove of trees that would be his memorial on earth. Islamic peoples regard a growing and "eternal" thing of nature, preferably a tree, as a fitting monument, and a comfortable Muslim of even diffident piety will usually be scrupulous in observing this tradition—a sensible one for a religion of the desert, where vegetation is rare and any that casts a shade is especially prized. The Chief agreed to show me his trees and as we strolled away from the house he resumed his discourse of yesterday.

Things had changed, he repeated, and a sign of the gravity of these changes was that he—of a lineage that had always been *Muhtars* and landowners—was no longer a farmer. Nor was he long to be *Muhtar*. After the coming election, next month, the incorporation of Balgat into Greater Ankara was to be completed and thereafter it would be administered under the general municipal system. "I am the last *Muhtar* of Balgat, and I am happy that I have seen Balgat end its history in this way that we are going." The new ways, then, were not bringing evil with them?

No, people will have to get used to different ways and then some of the excesses, particularly among the young, will disappear. The young people are in some ways a serious disappointment; they think more of clothes and good times than they do of duty and family and country. But it is to be hoped that as the *Demokrat* men complete the work they have begun, the good Turkish ways will again come forward to steady the people. Meanwhile, it is well that people can have to eat and to buy shoes they always needed but could not have.

And as his two sons were no longer to be farmers, what of them? The Chief's voice did not change, nor did his eyes cloud over, as he replied:

They are as the others. They think first to serve themselves and not the nation. They had no wish to go to the battle in Korea, where Turkey fights before the eyes of all the world. They are my sons and I speak no ill of them, but I say only that they are as all the others.

I felt at this moment a warmth toward the Chief which I had not supposed he would permit himself to evoke. His sons had not, after all, learned to fight bravely and die properly. His aspiration—which had led him, four years earlier, to buy a radio so his sons would hear the Korean war news and to see movies that would make them "wish more and more their time for military service would come"—had not been fulfilled. Yet the old Chief bore stoically what must have been a crushing disappointment. These two sons through whom he had hoped to relive his own bright dreams of glory had instead become *shopkeepers*. The elder son owned a grocery store and the younger one owned Balgat's first clothing store. With this news, curiosity overcame sympathy. I rattled off questions on this subject which, clearly, the Chief would rather have changed. As we turned back to the house, he said we would visit the shops after lunch and his sons would answer all my questions.

Lunch consisted of a huge bowl of yogurt, alongside of which was stacked a foot-high pile of village-style bread, freshly baked by the Chief's wife and served by his younger daughter-in-law. Village bread fresh from the oven is one of the superior tastes that greets a visitor. As I went to work with obvious relish, the Chief suggested that I eat only the "corner" of each sheet. Village bread is baked in huge round double sheets, each about the diameter of a manhole cover and the thickness of a dime. A large glob of shortening is spread loosely around the center between the sheets, which are baked together around the circumference. These sheets are then folded over four times, making the soft buttery center into a "corner." The corner is the prerogative of the male head of the household, who may choose to share it with a favored child. To invite a guest to eat *only* the corners is, in the frugal Anatolian village, a sign of special cordiality that cannot be ignored.

As I chewed my way happily through a half-dozen corners, I wondered who was going to be stuck with my stack of cornerless circumferences. Mama and the daughters-in-law? I asked about the children and learned that, as befits the traditional extended family, the Chief now had nine descendants living under his roof. Moreover, while some were taking to new ways, *his* grandchildren had been and were being swaddled in the traditional Anatolian fashion—for three months a solid mudpack on the body under the swaddling cloths, thereafter for three months a mudless swaddle. (Geoffrey Gorer's association of Russian swaddling with *ochi chornya* seemed due for an Anatolian confirmation, since Turkish eyes are every bit as lustrous black as Slavic eyes.) I glanced up at the large clock on the wall, which had stood firmly at 11:09 since I first entered the room at 9:16 the preceding day. It was clearly intended only as an emblem of social standing. In the very household where swaddling continued, possibly the first clock in Balgat (as once the first radio) had won a place. And though the clock was only decorative rather than useful, yet the hourglass was no longer visible. Times had changed. The Chief noticed my glance and suggested that we could now go out to see the shops of his sons.

We went first to the elder son's grocery store, just across the road and alongside the village "fountain," where Balgat women did the family wash as in ages past (though this would pass when the new municipal water supply became available at reasonable rates). The central floor space was set out with merchandise in the immemorial manner—heavy, rough, anonymous hemp sacks each laden with a commodity requiring no identity card, groats in one and barley in another, here lentils and there chicory. But beyond the sacks was a distinct innovation, a counter. What is more, the counter turned a corner and ran parallel to two sides of the square hut. Built into it was a cash drawer and above each surface a hygienic white porcelain fixture for fluorescent lighting. Along the walls was the crowning glory—rows of shelves running from "top to floor and side to side, and on them standing myriads of round boxes, clean and all the same, dressed like soldiers in a great parade." The Grocer's words of aspiration came leaping back as I looked admiringly around the store. His dream-house had been built in Balgat—in less time than even he might have forecast—and by none other than the Chief!

The irony of the route by which Balgat had entered history accompanied us as we walked in quartet, the Chief and I ahead, the sons behind, to the clothing store of the younger son. This was in the newer part of the village, just across the new road from the "bus station." The entrance to the store was freshly painted dark blue, a color imbued by Muslim lore with power to ward off the evil eye. The stock inside consisted mainly of

dungarees, levis, coveralls (looking rather like U.S. Army surplus
stocks). There was a continuous and growing demand for these
goods, the Chief stated solemnly, as more and more Balgati went
into the labor market of Ankara, first discarding their *sholvars*
(the billowing knickers of traditional garb in which Western car-
toons always still portray the "sultan" in a harem scene). In a
corner of the store there was also a small stock of "gentleman's
haberdashery"—ready-made suits, shirts, even a rack of neckties.

The younger son, who maintained under his smile of proprietary
pleasure a steady silence in the presence of the Chief, replied to
a direct question from me that he had as yet sold very few items
from this department of the store. One suit had gone to a pros-
pective bridegroom, but the Balgat males by and large were still
reticent about wearing store-bought clothes. A few, indeed, had
purchased in a *sub rosa* sort of way neckties which remained
to be exhibited in public. But wearing them would come, now
that several owned them, as soon as an older man was bold
enough to wear his first. The owners of the neckties had only
to get used to them in private, looking at them now and then,
showing them to their wives and elder sons, and some one of
them had to show the way. I remembered Tosun's rather nasty
comment about the Grocer: *"He even wore some sort of a necktie."* As one saw it now, the Grocer *had* shown the way, and it
was now only a hop, skip and jump through history to the point
where most men of Balgat would be wearing neckties.

The Grocer's memory stayed with me all that afternoon, after
I had expressed intense satisfaction with the shops, wished the
sons good fortune, thanked the Chief again and, with his permission, started out to walk among the alleys and houses of
Balgat. On the way, I absently counted 69 radio antennas on the
roofs and decided that yesterday's estimate of "over 100" was
probably reliable. And only four years ago, I counterpointed to
myself, there was but a single battery set in this village. The same
theme ran through my recollection of the numbers of tractors, refrigerators, and "unfarming persons." Several of these newly unfarming persons, recognizing their interlocutor of yesterday's coffee-
house session, greeted me as I strolled along. One stopped me
long enough to deliver his opinion of the Turkish-Pakistani pact
(strong affirmation) and to solicit mine of the proposed law to

give Americans prospecting rights on Turkish oil (qualified affirmative).

Weary of walking, I turned back to the coffee-house. The ceremony of welcome was warm and the coffee was again on the house. But the conversational group was smaller, this being a workday. Only eleven Balgati appeared to praise the weather and hear my questions. The group got off on politics, with some attention to the general theory of power but more intense interest in hearing each other's predictions of the margin by which the *Demokrat* party would win the elections next month. There was also general agreement, at least among the older men, that it would be better to have a small margin between the major parties. When the parties are competing and need our votes, then they heed our voices—thus ran the underlying proposition of the colloquy. "The villagers have learned the basic lesson of democratic politics," I wrote in my notebook.

The afternoon was about over before I got an appropriate occasion to ask about the Grocer. It came when the talk returned to the villagers' favorite topic of how much better life had become during the past four years of *Demokrat* rule. Again they illustrated the matter by enumerating the new shops in Balgat and the things they had to sell that many people could buy. There was even a new barber shop, opened last month by the son of the late Altemur after going for some time to Ankara as apprentice. "How are these new grocery shops better than the old grocery shop of years ago owned by the fat grocer who is now dead?" I asked. The line of response was obvious in advance, but the question served to lead to another: What sort of man had the Grocer been?

The answers were perfunctory, consisting mainly of *pro forma* expressions of goodwill toward the departed. I tried to get back of these ritual references by indirection. How had the Grocer dressed? Why had he been so interested in the life of Ankara? The light finally shone in one of the wiser heads and he spoke the words I was seeking:

Ah, he was the cleverest of us all. We did not know it then, but he saw better than all what lay in the path ahead. We have none like this among us now. He was a prophet.

As I look back on it now, my revisit to Balgat ended then. I

went back several times, once with gifts for the Chief's grandchildren, another time with my camera (as he had coyly suggested) to take his picture. On these visits I felt less tense, asked
fewer questions, than during the earlier visits. The last time I
went out with the publisher of a prominent Istanbul newspaper
("The New York Times of Turkey"), a dedicated *Demokrat* man,
who was eager to see the transformed village I had described to
him. He was enchanted with the Chief, the stores, the bus service
and electricity and other symbols of the history into which his
party had ushered Balgat. He decided to write a feature story
about it and asked permission to call it "Professor Lerner's Village." I declined, less from modesty than a sense of anachronism.
The Balgat his party needed was the suburb inhabited by the
sons of the Chief, with their swaddled children and their proud
new clock, their male "corners" and their retail stores, their fili-
opietistic silence and their movies that teach excitement. The
ancient village I had known for what now seemed only four short
years was passing, had passed. The Grocer was dead. The Chief
—"the last *Muhtar* of Balgat"—had reincarnated the Grocer in the
flesh of his sons. Tosun was in North Africa studying the Berbers.

II.

Modernizing Styles of Life: A Theory

> "I am thankful that the good God created us all ignorant. I am glad that when we change His plans in this regard we have to do it at our own risk."
> —MARK TWAIN

> "The United States is presiding at a general re-organization of the ways of living throughout the entire world."
> —ANDRÉ SIEGFRIED

THE PASSING OF BALGAT is but an instance of the passing of traditional society in the Middle East. The modernizing of ancient lifeways involves many Tosuns and shepherds, many grocers and chiefs, many sons of chiefs. For the stakes of modernization, as Mark Twain suggests, are deep and personal. Secular enlightenment does not easily replace sacred revelation in the guidance of human affairs. Sacred codes, once revealed and transmitted through the shepherd, provide simple rules of conduct for all the flock—who can remain ignorant or, more profoundly, innocent. But secular enlightenment each man must get for himself. Many individuals must struggle through the loss of ignorance-as-bliss in the making of a new secular "climate of opinion."

Western men need only reflect on the titanic struggles whereby, over the course of centuries, medieval lifeways were supplanted by modernity. Hindsight now summarizes these struggles as The Age of Exploration, The Renaissance, The Reformation, The Counter-Reformation, The Industrial Revolution. But well we know that this historical sequence worked itself out through millions of individual lives; that many suffered, others prospered, while their world was being reshaped in the modern image. In the end—and the end is not yet—all men of the West had acquired a new style of life.

A similar process is under way in the Middle East. The underlying tensions are everywhere much the same—village *versus* town, land *versus* cash, illiteracy *versus* enlightenment, resignation *versus* ambition, piety *versus* excitement. But the process reaches people in different settings and induces different dilemmas of personal choice. In Turkey a grocer exhilarated by the sight of a city must live out his life in a traditional village; in Iran a newly entrepreneurial peasant proudly owns the first store-bought suit in his walled hamlet but rarely dares to wear it among his envious fellows; in Jordan an illiterate Beduin chieftain professes the tribal law of the desert but plans to send his son abroad to school; in Lebanon an educated Muslim girl loves the movies but fears her orthodox parents; in Syria an under-educated, over-ambitious clerk dreams of being a Tito; in Egypt a young engineer has eaten pork in the West and seeks atonement in the Muslim Brotherhood. To locate these diverse figures in the modernizing Middle East is our aim. The parable of Balgat conveys some sense of the varied questions and answers, pleasures and pains, which modernization brings into the lives of people so variously situated. But Balgat is a miniature; what we need is a landscape.

Landscaping requires some principle of unity in diversity. The source of Middle East unity is a thorny problem of scholarship, complicated by the recent efforts of ideologues to impose a definition that will be politically usable rather than historically valid. Scholars seem agreed that the current ideologies tend to obscure and evade some real issues. The people of the area today are unified not by their common solutions but by their common problems: how to modernize traditional lifeways that no longer "work" to their own satisfaction. Some seek salvation in past pieties—the recourse to Islamic solidarity providing in this sense a parallel to the Crusades, which, in the name of orthodoxy, hastened the passing of medievalism and coming of modernity in the West. But, underlying the ideologies, there pervades the Middle East a sense that the old ways must go because they no longer satisfy the new wants. A world conference of leading Islamists recently concluded:

The disorder and poverty which rage in the Middle East . . . seem incapable of being remedied except by a greater solidarity among Islamic countries and by a general modernization of these countries. But though modernization is a tangible fact, only the pace of which might require control and acceleration, Muslim solidarity is only a fleeting, variable, uncertain supposition.[1]

Modernization, then, is the unifying principle in this study of the varied Middle East. The term is imposed by recent history. Earlier one spoke of Europeanization, to denote the common elements underlying French influence in Syria-Lebanon and British influence in Egypt and Jordan. More recently, following a century of educational and missionary activity, Americanization became a specific force and the common stimuli of the Atlantic civilization came to be called Westernization. Since World War II, the continuing search for new ways has been coupled with repudiation of the Western aegis. Soviet and other modernizing models, as illustrated by India and Turkey, have become visible in the area. Any label that today localizes the process is bound to be parochial. For Middle Easterners more than ever want the modern package, but reject the label "made in U.S.A." (or, for that matter, "made in USSR"). We speak, nowadays, of modernization.

Whether from East or West, modernization poses the same basic challenge—the infusion of "a rationalist and positivist spirit" against which, scholars seem agreed, "Islam is absolutely defenseless."[2] The phasing and modality of the process have changed, however, in the past decade. Where Europeanization once penetrated only the upper level of Middle East society, affecting mainly leisure-class fashions, modernization today diffuses among a wider population and touches public institutions as well as private aspirations with its disquieting "positivist spirit." Central to this change is the shift in modes of communicating ideas and attitudes—for spreading among a large public vivid images of its own New Ways is what modernization distinctly does. Not the class media of books and travel, but the mass media of tabloids, radio and movies, are now the dominant modes. Today's Middle East "chaos" is largely due to the shift of modernist inspiration from the discreet discourse of a few in Oxford colleges and Paris salons to the broadcast exhortations among the multitudes by the mass media.

This historic shift stimulated the inquiry begun in 1950, of which this book is the outcome. The role of new messages in the Middle East "transition" raised a breviary of empirical questions: who was changing? from what to what? how fast? with what effects? While the great debate over Permanence *versus* Change often obliges the Middle Easterner to declare himself philosophically on such questions, we investigate them here in a more limited sense. We focus on the personal meaning of social change—the transformations worked into the daily lifeways of individuals by these large historical forces.

That some millions of Turks now live in towns, work in shops, wear trousers and have opinions who, a generation ago, lived in the centuries-old *sholvars* symbolizing the agrarian, illiterate, isolate life of the Anatolian village is what modernization has already done to some people. That other millions throughout the Middle East are yearning to trade in their old lives for such newer ways is what modernization promises to most people. The rapid spread of these new desires, which provide the dynamic power of modernization, is most clearly perceived in the coming of the mass media. To see why this is so—to comprehend what the Middle Eastern peoples are experiencing under the title of modernization —we remind ourselves of what, historically, happened in the West. For the sequence of current events in the Middle East can be understood as a deviation, in some measure a deliberate deformation, of the Western model.

This observational standpoint implies no ethnocentrism. As we shall show, the Western model of modernization exhibits certain components and sequences whose relevance is global. Everywhere, for example, increasing urbanization has tended to raise literacy; rising literacy has tended to increase media exposure; increasing media exposure has "gone with" wider economic participation (per capita income) and political participation (voting). The model evolved in the West is an historical fact. That the same basic model reappears in virtually all modernizing societies on all continents of the world, regardless of variations in race, color, creed, will be shown in this chapter. The point is that the secular process of social change, which brought modernization to the Western world, has more than antiquarian relevance to today's problems of the Middle East transition. Indeed, the lesson is that Middle Eastern modernizers will do well to study the historical sequence of Western growth.

Taking the Western model of modernization as a baseline is forced upon us, moreover, by the tacit assumptions and proclaimed goals which prevail among Middle East spokesmen. That some of these leaders, when convenient for diplomatic maneuver, denounce the West is politically important and explains why we have chosen to speak of "modernization" rather than "Westernization." Rather more important, Western society still provides the most developed model of societal attributes (power, wealth, skill, rationality) which Middle East spokesmen continue to advocate as their own goal. Their own declared policies and programs set our criteria of modernization. From the West came the stimuli which undermined traditional society in the Middle East; for reconstruction of a modern society that will operate efficiently in the world today, the West is still a useful model. What the West is, in this sense, the Middle East seeks to become.

But these societies-in-a-hurry have little patience with the historical *pace* of Western development; what happened in the West over centuries, some Middle Easterners now seek to accomplish in years. Moreover, they want to do it their "own way." A complication of Middle East modernization is its own ethnocentrism—expressed politically in extreme nationalism, psychologically in passionate xenophobia. The hatred sown by anticolonialism is harvested in the rejection of every appearance of foreign tutelage. Wanted are modern institutions but not modern ideologies, modern power but not modern purposes, modern wealth but not modern wisdom, modern commodities but not modern cant. It is not clear, however, that modern ways and words can be so easily and so totally sundered. Underlying the variant ideological forms which modernization took in Europe, America, Russia, there have been certain behavioral and institutional compulsions common to all. These historical regularities some Middle East leaders now seek to obviate, trying instead new routes and risky by-passes. We alert ourselves to the novelty of these efforts by recapitulating briefly some essential elements in the modernization of the West.

1. The Mobile Personality: Empathy

People in the Western culture have become habituated to the sense of change and attuned to its various rhythms. Many generations ago, in the West, ordinary men found themselves unbound from their native soil and relatively free to move. Once they actually moved in large numbers, from farms to flats and from fields to factories, they became intimate with the idea of change by direct experience.[3] This bore little resemblance to the migrant or crusading hordes of yore, driven by war or famine. This was movement by individuals, each having made a personal choice to seek elsewhere his own version of a better life.

Physical mobility so experienced naturally entrained social mobility, and gradually there grew institutions appropriate to the process. Those who gained heavily by changing their address soon wanted a convenient bank in the neighborhood to secure their treasure; also a law-and-police force to guard the neighborhood against disorder and devaluation; also a voice in prescribing standards of behavior for others.[4] So came into operation a "system" of bourgeois values that embraced social change as normal. Rules of the game had to be worked out for adjudicating conflicts over the direction and rate of change. Who was to gain, how, and how much? As the profits to be gained from mobility became evident to all, conflicts over access to the channels of opportunity became sharper. The process can be traced through the evolution of Western property and tax laws, whose major tendency is to protect the "haves" without disqualifying the "have-nots."[5] It was by protecting every man's *opportunity* to gain that the modern West turned decisively in the direction of social mobility.

Social institutions founded on voluntary participation by mobile individuals required a new array of skills and a new test of merit. Every person, according to the new democratic theory, was equally entitled to acquire the skills needed for shaping his own "future" in the Great Society. The vigorous controversy over public education that agitated the eighteenth century produced a net affirmation of equal opportunity. In every Western country the verdict was pronounced that education should be freely available to all who wanted it, and in some countries whether they wanted it or not. Thus the idea spread that personal mobility is itself a first-order value; the sense grew that social morality is essentially the ethics of social change. A man is what he may become; a society is its potential. These notions passed out of the realm of debate into the Western law and mores.

A mobile society has to encourage rationality, for the calculus of choice shapes individual behavior and conditions its rewards. People come to see the social future as manipulable rather than ordained and their personal prospects in terms of achievement rather than heritage. Rationality is purposive: ways of thinking and acting are instruments of intention (not articles of faith); men succeed or fail by the test of what they accomplish (not what they worship). So, whereas traditional man tended to reject innovation by saying "It has never been thus," the contemporary Westerner is more likely to ask "Does it work?" and try the new way without further ado.

The psychic gap between these two postures is vast. It took much interweaving through time, between ways of doing and ways of thinking, before men could work out a style of daily living with change that felt consistent and seamless. The experience of mobility through successive generations gradually evolved participant lifeways which feel "normal" today. Indeed, while past centuries established the public practices of the mobile society, it has been the work of the twentieth century to diffuse widely a *mobile sensibility* so adaptive to change that rearrangement of the self-system is its distinctive mode.

The mobile personality can be described in objective and technical fashion. Since this is what the book is largely about, it will do here to define its main feature and to suggest the main line of its secular evolution. The mobile person is distinguished by a high capacity for identification with new aspects of his environment; he comes equipped with the mechanisms needed to incorporate new demands upon himself that arise outside of his habitual experience. These mechanisms for enlarging a man's identity operate in two ways. *Projection* facilitates identification by assigning to the object certain preferred attributes of the self—others are "incorporated" because they are like me. (Distantiation or negative identification, in the Freudian sense, results when one projects onto others certain disliked attributes of the self.) *Introjection* enlarges identity by attributing to the self certain desirable attributes of the object—others are "incorporated" because I am like them or want to be like them. We shall use the word *empathy* as shorthand for both these mechanisms. This condensation of psychoanalytic terminology has a pragmatic, not theoretic, intent—since our materials are simply not amenable to the more highly differentiated categories of Freudian vocabulary. Our interview data does not permit systematic discrimination between the introjective and. projective mechanisms. Nor does empathy denote sympathy or antipathy. In particular cases it may lead to either—"understanding" may breed dislike as well as affection.

We are interested in empathy as the inner mechanism which enables newly mobile persons to *operate efficiently* in a changing world. Empathy, to simplify the matter, is the capacity to see oneself in the other fellow's situation. This is an indispensable skill for people moving out of traditional settings. Ability to empathize may make all the difference, for example, when the newly mobile persons are villagers who grew up knowing all the extant individuals, roles and relationships in their environment. Outside his village or tribe, each must meet new individuals, recognize new roles, and learn new relationships involving himself. A rich literature of humor and pathos once dealt with the adventures of the country bumpkin in the Big City, the bewildered immigrant in a strange land. They had to learn their way in these new settings. Learn, in swelling numbers, they did. The story of the 19th century West includes this learning, which now enters the story of the 20th century East. Accordingly, we are interested in the mobile personality mainly as a social phenomenon with a history. Our concern is with the large historical movement, now becoming visible in the Middle East, of which an enlarged capacity for empathy is the distinctive psychic component. Our interest is to clarify the process whereby the high empathizer tends to become also the cash customer, the radio listener, the voter.[6]

It is a major hypothesis of this study that high empathic capacity is the predominant personal style only in modern society, which is distinctively industrial, urban, literate and *participant*. Traditional society is nonparticipant—it deploys people by kinship into communities isolated from each other and from a center; without an urban-rural division of labor, it develops few needs requiring economic interdependence; lacking the bonds of interdependence, people's horizons are limited by locale and their decisions involve only other *known* people in *known* situations. Hence, there is no need for a transpersonal common doctrine formulated in terms of shared secondary symbols—a national "ideology" which enables persons unknown to each other to engage in political controversy or achieve "consensus" by comparing their opinions. Modern society is participant in that it functions by "consensus"—individuals making personal decisions on public issues must concur often enough with other individuals they do not know to make possible a stable common governance. Among the marks of this historic achievement in social organization, which we call Participant Society, are that most people go through school, read newspapers, receive cash payments in jobs they are legally free to change, buy goods for cash in an open market, vote in elections which actually decide among competing candidates, and express opinions on many matters which are not their personal business.

Especially important, for the Participant Style, is the enormous proportion of people who are expected to "have opinions" on public matters—and the corollary expectation of these people that their opinions will matter. It is this subtly complicated structure of reciprocal expectation which sustains widespread empathy. Only in the lowest reaches of America's social hierarchy, for example, is it still discussed whether people *ought* to have opinions. In a climactic scene of *Sweet Thursday,* John Steinbeck relates how the Madam of a whorehouse prepares one of her hustlers, not really made for the business, to go out into the world of respectability. The first rule is to keep her mouth shut:

Next thing is opinions. You and me is always busting out with opinions. Hell, Suzy, we ain't got no opinions! We just say stuff we heard or seen in the movies. We're scared stiff we'll miss something, like running for a bus. That's the second rule: lay off opinions because you ain't really got any.

As Suzy moves from the anarchic margins of American life into solid citizenry, it is foreseen, she will learn to have opinions along the way. In the Middle East many more people have a much longer way to go. "How can you ask me such a question?" gasped the Balgat shepherd. His gasp resounded often in our interviews around the Middle East.

For, in any society, only when the accepted model of behavior is emulated by the population at large does it become the predominant personal style. The model of behavior developed by modern society is characterized by empathy, a high capacity for rearranging the self-system on short notice. Whereas the isolate communities of traditional society functioned well on the basis of a highly constrictive personality, the interdependent sectors of modern society require widespread participation. This in turn requires an expansive and adaptive self-system, ready to incorporate new roles and to identify personal values with public issues. This is why modernization of any society has involved the great characterological transformation we call psychic mobility. The latent statistical assertion involved here is this: In modern society *more* individuals exhibit *higher* empathic capacity than in any previous society.

As history has not been written in these terms, we were obliged to organize our own forays into historical data to establish a trace-line on the evolution of the participant society and the mobile personality. We restrain our account of these forays to some main lines which lead directly to the problem in hand.

2. The Mobility Multiplier: Mass Media

The historic increase of psychic mobility begins with the expansion of physical travel. Historians conventionally date the modern era from the Age of Exploration. Every Western schoolboy knows the names of Cabot, Columbus, Cortez and is dimly aware that they "opened new worlds." This was an initial phase in the modern expansion of human communication. Gradually the technical means of transporting live bodies improved and physical displacement became an experience lived through by millions of plain folk earlier bounden to some ancestral spot. Geographical mobility became, in this phase, the usual vehicle of social mobility. It remained for a later time to make vivid that each mobile soma of the earlier epoch housed a psyche, and to reconstruct transatlantic history in terms of psychic mobility. It is the contemporary historian who now distinctively perceives the mass immigration into America as a traumatic process of psychic encounter with the new and strange.[7] We accent the contemporaneity of the psychic dimension, because the moral injunction to "look shining at new styles of architecture" is something new in the world.[8]

The expansion of psychic mobility means that more people now command greater skill in imagining themselves as strange persons in strange situations, places and times than did people in any previous historical epoch. In our time, indeed, the spread of empathy around the world is accelerating. The earlier increase of physical experience through transportation has been multiplied by the spread of *mediated* experience through mass communication. A generation before Columbus sailed to the New World, Gutenberg activated his printing press. The technical history of the popular arts suggests the sequence. The typical literary form of the modern epoch, the novel, is a conveyance of disciplined empathy. Where the poet once specialized in self-expression, the modern novelist reports his sustained imagination of the lives of others.[9] The process is carried further in the movies and in radio-television dramas. These have peopled the daily world of their audience with sustained, even intimate, experience of the lives of others. "Ma Perkins," "The Goldbergs," "I Love Lucy"—all these bring us friends we never met, but whose joys and sorrows we intensely "share." The media create for us what has aptly been called "the world of the daytime serial."[10]

Radio, film and television climax the evolution set into motion by Gutenberg. The mass media opened to the large masses of mankind the infinite *vicarious* universe. Many more millions of persons in the world were to be affected directly, and perhaps more profoundly, by the communication media than by the transportation agencies. By obviating the physical displacement of travel, the media accented the psychic displacement of vicarious experience. For the imaginary universe not only involves more people, but it involves them in a different order of experience. There is a world of difference, we know, between "armchair travel" and actually "being there." What is the difference?

Physical experience of a new environment affronts the sensibility with new perceptions in their complex "natural" setting. The traveler in a strange land perceives simultaneously climate and clothing, body builds and skin textures, gait and speech, feeding and hygiene, work and play—in short, the ensemble of manners and morals that make a "way of life." A usual consequence for the traveler is that the "pattern of culture" among the strangers becomes confused, diverging from his prior stereotype of it and from his preferred model of reality.

Vicarious experience occurs in quite different conditions. Instead of the complexities that attend a "natural" environment, mediated experience exhibits the simplicity of "artificial" settings contrived by the creative communicator. Thus, while the traveler is apt to become bewildered by the profusion of strange sights and sounds, the receiver of communications is likely to be enjoying a composed and orchestrated version of the new reality. He has the benefit of more facile perception of the new experience as a "whole," with the concomitant advantage (which is sometimes illusory) of facile comprehension. The stimuli of perception, which shape understanding, have been simplified.

The simplification of stimuli, however, is accomplished at a certain cost. The displaced traveler's great pragmatic advantage is that he must take responsive action toward the stimuli presented by the new environment. However painful this may be—as when, to take a simple case, he has lost his way and must ask directions in a language of which his mastery is uncertain—overt action does help to discharge the traveler's interior tensions. But the passive audience for mediated communications has no such discharge channel; the radio-listener's personal response to new stimuli remains confined to his own interior. The inhibition of overt active response is a learned behavior and a difficult one. It was common, in the early days of movies, for persons strained beyond endurance to throw themselves or some object at the screen to stop the villain from strangling the heroine. Even the old media hands among the youngsters of today will sometimes, at a particularly agonizing moment in the television show, hide their faces.

Thus the mass media, by simplifying *perception* (what we "see") while greatly complicating *response* (what we "do"), have been great teachers of interior manipulation. They disciplined Western man in those empathic skills which spell modernity. They also portrayed for him the roles he might confront and elucidated the opinions he might need. Their continuing spread in our century is performing a similar function on a world scale. The Middle East already shows the marks of this historic encounter. As a young bureaucrat in Iran put it: "The movies are like a teacher to us, who tells us what to do and what not." The global network of mass media has already recruited enough new participants in all corners of the earth to make "the opinions of mankind" a real factor instead of a fine phrase in the arena of world politics. There now exists, and its scope accelerates at an extraordinary pace, a genuine "world public opinion." This has happened because millions of people, who never left their native heath, now are learning to imagine how life is organized in different lands and under different codes than their own. That this signifies a net increase in human imaginativeness, so construed, is the proposition under consideration.

3. The "System" of Modernity*

A second proposition of this large historical order derives from

* For a fuller discussion of the material in this section, see my paper "Communication Systems and Social Systems: A Statistical Exploration in History and Policy," *Behavioral Science* II (October 1957), pp. 266-275.

the observation that modern media systems have flourished only in societies that are modern by other tests. That is, the media spread psychic mobility most efficiently among peoples who have achieved in some measure the antecedent conditions of geographic and social mobility. The converse of this proposition is also true: no modern society functions efficiently without a developed system of mass media. Our historical forays indicate that the conditions which define modernity form an interlocking "system." They grow conjointly, in the normal situation, or they become stunted severally.

It seems clear that people who live together in a common polity will develop patterned ways of distributing *information* along with other commodities. It is less obvious that these information flows will interact with the distribution of power, wealth, status at so many points as to form a system—and, moreover, a system so tightly interwoven that institutional variation in one sector will be accompanied by regular and determinate variation in the other sectors. Yet, just this degree of interaction between communication and social systems is what our historical exploration suggests.

We differentiated two historical systems of public communication, Oral and Media, according to the paradigm: Who says what to whom and how? On these four variables of source, content, audience, channel the ideal types differ as follows:

	Media Systems	Oral Systems
Channel	Broadcast (mediated)	Personal (face-to-face)
Audience	Heterogeneous (mass)	Primary (groups)
Content	Descriptive (news)	Prescriptive (rules)
Source	Professional (skill)	Hierarchical (status)

In media systems, the main flow of public information is operated by a corps of professional communicators, selected according to skill criteria, whose job it is to transmit mainly descriptive messages ("news") through impersonal media (print, radio, film) to relatively undifferentiated mass audiences. In oral systems, public information usually emanates from sources authorized to speak by their place in the social hierarchy, i.e., by status rather than skill criteria. Its contents are typically prescriptive rather than descriptive; news is less salient than "rules" which specify correct behavior toward imminent events directly involving the larger population, such as tax collections and labor drafts. (Oral and media systems also differ sharply in recreational content, as we shall see, but we here focus on informational content.) Even these prescriptive messages are normally transmitted via face-to-face oral channels (or via such point-to-point equivalents as letters) to the primary groups of kinship, worship, work and play.

Naturally, few societies in the world today give a perfect fit to either of these idealized sets of paired comparisons. America closely approximates the model of a media system, but people also speak to each other on public issues and the personal influence of the "opinion leader" is strong.[11] Conversely, Saudi Arabia corresponds to the oral system but operates its radio transmitters at Jidda.* As we move around the world, subjecting our ideal types to empirical data, various elements in the patterns begin to shift. Most countries are in some phase of transition from one system to the other.

But two observations appear to hold for all countries, regardless of continent, culture, or creed. First the *direction* of change is always from oral to media system (no known case exhibiting change in the reverse direction). Secondly, the *degree* of change toward media system appears to correlate significantly with changes in other key sectors of the social system. If these observations are correct, then we are dealing with a "secular trend" of social change that is global in scope. What we have been calling the Western model of modernization is operating on a global scale. Moreover, since this means that other important changes must regularly accompany the development of a media system, there is some point in the frequent references to a "world communication revolution." We here consider the more moderate proposition that a communication system is both index and agent of change in a total social system. This avoids the genetic problem of causality, about which we can only speculate, in order to stress correlational hypotheses which can be tested. On this view, once the modernizing process is started, chicken and egg in fact "cause" each other to develop.

To formulate the hypothesis in a manner suitable for testing, we selected indices of three principal sectors—socioeconomic, cultural, political—which could be compared in oral systems and media systems. The "profiles" were as follows:

---

* Be it noted, however, that these State-owned transmitters produce but a single broadcast daily. See UNESCO, *World Communication* (1956), p. 94.

Sector	Media Systems	Oral Systems
Socioeconomic	urban	rural
Cultural	literate	illiterate
Political	electoral	designative

To sharpen the differences, these profiles are stated in dichotomous fashion. The dogmatic appearance of this formulation should trouble no one, for we test them empirically as continuous variables on which differences are calibrated. Just as there is no perfect media system so there is no perfectly urban, literate, electoral society. Our model is probabilistic, our measures are distributive, and our test of fit is correlational.

Our procedure was to construct a matrix containing data on urbanization, literacy, voting and media participation. We handled these as indices of public participation in the four "sectors" as a whole, by expressing our data as the proportion of total population possessing each attribute. Thus, we defined *urbanization* as the proportion living in cities over 50,000; *literacy* as the proportion able to read in one language; *media participation* as the proportion buying newspapers, owning radios, and attending cinemas (all three items being integrated into a single index number); *electoral participation* as the proportion actually voting in national elections (obtained by averaging results for the five most recent elections). Participation in these four sectors, so defined, was taken to represent participation in the social system as a whole. Recall that the participant style of modern society, as contrasted with the isolate lifeways of traditional society, hinges on the *frequency* of participation by individuals.

In the next chapter, and in the case studies, we shall examine more closely the *quality* of participation by different types of individuals in different countries. Here we wish to compare existing nations in terms of overall participation in the sectors essential for modernization. This requires a simple frequency measure, which we obtained from UNESCO and other UN data on most countries of the world—ranging from 54 to 73 in number on the different indices.*

---

* The statistics were used as reported in UNESCO *World Communication* (1951). These were checked against other UNESCO sources for typographical errors and against the UN *Statistical Yearbook* and *Demographic Yearbook* for errors of information and computation. Wherever significant differences appeared which could not be reconciled, the case was excluded

Simple correlation by pairs showed that each factor in the set was significantly related to each other factor.* In the present case, it was "statistically significant" that literacy correlated with urbanism at .64, with voting at .80, and with media participation at .82. Each of these correlations was investigated further, with generally confirmatory results, as when literacy was correlated with each item in the media participation index:

Media Participation Items	Correlation with Literacy
Daily newspaper circulation	.75
Number of radio receivers	.74
Cinema seating capacity	.61

It is obvious that newspaper circulation should correlate better with literacy than does movie attendance, the enjoyment of which does not require literacy. The high correlation of radio receivers leads, for explanation, in another direction. Whereas building cinemas (in which *imported* feature films are shown) requires no modern technology, the mass production of radio receivers does require a fairly high level of industrialization.

We subsume industrialization under our index of urbanization. This is a key variable in our "system," for it is with urbanization that the modernizing process historically has begun in Western societies. Our next task, having shown that literacy and media participation are highly correlated, was to establish their interdependence with urbanism. For the historical literature on this point, while allocating great influence to the growth of cities, is not clear on several important questions: if urbanization is a necessary condition of modernization (meaning that certain other changes can occur only in cities), then what are these other changes that

---

from our analysis. Otherwise all "self-governing territories" are included. The writer is unable to offer any definitive evaluation of these UN data which are assembled from reports prepared separately by each nation. There are national differences in definition of indices and accuracy of reporting. Whereas magnitudes of "error" cannot be checked systematically, the direction of error, in those cases I have checked, always tend toward overstating one's progress in modernization—i.e., underdeveloped countries are likely to report larger rather than smaller estimates of urbanization, literacy, voting, etc.

* Correlation is a statistical procedure to determine whether independent series of events, when their joint occurrence is enumerated, turn out to have occurred together more often than would happen simply by chance—and, if so, how much more often. Readers desiring elucidation of other statistical terms used in these pages may refer to the index of W. A. Wallis and H. V. Roberts, *Statistics. A New Approach* (1956).

regularly occurred in any society when urbanization occurred? If urbanization is necessary to start modernization, how much of it is necessary (what is the "critical minimum")? Is there a point at which modernization, once started, can sustain itself without much or any further urbanization (is there a "critical optimum" for urbanization)?

We formulated these questions, for testing, in three specific hypotheses: (1) that critical limits, minimum and optimum, can be established for urbanization within which literacy will increase directly as urban population grows in all countries; (2) that countries which have not reached the minimum limit of urbanization will also be predominantly illiterate; (3) that countries which have exceeded the optimum limit of urbanization will also be preddominantly literate. To test these hypotheses, we classified all 73 countries according to the data on literacy provided by UNESCO. We then found the mean urbanization for all the countries in each literacy group, as reported below.

Countries (N=73)	Literacy	Urbanization
22	Over 80%	28.0%
4	61-80	29.2
12	41-60	25.0
13	21-40	17.0
22	Under 20	7.4

Thus in all 22 countries less than 20% literate the mean proportion of population living in cities over 50,000 is only 7.4%. The "critical minimum" of urbanization appears to be between 7-17% of total population, for convenience one may say 10%. Only after a country reaches 10% of urbanization does its literacy rate begin to rise significantly. Thereafter urbanization and literacy increase together in a direct (monotonic) relationship, until they reach 25%, which appears to be the "critical optimum" of urbanization. Beyond this literacy continues to rise independently of the growth of cities. The surplus of 1.2% of urbanization in the second row is either insignificant, with only four countries, or else confirms the analysis. Between these limits of 10-25%, our findings indicate, the growth of cities and of literacy are closely interdependent.*

---

* These cutting points are somewhat arbitrary, of course, in the sense that their outcome is partly determined by the statistical input. Had urbanization been indexed by cities over 20,000 rather than 50,000 population, for example, the critical optimum on this continuum might well be located at

Having now established high pairwise correlations between urbanization-literacy and literacy-media participation, with critical optima for joint growth in each pair, we are in a position to suggest an interpretation in terms of historical phasing. The secular evolution of a participant society appears to involve a regular sequence of three phases. Urbanization comes first, for cities alone have developed the complex of skills and resources which characterize the modern industrial economy. Within this urban matrix develop both of the attributes which distinguish the next two phases— literacy and media growth. There is a close reciprocal relationship between these, for the literate develop the media which in turn spread literacy. But, historically, literacy performs the key function in the second phase. The capacity to read, at first acquired by relatively few people, equips them to perform the varied tasks required in the modernizing society. Not until the third phase, when the elaborate technology of industrial development is fairly well advanced, does a society begin to produce newspapers, radio networks, and motion pictures on a massive scale. This, in turn, accelerates the spread of literacy. Out of this interaction develop those institutions of participation (e.g., voting) which we find in all advanced modern societies. For countries in transition today, these high correlations suggest that literacy and media participation may be considered as a supply-and-demand reciprocal in a communication market whose locus, at least in its historical inception, can only be urban.

We shall later examine the idea that a common psychological mechanism underlies these phases—that it is the more empathic individuals who respond, in the first place, to the lure of cities, schools, media. Urban residence, schooling, media exposure then train and reinforce the empathic predisposition that was already present. On this view, the modern "style of life" can nowadays be acquired as a whole by individuals living in modernizing societies. This interpretation is quite plausible, but it does not clarify what happens to empathic individuals who are ready and able to modernize more rapidly and completely than their society permits. A

20% rather than 25%. Cf.: "An average rate of progress of less than 10% per decade is not sufficient to keep the number of illiterates in a country from increasing. . . . An average decennial rate of 25% or more seems to ensure an actual reduction in the number of illiterates in the total population." UNESCO, *Progress of Literacy in Various Countries* (1953), pp. 175, 178.

large and important class of Middle Easterners are in this position today. Our data on 73 countries, distributed over all the continents of the earth, indicate that many millions of individuals everywhere are in the same position. This further suggests that the model of modernization follows an autonomous historical logic—that each phase tends to generate the next phase by some mechanism which operates independently of cultural or doctrinal variations. To understand the position of those millions who may be caught in some historical lag today, we look more closely at our three phases.

The first phase, then, is *urbanization.* It is the transfer of population from scattered hinterlands to urban centers that stimulates the needs and provides the conditions needed for "take-off" toward widespread participation. Only cities require a largely literate population to function properly—for the organization of urban life assumes enough literacy to read labels, sign checks, ride subways. A population of illiterates might learn that they are not to smoke and spit in the subway, or that Express trains run on the local tracks between 5 and 7 P.M. But trial-and-error can be a wasteful societal procedure. The primitive social function of literacy, as of all skills, is to reduce waste of human effort. Its higher function is to train the skilled labor force with which cities develop the industrial complex that produces commodities for cash customers, including newspapers and radios and movies for media consumers. Cities produce the machine tools of modernization. Accordingly, increases of urbanization tend in every society to multiply national increases in literacy and media participation. By drawing people from their rural communities, cities create the demand for impersonal communication. By promoting literacy and media, cities supply this demand. Once the basic industrial plant is in operation, the development of a participant society passes into a subsequent phase. When voluntary urbanization exceeds 25%, thereby assuring the conditions of modern production, further urbanization no longer automatically guarantees equivalent increases in consumption. The need then shifts to modernizing the conditions which govern consumption.

Of this second phase, *literacy* is both the index and agent. To spread consumption of urban products beyond the city limits, literacy is an efficient instrument. The great symbol of this phase is the Sears-Roebuck catalogue. The mail-order house replaces the peddler only when enough people can read catalogues and write letters. In this sense literacy is also the basic skill required for operation of a media system. Only the literate produce the media contents which mainly the literate consume. Hence, once societies are about 25% urbanized, the highest correlation of media consumption is with literacy. We shall soon describe more fully how literacy operates as the pivotal agent in the transition to a fully participant society. Here we wish to suggest that by the time this second phase gets well under way, a different social system is in operation than that which governed behavior in a society that was under 10% urban and under 40% (roughly, less than half) literate. For, when most people in a society have become literate, they tend to generate all sorts of new desires and to develop the means of satisfying them.

It is this interplay of new desires and satisfactions which characterizes the third phase of modernization, namely *media participation.* Once people are equipped to handle the new experiences produced by mobility (via their move to the city), and to handle the new experiences conveyed by media (via their literacy), they now seek the satisfactions which integrate these skills. They discover, as did The Grocer in Balgat, the tingle of wondering "what will happen next"—the tingle which sounds the knell of traditional society, of routinized lifeways in which everyone *knew* what would happen next because it had to follow what came before. To satisfy this new desire requires the personal skill of empathy which, when spread among large numbers of persons, makes possible the social institution of media participation. This was the phase in which the West developed the "penny press," early symbol of the accelerating supply and demand for media products, which continues today with the pocket radio and the portable TV. It is characteristic of this phase, as the production-consumption reciprocal of media participation develops, that economists come to find production of radio sets a useful index of growth in total industrial production.[12]

For, rising media participation tends to raise participation in all sectors of the social system. In accelerating the spread of empathy, it also diffuses those other modern demands to which participant institutions have responded: in the consumer's economy via cash (and credit), in the public forum via opinion, in the representative polity via voting. Other studies had already shown high pairwise correlations between our indices and economic participation—e.g., around the world literacy correlated at .84 with per capita income and at .87 with industrialization.[13] Accordingly, we undertook to establish their connection with political participation, in such fashion as to determine whether the interdependence between these four participant sectors was genuinely "systemic."

We did this by multiple correlations of the four indices already described. This procedure enabled us to rotate each index in the matrix, thereby obtaining the simultaneous degree of correlation between it and all three of the other indices. Based on 54 countries (those reporting data on all four indices), the coefficients obtained in turn for each dependent variable are reported below.

Dependent Variable	Multiple Correlation Coefficient
Urbanization	.61
Literacy*	.91
Media Participation	.84
Political Participation	.82

* A notable feature of all literacy correlations was their stability, regardless of sample size. The correlation of .82 with media participation was for N=54 countries; for N=73 countries it was .84. (Standard deviation was 31.4.) UNESCO literacy data come grouped in five categories, each covering 20 percentage points. All other data were ungrouped.

The size of these coefficients demonstrates that the relationship between the four sectors *is* systemic. These independent tests of the participant style of life do in fact "go together" in 54 extant societies. Beyond this, their ascending order appears to support the historical phasing that has been sketched.

That the urbanization coefficient should be lowest is as expected. Our earlier data indicated that about 10% of the population must be urbanized before the "take-off" occurs. At this point it becomes "economical" to develop literacy and media; hence urbanization and other modernizing trends grow together for a period.[14] But after a certain degree of urbanization exists, then further growth of cities no longer affects other factors in the same degree. Our analysis locates this "critical optimum" at 25%, after which urbanization ceases to play a determinant role because enough people have been relocated in cities to assure the personnel requirements of modern production. As many countries in our sample long ago passed this urbanizing optimum, and since have turned to other factors to maintain self-sustaining growth, urbanization naturally yields the lowest (though still high) coefficient.

That the literacy coefficient is highest also supports our analysis.

Literacy is the basic personal skill that underlies the whole modernizing sequence. With literacy people acquire more than the simple skill of reading. Professor Becker concludes that the written word first equipped men with a "transpersonal memory"; Professor Innis writes that, historically, "man's activities and powers were roughly extended in proportion to the increased use of written records."[15] The very act of achieving distance and control over a formal language gives people access to the world of vicarious experience and trains them to use the complicated mechanism of empathy which is needed to cope with this world. It supplies media consumers, who stimulate media production, thereby activating the reciprocal relationship whose consequences for modernization we have noted. This is why media participation, in every country we have studied, exhibits a centripetal tendency. Those who read newspapers also tend to be the heaviest consumers of movies, broadcasts, and all other media products. Throughout the Middle East illiterate respondents said of their literate compatriots: "They live in another world." Thus literacy becomes the sociological pivot in the activation of psychic mobility, the publicly shared skill which binds modern man's varied daily round into a consistent participant lifestyle.

We come, then, to political participation. Democratic governance comes late, historically, and typically appears as a crowning institution of the participant society. That the voting coefficient is so high indicates that these 54 countries have achieved stable growth at a high level of modernity. In these countries the urban literate tends to be also a newspaper reader, a cash customer and a voter. The modern "system" of self-sustaining growth operates across the land in these 54 countries—as their cities sprouted suburbs, as their urban districts grew into "urban regions," their national increase of literacy and participation kept pace. This capacity to incorporate continuing social change within the existing framework of institutions has become a distinctive structural feature of the developed modern societies. In a century that has reinstated revolution as a method of social change, they have managed to adapt their own accelerated growth mainly by nonviolent procedures.

What of the other countries? What, in particular, of the 19 countries that had to be dropped from our multiple correlations (reducing our sample from 73 to 54) because they failed to supply data on themselves? Good social auditing is itself an index of modernity—only the rational modern perspective seriously believes that keeping records on one's past and present will help to shape future changes in a desirable direction; only modern institutions have developed the techniques of self-observation which sustain this belief. In our world survey, the countries with the least adequate statistical records tended also to be the least developed countries. What of them?

4. The Hurdles of Modernization

When the underdeveloped lands of the world are tested by our model of modernity, the enormous hurdles in the path to modernization stand out more clearly. What the West accomplished gradually over three past centuries is not so easy for the East to achieve rapidly in the present century.

Take the factor of physical mobility, which initiated Western take-off in an age when the earth was underpopulated in terms of the world man-land ratio. Land was to be had, more or less, for the finding. The great explorers took over vast real estate by planting a flag; these were slowly filled with new populations over generations. Since then, the earth's population has multiplied many times, while its acreage has remained about the same. Today exploration occurs mainly in outer space or inner psyche, while the world man-land ratio discourages international mobility. Immigration laws in the more developed countries are designed to keep underdeveloped peoples at home.

At home, in these countries, physical mobility still takes mainly the form of urbanization. But urbanization is no simple panacea for all ills. We have seen that its historic function is to stimulate take-off; thereafter it yields priority to other factors of self-sustaining growth. The critical limits of urbanization required in each country are a function of its population, more particularly of its man-land ratio. It is this which impedes take-off in many underdeveloped but overpopulated countries; where the man-land ratio is very high, urbanization is indispensable but hard to achieve according to rational plan. In such countries, natural increase tends to exceed growth of resources (including usable land) and population density rises steadily.

Sheer density of population, without countervailing urbanization, operates in turn as an anti-literacy force in most societies. Education is cheaper when pupils live close together and hence, other things being equal, density should be associated with greater literacy. But, without urbanization, other things are *not* equal— i.e., the production, distribution, and consumption of wealth are much lower. This has a direct depressing effect on all public services, notably free public education. Dense nonurban societies, where national income is relatively small, tend to maintain relatively fewer schools by public funds; also, since per capita income is lower and less widely distributed, fewer individuals can afford to attend school.

Hence, the more people there are in a given area, the smaller is the proportion being educated and the harder it is to get a rising proportion of literates among them—until they begin to be redeployed into cities. In sparsely settled lands the influence of urbanization is less marked and literacy rates will probably respond directly to rises in per capita national income. But in populous societies urbanization is the intervening variable and is crucial for the take-off toward increasing literacy. Only when dense populations show a significant rate of urbanization do literacy rates begin to rise. The interaction of density and urbanism as factors conditioning literacy may be represented in the figure below.

	URBANISM	
	High	Low
High (DENSITY)	High Literacy	Low Literacy
Low	High Literacy	Indeterminate Literacy

In countries of high urbanization, as our correlations have shown, literacy will also be high regardless of density (e.g., Britain and Western Europe). Where urbanism is low, generally literacy also will tend to be low. (This consequence is less marked in countries of low density, hence the classification "indeterminate literacy.") But it is very clear that low urbanism plus high density goes with low literacy in virtually all extant countries. To report only the most striking results of our several tests, correlation of literacy with density (defined as population per square kilometer) yielded a negative coefficient of —.60. This inverse relationship was about as consistently negative, for all 73 countries, as the correlation of +.64 between literacy and urbanization had been positive.

A similar result was obtained by correlating urbanism with media participation. For 54 countries the coefficient was .58. When the less developed countries were added, making a total of 73 countries, the coefficient dropped to .47. As striking as this decrease was the great "scatter" of data reported by the underdeveloped countries. Whereas the modern nations have achieved "optimum" relations between urbanism, literacy, media participation, the traditional societies exhibit extremely variant "growth" patterns (deviations from the regression lines). Some are more urban than literate, others more media participant than urban.

In the Middle East, two recent trends account for much of this imbalance. One has been the accelerated postwar movement to the capital cities in each country. This is "urbanization" for census purposes, but it seriously revises the historic meaning of the term. In Cairo, for example, there is a huge floating population with no home but the city streets. They attend no schools, do no work, get no cash, buy no goods. It would be more accurate to tally these involuntary urbanites as "internal rural refugees," but until some such auditing change is made the Egyptian census will continue to show a huge and growing surplus of urban over literate population. The second postwar trend is the rapid diffusion of cheap (or free) radio receivers among the rural populations of the Middle East. This again is an alteration of the Western model, in which media participation reflected a market mechanism —radios produced privately for profit were bought individually for pleasure. Radios distributed gratis by government facilitate "social control" rather than "individual participation"; they also explain why most Arab countries show an excess of radio-listeners over urban literates.

Such events introduce a new stochastic factor into the historical model of modernization—one that is not accounted for by the model. Such a factor is the effort by new governments around the world to induce certain symbols of modernity by policy decisions, in a sequence which disregards the basic arrangement of lifeways out of which slowly evolved those modern institutions now so hastily symbolized. A stochastic factor may be a genuine innovation which will remake the model; or it may be a risk taken in ignorance of the model. The evidence now available suggests that, in the Middle East, we are usually dealing with the latter alternative.

An instance is the new global fashion to install some voting mechanism as a symbol of modern desires rather than as a functional agency of modern governance. Democracy has become a world fad, spread across national lines by symbolic *diffusion*, rather than an institutional outgrowth of needs internal to an increasingly participant society. As a result, some modernizing countries show extraordinarily high ("ahistorical") voting rates. Indeed, whereas voting correlates highly with the other variables in the modern countries, sharp deviations occur in Asia and the Middle East. Thus Egypt, in 1956, ordered its impoverished rural masses to "vote" in a single-option plebiscite, which gave Nasser the 97% endorsement common in such performances. These great "underdeveloped areas" have in common the historic poverty of their resources relative to the soaring heights of their current aspirations. They are inadequately urbanized, industrialized and literate, relative to their urge rapidly to install the symbols of modern participant society.

This answers one question only to raise another. Since the stability of modern societies has been associated over past centuries with the whole "system" of participant behavior gradually evolved, how can these new societies-in-a-hurry hope to achieve stability while acquiring mobility? The question is not rhetorical; the writer does not believe that he knows "the" answer. History is a matter of secular trends, not eternal laws, and the persistence of a certain pattern of social change in the past does not mean that things must always be so. On the contrary, the very act of describing past trends and clarifying the conditions of their occurrence may help to shape policies that can redirect the course of history. We turn then to a key problem of modernization in underdeveloped countries: How have they gone about diffusing the capacity for psychic mobility, along with other capacities that historically have equipped people for efficient functioning in participant society?

5. The Model of Transition

Our historical model provided suitable terms for describing the degree of modernization present in a given society at a given time. The indices of urbanization, literacy, media and political participation discriminated efficiently the relative positions in 1950 of very many countries on all the continents of the world. But the model was static to this point. A dynamic component was needed to show how a country *moved* from one phase to the next, why an urban person regularly *became* a literate and a radio-listener and a voter. Such a dynamic component must connect institutional changes with alterations in the prevailing personal style.

We had already identified the characterological transformation that accompanies modernization as psychic mobility, with empathy as its mechanism. The questions now were: how can empathy be tested? how can the results of such testing be collated with the indices of participant behavior? What we needed to learn was whether a person who shows high empathy also exhibits the other attributes, and vice versa. Since empathy is an autonomous personality variable, it is not revealed by any census data, but must be elicited through psychological testing of individuals. At this point the Middle East survey supplied the missing link. The interviews contained a set of nine "projective questions" which we used to test each respondent's empathic capacity:

1. If you were made editor of a newspaper, what kind of a paper would you run?
2. What do you think you miss by not knowing what the newspapers have to say?
3. How do you think people who go to the movies differ from those who don't?
4. If you were put in charge of a radio station, what kinds of programs would you like to put on?
5. If for some reason you could not live in our country, what other country would you choose to live in?
6. Suppose that I could tell you anything you wanted to know about (this country): What two questions would you be most interested in asking?

7. What is the biggest problem that people in the same circumstances as yourself face in life?
8. What do you think people in the same circumstances as yourself can do to help solve this problem?
9. Suppose that you were made head of the government. What are some of the things you would do?

What these questions have in common is that they ask the respondent to imagine himself in a situation other than his real one. They are "role-playing" questions that require, for responsiveness, some capacity to empathize—to imagine what it must be like to be head of a government, editor of a newspaper, manager of a radio station, or even "people like yourself." The strenuousness of such demands upon persons untutored in empathic skills was underlined by the many respondents, in every country, who thought of suicide rather than imagine themselves in these exalted ranks. "My God! How can you say such a thing?" gasped the shepherd, when Tosun put such questions to him.

The historical course of empathy was underscored for me, while working on these interviews, by an advertisement that came through the mail one morning. Printed across the envelope, in bold red letters, was the query: "Suppose you were the editor of *Time* . . ." The circular letter inside described the typical workday of a *Time* editor. An American mass-circulation magazine mails such an item to millions of names, assembled from a variety of "lists," confident that the "teaser question" on the envelope will be comprehensible, interesting and entertaining. In the Middle East, for many millions, such questions are baffling, disturbing, and even impious: "It has never been thus!"

Our task was to devise a method to determine the degree of association between empathy, as tested by these questions, and the lifeways of modernity. The solution of this problem provided our theory of modernization with the dynamic component needed to analyze ongoing changes in the Middle East today. Our solution was to show, empirically, that persons who are urban, literate, participant, and empathic *differ* from persons who lack any of these attributes—and differ on a significant personal trait which is distinctive of the modern style. Such a trait is "having opinions" on public matters. Traditional man has habitually regarded public matters as none of his business. For the Modern men in a participant society, on the contrary, such matters are fraught with interest and importance. A broad range of opinions on public questions can be taken as a distinctive mark of modernity. Accordingly, the central schema of this study can be represented in the basic typology of modernization below.[16]

The Basic Typology

Type		Literacy	Urbanism	Media Participation	Empathy	Opinion Range
Modern		+	+	+	+	1
	A	−	+	+	+	2
Transitional	B	−	−	+	+	3
	C	−	−	−	+	4
Traditional		−	−	−	−	5

If modernization is the transition to participant society, then the direction of change in public communication is toward a constantly expanding opinion arena. The significant mode of participating, in any network of human communication, is by sharing a common interest in the messages it transmits—i.e., by having opinions about the matters which concern other participants. (Nonparticipation, conversely, consists of neither knowing nor caring about the messages relayed through a given network.) In a large public network, such as that of a nation, perfect participation is impossible—and perhaps undesirable. A network would hardly be manageable in which all citizens attended to all messages and expressed opinions on all public questions. There are determinate limits—maxima as well as minima—to the degree of participation appropriate for particular networks. The modernizing tendency is toward networks that can handle maximum participation, and concurrently to develop the participants needed to man these networks.

A person becomes a participant by learning to "have opinions" —further, the more numerous and varied the matters on which he has opinions, the more participant he is. To rank each respondent as a participant in the Middle Eastern opinion arena, we counted the number and variety of items in the questionnaire on which he expressed *some* opinion (i.e., did *not* say "I don't know" or "I have no opinion"). This enabled us to find a number for each respondent which determined his rank-order in the column headed "Opinion Range." Those in rank 1 had the most opinions, those in rank 2 somewhat fewer opinions, and so on down to those in rank 5 with the fewest (or no) opinions.

We then sought to determine whether, as hypothesized, the higher a person's opinion range, the more likely he was to score high on all indexes of modernity. And so, as the scale patterns show, it turned out. The top opinion-holders (rank 1) typically were literate, urban, media participants, and high empathizers. Among illiterates, those living in cities tended to have more opinions (rank 2) than rurals. Among illiterate rurals, those with a significant measure of media exposure scored higher (rank 3) than those without such exposure. This left a group which—in terms of literacy, residence, media exposure—should have been homogeneous in the opinion range, but in fact was not. Some of these individuals had significantly more opinions than the others. The only satisfactory way to account for this divergence was by our personality variable—empathy. For what distinguished these illiterate, rural, nonparticipant individuals (rank 4) from their peers (rank 5) was a keener interest in impersonal matters, a deeper desire to become participants of the opinion arena. They were marked less by their manifest ways than by their latent wants.

Once this was clear, our data fell beautifully into place. For the true Transitional is defined, dynamically, by what he wants to become. What differentiates him from his Traditional peers is a different *latent structure* of aptitudes and attitudes (see Appendix).[17] The aptitude is *empathy*—he "sees" things the others do not see, "lives" in a world populated by imaginings alien to the constrictive world of the others. The attitude is *desire*—he wants *really* to see the things he has hitherto "seen" only in his mind's eye, *really* to live in the world he has "lived" in only vicariously. These are the sources of his deviant ways. When many individuals show deviation in this direction, then a transition is under way in their society. In the next chapter, we show empirically how this transition is at work in every Middle Eastern country, with results that spell the passing of traditional society from that area of the world.

Here we stress that the transition to participant society hinges upon the desire among individuals to participate. It grows as more and more individuals take leave of the constrictive traditional universe and nudge their psyche toward the expansive new land of heart's desire. The great gap is passed when a person begins to "have opinions"—particularly on matters which, according to his neighbors, "do not concern him." The empathic skill which makes this possible is not highly valued in the traditional community. There people are taught to handle the ego with minimum awareness of alternatives to current practices—in the technical sense, compulsively. The Constrictive Self is the approved personal style. Self-manipulation, continuous rearrangement of the self-system to incorporate new experience, is regarded as unworthy of any person with "good character."[18]

The classic case is The Grocer of Balgat, repudiated on all sides as he sought to incorporate the new identities of his vicarious experience. The Balgati feared his opinions and called him "infidel." Tosun found his role-playing distasteful and wrote of him: "Although he is on the same level with the other villagers . . . he most evidently wishes to feel that he is closer to me than he is to them." The Transitionals, at various phases of modernization, are making their way toward an unclear future via a path replete with hard bumps and unsuspected detours. Their voyage entails a sustained commingling of joyous anticipations with lingering anxieties, sensuous euphoria with recurrent shame, guilt and puzzlement. From their changes of pace and their shifts of direction we learn how they perceive the terrain, its pitfalls and its promises.

A deep problem of values is imbedded in the life histories of these men-in-motion. The moral issues of modernization often are reduced to this: *Should* they want what they want? Since they want what we have, Western responses to this question usually reflect only our own value-dilemmas. Rather more relevant is the judgment of Middle Easterners on what they have and what they want. If we resist the temptation to adjudicate conflicting preferences among others, at least long enough to see how they adjudicate these options themselves, then we have a sounder basis than our own conventional values for moral judgment.

For example: a very powerful finding of our study is that Middle Easterners who are modernizing consider themselves happier than do those who remain within traditional lifeways. This is in striking contrast with the impressions conveyed by some observers, often from highly modern settings themselves, who feel that the undermining of traditional ways by new desires must be a net loss. Among such observers the passing of cherished images of passive peasantry, noble nomads, brave Beduin evokes regrets. But these regrets are not felt by the modernizing peasants, nomads, Beduin themselves, or felt less disapprovingly by them than by the moderns who study them and love the familiar way they used to be. Thus Tosun, the bright young modern from Ankara, gave his sympathy to the miserable intimidated Shepherd but only his indignation to the ambitious outspoken Grocer.

Deep sentiment for the splendid past can dim perception of its passing. So distinguished a commentator as Professor Hocking, when obliged to recognize the prevalence of modernist desires among Middle Easterners, does so with regret and even resentment:

> The most important single fact about these people, for the political discussions of the moment, is their rendezvous with CHANGE, the god of "modernity." They are in process of growth: and since this is so, they are no longer to be identified with what they were yesterday but rather with what they will be tomorrow.[19]

Sentiment here produces a misleading dichotomy. Yesterday is perceived as a splendid whole, now wholly gone. But this obscures the evident shaping of Middle East tomorrows by all their yesterdays and by what they seek each new today. There is no uniform Tomorrow just as there was no single Yesterday. It is precisely by "the political discussions of the moment," so impatiently dismissed by Professor Hocking, that the Middle Eastern future will be devised and revised through a succession of tomorrows.

I take respectful issue with Professor Hocking because the issue is central in the perspective of this book. One can admire great achievements of the past without despising small efforts in the present. It is as a monumental summation of small efforts that many great achievements can be viewed. One such is the western achievement of a Participant Society, which is a summation of desires for personal betterment that led through centuries of "political discussions of the moment" to institutions of civil liberty, public welfare and democratic governance. In our view, disdain for the transitory controversies of politics springs from an erroneous theory that the Long-Run is somehow independent of its own sequence of short-runs. Our effort is rather to study the relatedness of political, economic, communication behavior among the Middle Easterners who are piecing together the grand design of their future society.

Until now we have stressed the psychological dimension because the great dramas of societal transition occur through individuals involved in solving their personal problems and living their private lives. But certain of these dramas signify more for the future than others. Those Middle Easterners whose private lives have become permeated by the public questions will prove most enlightening for us. In the drama of modernization, those who have already incorporated the trends of the times (The Moderns) and those who have not yet been touched by them (The Traditionals) present a relatively static posture. The meaning of events is best clarified by those whom we perceive at the moment of "engagement"—a moment which occurs when an expansive Self, newly equipped with a functioning empathy, perceives connections between its private dilemmas and public issues. This is political consciousness, in the larger sense, and its acquisition distinguishes those who have been pierced by the present and in responding shape the future. The *Transitionals* are our key to the changing Middle East. What they are today is a passage from what they once were to what they are becoming. Their passage, writ large, is the passing of traditional society in the Middle East.

III.

The Passing of Traditional Society: A Survey

> "Systems have passed away before you. Do but travel in the land and see the consequences for those who did deny the messengers."
> —*Koran*, Surah III, 137

THE PASSING of traditional society from the Middle East is thus the passing of many traditional lives. All movements of social change alter the ways in which human beings live out their daily round. The process of modernization powerfully transforms individual lifeways. The move from the familiar and deeply personal life of a family farm in an isolated village to the strange impersonality of a "job" in a busy city crowded with unknown persons is one such transformation—probably the one that is most often experienced by modernizing individuals in the Middle East today.

But different figures also appear in this landscape. There are persons who would like to, but can not or do not, move alone to the city. There are villages to which, willy-nilly, the city comes— either via a new concrete road as in Turkey, or via radio as in Egypt, or via adventurous young villagers who shuttle to and fro as in Lebanon. By whatever method the city invades the village, its coming means that great dramas of reception *versus* rejection will be played out in the private lives of individual villagers. The poignancy is heightened for the modern observer, who knows that in some sense the city will always "win," by the great human cost added to these dramas because the actors are unaware that a rough draft of the third act is already written. It is possible that the characterological transformation required by modernization cannot

be produced without such conflicts of wills and ways. But awareness of the fuller process could lessen some of the needlessly tragic
results.

In the city, too, the modernizing landscape contains many
varied figures. Some migrants never penetrate the urban curtain
and live out their lives in a miserable daily dying. Others find in
the industrial discipline a full and satisfying life. Still others are
infused with new dreams of glory—imagining themselves at the
head of an Islamic brotherhood, or of a proletarian union, or of a
Titoist state defying all the mighty. Many, perhaps most, simply
try to learn a little more, get a little more, have a little more.

Those who already have much—whether of power, wealth,
status—also are obliged to rearrange their private lives, or at least
their private emotions, in terms of the changes wrought by modernization in the world they know. How shall a Jordanian *Qadi*,
official administrator of Islamic jurisprudence, reach proper decisions in a secularizing world when he cannot even quite make up
his mind about the movies? What shall an Egyptian journalist,
schooled in the great tradition of European liberalism, write in a
land inflamed by Arab nationalism and primitive xenophobia?
How shall a Lebanese girl, newly graduated from the university, with a taste for the arts, resolve the conflicts between her own
awakened desires and her father's traditional austerities? How, to
put the most general question, shall those who *have* dispose themselves toward those who *want?*

Such a landscape requires, as we put it in chapter II, some principle of unity in diversity. There we presented a principle of
unity—a theory of modernization that articulates the common compulsions to which all Middle Eastern peoples are subject. To ground
the theory in human history, we observed the operation of these
common compulsions over past centuries of modernization in the
West and recent decades of modernization around the contemporary
world. The unifying principle seems well grounded, but the question remains whether it helps to clarify the manifest diversity of
the living Middle East.

To answer this question requires data which faithfully record
diversity by permitting each relevant individual to speak for himself. Such data test any unifying theory by seeing whether the
regularities it postulates do in fact occur among diverse individuals.
The data of this book come mainly from a sample interview survey,

which gave living Middle Easterners the opportunity to speak for themselves. The case studies that follow will report the rich diversity shown in these interviews. This chapter aims to establish the regularities underlying the variety, seeking to test the theory against the data out of which it developed.

In reading this chapter, it is well to bear in mind the purpose of the book and the perspective from which it is written. The book seeks to explain *why* and show *how* individuals and their institutions modernize together. It denies a unique role to "human nature" or to "social determinism." Having no taste for beating dead horses, we do not even acknowledge these as issues, but go directly to a "behavioral" perspective. To wit: social change operates through persons and places. Either individuals and their environments modernize together or modernization leads elsewhere than intended. If new institutions of political, economic, cultural behavior are to change in compatible ways, then inner coherence must be provided by the personality matrix which governs individual behavior. We conceive modernity as a participant style of life; we identify its distinctive personality mechanism as *empathy*. Modernizing individuals and institutions, like chicken and egg, reproduce these traits in each other.

The book seeks, further, to exemplify this conception in the behavior of modernizing individuals and institutions in the living Middle East. To do this, I have made one book out of two enterprises—a theory of modernization and a set of case studies. This curtails the theory, a formal statement of which would require fuller presentation of economic, political, sociological and psychological data. It also curtails the case studies, for other events are occurring in each Middle East country than those we have selected for attention. The abridgement requires indulgence, then, from both social scientist and area expert. Being aimed at both, it may end by satisfying neither.°

The general reader may be less concerned with *these* matters, and more concerned that the book is written from a perspective which does not regard America today as an overindulged fat cow, chewing cud and yielding milk. Such a view is in vogue among Western intellectuals today, but this is *not* the way Middle East-

---

° The references in the back of the book do, however, lead the interested readers to fuller discussion of central points in the theory and the cases that have been published elsewhere.

erners see America. There, current political animosities coexist with the respect that leads to imitation. The case studies show how many variants are registered on any generalization about the Middle East today. But if forced to generalize, I would reverse the currently fashionable formula among Western intellectuals. What America is—to condense a rule more powerful than its numerous exceptions—the modernizing Middle East seeks to become. The meaning of public power and wealth for private comfort and fun is being learned.*

Those who regard this as ethnocentrism should try an exercise in self-analysis: Compare your own life with that of any Middle Easterner you ever knew. If you don't know any, try a different exercise: Ponder the French argument, before the League of Nations, against "a servile imitation of the schemes in force in Western industrial countries" by Middle East lands. This fine thought turned out, in the specific Syrian case, to be a defense of absentee landlordism against the wretched peasants and of anti-unionism against the impoverished proletarians. (Try *that* tune on a liberal harp!) Everyone opposes "servile imitation" as he opposes beating grandmothers. But no advocate of Middle Eastern felicity can properly oppose their quest for things they lack because, in his opinion, Americans have too much of these same things for their own good. Here again, abridgement of the argument may only say too much for some readers without saying enough for others. We turn, then, to the matter in hand and begin by telling how the survey was made.

1. The Story of This Book

The story falls into two main phases: first, organization of the survey, field work, and preliminary analysis of the data by the Bureau of Applied Social Research at Columbia University; second, a comprehensive re-analysis of the data and writing of this book in the Center for International Studies at M.I.T. The present writer participated in both phases.

The survey, started in September 1950, was completed in seven countries—Greece, Turkey, Lebanon, Jordan, Egypt, Syria

---

* Those with an appetite for intra-American polemics can follow this argument further in my "Comfort and Fun: Morality in a Nice Society," *The American Scholar* (Spring 1958).

and Iran. (The Greek survey, which served as a pretest for the interview schedule and sampling design, has not been reported in this book.) The interviews were made in each country by native scholars, usually teachers or advanced students at a major university, who were briefed and supervised by the American in charge. Interviews were made in the native tongue and subsequently translated into English by the bilingual interviewers or at the central office, where the interviews were also checked for accuracy and coverage. The questionnaire was so designed that if the interviewee was not a radio-listener or movie-goer, many subsequent questions automatically were not asked of him. Naturally, interviews with persons exposed to the media lasted longer than interviews with unexposed respondents. Since "filter questions" of this type were used throughout the schedule, the duration of interviews varied from one to six hours between different types of respondents. The basic questionnaire remained the same in all six of our countries. Minor variations were introduced, as the survey moved from one country to another, designed mainly to improve the questions or to adapt them to local circumstances.

It is not appropriate here to attempt a detailed account of the organizational and administrative problems which this pioneer survey encountered. Professor Glock has suggested the complications in a letter:

> Both Millard and Carlson outdid themselves in a job which involved all sorts of political negotiations and interpersonal operations which, unfortunately, cannot be properly recorded at this time. Working in the field was an 18-hour-day and seven-day-week job. There were clearances to be obtained, records to be kept, progress reports to be written, administrative red tape to be cut, and diplomatic functions to be performed in keeping government officials, interviewers and respondents happy about the project being done at all.[2]

In Iraq, indeed, the difficulties were so great that this country was dropped and Iran was substituted in its place. Elsewhere the work continued and about 2,000 interviews from all countries were received in New York starting in the Fall of 1951. Of these, approximately 1,600 (omitting all interviews from Greece and those from other countries which arrived too late or too incomplete to be used) have figured in the making of this book.

In the meantime preliminary analysis had begun. The first report to be completed was that on Turkey by the present writer, with the assistance of G. K. Schueller and Mary Stycos. This was followed by reports on Jordan by J. M. Stycos, on Lebanon by W. N. McPhee and R. B. Meyersohn, on Egypt by P. L. Kendall and B. B. Ringer, on Iran by B. B. Ringer and D. L. Sills, and a comparative report on the four Arab countries by P. L. Kendall and Elihu Katz.[3] These studies were reported in an impressive series of Bureau memoranda.[4] A comprehensive archive of reports made during the preliminary phase is available at the Bureau of Applied Social Research.[5]

The present re-analysis of the data was made possible by the Bureau, which invited this writer to undertake the job under the auspices of the Center for International Studies at M.I.T. The earlier studies had been made by different authors working on separate countries. Each analyst deliberately sought to test different hypotheses involving different sets of indices. Accordingly, a variety of non-comparable tabulations and conclusions appeared in their reports. The re-analysis undertook to recode and reprocess the original data again, using a single typology and common indices to test for comparable data in all countries. The scope of the re-analysis was restricted by the original data from the field. The open questionnaire was congenial to wide-ranging re-analysis, but the controlled sampling procedure imposed severe limits. Before specifying these limitations, it is appropriate to note that this survey was a pioneering application of modern research procedures in an area where such research is virtually unknown and where some of its basic requirements—e.g., census data—are either lacking or misleading. Under these conditions, the Bureau made a remarkable effort, which merits honorable mention in the annals of American social surveys.

Nonetheless, the reader who wishes to evaluate the conclusions for himself must be aware of the limitations imposed by the data. First, the sample in each country was purposively controlled to overrepresent the population of movie-goers, radio listeners and newspaper readers. The project's manual on "basic sampling procedure" gave the instructions below for simultaneously controlling the sample by radio-listening *versus* non-listening, urban *versus* rural residence, and sex. Beyond this, the sample was to divide radio listeners equally between those who do and do not listen to *foreign* radio; between respondents under and over 35 years of age; between high and low income respondents (with the specific cutting point for each country to be determined in the field). The sampling was confined geographically to three provinces in each country, to accomplish the field work with minimum cost of time and money and with maximum efficiency in deployment of interviewers.

The Sample: Simultaneously Controlled Characteristics

		% of Interviews
Radio Listener—Large Urban—Male		26.4
" " — " " —Female		6.6
" " —Medium " —Male		13.6
" " — " " —Female		3.4
" " —Rural —Male		13.6
" " — " —Female		3.4
Non-Radio Listener—Large Urban—Male		13.6
" " " — " " —Female		3.4
" " " —Medium " —Male		6.4
" " " — " " —Female		1.6
" " " —Rural —Male		6.4
" " " — " —Female		1.6
		100.0%

These controls imposed a limiting condition of some importance upon the re-analysis. No rigorous inference could be made from the controlled sample to the total population of any country. Within this self-imposed limitation, we have taken the liberty of suggesting some "national" inferences that seem plausible either (a) when the distributions of the data run together so consistently and significantly as to suggest an invariant, or highly probable, relationship between two attributes, or (b) when we have been able to compare these data with comparable figures given elsewhere for the population as a whole. (The latter procedure, as the reader must recall each time that it is used, is risky because statistics in every Middle Eastern country are incomplete and unreliable.)

Instead of working from sample to total population, therefore, we were obliged to work from sample to a theoretical typology. We have already outlined the main features of this typology and shown the global applicability of its indices to countries undergoing modernization. Here we wish to determine the regularities underlying the variations that appear in the six Middle East countries. Our theory of modernization requires that we specify regularities of institutional and personal behavior which will account for the social changes now visible in all the Middle Eastern lands.

The questions needing clarification are: *Who* is changing, in what *direction*, at what *rate?* The general response to these questions already presented by our theory can be recapitulated briefly.

From what to what? The direction of change is the same in all the Middle East lands. Everywhere the passing of traditional life-ways is visible; the secular trend is toward mobility—physical, social and psychic mobility. *Who is changing?* In every Middle East country the transitional people exhibit more of those charac-teristics we have already identified with the participant style: urbanism, literacy, media consumption and empathic capacity. We shall see, as our data unfold, that these entail an array of common sociological attributes such as age, sex, occupation: e.g., the literate young "unfarming" males (as they were called in Balgat) tend to lead the procession, but others follow close behind. *At what rate?* The rate of social change everywhere is a function (probably a linear function) of the number of individuals accruing to the transitional stratum. The more persons who are "going modern" in any country, the higher is its overall performance on the indices of modernity. Accordingly, the specified levels of achieved change vary widely from one Middle East country to another.

These variant levels of national achievement, in turn, explain the different impact of modernization upon persons living in the sev-eral countries today. The nation provides the channels through which individuals transform their own lives. Each person may de-cide for himself how to use the opportunities available to him. But it is the national posture which regulates the number and kind of opportunities that are available—how many, where they can lead, how fast. So, persons of the same type (in our typology) often lead quite different lives in different lands. To be a Traditional in Lebanon, where a modern communication network brings all types of people closer together, is quite a different life-situation from being a Traditional in Iran, where such people often live in vil-lages isolated from any urban centers and follow a daily round more akin to the Biblical epoch than to the twentieth century. A Modern in Syria tends to be an active and articulate young man, whereas in Jordan he is usually a disgruntled refugee from Palestine. Whereas Transitionals in modernizing Turkey are generally pro-ductive, optimistic and self-confident, their opposite numbers in Egypt are more often frustrated, dysphoric and ambivalent.

The logic of the relationship between the three types remains

valid *within* nations. In each country Transitionals score higher
on our indices of modernity than do Traditionals and lower than
do Moderns. But the *average* score of all Transitionals (as of the
other types) is higher in some countries than in others. This confirms the obvious fact that people live in places and that circumstances alter cases. But we wish to go beyond bromides and investigate the inner workings of these relationships. To determine the
relative positions of Middle Eastern individuals and countries on
a common scale of modernization, we used three central hypotheses: (1) if the mean scores for all three types are consistently
higher in country X than country Y, then country X is *more modern;*
(2) If the Transitional mean scores in country X are consistently
closer to the Moderns, then country X is *more dynamic;* (3) If
the mean scores in country X consistently show small differences
between all three types, then country X is *more stable.*

By "more modern" we mean that more people have gone further in transforming their traditional style of life, as scored by our
four indices. By "more dynamic" we mean that modernization is
occurring at a faster tempo—more people are changing more rapidly
in the directions stipulated. By "more stable" we mean that the
class-cleavages are less salient; accordingly, that modernization
is more likely to proceed without violent discontinuities of policy
and personnel (e.g., revolutions, *coups d'état,* riots, assassinations).

A very striking fact of Middle Eastern life today is that these
three attributes of modernism, dynamism, stability tend to go together. Turkey and Lebanon, the most modern of our six countries,
are also the most dynamic and the most stable countries (by the
definitions just given). The explanation appears to be that they
have passed their "take-off" points and are well launched in a
process of self-sustaining growth. This is *not* to say that they have
solved all their problems—which is an accomplishment of utopia,
not of modernization. It *is* to say that their problems are primarily
economic, that programs designed to solve these problems do not
include violent transformations of the social system as a method,
that political life has reduced the cataclysmic issues of ideology to
the manageable dimensions of planning.

The other four countries, less modern today, are also less dynamic (in rate of modernization) and less stable. The great postwar
events in Egypt, Syria, Jordan, Iran have been the violent struggles
for the control of power—struggles notably absent in Turkey and

Lebanon, where the control of power has been decided by elections. The omnipotence of politics, a lesson impressed on the 20th century by the Bolsheviks, has radically transformed the course of modernization in these less developed lands. Such proto-Bolshevization arises independently of, but then tends to converge with, their foreign policy positions in the bipolar world arena. This is a major problem in political sociology, and no serious student of social change in the living Middle East can ignore it.

We wish to come upon this problem, so to speak, from its proper social matrix. It is "no accident" that Turkey and Lebanon are democratizing while Egypt and Syria tend toward bolshevizing. (Jordan and Iran, we shall see, are not yet far enough along to be characterized.) On our analysis, Turkey and Lebanon are past take-off and set on a modernizing course, whereas Egypt and Syria seek to evade the historic route to take-off by trying a new bypass. It is no accident because, on the theory that has been set forth, political behavior is but one aspect of a behavioral matrix. People acquire the capacity for political participation by learning, under the permissive conditions of mobility, how to participate in all sectors of public life. The mechanism is empathy and its operation produces opinion on public matters. The outcome is a skill syndrome, a capacity to rearrange one's self-system on short notice, which flourishes in a setting of balanced urbanism, literacy, media participation. Our first task, then, is to provide data appropriate for ranking the Middle East nations as social settings conducive to mobility, empathy, opinion, participation.

2. Ranking the Nations: Societal Audits

As a starting-point, we assembled data on the principal indices of modernization for all six countries from 1950 census data. These are presented in Table 1. Before presenting these figures, it is necessary to state why they must be handled with considerable reserve.

First, Middle East statistics are a hazardous enterprise. Few governments in the area are properly equipped for accurate social bookkeeping. Even those which operate central statistical audits sometimes conceive their function as boosting morale rather than recording information. This leads to publication of figures which correspond poorly with any verifiable observations. Second, the absence of tested baselines complicates the work of efficient statistical services that have recently entered the area—UN, World Bank, Point Four and others. In Iran, where estimates of total population fluctuate between 15-20 millions, regional sample surveys instituted by Point Four can only limit the margins of error by a million or two either way. Even the modern Lebanese, owing to the Christian-Muslim ratio on which their internal governance is balanced, refuse to permit a systematic census. Third, in these circumstances the figures in Table 1 are only the best estimates that can be drawn from the sources that merit consideration. Fourth, these estimates refer to 1950, the year in which the bulk of our interviewing was done. Since then, several important changes have occurred—e.g., the extraordinary growth of mass media in Turkey, which by now puts her clearly in the top rank on media production and consumption. That Turkey has also, by now, survived the three most democratic elections in Middle East history also sets the framework.

Table 1—Auditing Modernization (1950)

	Turkey	Lebanon	Egypt	Syria	Jordan	Iran
Population (in millions)	21	1.3	21	3	1.3	18
Urbanization (%):						
Cities over 20,000	15	23	28	27	9	21
Cities over 100,000	8	16	19	21	0	13
Literacy (%)*	30	60	15	20	20	10
Voting (%)	36	11	—	26	14	—
Media Consumption (per 1,000):						
Daily Circulation	16	81	17	19	8	5
Radio Receivers	16	36	12	15	1	3
Cinema Seats	9	19	10	8	6	4
Media Production:						
No. of Dailies	72	45	55	33	5	20
Transmitting Power (KW)	540	4.5	81.1	11.8	20.5	31.5
Feature Films per Yr.	15	—	45	1	—	1
Education (%)†						
Elementary	7.6	11.5	6.6	9.0	6.1	3.8
Vocational	.20	.30	.15	.05	.02	.007
Teacher Training	.07	—	.06	.03	.002	.007
Universities	.09	.24	.18	.07	—	.02

* Indices of literacy vary widely, and so do estimates. These figures approximate the median of available estimates.

† Computed as proportion of pupils in total population (since there are no comparable figures on school-age population).

If read with these cautions in mind, and with some knowledge of the context, then Table 1 helps to clarify the Middle East landscape. Of our six countries, three are big and three are small. But there are differences within each group. Only Turkey among the big countries has its population fairly evenly distributed over its total surface. Both Iran and Egypt comprise vast uninhabited deserts—but Egypt is one of the world's most densely populated countries, whereas Iran has room for growth. There is demographic variation also in the smaller countries. Tiny Lebanon, least equipped for internal expansion, has by emigration extended its human frontier overseas and continues to grow. Syria, with the largest growth-potential, gives fewer signs of development. The relationship between present boundaries and future frontiers sets style and tone for persons living in these places: Lebanese feel free to go almost anywhere; Syrians feel more obliged to stay where they are. These matters go beyond societal audits to the type of data we shall present next.

On our theory, let us recall, it would be misleading to consider each index as an equally valid independent measure of modernization. More important is the balance between indices and their joint rates of growth in each country. The problem, for countries acquiring mobility, is how to maintain stability. Excessive growth in one phase of modern life, as compared with other related phases, often does more harm than good. We shall see this illustrated by the extraordinary rate of Egyptian urbanization. Responding to population pressure rather than public policy, this movement off the land has simply displaced a portion of rural misery into the cities without stimulating growth in the skills required for true urbanization. Similar imbalances overcrowd the metropoli in Syria and Iran, while the towns fail to grow. The high figure for elementary education in Syria also bespeaks an erratic leap rather than cumulative, movement. Outraged by French policy, newly-independent Syria virtually destroyed the school system developed under the French mandate and rapidly installed its own. This involved a large effort by the new government, but the figure reported in 1950 represented a take-over rather than a take-off. It can hardly be maintained as a growth-rate through dispersed rural Syria with vocational training at .05% and teacher training at .03%.

The Turkish figures show a better balance, representing a somewhat slower rate of growth, but growth that has been effectively maintained over three decades. It is, indeed, the remarkably sustained process of balanced growth that makes Turkey the area's outstanding example of modernization on our terms. As of 1950, Lebanon was "more modern" than Turkey on several indices. But if the 1950 table is taken as one point in a time-series extending over the three decades 1927-57, then it becomes clear that Turkey is modernizing at a faster tempo and is therefore "more dynamic." Moreover, Turkey has succeeded in keeping a more balanced ratio among the rates of growth in all sectors, an indication that Turkey is "more stable" which is supported by its extraordinary development of participant politics since 1950.

The balanced modernization of Turkey is most clearly contrasted with the erratic social change and political instability exhibited by Egypt. With roughly the same total population, Egyptian urbanization was just twice as large as Turkish in 1950. But a glance at the relationship of urbanization to the other sectors shows why this did not constitute modernization in Egypt. Whereas Turkey had gradually attained the critical minimum of 10% required for take-off, Egypt had already passed the critical optimum of 25%. Moreover, Table 1 shows a high degree of balance between urbanization and other rates of growth in Turkey, as compared with extreme imbalance in the Egyptian matrix. An important index of balanced urbanization is the growth of literacy. Since Egypt was twice as urban as Turkey it should, on our analysis, be something more than twice as literate. But its literacy was, in fact, half as high as Turkey's in 1950—i.e., to match Turkey's urbanism-literacy ratio, Egypt would require over 400% more literates than it had. This conforms to the global ratio reported in Chapter II, which showed that when urbanization exceeds 25% literacy should be over 60% and growing.

Such imbalances tend to become circular and to accelerate social disorganization rather than self-sustaining growth. Since 1950, Turkish literacy has increased steadily and at an appropriately swifter rate than urbanization; Egyptian literacy has barely kept pace with its swelling population and not at all with its overflowing capital cities—which are increasingly filled with homeless illiterates. The educational data in Table 1 tell the story. The 1% difference in elementary education means that each year Turkey produces almost a quarter-million more literates than Egypt, whose rate of population increase would require that she quadruple her annual production of literates merely to match the Turkish ratio. The educational percentages further show that Turkey is producing each year over a million more vocational graduates and teachers, the human "multipliers" in diffusing literacy and other skills, whereas Egypt's ratio should double Turkey's simply to service its urban sector at the same level (and approximately redouble to service its greater population increase).

Instead, we find Egypt outproducing Turkey educationally only at the university level, which supplies relatively few skills that are immediately utilized in rural Egypt and hence tends to increase imbalance and instability. A similar imbalance, relative to the literacy rates, appears in the Egyptian figures for media production-consumption as compared with the Turkish data. (The extraordinary figure of 540 KW transmitting power is erroneously reported as Turkish; this represents a huge transmitter installed by the United States, for its own use, at Istanbul.) Most striking, of course, are the comparative voting figures, which have diverged even more sharply since 1950—with three genuinely participant national elections in Turkey as compared with one Egyptian plebiscite designed to ratify the Nasser dictatorship.

In the case studies which follow we shall examine the statistical matrix for each country in detail. Here we wish to show how the order in which the countries are ranked corresponds with the attributes of the three personal types in each country.

3. Persons and Places:
Deviant Phases and Divergent Styles

Recall that modernization, in our view, is a secular trend unilateral in direction—from traditional to participant lifeways. This common process entails certain important regularities of social change throughout the Middle East. But there are national deviations because the individual countries are passing through different phases at a particular period of time. By making explicit the regularities we document the process; by noting the deviations we locate each country in its proper phase. The divergent behavioral styles associated with these deviant national phases reveal the impact of places on persons.

Of our six countries, then, Lebanon started earliest and had reached the most advanced stage by 1950. Turkey, showing more rapid and comprehensive modernization over the past three decades, has by 1958 overtaken Lebanon in many sectors. Jordan and Iran are the least modern countries. Jordan in 1950 was a tiny desert shaykhdom that had just been galvanized by the acquisition of new territory and a mass of Palestinian refugees, twice as numerous as the indigenous Transjordanians and much more modern in every way. (This huge refugee element explains the numerous deviations in the "national profile" of Jordan.) Iran, large and populous, was struggling to awaken from the deep sleep of centuries under the impetus of Mossadegh and the oil nationalization. Syria and Egypt are the complex intermediate cases. Syria exhibits a top-heavy elite in an underpopulated, still quite agrarian, land with inadequate resources. Egypt, with a rich agricultural production sustaining one of the world's most overpopulated areas, was still governed by Farouk in 1950. Since then, under military dictatorship, it has revived an historical claim to Arab leadership. This claim has diverted the new Egyptian elite from domestic modernization into a political arena strained by competing claims against its own large ambitions.

To make this ranking of countries plain, the rows of all tables are arranged in decreasing order of modernism—Turkey and Lebanon at the top, Egypt and Syria in the middle, Jordan and Iran at the bottom. The types are also ordered by degree of modernism—Traditional at the left, Transitional in the middle, Modern at the right. Where an index of modernization is being tested, the coefficients should increase from top to bottom and from left to right—the lowest appearing at bottom left and the highest at top right. The paradigm for such distributions is:

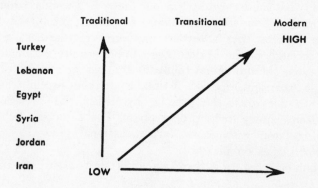

We begin with the array of sociological attributes, by type and country, presented in Table 2. These data document the generalization, for our sample, that modernizing Middle Easterners in 1950 tended to be young unmarried males, relatively well-off, and recruited among minority groups—in higher proportions than in the total population. (In addition to such diverse Christian minorities as Copts, Greeks, Armenians, this generalization includes also the Druzes and Jews. But as the two latter groups tend not to reveal their religion, Table 2 counts only declared Christians.)

As these data compare only differences between the types in each country (not comparable samples between countries), we expect the numbers to increase horizontally within each country but not vertically between countries. The horizontal increase is quite regular and in some cases dramatic—e.g., the clear majorities registered for males in all countries, and for young unmarried males in the four Arab countries. Females appeared more frequently as Moderns in countries where the Sunni branch of Islam does *not* dominate the social order and where there are many Christian Moderns. In Egypt and Syria, with many Christian Moderns, the Sunni Muslims *do* dominate. In Turkey, where the Christians are all Modern (though greatly reduced in number since expulsion of the Greeks) and where Muslims are Sunni, the high proportion of women as Moderns is due to Atatürk's separation of church and state three decades ago, together with his deliberate policy of coeducation and "lifting the veil." Sunni Islam, in the absence of a countervailing Christian influence, has tended to keep women in a traditional style of life.

On one point, data in Table 2 do show an important deviation. This is in the final column giving the "average of differences" between the three types in each country. The two lowest countries show differences approximately equal to those for the two highest countries. This requires a corollary of our hypothesis that the smaller the differences between the types the more stable the country. The capacity to maintain stability while modernizing at a rapid rate is shown only by Turkey and Lebanon. In Jordan and Iran, where modernization was barely visible in 1950, the small differences doubtless reflect the persistence of traditional relationships for most people. The likelihood is that, in 1958, post-British Jordan and post-Mossadegh Iran show the impact of modernization by larger differences between the types than existed in 1950.

Table 2—Sociological Attributes by Type and Country

	Total Number*			% under Age 30			% Unmarried			% Female			% Christians			% Well-off			Average of Differences†
	A	B	C	A	B	C	A	B	C	A	B	C	A	B	C	A	B	C	
TURKEY	99	35	123	27	40	45	20	26	41	19	27	29	0	0	.8	12	26	45	34.0
LEBANON	103	46	113	30	41	52	22	30	60	19	22	25	29	41	45	8	17	44	38.2
EGYPT	91	46	122	29	46	56	17	26	51	13	61	16	2	2	24	0	15	28	83.6
SYRIA	93	29	78	25	41	60	19	34	53	6	20	14	19	28	42	2	34	52	62.4
JORDAN	97	50	116	28	28	46	24	26	52	15	20	23	6	12	23	6	20	21	34.4
IRAN	48	27	53	31	53	58	10	20	34	14	7	17	8	13	26	6	20	19	37.2

* All comparative tables in this chapter are based on the numbers of respondents who were asked comparable questions in all countries. The whole numbers are smaller, therefore, than those presented later in the case studies. The average of differences between types also is generally smaller than in the case studies.

† We obtained this figure for each country by summing the differences between the three types in each column. We then added the sums of these differences for all five columns and divided by 5, producing an average of differences per country. The formula was: $X = [(C - B) + (B - A) + (C - A)]$; in the two cases where A > B and B > C, the order was reversed.

Especially in Jordan, where the highly modernized Palestinian refugees had barely begun to disrupt traditional relationships in 1950, the subsequent impact of their activities is likely to be visible in 1958.

A striking illustration of the hypothesis is the far greater distance between the types in Egypt and Syria. That these two acute "trouble spots" are the least stable lands in the Middle East is shown by every test in our battery—as by common observation. Why they have been so deeply shaken by the crisis of modernizaiton is indicated by the enormous cleavages between the divergent styles of life. In this context, other items in Table 2 become salient. We note, for example, that Egypt shows about the lowest proportion of females among its Moderns but very much the highest proportion among its Transitionals. No artifact of our sampling procedure alone could explain this difference between 16% and 61%. A more likely explanation is the unusual sequence of educational opportunities and vocational obstacles which shape the life-history of many Egyptian women. The point is clarified by comparison with the most modern and least modern countries. In Turkey, where women who receive education are also permitted (indeed encouraged) to take jobs, they tend to develop a consistent Modern style. In Iran, where most women receive neither education nor employment, they remain quite Traditional in their ways. In Egypt, many women receive education but then are blocked by tradition from mobility and vocational opportunities. It is still "unseemly" for a woman, outside certain sections of Cairo, to be seen alone in a public place where men are admitted—whether it be a movie or a museum. Accordingly, Egyptian women with some education but few outlets tend to cluster in the Transitional group —no longer quite Traditional, but not yet Modern. This frustrating experience may explain the growth of Egyptian feminist movements, such as that led by Dr. Doria Shafaq, and their increasing claim on public attention during the past few years.

The deviant case of Egyptian women throws light on the position of Transitionals throughout the Middle East. Our general proposition that Transitionals normally occupy an intermediate position on the indices of modernism, between the Traditionals and the Moderns, is heavily documented in the case studies. One qualification has already been stated: in more dynamic countries (those modernizing more rapidly) Transitional scores will tend to be closer to Modern scores. Two further corollaries appear to be valid: in more traditional (less dynamic) countries Transitional scores will tend to be closer to Traditional scores; and finally, in intermediate countries Transitional scores will show more extreme fluctuations between the polar types from one index to another.

The central role of the Transitional hinges, as we have seen, upon his *mobility*. The Transitionals are, literally, the men-in-motion of the Middle East. This is sometimes obscured in the case studies which, designed to gauge the degree of modernism achieved in 1950, deal with urbanization as the proportion of people living in cities at that time. This static measure naturally shows the highest proportion of urbanites among the Moderns, most of whom were born in cities. But the genuinely mobile persons are those who, having been born in rural places, *moved* to cities in their own lifetime. To compare our respondents on this test, we collated all answers to the questions where they had grown up and where they were living today. Those who had moved to a larger place or to a different province than their birthplace were classified as "mobile," with the results shown in Table 3.

Table 3—Mobility by Type and Country

	Traditional	Transitional	Modern	Total
Turkey	11%	20%	8%	39%
Lebanon	9	11	10	30
Egypt	1	17	5	23
Syria	5	7	4	16
Jordan	16	10	10	36
Iran	2	7	10	19

Among the living generation, Transitionals tend to be the most mobile. Turkish mobility is highest across the board, with the Turkish Transitionals distinctly ahead of their peers elsewhere. Noteworthy, in both Turkey and Lebanon, is the high mobility achieved by the Traditionals as well—which gives these two countries a more balanced distribution between the three types, at a high level of mobility, than is found elsewhere. In Egypt, frequent movement among Transitionals is accompanied by virtually *no* mobility among Traditionals. (The imbalance is expressed by the sum of percentage differences between the three types—32 in Egypt as compared with 24 in Turkey and 4 in Lebanon.) In Syria and Iran, mobility is extremely low and erratically distributed among the three types. Iran is the one country in which Transitionals score lower than Moderns, for in 1950 Iran a Transitional type had barely begun to emerge. The Jordan mobility profile deviates from all regularities owing to the Palestinian refugees, whose "mobility" was in fact a forced migration after the 1948 war with Israel.

One important correlate of mobility, for this study, is its tendency to increase media exposure. We have already seen that media exposure increases with modernity by types. Here we wanted a comparative measure to see whether mobility and media exposure go together by countries. We formed a weighted index of exposure to each of the media—e.g., daily newspaper reading scored 4, several times weekly scored 3, once weekly scored 2, less than weekly scored 1, and no reading at all scored 0. Combined with similar weights for radio-listening and movie-going, this gave us an index of media exposure which ranked individuals on a scale from 0 to 12. The proportion of high scorers (over 10 units) in the total sample for each country is reported in Table 4.

Table 4—High Media Exposure by Countries

Turkey	35%
Lebanon	29
Egypt	22
Syria	23
Jordan	29
Iran	13

The rank-order of the countries on media exposure corresponds perfectly with its mobility profile. The Turkish lead in media consumption, as in mobility, was already substantial in 1950. Even the usual deviation caused by the refugees in Jordan corresponds with its deviation on mobility. The attitudinal element which links mobility and media so closely is shown in Table 5 below. In the Middle East, the media are still so new that their title to existence is a highly controversial matter. Many respondents in each country, especially among the Traditionals who had never been exposed to them, regarded radio as a "devil's box" and movies as sinful. Among the Arabs, who are more respectful than Turks and Iranians toward the Islamic injunction against pictorial representation of human beings, there is also a wider *malaise* about the disruptive impact of the media upon their chances of salvation.

Transjordanians even attribute the ills that befell the Palestinian refugees to God's wrath over their consorting with these new-fangled media. "Look at the Palestinians," said one Transjordanian respondent, "they listened to the radio and God destroyed them."

In our case study of Jordan, we shall look more closely at these attitudes. Here we wish to compare their distribution among the Transitionals in the four Arab countries (the questions asked in Turkey and Iran are not directly comparable). Accordingly, Table 5 reports the proportion of Transitionals in each country who—when asked what they thought of newspapers, radio, movies—expressed approval of these media.

Table 5—Media Approval among Transitionals

	Newspapers	Radio	Movies
Lebanon	70%	89%	85%
Egypt	44	46	55
Syria	35	35	42
Jordan	58	82	47

The Transitionals approve of the media in proportions corresponding to their mobility. In Lebanon, where the young Transitionals already use their media-exposure as a wedge into the traditional structures of power and prestige, approval is highest for all media. (The lesser approval of newspapers, we shall see in the Lebanon chapter, was mainly a reaction against recent trends in the Beirut press.) In Egypt and Syria, media approval is generally low, with movies the most favored. This preference, reflecting Egypt's growing production of feature films, has probably increased its lead since 1950. In Jordan, the Palestinian refugees intensely disliked most of the newspapers available to them (controlled by non-refugee editorial policies) and had few opportunities to see movies. Their extreme preference for radio reflected the availability in refugee camps of radio receivers, their only channel of news from other sources (e.g., Cairo).

The importance of media exposure, in our theory, is that it enlarges a person's view of the world ("opinion range") by increasing his capacity to imagine himself in new and strange situations ("empathy"). When we tested empathy by our battery of projective questions, the respondents rank-ordered themselves by type and country in perfect correspondence with our hypothesis. To see more closely the connection between empathy and media attitudes, we classified all responses to the question "If you were made editor of a newspaper, what kind of a paper would you run?" Underlying the variety of responses, there was a certain cluster of attitudes that came closest to the approved modern attitude. This stressed "independence, impartiality, objectivity" as primary attributes of newspapers. We then tabulated the proportion of respondents, by type and country, who stressed these three attributes. The results, which index the incorporation of modern press standards, are shown in Table 6.

Table 6—Empathy to Modern Press Standards

	Traditional	Transitional	Modern
Turkey	42%	55%	59%
Lebanon	33	50	33
Egypt	19	42	36
Syria	26	40	35
Jordan	15	57	38
Iran	6	18	26

The distribution shows a consistently higher proportion of Turks across the three types. In both of the advanced countries, Turkey and Lebanon, it is among the newly-participant Transitionals and many Traditionals that the importance of an "independent, impartial, objective" press has been widely diffused. (The Lebanese Moderns were preoccupied by recent unpopular trends in the Beirut press.) In Egypt, Syria, Jordan the lower regard for modern press standards among the Moderns seems related to a more profound *malaise*. In these countries, a substantial segment of Moderns are the radical young intelligentsia dedicated to deep and rapid social change. The newspapers they read in 1950 were, by and large, controlled by the ruling elite—often liberals of 19th century vintage—who appeared to the young radicals as defenders of their vested interests. Counter-elite attacks since 1950 have transformed this situation. It is likely that in 1958 many more Moderns in Egypt and Syria, now satisfied with the radical line taken by their press, would give more attention to press standards than when they were preoccupied by acute issues of press ideology.

But our data refer to 1950 and our focus is on the Transitionals. That so many could imagine themselves in the strange role of newspaper editors, and that their imaginings took so modern a form, indicates the spread of empathy among them. The enlarging of perspectives, which accompanies empathy, is indicated by the content of their news interests. Each respondent was asked to recall the last item of news he had received. A person's answer to such a question usually reflects the habitual "screen" of perception and memory through which he filters incoming information. We classified the news items recalled by the respondents in categories showing an increasing range of news interest: personal, family, community, national, international. The proportions recalling international news are reported in Table 7.

Table 7—News Range: Recall of International Items

	Traditional	Transitional	Modern
Turkey	81%	64%	82%
Lebanon	39	54	69
Egypt	35	40	59
Syria*	31	45	58
Jordan*	29	39	62

* Refugee respondents in Syria and Jordan recalled mainly items dealing with Palestine. Following their own perspective, we classified such items as home rather than international news for these groups. Iran is not included because no directly comparable question was asked there.

This distribution corresponds to our paradigm, rising steadily from left to right and from top to bottom. The principal deviation —the extremely high proportion of Turkish Traditionals recalling international news—turned out to reflect a widespread (and rather single-minded) popular interest in the Korean War, to which a Turkish brigade had just been committed with immense publicity through all news media. Hence, this constitutes a special case of, rather than an exception to, the regular increase of interest in international news from Traditional to Modern types and from less to more advanced countries.

Empathy shows in the "news range" of an individual because this illustrates his interest in matters beyond his immediate personal and local concerns—in matters which, as Traditionals put it, are none of his business. Empathy shows as well in a person's "opinion range"—his capacity to form and express views on a variety of matters which are also, in the Traditional's sense, not directly his business. To test this, we formed an Opinion Index by drawing eleven questions from different sections of the interview bearing on different matters of large public importance. By his answers to these questions, each respondent revealed the number and variety of matters on which he had opinions. Each cogent answer was scored 1, each "no opinion" was scored 0. The maximum possible score per respondent was thus 11 units. The average score for each type in each country was then computed, with results shown in Table 8.

Table 8—Opinion Range (Index Units)

	Traditional	Transitional	Modern
Turkey	6.0	7.9	8.2
Lebanon	6.2	7.0	8.0
Egypt	4.3	6.0	7.5
Syria	6.6	7.6	8.0
Jordan	6.3	8.0	8.0
Iran	4.1	5.6	7.8

In such a scoring procedure, small variations register large differences. The .7 lead of the Turkish over Egyptian Moderns, for example, signifies that the same number of Turks gave about 100 more answers out of a possible total of 1353 answers. The consistent increases in opinion range by type and country (with somewhat lower scores than expected in Egypt) thus conform to our paradigm. As individuals and their nations move toward modernity, a systematic process of opinion-formation comes into play. The growth of a Public Opinion becomes manifest as more and more people increase their news and opinion range—the number and variety of public matters on which, though none of their personal business, they show interest and express opinions.

A Public Opinion grows out of the expectation that many people will have views on public issues; it is sustained by the reciprocal expectation that what people think about such issues will make a difference in their solution. This structure of reciprocal expectations —that people will have opinions and that their opinions will count —requires a widespread sense of deference toward *vox populi.* Individuals must believe that their own opinions combine with the opinions of others to express a "popular will," which is a major channel of access from the governed to their government. It is not necessary to believe that the will of the governed must always be heeded. But it must always be heard and sometimes be heeded.

To see how widely these reciprocal expectations had spread among Middle East respondents, we collated their answers to two questions. One asked them to name the biggest problem facing

them as individuals and facing their nation. Subsequently, they were asked what they could do to help solve these problems. Of those who said they could do nothing, some gave "objective" reasons (e.g., "the nature of the problem" or "no solution is possible"); the others cited "personal" impotency (e.g., their inability "to go against religion or fate"). The proportions citing personal impotency are given in Table 9.

Table 9—Personal Impotency

	Traditional	Transitional	Modern
Turkey	35%	33%	33%
Lebanon	51	35	40
Egypt	63	73	51
Syria	90	92	37
Jordan	52	57	45
Iran	63	100	72

The sense of personal impotency increases fairly steadily, within each type, as the scale descends from most to least modern countries. (One discounts, as usual, for the Palestinian refugees in Jordan.) This is particularly marked among the Transitionals, for their steady increase by countries goes with extreme fluctuations by types within each country. In the advanced countries, the Transitionals are closer to the Moderns, as they should be on such a basic self-image as personal impotency. In Turkey, indeed, the Transitionals are identical with the Moderns; there the Transitionals are already men-on-the-move, with a relatively developed sense of self-confidence. In the less advanced countries, the Transitionals are closer to the Traditionals and feel themselves to be even more impotent about their private and public problems. The Egyptian Transitionals, with their large component of frustrated females, score markedly higher on impotency than the Traditionals. They, and their Transitional counterparts in Syria, lag far behind the aggressive young Moderns who, less constricted by fears of impotency, have made postwar politics in both countries so full of alarums and excursions.

These results point to quite basic differences in the personal meaning of modernization at different phases of the process. When persons of the same type differ so sharply on their capacity to cope with their environment, then the differences in their environment are likely to be large. Since participation is based on the expectation that what one says and does will matter in the world, the sense of personal impotency indicates the absence of a basic requirement for participation. The distribution in Table 9 shows what a difference it makes to persons of each type whether they live in a society that is opening even if not yet open, advancing even if not yet very far advanced, adaptive to new people in new roles.

Most of all does their societal setting matter to the Transitionals. They are the men-in-motion who have made a heavy psychic investment in social change; but where they can go, how far and how fast, is limited by the availability of channels and adaptability of institutions in their society. This would explain why Transitionals in modernizing Turkey and Lebanon feel themselves to be just as potent as their most modern compatriots, whereas in distraught Egypt and Syria they feel even less potent than the Traditionals. Further, personal impotency is perceived by Traditionals as their natural role of ancient acquiescence. But for Transitionals, with their new aspirations, the old passivity is experienced as frustrating and the sense of impotency causes deep unhappiness.

This brings our scrutiny of divergent personal style to the "ultimate" question of happiness. We have little to report on any question regarded as ultimate, but the interview schedule did pose two questions that show us how happiness was distributed, by type and country, among the respondents. The first question asked each respondent whether he was happy or unhappy ("fairly" or "very") with his life. Very many didn't know. Of those who did know, the Moderns were the happiest type in each country, and in all types the Turks were the happiest country. The proportions declaring themselves "fairly unhappy" or "very unhappy" are given, in Table 10, in order to show next the reasons for unhappiness.

An important result of the distribution is the showing that Traditionals consistently register the most unhappiness in all countries. It must surely interest observers who regret the passing of traditional society from the Middle East to note that those who embody tradition are most unhappy while those seeking to forsake it become increasingly happy in the measure that they succeed. The Moderns are happiest except in the two most traditional societies, Jordan and Iran, which provide them with few satisfactions. The Traditionals are happiest in the chaotic intermediate countries, Egypt and Syria, which provide them with few opportunities to change their ways.

On the basic question of happiness, then, our paradigm and its corollaries are nicely illustrated. Unhappiness decreases from left to right and from top to bottom, with deviations where they should be on such a question. Transitionals, in the two modernizing countries, are closer to the Moderns. In the other four countries, they are closer to the Traditionals. (Their erratic position in the two lowest countries is due to the extreme unhappiness of the Moderns—in Jordan, over their actual displacement from Palestine; in Iran, over their threatened displacement by Mossadegh.)

Table 10—Unhappiness

	Traditional	Transitional	Modern
Turkey	29%	17%	14%
Lebanon	43	18	18
Egypt	40	41	19
Syria	41	40	13
Jordan	52	42	54
Iran	52	33	42

It seems reasonable to suppose that unhappiness distributes according to our paradigm because it is associated with other attributes that have shown a similar distribution. Happiness, like these other attributes, seems to express a ratio between desires and satisfactions for persons of each type in different settings. In Turkey and Lebanon, where modernization has opened enough channels and adapted enough institutions to provide a good ratio of satisfactions to desires, happiness is evenly distributed at a high level among the modernizing persons because they tend to get what they want. In Egypt and Syria, individual aspirations exceed social capacity to provide satisfactions—so that happiness is more common among the Moderns, who already have what they want. But Transitionals, who want what they cannot readily get, are quite unhappy.

Unhappiness is distributed in close proximity to the sense of impotency and the lack of empathy. It seems clear why this should be so. Confidence in one's capacity to solve the private and public problems he considers most important is a liberating expectation. It heightens euphoria and stimulates innovation—the empathic awareness of "variousness and possibility" which Lionel Trilling finds in the distinctively modern liberal imagination. The reverse conditions spread dysphoria. The sense of impotency tends to diminish empathy and constrict imagination. Why dream of a better life when one is powerless to do anything to make it come true? It appears that the widespread unhappiness among Transitionals in Egypt and Syria expresses the disjunction, in this sense, between their empathy and their impotency. They have acquired the personal dreams but they feel impotent to perform the social deeds. This syndrome may explain the unstable, and occasionally explosive, quality of public life in those countries. Frustration of the quest for a more satisfying life can produce chronic melancholy and acute rages.

Connections of this order, between private and public styles of life, require detailed exploration in each country. Comparative analysis has shown us the regularities that occur as different types of Middle Easterners in different countries respond to the common compulsions of modernization. The interaction between individual personality and social setting, under these common compulsions, produces a remarkable array of regularities on such apparently diverse matters as mobility, media exposure, media approval, empathy, news range, opinion range, self-confidence (personal potency) and happiness. These attitudinal and behavioral regularities show how individuals in the Middle East lands adapt to their environment. Now we wish to investigate the different environments with which individuals living in the various countries are confronted. For this purpose we turn from comparative analysis to the method of case studies.

4. The Cases in Hand

The case studies stress the distinctive features of each Middle Eastern country. In each country, that aspect of modernization which illustrates its salient current problems is discussed. While we look for the connections between communication, economic, and political behavior in each country, the specific topics vary from one country to another. In Turkey and Lebanon we focus on sociology of communication, in Egypt and Syria on politics. By following the "natural contour" of current events, we become involved in highly controversial issues. Partisan to modernization, our own judgment on some of these issues is made apparent to the reader. But the data are sufficiently abundant that the reader can form his own independent, and quite contrary, judgments.

The case studies aim at depicting more vividly the particular environment which surrounds people living in each country. Instead of repeating parallel results obtained on the same rigidly applied indices in case after case, we provide the reader with some fresh material on each country. The danger is that the abundance of particularities will obscure some essential regularities. It may help the reader to perceive the connections between cases, if he is alerted in advance to the procedures used.

We were able to take considerable latitude in defining the types in each country because our typology is basically a correlational matrix. This means, as already shown, that one can legitimately start with any item in the matrix and use it as a base line from which to discuss any other item in the matrix. It is even permissible to use several of the items to represent the matrix as a whole—where the coefficients of multiple correlation obtained from empirical data showed these items to have a "systematic" relationship among different individuals, from different countries, responding to a diversified battery of questions.

The reader will recall that all respondents were classified as Moderns, Transitionals or Traditionals by their score on the opinion range. Subsequently, high correlations were established between these scores and those on urbanization, literacy, media participation and empathy. This enabled us to speak of Moderns with respect to any of these items or all of them together. A formal justification for this procedure is presented in Appendix C, where a latent structure analysis shows more rigorously the consistency of the typological patterns denoting different "styles of life." This entitles us to refer to Moderns in one place as those scoring high on the opinion range; in another place as those scoring high on empathy; in still other places as those who are urban, literate, and media participant. Where necessary to avoid confusion, we indicate the specific referent of the terms Modern, Transitional and Traditional. Here we simply alert the reader to the logic which permits us to vary these references so freely.

Our formal title to these variations would avail us little without the rich and varied data provided by the Bureau's multidimensional interview schedule. This very open questionnaire, which is reproduced in full at Appendix A, departed from the restrictive hypothesis-test mold in order to provide subsequent analysts with opportunities for a "fishing expedition." An open questionnaire, which draws upon the researchers' own empathy for what is possible and what is probable in a new and strange area, enables them to learn many valuable things which in advance they could not even know that they would want to know. In this respect, the Bureau questionnaire can serve as a model for future efforts to apply modern American research procedures in the less developed areas of the world.

We begin with Turkey as the area's most impressive example of modernization—impressive in that it has steadily evolved, and continues to evolve, along lines laid down by a revolutionary dictator over three decades ago. Atatürk's genius as a social planner was to see "economic development" within a comprehensive behavioral matrix. To raise industrial production, Atatürk began by simplifying the national language, separating religion, installing schools, building roads, creating cities. By such institutional innovations he undermined the props of rural isolation and encouraged traditional Anatolians to come into the modern world. He degraded the fez and the veil—symbols of traditional demeanor—and publicized his own portrait in formal Western attire. He invented *Halk-evleri* (Peoples' Houses) and put radios in them so that people could receive "the news" and discuss it. (That he decided what was news and what were appropriate opinions irritated some observers, but this diminished as he silenced some and others noticed that he was usually right.) Within this matrix of behavioral and institutional innovations, Atatürk also built cement factories and initiated a sturdy republic. Economic development and political modernization thus were located in a psychosocial setting that made possible the spread of a genuinely participant style of life.

The story of Turkey under Atatürk is so striking a case of mobility wedded with stability that we take a separate chapter to describe it. Chapter IV gives special attention to the "communication revolution" initiated by Atatürk—its antecedents and its consequences. In chapter V, we report the attitudinal posture of Atatürk's republic as revealed by our interviews in 1950—indicating, where possible, the continuing modernization that has occurred since the survey was made.

We then report on the four Arab countries, taken in the order of their modernity. Chapter VI deals with Lebanon, whose long history of modernization shows in the locus of its current issues. Politics has been reduced to questions of program rather than principle. Even the potentially explosive issue of the Christian-Muslim ratio (which would torpedo any government in Egypt and Syria) has been managed by reasonable continence and judicious compromise. Lebanon's are the modern problems—salient since the 19th century—of capital investment, the younger generation, the emancipation of women. Accordingly, we give special attention to these problems in the case study of Lebanon.

We next turn to the two intermediate countries, Egypt and Syria. Theirs are the 17th century problems of mobility and urbanization, capital formation and industrialization, social rationality and the idea of a public policy. But these problems are altered by their appearance in the 20th century. Egypt, in 1950 still governed by Farouk, showed signs of that ambivalence among the elite which subordinates any consistent line of public policy to the need for private gratifications. This has since evolved into the "Nasser syndrome," which we describe in chapter VII. Syria, with a real growth-potential that still remains unused, exhibited in 1950 the propensity for extremist politics which since has produced the series of *coups d'état* that made her, by 1958, the main outpost of Soviet influence in the Middle East. There is an embarrassing look of hindsight in these two case studies now that Nasser rules both lands in a United Arab Republic. But both chapters were drafted in 1954, when Naguib ruled Egypt and Shishakli ruled Syria. Our subsequent revisions have incorporated no up-to-date references to Colonel Serraj, whose portrait fits into the gallery of "Young Effendis" in chapter VIII. If we mention that the final sentence on Syria ("In the current situation, extremists can take heart") was written in 1954, it is not to establish ourselves as prophets but to indicate that there may be some predictive power in the data we are reporting.

We turn, in chapter IX, to Jordan. This is a very special case —a desert shaykhdom of Beduin tribesmen, under British dominion, newly overrun in 1950 by a horde of Palestinian refugees twice as numerous and much more modernized than themselves. Our preceding account of Middle Eastern regularities has shown that one such regularity is the phrase "with the usual exception of the Palestinian refugees." The most modern subpopulation of Muslim

Arabs is living in the least modern country of Muslim Arabs in our survey. The plain consequence, of course, is that the Hashemite Kingdom of Jordan constitutes not a nation in any recognizable sense, but a nominal state with two substantial bodies of population. Although both are Muslim Arabs, this is a case of "culture contact" between peoples who are virtually foreign to each other. Our discussion of Jordan is organized around this most salient of current problems in the Middle East.

Our final case study deals with Iran—Muslim but not Sunni, on the margins of the Middle East but not Arab. Like the Turks, the Persians once directed a great empire, but so long before the Ottomans that their administrative skills were largely dissipated. Reza Shah was no Atatürk, among other reasons, because he lacked the corps of skilled lieutenants to instrument a modernizing program of social action. Iran has been adrift upon the sea of world politics; and world politics in 1950—as since then—has been bipolarized between Washington and Moscow. The impact of bipolarization has shaped the recent history of the Middle East in ways that cannot be explained purely by psychosocial regularities and secular trends. The Middle East will be different, for decades to come, because its dynamic phase of modernization coincided with the Cold War. Policies have prevailed that would otherwise have failed; people have gained who would otherwise have lost (or been obliged to place their bets differently). No country in our survey exhibits the Cold War impact so clearly as Iran in 1950; accordingly our chapter on Iran is organized around this disputatious theme. With Iran we conclude the case studies, to which we now turn.

The New Turks

IV.

Turkey: From the Past

"Our enemies make us laugh; our friends make us cry!"
—TURKISH PROVERB

"For centuries, until the current era, nothing new and very little good happened to the masses."
—D. E. WEBSTER

TURKEY is not yet a Modern society in our sense; but it is no longer a Traditional society in any sense. The Muslim Institution has been separated from the secular state. Though Koranic codes are still heard in the mosque, a Constitution now is law in the land. Where once a Sultan reigned, a president now governs. The Republic has ceded a large domain to individual reflection and majority rule. The women of Turkey have removed the veil; the men have laid aside the fez. The children now grow up in skirts and trousers instead of *sholvars*, and go to schools where they no longer memorize the Koran but instead learn to read and write. To facilitate the modern miracle of free public education, the antique Arabic orthography was replaced by the simpler Western script.

These great deeds constitute a unique "revolution" in the series that followed World War I—one which has *neither* revised its goals *nor* lost its dynamism. Its momentum survived the reversal of Atatürk's party in the 1950 election. Indeed the added stimulus of a new party come to power, unexpectedly and for the first time, released a great burst of energy into the channels of social change. Within a year, the spectacular road-building program was under way, a modern Turkish brigade was fighting in Korea, and construction of the largest radio transmitter on the Eurasian continent was started in Istanbul. This sequence of events underscores the theme of our inquiry—the "systemic" role of communication in modernization.

It was Atatürk's sustained perception of the behavioral unity needed for the variegated modern style of life that gave to his revolution its special character. Challenging Sumner's dictum that "stateways cannot change folkways," Atatürk aimed at nothing less than reshaping a traditionalized society by transforming the daily deeds and desires of the people—first the new elite, then the ancient mass. From the very start, Atatürk preoccupied himself with details of deportment that seemed picayune to his more rigidly ideological contemporaries leading the revolutions that erupted throughout Europe at this epoch. His model was the "modern Western style" and his method was the production of "new Turks."

Of special relevance to the continuity of the revolution Atatürk initiated is the role he assigned to *communication*. To change the thoughtways of a people, Atatürk perceived that he must transform the existing network into a system of mass communication. The need was easier seen than satisfied. In a society whose illiterates exceeded 90% of the population, the job had to be done for the long run and from the very bottom. Accordingly, Atatürk began with his famous decree changing the orthography of the Turkish language.

To undermine the "oriental mentality" which interdicted republican development, Atatürk set out to promote mass literacy. For this a more efficient instrument than Arabic script was needed, so Atatürk decreed it into existence. But if stateways do change folkways, they do so only gradually in the course of time. Hence, while his New Turks were laboriously acquiring the written word, Atatürk went to them with a vigorous campaign by the spoken word. He created throughout the barren villages of Anatolia the network of *Halk-evleri* (People's Houses) which served as message centers for transmission of the new republican mystique, via Party directives, to the unlettered masses of rural Turkey. Next he put radio receivers into these *Halk-evleri* so that the villagers might receive the new word directly from its source.

As the "communication revolution" pursued its course, early enthusiasm encountered later currents of frustration. In 1949 M. W. Thornburg, reviewing the Turkish economy, raised the question: "Why does a popular revolution, after nearly a quarter century of glamorous successes, leave most of the people—perhaps 18 out of the 20 million—almost where they were before?"[1] By 1949 the Revolution had run its course for exactly a quarter-century. Compared with the modern Western countries Atatürk admired, Turkey had a long way to go. But compared with the situation Atatürk inherited in 1924, great strides had been made. The picture Thornburg presented as an impasse in 1949 was unduly somber. A resume of the communication situation in traditional Turkey shows that the quarter-century's achievements now appear as a midpassage.

1. The Ottoman Context

The Ottoman Imperium comprised not merely a variety of illiterate populations but an *anti*-literate elite, who regulated the daily round of public life by maintaining exclusive control over key points of contact between individuals and their larger environment. In 1554, Oghier Ghiselin de Busbecq, imperial ambassador at Constantinople, wrote of the Turks:

They have never been able to bring themselves to print books and set up public clocks. They hold that their scriptures would no longer be scriptures if they were printed; and if they established public clocks, they think that the authority of their muezzins and their ancient rites would suffer diminution.[2]

Oral communication was the rule under the Ottoman dispensation. "The news" was carried from one locality to another by public criers, itinerant preachers, and merchant caravans; it was then orally relayed through the corresponding milieux of each locality, such as the coffee house, the mosque, the market place and caravansery. The contents of "the news" reflected the utter dependence of the populace upon a remote center. According to Ahmed Emin Yalman:

Thus were made public government laws, regulations, and orders, military news, the appointment of a new governor, dates of religious festivals, funerals of prominent people, arrival or departure of caravans and ships.[3]

Such a communication structure served as an administrative technique of social control, not as an instrument for shaping an enlightened public opinion. For, in truth, public opinion in the modern construction was non-existent in the Ottoman system. Communications were designed not to enlighten and persuade opinion, but to prepare and prescribe behavior. The integration of this communication structure into the general system of Ottoman administration is indicated by the fact that the public criers were not used for official announcements to non-Muslims. In this case the communal heads of the *millets* (the special Ottoman institution for religious minorities) were summoned to receive the news in behalf of their constituencies. In the Ottoman system it was natural that the message-intermediary should also be the power-intermediary.[4]

Such a network of oral communications had to be ramified. Proclamation of government and commercial notices was the special task of the *dellal* (town crier).[5] Religious and police announcements were made by the *bekci baba*—a personage of note who served as water-carrier by day and watchman by night. Attached to his district police station, he would beat drums and announce the holy month of Ramadan or any other religious *bayram* (holiday) and would give warning of a fire in the district. The Ottoman system was persistent. The author of a current biography recalls how, as a youth in Istanbul, he would awaken to hear the night cries of the *bekci baba*.[6] Even deeper is the impress left by the *musdajis* ("bringers of tidings"), old women whose job it was to transmit news of the arrival of a new child and invitations to its grand reception.[7] Their competitors, and sometimes collaborators, were other old women who served as itinerant vendors. With their easy access to the harems, these hardened females were admirably situated to act as competitive relay-channels for amorous messages and as catalysts for intrigues of various descriptions. In Turkish folklore the sinister figure of the "old woman" recurs at a crucial turn of the tragedy.[8] Turkish ladies still alive can vividly recall their childhood fear and loathing of these potent old crones.[9] The oral tradition was deep and persistent; even among the literate class, in this country, "it is still customary . . . to send both business and social messages by word of mouth."[10]

Another impediment to the spread of printed communication was the institutional opposition of the Muslim clergy. The illiterate peoples of Islam had long been taught to regard The Word as sacred and to pay reverence even to paper, on which the name of God *might* be written. The perspicacious de Busbecq records widespread beliefs among 16th-century Turks concerning the sanctity of paper.[11] Religious respect for paper did not entail a desire for imprinting it. The first printing press did not appear in Turkey until 1728, three centuries after its invention in Europe.[12] Ubicini reports the opposition stimulated by the project:

On the first rumor of the proposed innovation, alarm arose throughout Constantinople. The Ulema, under the pretence of zeal for the safety of the Sacred doctrines and traditions, but in reality dreading some attack on their own power, professed to regard the new project as profane. The emanations of human intelligence, they alleged, having been always handed down to posterity by writing, ought not to be subjected to any less careful mode of transmission.[13]

One result of orthodox opposition to print was that the non-Muslim minorities took the lead. In closer touch with Europe, and mindful of all techniques that could strengthen the cohesion of their groups, the minorities brought their own printing presses into Turkey as soon as they became available in the West. Yalman dates the Jewish press from the 15th century, the Greek and Armenian presses from the late 16th and early 17th centuries.[14] Ubicini adds that an early product of the Hebrew press in 1488 was, significantly, a Manual for Children.[15] By 1520, indeed, the Salonican Jews had a famous Talmud Torah, in a building which housed also a complete system of secular education from grammar school to academy.[16] Thus, the non-Muslim minorities of Turkey gained several centuries in the education of their young and the transmission of skills in modern communication. They have retained this lead to the present day, with interesting consequences, as we shall see, for the current shape of communications throughout the Middle East.

Meanwhile, the Muslim majority moved ahead slowly, at a rate barely perceptible in the retrospect of centuries. The Turkish press installed in 1728 quickly lapsed into disuse, during the next period of continuous and disastrous wars, and had to be "reestablished" in 1784 by Selim III. Searching for ways to rehabilitate his declining domains, Selim used the press not for spreading popular enlightenment but for stimulating the enfeebled elite.[17] According to Creasy, the revived press was highly specialized:

Many European works on tactics and fortifications were translated from the French and published by the Sultan's orders, under the inspection of the Turkish mathematician, Abdurrahim Effendi.[18]

As printing foundered, so secular public education never really got started under the Ottoman dispensation. Secondary schools were instituted in 1860, but whatever pupils there were went mainly to the *Medresses.* These centers of primary religious instruction were run by the *'Ulema,* or "learned men" whose learning had terminated with medieval commentaries on the texts of Aristotle. Halide Edib, Turkey's foremost woman writer, says that "the Medresses remained up to the end of the last century what they were in the 13th century."[19]

The Ottoman regime failed to unify its diverse peoples through communication and education. Sir Mark Sykes, on the eve of the Young Turk revolt, reported an interview with a renowned Kurdish ecclesiastic:

> He told me that he had the keys of a library of 3,000 volumes in a large *tekke* near Van; it contained no books in any other script save Arabic, but there were perhaps forty or fifty volumes in Kurdish, several works on divination and magic, and one on the Albanian method of drawing auguries from the bones of lambs.[20]

By such communications, leading Kurds of this hinterland could hardly be rallied to the support of the imperial center. How could be rallied, more generally, a population of 13 million in which 1% were literate in 1908?[21] In fact, they were not rallied and the Ottoman Empire crumbled.

2. The Atatürk Vectors:
Ways of Participation

In chapter II we described the secular process of modernization as a sequence of four phases in social participation: urbanization, literacy, media, voting. Urbanization comes first in our schema because all that one means by modern society requires, as precondition, a certain minimum of population agglomerated in cities. Below 10% urbanization *no* society in our survey rated as modern on the other indices (literacy, media, voting); above 25% practically *every* society rated as modern by this test. These limits therefore fix an essential minimum and a critical optimum for the index of urbanization on the scale of modernization. Clearly, the denser the total population (i.e., the higher the ratio of persons to acreage) the more urgent the need for urban agglomerations.

Turkey as a Transitional Society has followed the urbanizing pattern, but within a relatively benign geohistorical context. A special feature of the Turkish situation, radically different from the demographic position of Egypt, has been the relative absence of Malthusian pressure of men upon land. The internal need for massive urbanization was less intense than elsewhere; nor, since Atatürk abstained from international commitments, were external pressures permitted to force the tempo. When Atatürk undertook to modernize Turkey, the Traditionals were still in their villages and his task was to stimulate rather than control. Conversely Nasser's Egypt, which is heavily involved in Cold War politics, must cope with millions who have already streamed into the capital cities and have acquired wants that must rapidly be satisfied or controlled.

Hence, the founding fathers of the Turkish Revolution were under no urgent pressure to achieve urbanization in a hurry and by draconic measures. The one need felt as pressing by Atatürk was for a capital city in Anatolia; the consequent rise of Ankara is a tribute to the *systemic* demographic strategy he evolved. For Ankara's growth was not permitted to disorder the rest of Anatolia. Atatürk's inaugural platform had postulated a new life for the Turkish village, but *qua* village. The village was not to be modernized by being urbanized, but rather by being equipped to live as a modern village. This theme underlay the *Köy Kanunu* (Village Law of 8 March 1924), the first extensive code of laws passed by the Grand National Assembly after the Republic was proclaimed.[22] It underlay, too, the ensuing sequence of practical measures: one such was the institution of agricultural instruction for village youths during their military service; another was the formation of agricultural credit cooperatives through the central *Ziraat Bankasi* (Agricultural Bank).

The most spectacular measure was the creation of a system of *Köy Enstitütü* (Village Institutes). This was designed to provide a practical primary education for villagers, who would then return to their villages to instruct the others—i.e., a self-accelerating system for education of villagers by villagers that would entail minimum involvement of urban resources. The specific ideology of Villagism had its place in Atatürk's program of controlled and measured urbanization. Its success appears in the figures for urban growth as of 1950.

Table 1—Growth of City Population[23]

Year	Population in Cities Over 20,000	Population in Cities Over 50,000	Population in Cities Over 100,000
1927	12.5%	7.7%	6.2%
1935	13.0	8.0	6.4
1940	13.7	8.6	6.4
1945	14.1	9.5	7.4
1950	14.7	10.2	8.3

Only in 1950 did Turkey finally cross our symbolic lower limit of 10% population in cities over 50,000 and thereby officially enter the range of Transitional societies. It is the overall pattern of balanced and cumulative growth that distinguishes the Turkish route to modernization. The main fact not revealed by the table is that urbanization has been largely confined to western Turkey. Geographical mobility has touched, as yet, only a portion of the Turkish population. The 1945 census reported that 16.3 million native Turks were still living in the same province where they were born; only 1.7 million had been born in a different province.[24] This means that urbanization is yet to come throughout eastern Anatolia. Its instigation may well date from 1955, with the first all-weather Anatolian throughway from Istanbul to Van in the remote eastern border province neighboring Iran. In this Anatolian area live about 8 million people, over a third of the Turkish population.[25]

A second fact revealed only by detailed breakdowns is the significant measure of pre-urbanization and suburbanization that has occurred. Turkey is no longer a land of three metropoli with one hinterland; in its western half today is a network of smaller urban centers with radial zones of influence. As a new city develops, it "magnetizes" the surrounding countryside. Some villages well situated along its roads of access tend to grow as distribution-points for its trade and dormitory-towns for its labor force, whereas other villages intervening between these nuclei tend to diminish. The dramatic transformation of Balgat, in four brief years, from a stagnant village of under 500 souls to a "dormitory town" housing over 2,000 and finally to a "suburb" of Ankara is but one instance of the process. Its extent is indicated by the fact that there are now, besides the five great cities, a dozen centers with over 50,000 population and nearly 50 centers with over 20,000 population.[26] Meanwhile, in the decade 1935-45, the population of villages under 500 decreased by 6.5%, while those over 500 increased by 6.8%.

These proportions involve shifts of approximately 2 million people from smaller to larger villages. During the same period, over 800 villages "disappeared" completely—just as Balgat "disappeared" in 1954.[27]

The impact of urbanization upon economic participation is registered, first, in the occupational census. People move to cities mainly to find new jobs; or take jobs mainly to live in cities. Between 1927 and 1945 employment in the agricultural sector (farming, forestry, fishing) declined slightly over 5%. A corresponding rise was distributed between industry, commerce, and public administration.[28] This involved a major occupational shift *between* sectors for over a million persons.[29] Again the detailed breakdowns are revealing, even for the less dramatic occupational shifts *within* sectors. They show, for example, a relative decline of employment in village-produced consumer goods (textiles, food and drink, tobacco), matched by substantial increases of employment in production goods. Mining doubled, machine tools and energy sources virtually quadrupled, and a chemical industry came into existence. The numbers involved in these shifts are small, but the 1945 figures of a mere 2,557 employed in chemicals takes on a different aspect when seen alongside the comparable figures of 890 in 1935 and 0 in 1924.[30] These occupational shifts correspond to urban growth in Turkey, moderate in tempo, but far more rapid and balanced than the pattern typical of the Middle Eastern area.

Along with these shifts has come significant growth in per capita income distribution. We shall have occasion to compare income data in Turkey and elsewhere, showing consistent advances among the Turks. That their situation in 1949 was deplorable as compared with U.S. standards has been suggested by Thornburg. But the improvements then already wrought in the daily life of living Turks is indicated in Table 2 below compiled by R. D. Robinson.

This table is a human document which speaks eloquently for itself. We underline only the three communication items at the top and bottom of the list. In 1929 movies were non-existent in Turkey; by 1949 it was the commodity to which the ordinary Turk gained access on the terms of closest equality with the ordinary American. In 1929 a Turkish newspaper cost as much as a pound of bread;[32] by 1949 it cost 33% less and brought the Turk's price much closer to what the U.S. worker paid for his paper. In access to a radio of his own (as we have seen, a good index of advanced

Table 2—Value of Labor in Turkey and U.S. (1949)[31]

To Buy These Things:	An Ordinary Turkish Worker Takes at least This Long: Hours	Minutes	An Ordinary U.S. Worker Takes at most This Long: Hours	Minutes	Time Ratio, Turk to American
A radio	500	0	12	30	40:1
A pound of sugar	2	45	0	5	33:1
A kw-hour of electricity	0	48	0	2	24:1
A 5-gallon tin of kerosene	23	20	1	2	22:1
An automobile	20,000	0	1,145	50	17:1
A pair of shoes	130	0	10	0	13:1
A pound of potatoes	0	36	0	3	12:1
A man's suit	333	0	33	20	10:1
A pound of cheap soap	2	30	0	15	10:1
A quart of milk	1	30	0	11	9:1
A package of cigarettes	1	0	0	10	6:1
A pound of wheat flour	0	28	0	5	5 ½:1
A pound of bread	0	32	0	7	4 ½:1
A bottle of beer	1	10	0	15	4 ½:1
A cup of coffee	0	20	0	5	4:1
A cotton dress	23	20	6	40	3 ½:1
One egg	0	10	0	3	3:1
A pound of onions	0	16	0	6	3:1
A daily newspaper	0	20	0	6	3:1
Admission to a cinema	1	0	0	30	2:1

(a) Assumes a wage of 3.00 Turkish lira per ten-hour day, or 30 kurus per hour. This wage is generally considered to be high.

(b) Assumes a wage of $9.60 per eight-hour day, or $1.20 per hour. On the basis of statistical evidence, this would seem to be low.

industrialization) the Turk compared on least favorable terms with the American. Even in 1949 this gap was bridged by wide distribution of community radios through the *Halk-evleri;* since then individual ownership has increased many times over (see Table 5 ff.). The growth of media, along with the parallel growth of literacy, provide the production-consumption reciprocal for a commodity which lay at the heart of the Turkish revolution: i.e., Enlightenment. It was to spread information and opinion, and thereby participation through consensus, that Atatürk engineered the Republic largely as a "communication revolution." In his conception, this was the essential companion of urbanization, designed to transform the Turkish psyche as cities transformed Turkish behavior.

3. The Communication Revolution

Communication begins with language. Atatürk, taking first things first in his usual way, started with a revolutionary shift from

Arabic to Western script. Widespread literacy is an indispensable
condition of the modern style of life, urban version. The efficient
functioning of a city presupposes an economy of discourse for
which the essential commodity is print—produced by media and
consumed by the literate. Again, Balgat dramatizes the historical
logic of the transition to literacy. So long as it was a Traditional
village, the Grocer managed to run his affairs with a dozen un-
labeled sacks. In the city grocery which he admired, however, the
attractive rows of cans concealed their contents in the approved
hygienic manner. The illiterate is an inefficient customer in a
modern shop; to make intelligent choices the consumer must be
able to read the descriptive labels and compare their prices. This
presumes the 3 R's.

On a more complex level, literacy transforms personal perspectives precisely by accumulating such alterations in the simple
routines of daily behavior. The urbanite requires more *concepts*
to organize his percepts efficiently. The process by which his movements in a grocery store eventually lead to the meal on his table
requires reading and computing at every turn, operations which
serve no function in the villager's daily round. Mental operations
of the urban sort grow and flourish only in a setting where the
required skills are widely spread. It was this larger sense of literacy
that Atatürk intended when he proclaimed: "The cornerstone of
our cultural policy is the suppression of ignorance."[33]

So Atatürk ruled that "the most productive and important duty
of the state is public instruction."[34] The secular drive of the new
Republic infused its educational program, as the mystique of
Villagism shaped its course. Major emphasis went into the ingenious system of Village Schools and Institutes, by which the
slender resources of available literacy were to prime a self-
accelerating process of practical basic instruction among villagers.
It is, however, more difficult for the ignorant to acquire the habits
of literacy than for the penurious to acquire the sense of cash.
Educational diffusion was a tougher problem for Atatürk than
occupational redistribution, since its advantages were less self-
evident and hence the motivations of the populace less easily
aroused. In such case Atatürk proceeded in the fashion of Bona-
parte rather than Talleyrand. A sweeping ukase decreed that the
new village schools would be built by the villages themselves;

and a very large proportion were built in fact by the forced labor and money contribution of the villagers. To ensure that once built they would be used, Atatürk, with the canny sense of social control typified in Ottoman administration at its most efficient, further decreed that the village teacher would henceforth occupy a place in the Village Council.

The situation of urban teachers in the rude village setting during the early years was hard. One pioneer teacher stressed the communication void:

> The village was small and primitive, lacking even a coffee house. Mail arrived but once or twice each week. There was not a single radio instrument for receiving news and music from the outside world. Lying at the edge of the peninsula, it had no traffic passing through it. There was not a single resident whose educational background made him a congenial companion.[35]

The teachers were often ostracized and even beaten by the villagers. Their experiences have created a distinct literature. A vivid autobiographic account is *Çalikuşu* ("The Wren"), the story of an Istanbul girl assigned to teach in Anatolian villages, which became the first "best-seller" in Turkish literary history (20,000 copies in 26 years).[36]

A village teacher of the second generation, Mahmut Makal, who at age 19 had been embattled by those he wanted to teach and then thrown in jail, has since written an extraordinary document which is both passionate autobiography and descriptive sociology. His *Bizim Köy* ("Our Village") highlights the slow tempo, bitter struggle, and often meager fruit of the search for modern enlightenment in traditional society. It is a noteworthy corrective, however, that this harsh account has itself become the all-time best-seller of Turkey. At the rate of 50,000 sold in four years, *Bizim Köy* is probably the only book that has been read by more living Turks than have read the Koran. That its author is a born villager, bred by the Village Institutes, suggests that the fruit of the young growth, if sparse, can be nourishing. That there now exists in Turkey a market of over 50,000 people able to buy the book, and an audience possibly six times as large able to read it, is a datum which suggests that economic participation via cash, and psychocultural participation via literacy, have grown together in significant measure.[37]

Progress through the Village Institutes is slow. Many of these people learn to read, painfully, but not to write. They acquire bare literacy, but not the literate way of thought. They can sign their names and decipher tax notices, but they remain on the periphery of participation—as we shall see in our later case studies of the "low Transitionals" in Turkey today. The government classifies these persons as "illiterates knowing how to read" and they composed 35% of the illiterate population in 1945.[38] The primary school population shows a fivefold increase—from 337,000 in 1923 to 1,600,000 in 1950 but this leaves the great majority still outside the educational institution.[39] Even this moderate scale of achievement has been possible only by the ingenious use of all opportunities, including some outside the formal educational structure. During their military service, illiterate conscripts are taught enough 3 R's, hygiene, and citizenship to qualify for admission, after discharge, to Village or Trade Institutes. The government also has increased its own "priming" function; the education component of annual government expenditures has risen from 5% in 1939 to 12% since 1950.[40]

The priority on rudimentary education was accelerated in recent years as it became clear that a new elite was on hand, committed to the Republic in principle and competent to operate it in practice. During the period 1946-51, a total increase of 3,000 schools was recorded, of which about 2,000 were elementary and only 150 were secondary schools.[41] This continues Atatürk's policy of "suppression of ignorance" on a wide front which, slowly but steadily, has paid off. The decade 1935-45 registered a 10% increase of literacy (reading *and* writing) in a constantly rising population.[42] This was unique in the prewar Middle East and the figure is focused by regional comparisons. In 1953, while Eastern Anatolia was lowest with only 20% literacy, Western Anatolia and Thrace had attained the overall figure of 50% literacy.

This is precisely the lower limit of literacy fixed by our global study, corresponding to the lower limit of 10% urbanization, needed for the transition to self-sustained growth. Western Turkey entered the modern world on both these indices in the "correct" symbolic proportions—an extraordinary display of balanced modernization. Turkey's internal stability during rapid transition, reflects these close growth-ratios between literacy and urbanization, as summarized by the 1945 figures in Table 3.

Table 3—Literacy by Sex and Place[43]

Size of Place	Male	Female	Total
Cities over 30,000	72%	48%	62%
10,000-30,000	63	32	49
Rest of Turkey	36	11	23

This table also shows the especially liberating effect of modernization among urban women. Removal of the veil was a symbolic gesture that affected primarily city and town women, since village women had rarely veiled. In places larger than 10,000, whereas male literacy is not quite double the rest of Turkey, female literacy has trebled the rural growth rate. The same impact is recorded in the occupational distribution. In the 1935-45 decade, female employment in the new urban industries consistently multiplied tenfold and hundredfold—the more significant in that the process began, in most cases, from near-zero.[44]

The relatively rapid advances among women, matched and exceeded by advances among youth of both sexes, gave a special impetus to the psychocultural transition. For, while males in modern society typically spend a major portion of their waking hours at work, women and children typically have more leisure. When supplied with media, and equipped by literacy to enjoy their use, the female and youthful segments of the population typically become major participants in the modern communication system.

Thus, the number of Turkish periodicals devoted to children and education spurted from 15 in 1945 to 50 in 1950. This rate of increase proved to be excessive and one year later the number of such periodicals had been cut back to 27, still a noteworthy increase over 1945 but a more moderate one.[45] Thus, too, Radio Ankara introduced in 1952 a daily "Hour of the Child" which is a substantial block of time in a limited programming schedule that traditionally has been devoted mainly to political news and discussion.

The comparable acceleration of media participation among women is shown in Table 4 by their relative increase over men, year after year, among registered readers in public libraries. While the male readership is much larger and has increased steadily, among women readers this population has more than doubled. Public libraries, of course, are mainly metropolitan institutions;

and capital cities dominate the world of books in Turkey as they do in more developed countries. Other printed media have, however, been decentralizing at a steady rate. During the 1946-51 period, 149 new printing presses went into operation. Of these 54 went to Ankara (total 66) and 33 to Istanbul (total 266); the remaining 62 presses were distributed among the smaller urban centers. By 1951, only 6 of the 63 Turkish provinces had no press and 17 provinces had five or more presses.[47]

Table 4—Public Library Readers, by Sex[46]

Year	READERS Male	Female
1936	719,089	53,466
1950	772,963	118,392

A major link between urbanization and modern communication systems is electricity, the source of power which operates printing presses, transmits radio broadcasts, and illuminates motion pictures. Turkey, having completed the electrification of its provincial centers, is now electrifying parish centers and, before the decade ends, should be into the final phase of village electrification.[48] Progress in the electrification program is matched nicely by the distribution of radio sets shown, by size and type of place, in Table 5.

Whereas the total figure doubled from 1945 to 1951, increases in the smaller centers trebled. The province centers show directly the impact of earlier electrification. The numerically smaller increases in parish centers and villages reflect, as a special feature, the widespread distribution of cheap battery sets prior to the

Table 5—Distribution of Radio Sets[49]

Size of Place	1945	1951
Province Centers	106,045	208,424
District Centers	45,130	126,110
Parish Centers	14,502	41,301
Villages	10,585	36,435
Total	176,262	412,270
Type of Place		
Homes	161,341	379,720
Public Places	13,926	30,680
Other Places	995	1,870
Total	176,262	412,270

1950 election campaign. Each of these sets, which mainly account for the increased distribution in "public places," brought broadcasting to an entire village for the first time. Another such spurt occurred prior to the 1954 election, registering a further 50% increase in the total radio sets. The growth of film and press have, proportionately, kept pace. In this way psychic participation through media and political participation through voting come to reinforce each other even in rural Turkey, with consequences we shall shortly explore in detail.

With but two national elections reported, trend-data are inconclusive on the tempo of political development. But the available figures do establish that electoral participation (the fourth variable in our global model) has been extremely high. Naturally, participation is most marked in the five great cities, as shown by the following proportion of eligible voters in 1954 who *actually* cast their ballots: Ankara 96%, Adana 93%, Izmir 89%, Bursa 85%, Istanbul 75%. These figures are striking even if somewhat inflated. Such a turnout might be expected in Ankara, a vibrant new capital city which senses itself to be the nerve-center of a great adventure in social change, but few observers foresaw the extent to which the entire country participated in both elections.

Table 6—Electoral Participation[50]

Election	Eligible Voters	Votes Cast	Participation Rate
14 May 1950	8,905,576	7,916,091	88.9%
2 May 1954	10,259,452	8,300,000	80.9%

In the retrospect of 1970, the extraordinary rate of 88.9% in 1950 may be seen as a first enthusiastic response to a new opportunity for political participation. If so, there is by now sufficient historical evidence of Turkish stability to justify confidence that a voting level appropriate to the over-all scale of participation will establish itself. For it is precisely this persistent quality of dynamic equilibrium that has given the Turkish Republic its distinctive place among the modernizing societies of the twentieth century.

There is no implication here that an excellent principle produces invariably excellent results. Much of what has been done, and continues to be done, in the name of the Turkish Republic wears an unlovely aspect in the eye of a Western observer. Coercion has been called in to pinch-hit for persuasion on many occasions, not because the opposition had filled the bases with winning runs but because the manager was nervous. Arbitrary abuse of the central power recurs too often to be overlooked in any serious account of Turkey today. While the voters were triumphantly participating in the 1954 election Hüseyin Cahit Yalçin, editorialist of the opposition People's Party paper *Halkçi* and dean of Turkish journalists, was confined in the Usküdar prison at Istanbul, sentenced to 26 months for editorials displeasing to the government.[51] Similarly, when the editors of another opposition party paper *Millet* accused the government of dictatorial methods in August 1954, the government promptly justified the charge by clapping them in jail.[52] A more rational course might be expected from a government which, having just been re-elected to office by a huge majority, could afford to act with self-confidence.

If authoritarian ways persist, however, they are less frequent and widespread than earlier repression; and the countervailing force of the mass media makes itself increasingly felt. Just as the earlier arrest of Mahmut Makal was nullified after an outburst of public protest, so the arrest of Yalçin stimulated a large press campaign to obtain his liberation. This is a noteworthy item in the sequence of Turkish modernization. A decade ago there was no opposition press to protest at all. Today, such a press exists and is heard; tomorrow its voice will be heeded. By such a characteristic evolution, probably, Turkey will finally incorporate in systemic form the difficult modern perception that an opposition is to be outwitted, not outlawed.

This follows, in large measure, from the favorable circumstances in which Turkey's republican politics originated and developed. The world political arena was not bipolar in 1924-44, hence Atatürk's policies were not threatened by that invasion of external power linked to organized internal issues which has made stable governance in postwar-II Egypt, Syria, Iran so difficult. Atatürk was able to rally his cohorts behind a program of national modernization without the intrusion of the world oil politics that downed Mossadegh, the world strategic struggles that detoured Nasser, and the world ideological conflicts that have split the elites in both countries as in Syria and Jordan. The Ottoman Empire had developed a tradition of governance among its educated classes, rather than the traditions of profitable acquiescence or irresponsible opposition under foreign tutelage which spread through the

Arab lands. Of great importance, as we have seen, was Atatürk's favorable demographic heritage—a set of land-man ratios that made rational planning of large-scale modernization feasible. All these predisposing factors, put to good use through foresighted policies and efficient administration, made possible the balanced growth at a steady rate which underlies the Turkish political revolution. What makes Turkey's political stability over three decades so "revolutionary" is that these decades have witnessed the emergence of the only truly democratic, multiparty system that incorporates the consent of the governed through widespread electoral participation. This brief summary does not ignore that Atatürk's methods were often dictatorial, and that relics are still evident in onslaughts upon those civil liberties which a participant system requires. It does foresee the reduction of such short-term measures by the party in power in behalf of the longer-run gains that accrue to a participant polity from the incorporation of opposition.

Such prophecy of the Turkish future is based, as all forecasting must be, upon the Turkish paths to the present. The process of psychic liberation has, in the course of three decades touching three generations, become systemic in the Turkish Republic. When both major parties are committed by their past and their present to the increasing production of "New Turks," the process can no longer be seriously disordered by the results of an election. The production of "New Turks" can now be halted, in all probability, only by the countervailance of some stochastic factor of cataclysmic proportions—such as an atomic war. As this would invariably bypass the results of *any* social research in the present, we confine our discussion of Turkish transition within the set of historical conditions that has been outlined. Within this framework, however, we seek to determine its meaning in the profound sense that the Turks themselves have assigned to the production of "New Turks" —i.e., the integral transformation of personality.

4. Toward New Turks

An effort of imagination is required to perceive the specific personal meanings of a social fact. Imagination is inadequately served, for this purpose, by the diffuse imagery associated with the familiar labels, such as a barter economy. Historically, in any society, the "sense of cash" is an acquired trait. It has to be learned, often painfully, by a large number of people before their society can negotiate the perilous passage from barter to exchange. Consider, for example, this sentence on the traditional Anatolian peasantry by Professor H. A. R. Gibb:

> We may suppose the *re'aya* to have been animated hardly at all by any idea of gain, and to have worked their land with a minimum of effort and very little knowledge.[53]

Gain, effort, knowledge—these are huge categories of discourse. For any adequate comprehension of the personality transformation which accompanied the shift from barter to cash in contemporary Turkey, we are obliged to take these large terms in their historical sense. What has been acquired in one generation, among a population that had always been ignorant and indifferent, is precisely the sense of gain, effort, knowledge which came over centuries to guide personal behavior in the modern participant society.

A profound cleavage is discernible, naturally, between those Turks who have acquired the participant style of modern life and those who have not. We distinguish these polar groups, respectively, as The Moderns and The Traditionals. Between them lie The Transitionals, those increasingly numerous and future-containing Turks whose story has poignancy for the restless souls now appearing in every underdeveloped land of the Middle East. One must be careful in dealing with such "ideal types." This method has the advantage of clarifying the regularities of biography and personality which distinguish one social type from another; its disadvantage is that the boundaries are too sharply etched and the final portrait sometimes belies the subject simply by its excessive clarity. We have here sought the gain without the loss, first by constructing a threefold typology (rather than the usual dichotomy which may induce excessive polarization); then by proceeding in fairly strict empirical fashion on the crucial points. We began by sorting out the Turks in our sample according to conventional sociological indices: age, sex, residence, socio-economic status. This gave us a classification of limited analytic utility, since the resemblances between members of each group were restricted to precisely those traits and no others.

We advanced the matter somewhat when we sorted further by the criterion of media-participation: the frequency with which each person read newspapers, saw movies, and listened to radio broadcasts. It is clear why this should differentiate individuals in a society where the mass media are relatively new and meager, hence where media exposure is a distinctive experience for most people. In modern Western society, where all who read can run, "the news" is a pervasive element in the daily round and can hardly be avoided. But in Turkey, there coexist two quite different social settings. A Modern setting operates in the cities of Western Turkey, where flourish a system of media, a literate corps of "communicators" and "audiences," a continuous and comprehensive coverage of world events. In the Traditional setting that prevails throughout the hamlets and villages of the Anatolian steppe, however, there are practically no theatres, few radios, and scant newspaper circulation. There *oral* communication provides the rudimentary equivalent of entertainment and enlightenment which, in the Modern setting, people obtain through the mass media. In a Turkey so bifurcated, one might expect a man's status and psyche to be much more closely related to his communication situation than would be the case in a media-saturated modern society.

Such correlations did, in fact, appear as between the "pure" Moderns and Traditionals. However, as we moved from the ideal types deeper into empirical data, lines regularly crossed. Certain low-status persons with high-media exposure exhibited attitudes akin to the Modern style, while others in the same status remained closer to the Traditional outlook. The most satisfactory way of accounting for such variations turned out to be the personality variable of empathy, shown by the capacity for ready ego-identification in new situations. This defined the Transitionals in such a way as to separate them consistently from Moderns and Traditionals. At the same time, capacities for identification could be rank-ordered to discriminate differences of degree *among* Transitionals.

The portraits we have drawn accent the psychic mechanism upon which turns the future development of a participant style among Turks, with special attention to the engagement of this mechanism in the developing communication system. They are to be understood within the historical context we have sketched of social change under the Republic. A corps of Moderns existed in Turkey, almost exclusively in Istanbul, over many pre-Atatürk generations. It was reinvigorated by those who made the Revolution and has been steadily incremented by the "New Turks" who

grew throughout Western Turkey under their tutelage. The increments have begun to come, only in the past generation, from the
vast inert population of Traditionals that still prevail throughout
Anatolia. Those who have disengaged themselves from the traditional mass and moved toward the life-styles of modern men are
the Transitionals. In the growing number and influence of these
men-in-motion will be written the next phase of the Turkish
story. To perceive more clearly the lines of evolution among these
Transitionals, we look first at the Traditionals whence they came
and then, in the next chapter, at the Moderns whither they go.

5. Traditionals: The Constrictive Self

Western man began, decades ago, to agonize over "the man
with the hoe" who seemed, in Edwin Markham's words, "bowed by
the weight of centuries . . . stolid and stunned, a brother to the
ox." Only more recently, however, have we applied techniques for
obtaining more precise description of what happens to men routinized in the age-old lifeways of Traditional societies. It is especially
fortunate for our present understanding that scholars trained in
these techniques have recorded their observations of Turkish village life in several phases of transition.

A doctoral dissertation by J. A. Morrison described how the
peasants of Alişar, a village of 292 souls and 58 households located
in the Kanak Su Basin of Central Anatolia, lived in 1932 "much
as did the occupants of the *hüyük* three thousand years ago." Moreover, this situation appeared to the Alişar villager as quite normal,
since he neither knew nor sought any other way of living. Morrison
reported:

> The Anatolian peasant is singularly incurious about almost everything
> that does not directly concern his daily life. To the average peasant, any-
> thing that happened more than fifty or sixty years ago is "çok eski"
> (very old), regardless of whether the event took place one hundred or
> one thousand years earlier. Asked how old his village is, he will answer
> with exasperating vagueness not unmixed with satisfaction "çok eski."[54]

The quality of "exasperating vagueness" has been described
by Muzafer Sherif, an American social psychologist of Turkish
origin, who in 1944 conducted a series of studies in five Turkish
villages. These were ranked in terms of their *degree* of contact
with the products and facilities of modern technology. Within each

rank he then compared the responses of the villagers on "a few basic phenomena dealing primarily with the units, precision, and scope of space, distance, and time perceptions . . . conceptions of the alien or strange, and of wealth." Sherif's findings confirm our basic proposition that *mobility tends to be systemic,* i.e., physical, social and psychic mobility "go together" in every village. His general summation is that: "The radius of the world in which the individual lives his daily life widens *in proportion to* the degree of contact with modern technology."[55]

The specific results from which Sherif draws his conclusions are very instructive. The sense of cash, for example, develops in proportion to the degree of contact with modernity. In every village the local scale of riches is fixed at both extremes by the limits known to the villagers, each of whom determines his own status by his relative position on the scale. In the most isolated of his five villages, Sherif found that "the greatest sum of money one can actually conceive of is about $80 for women and around $800 for men"; in the most advanced village, imagination soared to $5,000. The notion of "wealth" as a potentially indeterminate quantity, whose appropriate metric is purchasing power, appears only in those villages which have already begun to shift from a subsistence to a cash economy. With increasing exposure to the supple scope and limits of monetization develops the "sense of cash."

So, too, with the sense of space, distance, time—the geotemporal universe. Only in the measure that they come into contact with urban society do villagers acquire the concepts, indeed the language, of precise and standard units. Sherif found that the villagers could estimate distances with any accuracy only in terms of travel by foot. Guesses of distances any of them had covered by a conveyance were extraordinarily erratic. "They have no idea how far these distances really are. They cannot translate them into terms of walking time, their real psychological distance unit." In Karlik (most isolated) the older men believe that the province of Van in Turkey is farther away than is Galicia, which is now in Poland and is in fact several times more distant than Van. The belief is due to several oldsters who served in both provinces during World War I; but they went to Galicia on the train, while they had to walk most of the way to Van.

Also, in Karlik "only a few villagers know the names of the

days of the week and of the calendar months." Even in Beşikdüzü (least isolated) only 80 of the 842 villagers use a calendar or a timepiece. Recall, in this connection, the purely decorative clock in the guest room of The Chief in Balgat. Hours are identified by phases of the sun; days by markets in the vicinity (e.g., Tuesday may be "two days before the Görele Market"); months and seasons by the farming routine ("hazelnut-gathering time"). Events of past years and decades are located in terms of wars experienced and other memorable, usually catastrophic, events. Small wonder that Morrison's villagers could only reply, with "exasperating vagueness," *çok eski!*

Such psychic traits as Sherif describes interact endlessly with the established institutions of Traditional society, from which they derive and which in turn they reinforce. These institutions usually are authoritarian, patriarchal, changeless; the values they enjoin are loyalty, obedience, inertia. The whole complex forms a "courage culture," in which absence of curiosity is a primary component ("theirs not to reason why, theirs but to do or die"). The absence of curiosity goes together with the absence of knowledge in a reciprocal equation; ignorance and immobility are twin growths. Sir James Frazer has shown, for a variety of Traditional societies, the persistent interaction between superstition (absence of knowledge) and stability (absence of change).[56]

The key to the equation is communication, the social system of messages by which beliefs are transmitted between and within generations. The folklore of Anatolia is instructive in this regard. In these ageless tales, change is regularly identified with evil. Prominent among their population of malevolent beings, for example, are the *Jinns*, whose distinctive trait is the power to assume any shape they wish. Changeability, in such a context, is perceived as *shameful*. By contrast with the modern pluralist conception of personality in which "adaptability" figures as a major virtue and an indispensable skill, the Traditional man is cut once and for all to a familiar pattern. The mold is the same for all men of the same age and rank. The persistent deviant is not merely the odd "eccentric" or amusing "character" of tolerant modernity; as a threat to village rigidities he risks instead the grave reprisal of becoming the village "idiot" or "outcast." Such a setting does not encourage exploration among strange identities or experiment with unfamiliar roles. Ego-identification becomes compulsive, empathy is lacking, and a Constrictive Self becomes the approved personal style.

The taciturnity of villagers is a specific communication aspect of life in a "courage culture." Words are terribly awesome matters to Traditional man, who knows relatively few of them and uses them with some difficulty. Modern children learn young that "sticks and stones can break my bones, but words will never harm me." The Anatolian proverb says: "The hurt of a stick dies away, but words hurt forever." The extreme susceptibility of Traditional Turks to the danger of words has shown itself in legal measures adopted to prevent ridicule of persons. The Republican government, under the war-heightened tension of 1940, ordered a censorship of all Western publications; every word derogatory to the Turks was to be excised or the entire publication removed from circulation.

On the behavioral level, oral passivity is often associated with physical aggressiveness. This is the theme of H. G. Dwight's striking tale of "Memish," a mild Anatolian servant, who brooded long over a man who had called him afraid of a knife; then used all his meager savings to buy a knife and kill the man, with pride but without pleasure, in a fair fight.[57] The general point has been well made by Dr. Eleanor Bisbee, warm friend and keen observer of the New Turks: "Frustration in Turkey, bitter enough for violence, can often be traced to the inarticulateness of the illiterate, who defend themselves with blows when their words fail."[58]

In polar contrast to the Traditional "courage culture," where the constricted self is routinized in the performance of duty with loyalty and obedience committed once for all, is the Modern type of "ingenuity culture." Here the appropriate personal style is the expansive, desirous, seeking, acquiring individual. In the Modern milieu a man gets on by his wits in new opportunities, not by his inertia in familiar routines. In the perceptual apparatus of Modern men, all scales are in principle infinite until proved otherwise. He locates himself not at some fixed point in the rank-order of things known, but at some moving point of desire in a scale of things imagined. Aspiration, curiosity, know-how overcome constriction, impassivity, ignorance as Traditional men move toward Modernity. Participation replaces isolation, effort replaces acquiescence, initiative replaces inertia. It exaggerates, but probably does not falsify, the time-space perspectives of Modern man to say "the sky's the limit!" and "the world's my oyster!" Few indeed are those, even among the most modernized, who go all the way in consistently living out such a perspective. But how much longer is the way when one starts with people for whom the largest fortune conceivable for a woman is $80; in a society where units of time and space are hardly known; among a population who see the future as always strange, hence ominous, and the past only as a diffuse *"çok eski!"*

To cover this terrain more systematically, showing how the changing styles of life had worked themselves out in the setting of the Turkish Republic as of 1950, we turn directly to the results obtained by interviewing a varied sample of Turks. Here, insofar as is consistent with clarity, we shall let the Turks speak for themselves.

V.

Turkey: Toward the Future

"On progress we shall set our heart. We shall skip
five hundred years and not stand still."
—ZIYA GÖKALP, *Esnaf Destani*

THIS CHAPTER disengages the Transitionals from the
matrix of traditional attitudes we have just sketched and compares
the three types among the respondents. To test the role played by
the "communication revolution" in Turkish modernization, we
made an independent classification of our respondents according
to their exposure to mass media. The results gave a very close
fit to the expectations derived from other indices in our typology
of Moderns, Transitionals, Traditionals. Turkish Moderns were
found to be the heavily-participant individuals who regularly read
a daily newspaper and listen to the radio. Most of the Traditionals
never (or hardly ever) do either and show little interest in the
media. Transitionals occasionally are exposed to both; moreover
their media exposure is limited by circumstances rather than desire
—they would like to participate more often than they can. We then
cross-tabulated these media-groups with each sociological attribute
to see where variance occurred. Our findings confirmed the consistent relationship between media-exposure and biographical attributes that had been hypothesized. The three groups (defined
only by media exposure) distributed themselves quite as expected.
Table 1 shows the proportions of each type who are younger literates living in cities, with relatively higher income, occupation, education. The differentia that count most in the disengagement of
Transitionals are occupation, education, and of course literacy. The
job is a major source of enlightenment, a channel through which ex-

Table 1—Social Correlates of Media Exposure

Upper Levels	Moderns	Transitionals	Traditionals
Urbanization	81%	61%	35%
Income*	85	68	43
Occupation†	75	51	18
Education‡	70	46	8
Literacy	98	71	19
Age: Under 50	86	83	66
No. of respondents§	(105)	(105)	(49)

* Interviewer's estimate.
† Professional, clerical, and entrepreneurial occupations.
‡ Above elementary schooling.
§ The numbers in each table for Turkey are as above unless otherwise stated.

perience of the larger world is acquired. Preconditions are schooling and literacy. Access to these channels differentiates modern men from their ancestors; and the distribution of such access is a fair index of modernization in any society.

Having differentiated our subsample by frequency of exposure to all media, we asked whether there were consistent differences in exposure to the different media. Each respondnt had been asked to recall the source of his last piece of news, with results shown in Table 2. The Moderns acquire what they consider "news" mainly through the *media* system, recalling equally radio and newspaper items. The Traditionals receive their news mainly through the *oral* system. The Transitionals participate in *both* systems. They recall newspaper and radio items, but word-of-mouth also figures often as a source of news. This is one of several results to be reported which indicate how Transitionals operate as a media-oral relay between the two separate "worlds" represented by these systems.

Table 2—Source of Last News

	Moderns	Transitionals	Traditionals
Newspaper	54%	46%	8%
Radio	39	26	10
Word of mouth	6	26	78
No news	1	2	4
Total	100%	100%	100%

The cumulative character of media participation was underlined when respondents were questioned in detail on their media habits. As Traditionals show little or no exposure, these questions were asked only of Moderns and Transitionals. The responses, in Table 3, show that the more habitual newspaper reader is also the more likely reader of *several* papers, the more regular radio listener is also the more likely listener to *several sources* (including foreign stations).

Table 3—Media Habits

	Moderns	Transitionals
Among Newspaper Readers:		
Read Two or More Papers	85%	58%
Among Radio Listeners:		
Listen to Foreign Broadcasts	67	44
Among Foreign Listeners:		
Heard BBC	83	63
Heard Voice of America	51	37
Heard Radio Moscow	17	11

Media participation thus tends to be centripetal. As radio and press diffuse through different social strata and geographical areas, they tend to converge on the same people in the same places. This may explain why hopes for achieving quick milennia of modernization through the media alone usually have been disappointed. Such hopes are based on too simple a theory of the communication function. In accomplishing social change, the flow of influence between media and institutions is not unilateral but reciprocal. One does not penetrate traditional barriers of isolation, ignorance, indifference simply by installing a radio. What is changed, for example, when the radio is installed at a mosque, under charge of the local *Imam*, who turns it on exclusively for broadcasting the daily calls to prayer and then turns it off again (as I witnessed in the Persian town of Gom)? While the media system tends to become self-accelerating once in operation, its initial tempo of diffusion among new audiences is slow.

Given the media's centripetal tendency, particularly marked during the early phase, it is natural that the cleavage between the enlightened and the unenlightened should remain great in Turkey today. Consider these responses, in Table 4, to questions testing level of information on current world affairs.

These distributions are as expected, but the importance of media participation is indicated by the substantial increments of information among Transitionals over Traditionals. Transitional awareness of such remote matters shows how the horizon widens,

Table 4—Concentration of Information

Information About:	Moderns	Transitionals	Traditionals
United Nations			
What it is	82%	55%	10%
Where it is meeting	72	50	10
Who is Sec'y. Gen'l.	52	26	2
Marshall Plan	28	21	9
Foreign Peoples			
Americans	48	41	16
British	41	30	14
Russians	4	3	2

exposure deepens, and enlightenment increases as the media penetrate into new strata and areas. The conjunction is clearer when these responses are collated with a battery of items, as in Table 5, testing direct and mediated exposure to the foreign world.

Both direct and mediated experience increase with modernization. The 10% of Traditionals who visited a foreign country are oldsters (like the Chief) who did so during their military service. The "contacts" with Americans and other foreigners signify the unforgettable experience of seeing a modern-dressed man appear in their village. (Some of the urban Turkish interviewers reported being taken as "foreigners" by Anatolian villagers.) By contrast, the Transitionals show a substantial increment of mediated over direct exposure to the outer world. This is partly due to the special function of the *pictorial* media in widening the horizons of semi-literate and non-literary people. Visual images being more easily comprehensible, films and magazines often diffuse more rapidly among such a population. Apart from this, the results underscore the more general concurrence between

Table 5—Foreign Exposure: Mediated and Direct

Exposure	Moderns	Transitionals	Traditionals
Know a foreign language	54%	33%	12%
Direct			
Visited a foreign country	37	22	10
Foreign contacts in Turkey	59	47	18
Know individual Americans	48	41	16
Mediated			
Attend movies	88	63	27
Prefer American movies*	68	48	23
Read foreign magazines*	82	69	33

* Among movie-goers and those who know a foreign language.

direct and mediated exposure to the wide world. Participation tends to be a consistent lifestyle.

Indeed, where the ratio between the two modes of experience shows an excessive disjunction, the explanation is likely to lie outside the range of newly-acquired information. For example, more Traditionals expressed opinions about Russia than one would expect from their general level of information on other questions. Inspection of these opinions revealed, however, that they derived not from current information, but rather from the traditional stock of Turkish folklore. Any question dealing with Russia is likely to evoke from Traditionals such stock responses under the guise of current opinions. Respondents were asked first to express a judgment on the policy toward Turkey of several nations, then later on the peoples of those same nations. Those expressing some definite opinion are distributed in Table 6.

Table 6—Opinions on Foreign Policies and Peoples

Expressed Opinion on:		Moderns	Transitionals	Traditionals
Policies:	British	92%	83%	51%
	American	99	90	60
	Russian	99	93	80
Peoples:	Britishers	95	78	45
	Americans	98	86	57
	Russians	85	82	69

Much of this table is as it should be. There is generally more opinion of policies, which can be learned from media and media-oral relays, than of peoples. American policy and people are both fairly salient in Turkey, as official Americans have been there in quantity since 1948. That so many Traditionals, in their isolation from current events, should express definite opinions on Russian policy and peoples suggested at first some special break-through by the media system. The content of their opinions indicates, rather, that the whole folkloristic inventory of traditional sayings about "the Muscovite" (a symbol used for generations to frighten naughty Anatolian children) provided their stock of responses on these ostensibly current questions. Fortunately, there is an independent confirmation of this interpretation elsewhere in the interview materials. When asked directly, in a separate set of questions, whether they had any current information of the Russians, only 2% of the Traditionals claimed such knowledge.

1. From Tradition to Transition

For, in truth, the data just presented on media, news, opinions show that most Turkish Traditionals remain contained within their familiar little universe of family, mosque, village. They remain uncurious about the larger world, unresponsive to its occasional impingements—so long as they remain occasional. When the impinging stimuli become too pervasive to be ignored, the Traditionals turn rejective. This is a normal mechanism of ego-defense for the constrictive personality—defense by total rejection, rather than by partial incorporation in the expansive Transitional style. But once such "instinctive" rejection comes to require defensive verbalization, signifying a need for self-reassurance among the Traditionals, then a process of change is under way. A fine example of how this phase was operating in 1950, in the village of Sakaltutan (near Kayseri), has been described by Paul Stirling:

> The villagers do not think of the village as a changing society and children accept their father's point of view more or less without question. Although most of the young men have been to the cities and seen the modern generation of Turkish girls in Western dress about the streets, and been to American films, they state not only to me but to each other that their own customs are better. The only time I heard the opposite view it was greeted with a storm of protest.[1]

Dr. Stirling's account shows how, while tradition still rules, transition gets under way. When people feel obliged to defend tradition they are no longer simple Traditionals unaware of alternatives. In Balgat, the villagers vociferously defended the good old ways against the "infidel" Grocer in public, but went to him privately for advice on what they should do in Ankara. So, the "storm of protest" against the exponent of new ways indicates which way the wind was blowing in Sakaltutan. In an earlier period the responsive storm would more likely have taken the form of a chill indifference. Had the offender persisted beyond tolerable limits, he might have been condemned as an idiot or punished as a heretic. In neither case would "most of the young men," as Dr. Stirling reports, have been likely to "state not only to me *but to each other* that their own customs are better." They would have felt no such need for mutual self-reassurance.

In villages that remain Traditional, no voices need be raised to defend traditional ways because no other ways are on the agenda. It is a distinctive trait of Traditional society that it promotes no alternatives to itself; hence the corresponding psychic trait of the Traditional villager is that he lacks "curiosity." The sense of variousness and possibility develops as a specific feature of Modern society, where changes in the daily round of life are frequent, the unexpected may happen at any time, and people must be prepared to make choices.[2] The secular evolution of curiosity as personal trait and social utility is a phase of modernization closely linked to the rise of mass communication—which taught large audiences to ask questions, perhaps more effectively than it taught them to find answers. It was, again, the highly empathic Grocer of Balgat who said he preferred American movies because: "They are exciting. They make you ask, what is going to happen next . . . ?" Everyone knows what happens next in a traditional folk story—as in most Turkish movies I have seen.

At different points in the Turkish interviews, respondents were asked what they would like to know about the world, about various countries, about specific events they had heard of only vaguely. The Moderns, with the Transitionals just behind them, demonstrated an abundant curiosity; there were all sorts of questions they wanted to have answered. The Traditionals, typically, could find few questions to ask. Most of them said that there wasn't anything they cared to know. Some, who wished to be polite to the interviewer, did search out questions to ask. Those were invariably personal, often purely sensory, and clearly derived from immediate concerns of their actual life rather than imaginative curiosity about life elsewhere. About America, an object of relatively high interest among all Turks, Moderns asked big questions of an impersonal order—involving ideology and social institutions, general economic conditions, problems of public policy. The Traditionals asked: "Is it cold there?" . . . "Are the people friendly?"

The Traditional's incapacity to establish connections between himself and the larger world is the key to his perspective. His personality has been socially disciplined to constrict imagination to the familiar time-space dimensions of his daily life. Even on the simplest level of generalizing from self to a larger universe, the trained incapacity of the Traditional is evident. All respondents were asked to name "your biggest problem," for example, and there was marked convergence on economic troubles. But when asked later to name Turkey's biggest problem, the Traditionals failed to generalize as compared with the others.

Table 7—Generalizing Personal Problems

Economic Problems Most Important:	Moderns	Transitionals	Traditionals
For ME	64%	59%	67%
For TURKEY	52	21	8

Only one of twelve Traditionals was able to connect his personal economic problems with those on the national level. It is fair to say "able" rather than "willing," for most Traditionals simply did not name *any* alternative problem before the nation. Confronted with so awesome a demand upon their capacities, they fell silent altogether.

The consistent incapacity to link oneself to the outer world underlay most of the regularly recurring differences among the respondents. These differences could not be due simply to "national character," since all the respondents were Turks. Nor were they due simply to "class differences" in wealth or status or residence, since persons similar on these criteria nevertheless were found to differ in their perspectives. The most satisfactory way of accounting for these differences was the personality variable of empathy, seen as the mode of articulating a person's governing style of life. To condense the results which document this theme, we constructed two sets of indices—on empathy and dysphoria.

Each was tested by a dispersed series of projective questions, answers to which required the respondent to imagine himself in an unfamiliar role, place or time. Three questions illustrate the pattern of response for the entire series. At one point (after he had identified the biggest problems facing himself and the nation), the respondent was asked what he would do about these problems if he were the president of Turkey. This is a role-identification question, typically requiring heavy demands upon the self among pre-Modern persons. At another point a simpler demand was made upon empathic capacity: the respondent was asked where he would choose to live if he had to live elsewhere than Turkey. If he refused to imagine living elsewhere, the interviewer probed: "But if you *had to* live elsewhere . . . !" At still another point, the respondent was asked how he would feel about living in the United States. This is the least demanding sort of projective question, since it specifies part of the alternative situation and can be answered by simple acceptance or rejection without adding imagined specifications. The results on these three questions are given in Table 8.

Table 8—Empathy Index

Ability to Imagine:	Moderns	Transitionals	Traditionals
. . . being Turkish president	86%	63%	35%
. . . living outside Turkey	94	74	49
. . . living in United States	100	98	74

These figures speak, to a certain point, for themselves. It is at the point where they stop speaking for themselves that the student of Turkish (or human) behavior must ponder them. It makes common sense to reflect that, after all, one cannot reasonably expect to ask an Anatolian (or any other) peasant what he would do as President and get a comprehensive answer. This is obvious upon statement. But it is as a start rather than a conclusion that one needs to take this obvious point. For the figures also show that some Anatolian peasants, although living in the same social setting as their silent peers, *can* answer such questions, i.e., practically all Transitionals and three out of four Traditionals could imagine living in the United States.

Clearly, in a more fully developed participant society, most people can answer all such questions with ease. Recall the circular letter we mentioned earlier which asked: "Suppose *you* were the editor of *Time* . . . ?" It assumed that potential subscribers would not be disturbed and lost, but rather pleased and won, by the demand that they imagine themselves in a role which obviously none of them had ever actually experienced. The American assumption is the more striking when compared with results obtained in the Turkish survey by asking: "What would you do if you were editor of a newspaper?" Most Traditionals simply could not imagine what they would want to do. As Turkey approaches closer to the "modern Western style" it has chosen as its model, empathy will spread and the number of non-responders on such questions will be reduced. In a participant society, even the broad rural and lower-income strata are willing and able to have ideas on what the President "ought to do," to imagine living elsewhere than their birthplace, to express views about the future.

This involves nothing less than a personality transformation of major proportions. Perhaps the deepest insight the data give into the gravity of this change is the prevailing dysphoria in the daily round of life among the Traditionals. The feeling that this must be so is expressed by their own Traditional proverb: "Our enemies make us laugh; our friends make us cry." In the world of the Traditionals, the sense of life is dull, heavy, gloomy. "Never have I seen such a colorless, shapeless dump. The main color is gray . . ." wrote the Ankara-bred interviewer Tosun on his first exposure to Balgat. The dysphoric tonality of Traditional life *for those who live it* is documented by another set of questions. One asked simply, and in quite general fashion, whether the respondent felt himself to be "happy or unhappy." Another, much later, asked what his reaction had been to the last piece of news he had received. A third asked what the respondent felt he could do to help solve Turkey's problems. The responses are given in Table 9.

Table 9—Dysphoria Index

	Moderns	Transitionals	Traditionals
Feels unhappy generally	15%	20%	33%
Felt unhappy about last news (i. e., sad, sorry, angry)	39	46	62
Feels unable to help solve Turkey's problems	45	53	86

The complex of gloom condensed by these figures is difficult to reconstruct for those who live in a participant society fashioned in the century of optimism with the ideology of progress. Clarity on how we evaluate this is therefore essential. Nowhere on this page or in this volume is the implication intended that Modernity is utopian or that Americans, as the most modern people in the sense we use this term, are therefore the best and happiest. Neither by this caveat is the contrary intended. There is simply no net judgment of this order made or needed in this book. What our study underscores is that Modernity and Tradition are even more radically different from each other than is commonly acknowledged, that bridging the difference hinges upon a transformation of personality along with a remaking of institutions, that this modernizing process is underway among a large number of Middle Easterners. Our data on happiness show why so many Middle Easterners are willing to undergo the difficult process of modernization—they simply are too unhappy with the old traditional ways to resist an opportunity to try something new.

The first line of Table 9 tells us that one of every three Traditionals declares himself to be an unhappy person, a proportion very much higher than among the other types. The second line has special relevance for communication. When a person is asked to tell the last piece of news he heard, a complex screening process is activated—i.e., selective recall from a selective memory which has selectively stored the original selective perceptions of the respondents. That two of every three Traditionals, as a regular outcome of this process, select for recall a "last piece of news" which made them feel unhappy is a solid indication that sadness is the dominant tonality of their setting, that dysphoria is the approved and expected mood. What one "recalls" of the news is also what one uses as subject matter of conversation with friends and acquaintances. The prevailing gloominess of Turkish village conversation (as indeed of its "popular" movies and press) is documented by this result.

It reflects also the fearful views of the outside world that interact with the overwhelming pessimism about the future, and the helpless futility of efforts to make it better, as expressed in the third line. The Modern impetus to make a better world is absent from the Traditional psyche, because Modern confidence that such a world is feasible is absent from its perspective. In obeisance to the fatalistic rule of Kismet, the Traditional lives under the narcosis of resignation. Roughly nine of ten Traditionals felt that neither they personally nor "people like them" could do anything to help solve their own or Turkey's problems.

To transform passivity of this order into a sense of participation takes some doing, but we have seen that the Turkish Republic has been doing it at its own pace. It is clearly the case that, by objective measures, Traditionals in Turkey are decreasing and Transitionals are increasing. Less obvious, in any detail, is the personality transformation entailed by the institutional changes. Our understanding of the results reported above becomes more vivid when we see how the general themes articulate themselves in particular cases. An illuminating terrain is the reaction to new sorts of information, particularly those messages distinctively carried through the developing mass media. We turn, then, to a closer look at some individual cases which illustrate the general propositions.

2. Constriction and Communication

A first item to note is the response made to the interview situation itself. Balgat illustrates two main ways of responding that are quite characteristic. The Grocer sought to make the interview an occasion for psychic rapprochement with the Modern young interviewer Tosun; he "evidently wished to feel that he is closer to me than he is to the other villagers." Along with this, the Grocer answered all questions freely and fully. The Chief, however, remained wholly disengaged from the urban interviewer—neither friendly, nor hostile, but simply observant and self-contained. He answered questions with regard only to his own interests rather than Tosun's. Hence the Chief, as interviewee, was a man of few words on many subjects and many words on a few subjects.

The intent of these remarks goes beyond their limited relevance to the technique of interviewing. The manner in which persons perceive the interview situation is a datum on their readiness and competence to participate personally in essentially impersonal social enterprises. It is axiomatic among American communication specialists that most Americans are not at all intimidated by opinion surveys which demand their views on great men and great matters well outside their actual experience. On this axiom is constructed the American advertising industry, unparalleled in history as an economic institution and also as a communication agency for enticing personal participation in American society. Living in such a setting, Americans seem to find few demands upon their empathic capacity exorbitant. When interview technicians discuss the questions they will ask a "national cross-section," it rarely occurs to them to worry about the limits beyond which American imagination will not function in principle. The population is accustomed to projecting themselves into strange roles and situations, and they enjoy exercising their skill. Indeed, a more common complaint about opinion polls heard among ordinary Americans is that the pollsters do not get around to them.[3]

The contrast with the social psychology of the interview situation among Turks is striking. How little they perceive the essential impersonality of the situation is clear from the excessive preoccupation of Turkish interviewees with what the interviewers might think of them. With extraordinary frequency, for example, inter-

viewers were thanked profusely for their personal interest. Said
one 47-year old illiterate villager after a three-hour interrogation:
"You are the nicest *effendi* I have ever known. No other *effendi*
has ever cared to know my thoughts on so many things." The
meaning of impersonal communication simply has not penetrated
in such measure that question-and-answer can be handled, psychologically, as a game.

In participant societies, where the mass media have taught
people how to communicate socially without being personally
"engaged," the question-and-answer game is played with uninhibited
pleasure by the populace (witness the "vox populi" feature in most
newspapers and the "quiz show" that dominates radio-TV programming). Among Traditional Turks, who have not yet learned
the participant style taught by the mass media, the situation of
question-and-answer is deadly earnest. Words count for much, we
have seen, with the Traditionals; and one does not speak lightly
on weighty matters. Consider the following array of responses to
the question where one would live if he could not live in Turkey:

I could not live in any other place. (Why?) Because I love Turkey.
(If you were forced to leave Turkey?) I would kill myself. (001: House-
maid, age 25, illiterate, poor)°
God forbid! I would rather die than live somewhere else than in
Turkey. (Why?) Because this is our country. (021: Worker, age 30,
illiterate, destitute)
I would rather die than live. I would not want to go anywhere. If
all go I would go. If nobody goes I would choose death. (089: House-
wife, age 24, illiterate, poor)
Would not want to live in any other country. I cannot leave my
people. Wherever my nation is I want to be there. (If you had to go?)
Nowhere. I would rather die. (116: Horsewagon Driver, age 29, illiter-
ate, poor)
I would rather prefer to die. (127: Farmer, age 58, illiterate, poor)
I would rather die. (186: Doctor, age 53, college, moderate)

These respondents exhibit one common trait: they can more
easily imagine destroying the self than making the effort to project
it beyond the familiar world into the strange. In the foregoing
quotations we deliberately chose a wide spread of sociological
characteristics (sex, age, occupation, education, economic status)

° For each quotation, the interview number of the respondent is given,
along with his occupation, age, education, economic status. The latter is
scored on a five-point scale: destitute, poor, moderate, well-off, rich.

to emphasize that this is a *psychological* trait. It recurs wherever a constrictive personality is found, even when the personality belongs to a college-educated doctor in fair economic circumstances. But the incapacity to take questions casually, to project "impersonally" into the situations they define, is especially marked in that social setting where Traditionals are the rule.

Constrictiveness, moreover, is more than a "trait." It is a "self-system," in Harry Stack Sullivan's phrase, a consistent way of organizing one's self-defenses against the threatening beyond. Consider the 30-year old worker, illiterate and destitute in his village near the Black Sea, who invoked God and death to save himself from the apparently worse fate of imagining himself living elsewhere. His tone on questions of the projective order ranged from the laconic to the shrill; but his underlying response never deviated from the evasive and rejective. He was terrified by the question as to what he would do if he were President of Turkey and again invoked God to preserve him from ever thinking of such a thing. He was less intensely agitated by the questions as to what he would do if he were editor of a paper or manager of a radio station; but he still replied, though without seeking aid from the Deity, that it would be "unseemly" for him to imagine himself doing such things. Even when asked what he considered the biggest problems facing Turkey, this man, raised in a coastal village across the Black Sea from the Soviet Union, could only reply: "I don't know." By this time he had probably been intimidated and exhausted by the interview situation.

For it is evident that this young man has not been trained to receive, retain, and relay opinions about the world outside his daily round of life. He is not interested in things foreign; when asked what he would like to know about other lands he replied: "Nothing." When asked his impressions of various foreign peoples, he said: "I don't know; they are all infidels." Indeed, in the whole series of questions dealing with mediated news of the world external to his village, the one positive expression was that he sometimes liked to listen to the newspaper being read. Why? "They tell things in a nice way, everything about governors, commandants, officials." When probed further about his interest in these important people, he continued (under continuous stimulation) as follows:

Yes. They are big. They do big things. (Why do these big things interest you?) They are our leaders. What would happen to us if something would happen to them? (What would happen?) We would all be lost. We could not do a thing without them. (Why not?) They are our masters. We all depend on them.

This illiterate Black Sea worker still perceives politics in the non-participant way which prevailed through the Ottoman centuries. Then, as we have seen, the messages that counted were prescriptive, usually dealt with war and taxes, and typically originated in the Sultanate. From the center "news" was relayed through controlled channels to fixed points on the circumference. Whatever the Sultan (or his spokesmen) chose to define as news *was* news—his engagement in a war, his travels through the lands, the state of his health. The outer world of space and time were defined by the moments of the monarch.

Just so, the Black Sea worker thinks of the newspaper solely as a way of being informed, at appropriate distance, about the doings of "our masters" without whom "we would all be lost." The newspaper for him is no vehicle of opinion, neither for hearing those of others nor for selecting some to make his own. What would a man want with an opinion if his fate is in any case decided for him by those whose proper role it is to decide such matters? Opinion is simply irrelevant in such a perspective. All he wants is a court chronicle of those great men on whom "we all depend."

The irreality of psychic participation (opinion) without a sense of political participation is very clear to the Traditionals. A 48-year old cobbler, born and raised in the Izmir province, replicates the pattern of the 30-year old Black Sea worker. He does not go to movies or listen to the radio. Nor, though he claims to be literate, does he read newspapers. He is not interested in world news, nor in local-regional news. His only news interest is to learn, in small doses, about the doings of the central government. This interest is focused clearly on "our masters" rather than "my opinions." When asked whether he ever heard controversies over the news, he mentioned recently witnessing an argument between two acquaintances over the wisdom of sending Turkish troops to Korea. When asked what he thought of this, the cobbler replied: "A silly argument. Nobody is asking our opinion. There are learned people. They *know* what is right and what is wrong better than we do."

The Traditional does not participate in shaping public policy; nor does he feel that he "should" (is expected to) participate; nor

is he particularly interested in (desirous of) participating. For
him enlightenment signifies incuriosity and practical wisdom coun-
sels ignorance. The 58-year old farmer, who was very firm in his
conviction that he missed nothing by ignoring the radio, stated
the case for constriction very concisely: "Even if I had enough
money, I would not buy a radio. (Why?) *I don't like too much
news.*" He dismissed all imaginative fiction as "nonsense stuff and
not real." His interest in media was restricted to but a single category: "I like to listen while my son reads the Korean war news. I
get excited and even with my old age I want to go there and fight."
The Traditional's only public role is to fight; the rest is not his
affair. The 29-year old horsewagon driver echoed these sentiments
of the farmer twice his age in a different province. On the question
whether he missed anything by ignoring newspapers and radio,
he said: "I lose nothing because I am not interested in *things which
do not concern me.*"

Throughout the Traditional interviews resonates this empty
space between the private and the public arenas, this zero or near-
zero contact between oneself and the larger world. The Traditional
cares nothing, wants nothing, can do nothing about this world.
Particularly poignant is the resignation of Traditional women, disturbed about their menfolk in Korea, who repeat solemnly they
can do nothing about this. In modern society, where war is perceived in many dimensions and policy alternatives are publicly
debated, women can and do express opinions on recruitment and
rotation policies, rationing and price control, and an array of other
"issues." The Traditional Turkish women can *only* wait and pray
while the men fight.

The praying-female and fighting-male postures are classic in
the Traditional repertory of personal deportment. They activate
the intense feelings of dependence upon authority we have noted,
and provide the major outlet for aggressiveness in the Traditional
system of values which codifies rational behavior for a "courage
culture." The self-imagery of Turks in this dimension is widespread
and persistent. When asked for two words best describing the
peoples of different lands, the Turks identified themselves mainly
in terms of *bravery* and *loyalty,* the most compulsive symbols of a
"courage culture." This emphasis is univocal, of course, among the
Traditionals. *Every one* of the persons quoted above, who would

sooner imagine suicide then leaving Turkey, responded to this question with two words in the following list: "brave, heroic, fighters, unafraid, honest, true." But these values persist, as words often do, after their references have changed, even among Turks who have passed beyond the Traditional orbit of life. That the Turkish social setting still showed many traditional elements, in 1950, is indicated by the distribution of symbols among the entire sample.

Table 10—Symbols of Peoples

Turks		Americans		British	
Brave	120	Industrious	59	Cold	56
Loyal	57	Kind	58	Sober	34
All others	128	All others	122	All others	96
	305		239		186

Russians		French	
Wicked	45	Gay	41
Cruel	41	Pleasure-loving	34
All others	84	All others	46
	170		121

N.B. As many of the 259 respondents could not think of two words (or even one word), no column reaches the maximum possible total of 518 choices.

These results fit well Lord Macaulay's brilliant distinction between "courage cultures" and "ingenuity cultures," whereby he sought to explain the high moral tone of prevailing opposition in a still medieval Italy to the modern perspectives of Machiavelli. The Machiavellian behavioral code based on ingenious "success" formulae struck his contemporaries as "unseemly" for loyal men and "unworthy" of brave men.[4] Even today, when Turks wish to express positive sentiments toward others, they do so in the affiliated symbolism of courage-loyalty. When they wish to express hostility, as toward the Russians, they merely transpose courage into "cruelty." Conspicuously absent from these Turkish judgments is the symbolism of ingenuity. It seems less relevant to one's judgment of a people whether they are intelligent, efficient, successful. This contrasts sharply with the judgments expressed by people living in more modern societies, among whom, as shown by UNESCO surveys of national stereotypes, the symbolism of ingenuity-success plays the most active role.[5] It contrasts also with the perspectives of the Modern segment within Turkey.

3. Moderns: The Big Picture

The Traditionals compose a very substantial proportion of the Turkish population, well over half even today. But they neither have nor seek a shaping influence over the Turkish future. The "creative minority" of Moderns, perhaps now 10% of the population, provided the elite that shaped Turkey's recent past and model its future. These are the urban, educated, relatively well-off Turks who run all of the government (still a virtual monopoly of top power) and most of the private enterprises. These control and consume the largest shares of the social values that are highly prized, e.g., income, safety, deference.[6]

The Modern link between mediated communication and personal perspective is implicated in the response of a 22-year old Turkish student, when asked what sort of paper he would run if he were its editor:

A paper that will interest the whole world. I believe that we will have a world government one day in the future. There will be no border barriers . . . I would introduce the backward areas of the world to the whole humanity. I would tell about their customs and ways and generally about their life. I would boost the idea of traveling all around the world.

No rejection or evasion here; no dumb silence or frightened retreat before the "unseemly" question. This young Modern speaks in a language which would sound natural to a student World Federalist anywhere. But it would surely sound strange to Traditionals in his own country, whose morality requires compulsive loyalty to family, mosque, and nation.

Alongside this ready identification with the "whole world" and "whole humanity" goes an equal facility at rearranging the self-system on short notice. Once an expansive personality incorporates such global symbols and abstract entities, the empathic mechanisms become skilled in orienting rapidly to new situations and unfamiliar roles. The moderns have no difficulty imagining themselves as President of Turkey. By comparison with the blank and frightened replies of most Traditionals, their responses to this question are ready and full:

I would adjust the taxes according to social justice. . . . To base the economic policy on a liberal doctrine. I would like the government to do things private enterprise cannot do. . . . To follow a peaceful foreign policy, basing my actions on the UN Charter. (020: Lawyer, 22, college, moderate)

To have safety from aggression, I would try to have friendlier relations with other countries. To make the country better its standard of living. I would give wide scope to foreign capital and safeguard it. To modernize our agriculture and organize it in the shortest possible time. (138: Tobacco merchant, 40, high school, moderate)

I wouldn't have obligatory universal military training. I would ease the customs law. I would give more freedom to the press. (027: student, 22, college, moderate)

I would defend the idea of a preventive war. (030: Government Official, 37, college, moderate)

I would raise the standard of living. I would try to wipe out the illiteracy and raise the cultural standard. Take steps to make the newly-established democracy in our country permanent. Separate matters of religion from matters of state. (029: Businessman, 40, high school, well-off)

I would try to have a strong army. I would build good roads in every section of the country. I would give big importance to the air force. I would try to give the people an easier way of life. I would have a strong police to take care of thefts and murders and such. (095: Butcher, 51, grammar school, moderate)

I would give farm machinery to the farmers. I would irrigate the dry land. I would build factories. I would work night and day to better the living conditions of the country. I would lower the unnecessary taxes. I would provide jobs for the unemployed. (120: Mason, 49, high school, moderate)

These attitudes are found mainly among the younger, urban, relatively well-off, and educated minority. But, here again, the responses were selected to show that high empathy is essentially a *personal* characteristic that occurs among groups that are sociologically diversified. It is found among 40-year old businessmen and 50-year old artisans (butcher, mason) as well as 20-year old lawyers and students. This spread of empathy is facilitated in societies where mediated communication is available to supplement, or replace, the "big picture" of the world elsewhere acquired only through higher education.

Modern Turks, then, are on familiar terms with the world. They exhibit the cosmopolitan perspectives which identify the modern style everywhere. This appears in their remarks about the countries other than Turkey in which they might choose to live. No Modern would rather die than live elsewhere. Indeed, many Moderns express willingness (even desire) to live in various foreign places—

and for very cogent reasons. For example, a radio announcer said that he would like to live in France because of the "elite environment":

There—I believe—in Paris, exists the choicest little cultural society in the world. (123: 20, college, well-off)

Another Modern would like to live in the United States for reasons that suggest the "Transitional" path by which he came to hold his present views (the compulsive avoidance of dirt; the desirous attraction to wealth):

They have a clean and rich life there. I like to live among rich people. (094: 39, Grammar school, moderate)

Reasons equally characteristic of the Modern style are given for *not* wanting to live in certain foreign countries. Instead of such blanket condemnations as "all foreigners are infidels," which recur frequently among Traditionals, the responses of the Moderns are specific rather than stereotypical. One student gives a direct "communication" reason for not wanting to live in Soviet Russia:

We don't know what is happening behind the Iron Curtain. I would not like to live in a place I couldn't get any information about. (077: 28, college, moderate)

Such concern for information would hardly occur to the Traditional, who does not participate in the communication network even within his own country. Only to the Modern perception would it occur naturally to use a phrase like "Iron Curtain" to designate the repression of public information, for only Moderns sense this lack as something almost physical.

From intense participation in the communication network derives a heightened awareness of the interaction between Self and Others. Indeed, some Modern Turks reveal the same sensitivity to what others know and think about them as do the "other-directed" persons whom David Riesman has characterized as the prevailing modern type in America.[7] A young merchant is dissatisfied with American attitudes toward Turkey because:

They know something about Turkey of 30 years ago, and think we are still back there, in spite of the tremendous changes that have taken place. (085: 37, high school, well-off)

He is not alone in his concern that Turkish "modernization" should be recognized. An educated housewife is equally pained with Americans for the same reason:

> Most of them don't even know of our existence, and some who do know think we are living in the days of our ancestors. (042: 36, college, moderate)

These views reveal a common sensitivity to public attitudes in the West, including the use of modernism as a standard of judgment. A tobacco executive even declares that he would not like to live in Britain or America because these countries are *not modern enough:*

> I don't like conservatism. They are the same people they were 500 years ago. (138: 40, high school, moderate)

Not many Modern Turks are quite so defensively sophisticated. Some take very literally the communication content to which they are exposed and these appear to be a little old-fashioned. An agricultural engineer, for example, explains his desire to live in the U. S. A. thus:

> Ever since I was a child I used to dream and think about people. I used to imagine all people equal, having nice homes. In my imagination I used to send their children to school and educated them. Now, as an adult, I know that America is that country I used to dream about. (014: 36, college, moderate)

Other Moderns respond in the qualified fashion of people who know too much to give simple answers to complex questions. A 35-year old doctor would like to live in the United States because:

> My profession is very advanced there. I could speak freely and air my views the way I wish.

On the other hand, he considers American policy toward Turkey unsatisfactory and he is quite articulate about his reasons why:

> Turkey is the most vulnerable country for a Russian attack. That is why they did not accept us into the Atlantic Pact. In this way the Americans spoiled a perfect chance of having a fortress against the Russians. . . . Also their capitalists are using us for exploitation. They give miserable prices for our tobacco. They act as if we were an American colony.

These two statements show the Modern differentiating skill in relating self to others. The moderns can identify readily with a

variety of foreign countries, can imagine themselves living elsewhere for a variety of reasons, can distinguish between policies and
peoples, can differentiate their personal from their political identities. This doctor can admire Americans for professional and personal reasons, while rejecting American policy. Traditionals do
not make such distinctions.

A few Turkish Moderns have learned to empathize so skillfully
that imagination carries them *beyond* familiar reality to its shadowy
periphery. Such Turks exhibit a *Weltmühe* and *cafard* that is found
more commonly among certain "ultra-modern" types of Europeans.
Born and raised in Istanbul families long intimate with European
ways, educated at the Sorbonne and infected with the *rive gauche*
legends of van Gogh and Gauguin, these ultra-modern Turks find
the strenuous efforts of national modernization a bit tiresome and
plebeian. One such respondent would like to live in Tibet, another
in Tahiti. A third does not even require anything so concrete as a
place-name, but can project himself into a purely abstract idea of
remoteness. To the question where he would like to live, this banker
replied simply: "On a small island, far away and empty." His
reason indicates the *weltfremd* attitude which has become familiar
in the modern West as the "problem of alienation." He would not
like to live anywhere else than his empty and remote island because:

> There is not much difference between any populated and so-called
> civilized city in the world. I have seen most of them and have not been
> impressed. (042: college, well-off)

The perspective of modern Turks is very clearly related to their
specific attitudes toward communications. Contrast the habitual
apathy toward news among Traditional Turks with this educated
merchant's explanation of his interest in foreign news:

> I want to know what is happening. I want to get different opinions
> on it, and get a clear and unbiased idea. I want to find out where the
> world is heading. (143: 55, college, well-off)

This might well stand as a concise summary of the modern view
of news and the function of public information transmitted through
mass media. The notion that "the world is heading" *somewhere*
underlies modern notions of a "big picture." Unlike traditional
eschatology, which saw the world as heading toward some pre-
ordained doom or golden age located in a hereafter, the modern

perspective sees history as a "secular process" in which events are related to each other in a sequence that can be analyzed and even altered by living observers.

Another Modern attitude toward the press is a young housewife's response that, if she were editor of a newspaper:

> I would run an opposition paper. I would be in opposition to the party in power, whichever it might be. I would criticize. That's the main function of the paper. (078: 28, college, moderate)

The Modern constellation of attitudes appears also in their comments about radio. As compared with the Traditionals' compulsive loyalty to the old and familiar, the Modern Turk shares the pervasive desire for novelty and variety which marks the modern style everywhere. When asked why he prefers the BBC to domestic stations (which he considers "not worth a damn"), a student replies "Novelty." This orientation is further illustrated by his explanation why the war news, at first novel, no longer interests him:

> This last war has lasted over ten years and . . . I am bored. (037: college, moderate)

A mechanical engineer prefers American musical programs (AFN) to Turkish because of their "Variety—new songs as well as old ones." Asked what he would do if he were a station manager, he replies:

> I would first make a poll to determine the needs of the people. (023: 25, college, well-off)

Here, incarnate, is the modern attitude toward communication—"feedback" and all.

Another aspect of the modern style—what Veblen called "conspicuous consumption"—is revealed in the comment of a housewife:

> Everybody who is somebody listens regularly to the news. (075: 48, college, well-off)

The modern middle-class view is generalized by a student, who explains why Americans have the best entertainment programs:

> It is the result of free enterprise and democracy. This is too deep to go into, but I can say that free enterprise gives the best living conditions and money will always buy the best entertainment. Therefore the Americans have the best programs. (077: 28, college, moderate)

A final aspect of the modern style in communication behavior among these respondents is their "propaganditis"—their alertness to source and method in their foreign news.[8] A housewife appraises the BBC's vigilance against verifiable inaccuracies, displaying a truly modern sense of relevant evidence and tentative conclusions:

Up to the present the BBC has been a reliable source. They never say anything that is liable to blow back into their faces. (005: 26, college, moderate)

A merchant, making explicit a typical reaction of propaganda-allergic modern listeners to "loaded" presentations, prefers the BBC because:

They give bad news as well as good news and thus make me feel that they are not trying to shape the facts so that news favors their side. They always give you both sides of the argument. (085: 27, high school, well-off)

Preference for "both sides of the argument" is a Modern notion limited, even in the most developed societies, to relatively small segments of the population. A valuable set of experiments has shown that this trait develops mainly among habitual participants in the communication network. Americans whose media exposure is only occasional are more likely to be persuaded by the vigorous presentation of a "one-sided" case. It is among those Americans for whom media exposure is a regular part of daily life, and who are therefore likely to be exposed to the countervailing arguments in due course, that the presentation of "both sides" is a condition of persuasion.[9]

When media participation attains this degree of subtle discrimination and supple responsiveness, then the society contains a cadre of Modern persons who shape its opinion arena. The Modern Turks, who today view the world around them in terms of "the big picture," provide the model toward which flow the aspirations and energies of those who will shape its future. We turn, finally, to a closer look at those Transitionals who are making their way in the modernizing stream.

4. Transitionals: The Widening World

Between the Traditionals firmly rooted in the ways of the Ottoman past and the Moderns, who have incorporated the "modern Western" style that Atatürk publicized as a model, there is the substantial number (perhaps 30%) of Turks who have been labeled Transitional. These individuals no longer exhibit the constrictive personality and compulsive empathy of their traditionalized countrymen, but they have not yet achieved the expansive cosmopolitan style of the Moderns. They are men in motion, and they have in common both the direction and mode of their mobility.

The Transitional Turks are in process of self-transformation. They are persons marked by aspirations for a future which will be better than the past, but they have not yet acquired a comprehensive set of new values to replace the old. Hence they exhibit *ambivalent* feelings about the choices between old and new which must be made along the way. It is this conflict of values—continued loyalty to the old, growing desire for the new—which differentiates the decisions and shapes the behavior of the Transitionals. The conflict exhibits various forms. Sometimes ambivalence takes the form of uncertainty and indecision. For example, whereas Modern respondents have clear and definite opinions about foreign countries, one young Transitional student responded as follows to the question whether he would like to live in America:

> I am not sure about this country. Things I hear differ so much. Some people love it—progress, technique, and all. Some find the people dull, suffocating, without individuality—too specialized, with no wide range of interests. I don't think it would be the worst place to choose. Anyhow, it would be a great risk, because once you get there you are stuck.

While modernized enough to be interested, differentiating and critical, he has not yet acquired the sense of uninhibited mobility which underlies the experimental perspective of the genuine Modern. He is "not sure"—a move would involve too great a "risk"; if it didn't work one would be "stuck." The notion that one can "try it out" without completely engaging oneself, the sense of tentative exploration in which both psyche and soma are only partially committed and can easily be withdrawn, this medical student has not yet acquired.

Ambivalence also takes the form of self-contradictory preferences. On the same question, a 54-year old doorman said first that he would not live anywhere else than Turkey. Probed by the interviewer, he next said: "If I had to live elsewhere, I would live in a Muslim country." The religious motivation appeared to be paramount in his explanation. But further discussion elicited the contradictory response that he would live in the United States. Why? Because: "I hear that everybody there is rich."

Among younger Transitionals, ambivalence often shows itself in incompleteness and inconsistency of attitudinal structures. Such persons exhibit modern views on various matters, but do not carry them through to their logical—or, more cogently, psychological— consequences. They abandon these views midway and often, as a result, present curious lacunae in their perspectives. A taxi driver, for example, would like to live in America "because life, I hear, is much easier there." When asked what he would like to know about the country, he replies: "All I want to know is how to get there. Once I am there, I am sure I can manage." This is the perspective of modern man, activist agent of his own destiny, with none of the fatalism and quietism which prevails among Traditional Turks.

Quite a different picture emerges, however, from the same man's responses to other projective questions. Asked what he would suggest to improve domestic radio programs, he replies: "*Who am I* to criticize the whole nation's radio?" Asked what he would do if he were manager of the radio station, he replies:

> What a question again! I don't know how to deal with my own business and you ask me what I would do with the radio house. . . . I listen when and if they play, and what they play I have to listen to and be thankful. (047: 36, Grammar school, poor)

This is rather the voice of the obedient Traditional, passive member of an environment in which most important decisions are made by his betters and are quiescently enacted by him. It is illuminating that his inconsistency comes between facility at empathizing in space and unreadiness to project himself in status.

Unlike the Traditional Turks who regard their station in life as "given" them by an allocation from Allah, this young taxi driver *does* have aspirations for a better life—he could be called "upwardly mobile." Only, to achieve these aspirations he would have to get out of the society in which his self-image has been traditionalized. This may account for the note of activism and self-confidence that enters his response when he imagines getting on in America: "Once I am there, I am sure I can manage." No talk, at this point, that "I don't know how to deal with my own business."

The root difficulty of many Transitional Turks is this conflict between new aspirations and old traditions. To satisfy the desires without violating the loyalties it often seems necessary to go somewhere else than where one is. The historic link between physical and psychic mobility thus reappears in the changing Turkish society of today. It is epitomized by the Balgat Grocer who had his "eye at the higher places," but felt that to achieve his ambitions he would have to "get out of this hole" and move to the city. The taxi driver, who also desires an "easier life," feels that he would have to leave his city and go to America to get it. This situation is typical for Transitionals.

Some Transitionals have found neither opportunity nor courage to seize this dilemma firmly by the horns; these continue in ambivalent suspension between desires and compulsions. Many try, somehow, to slip between the horns by small-scale movements. Even this, however, means changing the locale in which one has been traditionalized in order to achieve the new conditions one desires. Hence, most Transitionals are men-in-motion. Of a Transitional group studied closely, a majority were born in villages or small towns, but nearly all *now* reside in or near urban centers. This move from country to city is characteristic of modernization throughout recent history. It is interesting, too, that more Transitionals have moved toward Ankara, the Anatolian city, than toward cosmopolitan Istanbul. It seems appropriate that Transitionals should tend toward an environment intermediate between the traditional hinterlands and the cosmopolis.

Restlessness and striving are fairly widespread among Transitionals on the move. Responding to the direct question: "In general, how do you feel about your life?" one out of every five Transitionals described himself as "fairly unhappy" or "very unhappy." When next asked: "What makes you feel this way?" nearly two-thirds gave reasons based on the inadequacy of their material resources. Most of these are employed in cities; some are still on farms. In both cases, they tend largely to be dissatisfied with how they make their living and how much they make.

In explaining their discontent in economic terms, the Transitionals differed sharply from the Traditionals, who mainly gave reasons for unhappiness classifiable as "fatalism and religion." The Transitionals revealed also a characteristic ambivalence on religion. Two of every three Transitionals had, on a direct question, asserted their religious beliefs to be quite important to them. On the behavioral level, however, these beliefs seem to have lost their directive force; and it may be that, in these matters, actions speak louder than words. For example, whereas most Traditionals go to the mosque "very often," nearly two-thirds of all Transitionals (including half of those who claimed religious beliefs to be important to them) said they "seldom" or "never" go to the mosque. Among those whose piety has faltered, reasons for discontent were almost always explained in "material" rather than "spiritual" terms. Secularization shows itself in the cleavage between inherited doctrines and acquired desires.

This cleavage opens one gap through which psychic mobility has spread. On the question: "What is the biggest personal problem for people in the same circumstances as yourself?" 72% of all Transitionals gave responses classifiable as *economic*. They were next asked: "What can you do about it?" Compared with the overwhelming passivity and fatalism of the Traditionals, relatively few Transitionals said merely "nothing." Even among those who made no specific suggestions for action, two-thirds gave some cogent reason why he personally could not cope effectively with the problem he had specified. Some attributed ineffectiveness to their status, others to their lack of requisite skills, and the largest number to an analysis of the "nature of the problem." A fairly large minority of those who answered, however, did put forward some concrete idea as to appropriate action they might take.

This quality of *activism* differentiates the Transitionals from the Traditionals and relates them to the Modern Turks. The difference shows in their views as to what can be done about the "biggest problem facing Turkey," as each respondent had himself defined this problem in a preceding question. A substantial minority of the Transitionals had some quite definite proposal as to what could be done to solve the biggest problem. On another question —what they would do if head of the Turkish government—only a rare Transitional exhibited the complete lack of empathy which was so pervasive among Traditionals. About one-third of the Transitionals who gave some response were unable to follow this up by imagining the concrete measures they would take in this august role; but the rest, like the Moderns, put forward quite specific programs for action. Of these, by far the greatest number were classifiable as "economic measures."

These characteristics sharply differentiate the process of opinion-formation among the Transitionals. Quite consistently they express more varied opinions on more varied subjects, and in more positive fashion, than do their Traditional compatriots. To exhibit these consistencies, we compared the over-all responsiveness of the three types on the total interview schedule, with results shown in Table 11. First we computed the average number of respondents on all 42 questions which had been asked of all interviewees. This procedure made the Traditionals appear to be more responsive than if we had counted the answers to *all* questions—since they had not been asked many questions precisely because of their nonresponsiveness on preceding "filter" questions. Despite this advantage, the frequency of response among Traditionals is significantly lower, as shown in the first row of Table 11. Next we averaged, for each type, the number of responses given on all 19 questions to which each respondent could give as many answers as he wished—e.g., when asked to enumerate his preferred radio programs. On such questions each additional item enlarges and diversifies the respondent's area of choice. The results are shown as Variety of Response in the second row. Finally we compared the types on all 13 questions calling for a single definite response on some substantive public issue (e.g., "What should be done about poverty?"). Here we differentiated noncommital responses (e.g., "Something should be done") from those which committed the respondent to some definite opinion (e.g., "The government should control prices/ raise wages/subsidize farmers/ etc."). We then computed the average of commital responses, with results shown in the third row of Table 11.

Table 11—Components of Opinion Formation

	Moderns	Transitionals	Traditionals
Frequency of Response	95%	88%	73%
Variety of Response	49	42	32
Commitment of Response	87	83	77

In every case the Transitionals disengaged themselves consistently from the Traditionals and positioned themselves closer to the Moderns. Though a substantial proportion of them are still rural persons with low earnings in poor jobs, they have gained mobility through their literacy (see Table 1). Extending their distance from the Traditionals through the "mobility multiplier" of mass media (see Tables 2, 5) they steadily draw closer to the thoughtways of the Moderns.

By way of resumé, then, the Moderns, already within the audience for mass communication, are the currently active element in Turkish society. The Traditionals, on the other hand, are the quiescent segment of the society and do not participate significantly in either the new communications or other modernizing institutions. They do not attend to the output of the mass media; nor do they, in the normal course of events, want to think or do much about the problems these media describe. The Transitionals, moving from traditional ways toward a modern style, are the new source of social energy for the future.[10] It is they who are likely to bring into Turkish life the newer currents of thought and action that may emerge in the next years and decades. This probability gives the Transitionals their special significance both for communication and for social change.

They are acquiring psychic mobility, a personal capacity to identify widely and empathize readily. They are secularizing, acquiring a common concern with problems identified as socioeconomic rather than religious. They are becoming activist: problems are to be dealt with by policy rather than by prayer. On all manner of public questions, they have opinions, individually articulated and positively expressed. As their numbers increase they are bound to play a larger role in the future direction of Turkish society. What remains to be worked out is the shape of their political future.

The 1950 election, which turned out of office the Atatürk party that had governed continuously over the quarter-century since the Revolution, gave an important impetus to mass participation in political life. Professor L. V. Thomas has written of this event:

No feature of the nationwide political agitation was more remarkable to the "Old Turkey Hand" than the total disappearance of hesitancy or fear on the part of the common people as they discussed their government.[11]

In the spring of 1954 I accompanied Ismet Inönü and Kasim Gülek on a pre-election campaign trip to the Adana region. What had struck the Old Turkey Hands in 1950 was even more highly visible in 1954. In remote villages the peasants still rushed forward to kiss the hands of the candidates. But these were no longer simply "our masters." When the serious business of the election issues was put on the table, the men who spoke up, the local Transitionals, asked questions that were direct, tough, and insistent. The issues were not moral but economic, and of a crescendo pattern—the market price of crops, the amount of government support, the availability of consumer goods, the proposed legislation to give American companies prospecting rights on Turkish oil. These are not the questions of a quiescent peasantry, but of an alert electorate.

These elections have thus opened an avenue of mass political participation. In what measure this avenue will be broadened to encourage popular participation in shaping the national and international life of Turkey remains to be determined by future events. If the measure is large, as seems likely, then the next great accretion of public influence will go to those persons we call Transitionals. They are not now rich, informed, or powerful. But they exhibit the desire to become all of these things. As the Grocer of Balgat put it: "My eye is at the higher places." The further element is that the modernized elite of Turkey is well-attuned to the rising and spreading aspirations of the Transitionals. This goes far to explain Turkey's political stability in a Middle East elsewhere riven by conflicts within elites, between elites and aspirants.

As we turn from Turkey to the highly unstable Arab lands, we shall be obliged to deal with the passing of traditional society as partly the story of modernization *manqué* by reason of ideological schism and political cleavage. We make the transition by way of Lebanon—the Arab country which began its modernization earliest and, partly for that reason, has developed it farthest.

The Arab Worlds

VI.

Lebanon: Two Worlds in Small Compass

> "To be a Levantine is to live in two worlds or more
> at once, without belonging to either."
> —ALBERT HOURANI

LEBANON is the most modern Arab land today as an outcome of its history. Smaller than Connecticut, with little over a million inhabitants, Lebanon is no leader in natural power and wealth. Industrially, it has nothing that measures up to the Turkish steel complex of Karabük; its farming, based on intensive cultivation of small stony plots, is negligible compared to Egypt's highly organized agricultural system. Yet it scores well ahead of all Arab neighbors on every index of modernity. Lebanon has the highest proportion of people who live in cities; earn and spend cash; attend school and are literate; read newspapers, see films and hear radios.[1] To explain this requires an historical resumé.

The Lebanese early became attuned to a variety of modernizing influences from abroad—trade connections, Christian ties to European churches and to emigrant colonies overseas, widespread contact with Western missionaries and administrators. These religious, economic and cultural factors transformed village life while other Arab peasantries slumbered. Many issues raised by modernization remain unresolved, but Lebanon has moved farthest away from Arab-Muslim traditionalism. In its place there developed a modern set of specifically Lebanese perspectives and practices. Their distinctive mark is to interweave modernism more closely with Westernism than is permissible in any currently prevailing ideology in the Middle East. As the historical conditions under which this occurred are still operative in Lebanon, and clarify some of her current problems, we do well to begin by reviewing these Westernizing factors.

1. The Westernizing Factors

Lebanon has always been an *entrepôt,* a way-station for foreigners with exotic goods and ideas. Its ports convened people
from East and West in Phoenician, Roman, Byzantine, Arab and
Ottoman times. Among its merchants have flourished qualities of
enterprise and adaptability not associated with agricultural societies. Commercial exchange has been augmented by recent development as a regional center of education and recreation. Students
flock to the American University of Beirut and the Université de
St. Joseph, vacationers to the cool mountain resorts which provide
a major source of the national income. Increasingly, international
conferences and organizations make their headquarters in Beirut.
The national airport is a way-station for world airlines.

A distinctly Western political phase began, after the 1860
massacre of Christians by Druzes, when the Great Powers established an autonomous regime headed by a Christian *mutasarrif*
(governor). Subsequently, Lebanon's "public security and standards of social and political life advanced to a point not nearly
reached by any other province of the Ottoman Empire."[2] Thereafter the old saying became current: "Happy is he who possesses
even a goat's enclosure in the Lebanon."[3] Independence symbolized its uniqueness by affiliation with Phoenician ancestry. Even
Westernized Christians, such as the young poet Sa'id 'Aql, still
cherish this Phoenician link with the Mediterranean rather than
the Arab-Muslim world.[4]

The lifeways of Lebanese separateness deepened as a large
Christian population settled on the Mountain. Christian increase
was due to another important Lebanese tradition, that of *asylum*
for persecuted religious and racial groups, which also goes back
very far (to Byzantine and early Arab times). Christianity and
Westernization grew together. Channels of communication with
the West were ready-made for members of the Uniate, Orthodox
and Protestant sects. They, in turn, relayed Western influence internally. Leading Westernizers were the Maronite Christians (today about 30 per cent of the population), for their ties with Rome
and France provided their safety in a Muslim area. The first Arab
press was probably introduced by a Maronite scholar educated in
Rome early in the 17th century.[5] The first modern school was

founded in 1789 by a Maronite patriarch educated at an Italian seminary.[6]

Since the Ottoman *millet* system encouraged local communities to co-exist with minimum interaction, these Christian channels to the West operated mainly as closed circuits. As a result, independent rates of social change occurred within the Lebanese area, the Christians modernizing faster than others. But, in time, diffusion occurred. An instance was the Arabic literary renaissance. The flow of influence in this case illustrates the role of communication in social change. Since the Lebanese Christians controlled the channels of enlightenment (schools, presses, foreign contacts), Muslims seeking new ways throughout the area tended to move toward them. The newspapers and magazines initiated by Lebanese Christians in Cairo in the 1870's brought Muslim Egyptians into the Arabic cultural revival.[7]

European and American missionaries, by founding schools and presses, performed a modernizing function analogous to that of Western military instructors in the Ottoman officers' academies. Religious and military education were their respective aims, but a regular side-effect was the transmission of Western languages, ideas and personal ties to small but influential groups. Since the missionaries developed the only school system ranging from elementary to university level, Christians early outdistanced Muslims in literacy and learning. As late as 1941-43, Christians still constituted 70 per cent of the school population but only 53 per cent of the total population; and among Christians enrollment was 15.8 per cent compared to the Muslim 7.8 per cent.[8] Today almost 70 per cent of the total population is literate, with nearly universal literacy in the original Mount Lebanon area. There is no remotely comparable literacy rate in any other Arab land.

Whereas Christianity brought modern enlightenment, the political modernization of Lebanon is largely a French legacy. France entered the Middle East as protector of the Cross, by leading the Crusades; later Suleyman the Magnificent recognized Francis I as protector of all Christians of the Latin rite in Ottoman possessions. French predominance in the Levant is recorded in the Arabic language, where *Franji* (Frank) and foreigner are coterminous. Other Western powers were influential. Americans and Britons, active in education and commerce, made a strong impress. Some Lebanese adopted walking exercises, afternoon teas, and punctuality to the extent that they became known as the "Ingliz" to others.[9] The French, however, made the more massive quest for cultural pre-eminence and political power.

France created the separate state of Greater Lebanon, incorporating predominantly Muslim districts under a prevailing Christian element. There the French laid the basis for Lebanese modernization. Public order was firmly established, a modern ,code of contracts replaced the Ottoman *Majalla,* and a new legislative code was enacted.[10] French capital built ports, roads, railways and public utilities, and helped to develop the silk and cement industries.[11] The Constitution of 1926 made Lebanon the first Arab Republic and established a framework for representative government. But effective power was denied to indigenous leaders, and little was done to diffuse the political mentality that sustains a democracy. Instead, divisiveness and sectarianism were permitted (and sometimes fostered) to improve the French position. On balance, however, the mandatory regime was a net instrument of modernization—by what it accomplished directly and by the regular contact with a European social system which it provided.

Indigenous needs, the missionary movement, French governance —all played their part in developing a more cosmopolitan variety of person in Lebanon. Modernization was further accelerated by the profound changes which altered Lebanese village life long before they became visible in other Middle Eastern lands. Nothing similar occurred in the Turkish village, for example, until after World War II, with Marshall Aid tractors and roads. Their earlier modernization and higher living standards explain why Lebanese Traditionals are less traditional than villagers elsewhere in the area.

The Lebanese early acquired mobility. Large-scale movement of people—both urbanization and emigration—began in the late 19th century, when population growth and land congestion resulted in excessive fragmentation of holdings.[12] Peasants faced the classic choice of destitution or migration.[13] The special feature of Lebanese history is the high proportion of those who chose to move. An unfavorable ratio of population to land has not been sufficient to mobilize large numbers in other Middle Eastern areas. The ratio is much more unfavorable in Egypt, yet the *fellah* does not migrate. Nor does the Anatolian villager leave Turkey. In contrast, there are probably as many Lebanese living outside the homeland as there are in Lebanon.[14]

Educated Lebanese also migrated. Highly trained and seeking better opportunities, thousands went to Egypt under the British regime as subordinate officials, merchants and professionals. The largest numbers made their way to Latin America and the United States.[15] In Brazil, emigré Lebanese came to own 500 large industrial enterprises, including some of the largest textile plants in the world.[16] Emigration deepened with the permanent transfer of whole families, becoming a social force which touched all levels of the community.

Geographic mobility, historic antecedent of mass media in this role, was the key to social and psychic mobility. We associate this with our survey results which show that the Lebanese are today more facile empathizers than other Middle Eastern peoples. In Table 9, for example, under 2 per cent of Lebanese respondents could not choose another country if they had to leave Lebanon (as compared with huge resistance to this question elsewhere). The presence of relatives and countrymen overseas reduces the agony of forsaking familiar earth. As one farmer said, "It is easier to go to America because there are many Arabs there. I know people who have gone there." This personal link can create psychic familiarity and even the illusion of physical nearness. A pro-Communist laborer, who nonetheless would go to the United States rather than the Soviet Union if he had to leave Lebanon, justified his choice by saying: "America is nearer. Russia is very far and very wide. . . . We have no relatives with Russia, it is very far away." Large-scale emigration over past generations has shaped personal identification with the outer world among those who remained behind.

Concomitant with emigration was urbanization: villagers, while supplying a steady flow overseas, also built up the Lebanese cities. Today, almost a fifth of the population resides in Beirut; another fifth in Tripoli, Saida and Zahle. Between 1932 and 1951 the proportion of population in cities over 10,000 rose about 8 per cent (an absolute increase of 220,000).[17] Since there were not enough urban jobs to absorb this increase, many farmers did not quit their villages but took part-time work in nearby cities. The practice of temporary residence outside the village, rare before 1880, gradually became commonplace as Lebanon developed roads and acquired automobiles.[18] Many young farmers experienced part-time living away from their village as a work-routine.[19]

This high mobility had profound repercussions for villagers who moved and for those who remained behind. As remittances from relatives in cities or overseas dwarfed other sources of income, villagers acquired a new and lively sense of cash, which developed further with the increased use of mountain villages as summer resorts. Lebanese villagers acquired a taste for risk-taking, virtually unknown to the Syrian peasant who hoards his money or converts it into jewelry. With cash as the new gauge of value, land lost its sanctified status and became an item in the calculus of market price.[20] The alterations which mobility and monetization have long been working in the psychic equipment of the ordinary villager explain why there are relatively more Transitionals in rural Lebanon than in other Arab countries.

A more exact statement is that Transitionals in Lebanon are, by and large, far less traditional than their peers elsewhere in the Middle East. The modernizing process has carried so many Lebanese so much further into the 20th century that they face more modern problems in more modern ways than do their opposite numbers elsewhere. It is among Transitionals in rural Lebanon, for example, that the roles of youth and women are posed in terms parallel to Western discussion of these matters. In rural Egypt and Iran, these matters are not even salient yet as problems. Awareness that these role-conflicts are central issues for Lebanese Transitionals today is an outcome of our case study. But we wish to approach them, having reviewed the impact of communication upon Lebanese modernization in the past, by way of the communication data produced by the 1950 survey.

2. Media and Status

We first classified our Lebanese respondents by the media index used in Turkey.* This adequately differentiated the Traditionals—of whom 60 per cent were non-listeners to radio, compared with 6 per cent among all the others. But since the

---

* The Lebanese sample was designed to overrepresent the literate population living in areas where the mass media exert their greatest influence. Two urban residents were interviewed for every rural resident, three men for every woman, and the sample divided about equally between respondents in high, medium and low income brackets. Geographical concentration in the Tripoli, Saida and Beirut-Mount Lebanon districts was designed to assure adequate coverage of these three major regions, so different in historical and sectarian tradition.

Transitionals are so much further advanced in Lebanon than elsewhere, we needed a more refined measure to differentiate them significantly from the Moderns. The sub-classification in Table 1, separating those who listen only to domestic stations from those who listen also to foreign stations, filled this need.

Table 1—Types of Listening

	Moderns	Transitionals	Traditionals	Totals
Foreign Listeners	67%	33%	9%	116
Domestic Listeners	27	61	31	86
Non-Listeners	6	6	60	102

$$N = 304$$

The correspondence between lesser modernity and narrower listening scope is very close, but several questions remained—e.g., what are the important differences between domestic and foreign listeners? In Lebanon, the foreign listener hears not only foreign news and views, but also lectures on Arab history, favorite Arab songs, and superb Koran readings. One listener explained his fondness for BBC programs by saying:

> They fit into our life here in the Near East more than others. I like to listen to London because it has various programs about religion, culture and history of the Middle East. It is something concerned with us.

Conversely, the domestic listener may find an English or French language program in progress. In 1949, three of Radio Lebanon's news broadcasts were beamed in French, two in English and four in Arabic. Besides nine hours a day of Arabic broadcasting, there were two and one-half hours of French and one hour of English programs. French broadcasts were produced by the École Supérieure des Lettres (with a subsidy from the French Legation) and English programs were prepared by the staff of the British legation.[21] Given these facts, it was doubtful *a priori* that domestic listeners would differ significantly from foreign listeners. But quite different they turn out, in fact, to be.

The biographical data drawn from the interviews showed that each "radio audience" corresponds closely to a "social class." Table 2 presents the differences on education, literacy and standard of living. The three types of radio audiences differ consistently in socioeconomic class and, as further analysis showed, on an array of attributes involving status, behavior and outlook. On frequency of media exposure, on media preference and program preference there are wide and recurrent differences.

Table 2—Socioeconomic Status of Listener Types

	Foreign	Domestic	Non-Listeners
High education (lycée or college)	87%	34%	13%
Literate	95	71	50
Above average living standard	87	70	39
N* =	(116)	(86)	(102)

* These numbers apply for all tables unless otherwise stated.

Media exposure, we have noted, is centripetal. Radio-listeners tend to be reached by other media than non-listeners. As Table 3 shows, foreign listeners are more media-minded than all others.

Table 3—Exposure to Newspapers and Films

	Foreign Listeners	Domestic Listeners	Non-Listeners
See movies	85%	71%	37%
Read newspapers	90	72	46

It is a rare foreign listener who does not also read newspapers and attend movies. Domestic listeners take a high intermediate position, while non-listeners show a dramatic decline in exposure. Foreign listeners are also most regularly exposed to all media as shown in Table 4.

Table 4—Frequency of Exposure

	Foreign Listeners	Domestic Listeners	Non-Listeners
See movies weekly	63%	41%	42%
Read newspapers daily	68	61	44
Hear radio daily	90	67	—

The foreign listener is a heavy consumer of communications. One such young respondent (096) of Greek Orthodox faith, fluent in English, French and Arabic, sees movies three to four times a week. He reads regularly two newspapers, one published in Syria, the other in France. His content preferences are numerous and varied; he "usually reads" eleven parts of his newspapers, ranging from foreign news to novels and stories. Among the radio stations "best heard here" or "heard in the past month," he named BBC,

VOA, Damascus, Egypt, Beirut, Ankara and Belgrade. He also reads, at least occasionally, the *Egyptian Mail, Life, Time, True Story* and *Romance* magazines. This young man's involvement with movies and romance stories may be related to the fact that he was going through a courtship. He, like other young respondents, told the interviewer that he valued the media as a teacher of appropriate conduct in life.

At the other end of the spectrum are the non-listeners. An illiterate peasant woman—who had never attended the cinema, had no contact with the other media, and had never heard of Europe—speaks for extreme rural isolation. Her information comes, as in Biblical times, from the primary network of the woman's daily round. Asked how she got her news, she replied:

> From the neighbors; at the bakery when I go to bake the bread, and at the well where I get our drinking water. (Who tells you the news when you're at those two places?) All the women who go there. (What do they usually talk about?) About who is going to marry, who is going to have a baby, who went to Tripoli, and what for, who quarreled with whom and why. (185)

When news is equated to village gossip, face-to-face exchange suffices. This old woman explained that she did not miss reading newspapers because: "It's not for us, it's only for the men—they know how to read and they are more capable of thinking than we are." Nor did she miss the movies, explaining why by an item of Traditional wisdom: "When one has not been aware of the existence of a thing, one does not miss it."

Most Lebanese Traditionals do not exhibit this complete isolation from the mass media. Deprived as many of them are, they have been touched to the extent that desires, if not behavior, are modified. A destitute shepherd aged 26, unlike the village wife, *does* miss things of which he has become dimly aware. While he is not exposed to any of the media, devotes his leisure time exclusively to cleaning his nails, and invokes Allah to answer most of the interview questions, nevertheless this shepherd envies those who listen to the radio: "They are educated and understand." Even more does he covet the skills of the newspaper reader: "One learns about the world and happenings in Beirut while sitting in his home. . . . Papers tell many things. . . ." His feeling is made more poignant by its very vagueness—he does not know exactly what it is he is missing. When asked by the interviewer what the papers

write about, he answers: "Many things, I cannot say, because I
don't know, but I hear so." (286)

Selective perception enables Traditionals, exposed to the media
in limited dosage, to notice only those messages which confirm their
customs and values. The Balgat Chief found in movies mainly cherished resonances of traditional martial themes. Similarly, a poor
Lebanese woman aged 35, of Greek Orthodox faith, does not discover in movies the enticements of freedom and fashion. Instead
she learns "reliance on God." Radio helps her to withdraw into
her preferred dysphoric fantasies. When she tunes in Arabic music,
"I remember my relatives who died—and what a sad life this is."
Novel and distant matters do not penetrate her frame of attention.
She cannot bear to watch dancing other than the traditional
dabki,[22] and she refuses to hear news of foreign countries: "I
don't understand them and I don't bother." (031) A constrictive
personality shuts out the potentially expansive effects of the media
to which she is exposed.

But the modern media do enable others to create new identifications and thus to participate in the modernizing process. An
index is program preference—what people look for and listen for
in the media. Attitudes toward news are of central relevance here.
It was naturally among Traditionals that dislike for news was
most often manifested. One villager warned: "Those who listen
buy trouble for themselves. Because they worry themselves about
what is not their concern. They must stick to their work. *It* makes
them live, not wars in China." (012)

Conversely, preoccupation with the news characterizes the
Modern respondent. A retired Army major anticipates his daily
diet of information with the same pleasure as his victuals: "Just
as I wait for 12 o'clock to have lunch," he says, "so do I wait for
8 o'clock to hear the news." (024) The data show that 80 per
cent of the Moderns are interested in news broadcasts, as compared to 40 per cent Transitionals and 30 per cent Traditionals.
Also, 62 per cent foreign listeners, as compared to 55 per cent
domestic listeners, chose news as a favorite program. The foreign
listeners showed greater involvement: 53 per cent tuned in news
broadcasts daily, as compared to 28 per cent domestic listeners
who did so.

Among those interested in news, the foreign listeners were distinctly more concerned with international issues. Respondents

were asked to recall the news they had heard most recently—a useful indicator of attention and retention. They divided thus:

Table 5—Type of News Heard Most Recently

	Foreign Listeners		Domestic Listeners		Non-Listeners	
International news		71%		44%		34%
National news	22		30		32	
Local or community news	4		18		32	
Family news	0		8		13	
Other	3	29%	0	56%	2	66%
Total		100%		100%		100%
N =		(95)		(63)		(63)

This answered our *a priori* query whether people are foreign listeners because they care more about events outside Lebanon. As Moderns, their interests in fact encompass the world. While the other audiences also recalled international news items, their major concern was the domestic scene—family, local and community news. These were mentioned by foreign listeners hardly at all (4 per cent).

Closely related to news preference is media preference. The relevant differences are shown in Table 6, on the question asking how respondents got their most recent news.

Table 6—Source of Most Recent News

	Foreign Listeners	Domestic Listeners	Non-Listeners
Radio	51%	25%	4%
Newspaper	31	45	38
Word of mouth	18	30	58
Total	100%	100%	100%
N =	(109)	(73)	(79)

While non-listeners rely most heavily on oral communication, and domestic listeners turn largely to newspapers, a majority of foreign listeners depend on radio (especially international broadcasts) for the type of news that most concerns them.

Striking among the Moderns are the warm sentiments they express about radio. Americans of this type—the socioeconomic elite, cosmopolitan in outlook, heavy consumers of communication —are much less radio-minded. They turn rather to the printed media of books, newspapers, magazines.[23] When Lebanese respondents were asked to choose between radio and newspapers, the majority of Moderns chose the radio. This reaction stemmed not only from their low esteem of the Lebanese press, but also from their high regard for foreign radio. One Modern described his radio as an "electric newspaper, which keeps me in contact with the rest of the world." (024) Another, a well-traveled engineer fluent in four languages, called the radio "a splendid invention giving me . . . the feeling of not being isolated from the outside world." (025) Many said that they "could not get along without" a radio of their own (a more frequent sentiment, in America, among housemaids and other non-elite persons). And, indeed, 87 per cent Moderns as compared to 78 per cent Transitionals and 16 per cent Traditionals owned their own sets.

The foreign listener's intense interest in international news suggests an expansive outlook. This is documented in Table 7, which reports on an index of cosmopolitanism, made up of items that reveal interest and exposure to various sorts of international experience.

Table 7—Indicators of Cosmopolitan Interests

	Foreign Listeners	Domestic Listeners	Non-Listeners
Speak some English	71%	40%	7%
Recent contact with foreigners	70	55	28
Read foreign publications	68	10	4
Prefer U.S. films	84	63	47
Prefer Western music	56	19	—
Know United Nations	78	50	24
N =	(116)	(82)	(102)

The foreign listener is a Westernized man. Not only does he speak a foreign language, but he meets people from abroad and exposes himself to every form of mediated contact with the West. A remarkable proportion reads foreign publications. The Lebanese is much more likely than the Turk or Egyptian to be exposed to Western communications, as indicated in Table 8 by circulation figures for sample issues in 1953-54.

Empathy is the base of the Modern's interest in the wider world.

A young Lebanese girl, educated in a French school in Beirut, was able to identify with the far-away American soldiers to the extent that news from Korea made her feel "miserable . . . because American boys are losing their lives for no worthy reason . . ." (401) Another girl, a well-to-do Sunni studying at the American University, revealed an even more striking ability to identify herself with an American situation. Her most recent news was "the enormous bill Mr. Truman is presenting to Congress of nearly 90 milliard dollars." (How did you feel?) "I was shocked, plain shocked. I believe America is driving head-first into a crazy scheme of things which is going to destroy it. It's spending much more than its capital, financially and in human life and endurance." This student, it turns out, is a great fan of American popular music. She listens constantly to radio broadcasts of "American blues, waltzes, tangos and rhumbas." Conversely, she avoids Arabic music like the plague: "The music is horrid, the voices and instruments are intolerable, and each song takes a quarter of an hour to finish." Her reading fare also is almost entirely American—*Time, Life, Ladies Home Journal,* fashion and screen magazines—because "they are much more entertaining." This student's continuous mediated exposure to American life brings Washington's concerns closer to her than those of Beirut. She exhibits an extreme syndrome of cosmopolitanism—xenophilic incorporation of the foreign as a mode of uniformly rejecting most native secondary symbols.

Table 8—Comparative Sales of American Magazines

	Time	Life	Newsweek	Fortune	Combined Average Sales per 10,000 Inhabitants
Lebanon	1,226	652	355	26	17.5
Turkey	1,239	1,373	541	28	1.4
Egypt	1,452	1,779	407	56	1.7

Pro-Western Moderns have no corner on the foreign news market. Also heavily involved are Moderns hostile to Western policy, who combine ideological antipathy (the antonym of sympathy not of empathy) with a desire to hear Western broadcasts. As educated people they consider it necessary to know what is occurring in the world from the best available sources. An Anglophobe physician (who says the British "would gladly enslave all other nations for their own egotistical purposes of comfort and wealth") is nevertheless a BBC listener—because "they give the most accurate, precise and up-to-date news as compared to other countries. I have been listening to news from England for over 15 years and have never had to doubt their truthfulness . . ." He prefers international radio because the local Beirut papers feature "the most stupid news about trivial thefts, or the length of someone's moustache." (038)

A 29-year-old senior accountant at the Iraq Petroleum Company, who spends "approximately all" his leisure time in political party and trade union activities, also feels this need to see the big picture. Like the doctor, he has no particular fondness for the West, and is convinced that they broadcast to Lebanon in order to serve their own ends. But he explains, "I listen to foreign programs not because I like to, but because I want to understand the policy of that country towards world affairs and towards us here. . . . I want to compare its news with what I read in the Arabic press." (142) This sophisticated awareness of news as conditioned by source—the need to know *who* is saying *what* for what *purpose*—is typically an attribute of the Modern foreign listeners.

The Traditional, by contrast, does not treat "the news" as a complex autonomous reality to be apprehended only by a varied diet of information and opinion. He has a more "itemistic" approach. Unlike the doctor, he often is interested in local scandal and personal anecdote—the length of somebody's moustache. "Outside" news, when mentioned at all, related to Syria or other Arab lands. Typical recalled items were: the opening of a road between Syria and Lebanon; the death of an important man in his bathroom, allegedly the victim of poisoning; the formation of a new cabinet in Syria; the new association of Palestinian refugees designed to regain their homes and properties; the capture of a thief who hypnotizes people and then steals from them. In short, the major news items that were remembered dealt with national or local events, and often enough with gossip and scandals.

Among domestic listeners who occasionally dialed world news, there was a tendency to recall items with a special personal reference. A fisherman judges America unfavorably because he once heard that "the Americans do not allow people to catch fish on their shores." As for Russia, he says: "I will not live in Russia because they do not have a sea. I will choose Morocco. Because it is a sea country and they say it has lots of fish on its coast. I can fish as much as I like and become rich. (What will you do then?) I will buy a big motor boat and fish more." He feels that he understands the British: "They are fishermen." (107)

Aside from their concepts of news, the Lebanese differ on other indicators of modernity. Enlightening is the hypothetical choice of country if one had to leave Lebanon. Sorted according to educational level of respondents, the choices are shown in Table 9.

Table 9—Choice of Country by Educational Level

	USA	Latin America	Europe	Soviet Bloc	Arab Area	Lebanon Only	Totals
High education	49%	0%	25%	2%	8%	2%	(115)
Low education	49	10	7	4	18	1	(85)

There is a striking absence of persons (so prevalent elsewhere) who refuse to consider any move at all. Among those choosing the U. S., where there was no difference in frequency, there was great difference between the two groups in rationale of choice. The low-educated, in true Traditional style, chose the move that involved the least mobility. They justified their choice by saying there are large Lebanese colonies there; in imagination the U. S. becomes a displaced Lebanon. A cart driver said: "I know people who have gone there." A chauffeur added: "I have a cousin who went there and became rich. . . . I hope I can go there." Said a third: "There are Arabs there. I have some relatives there. In Russia I don't know anybody." (052) Few Traditionals could conceive of moving to Western Europe, where there are no substantial Lebanese colonies to provide the personal link. Those who did not choose the Americas tended to choose other Arab countries—again, the move involving the least mobility. By contrast, one of every four Moderns chose a West European country. Their ready capacity to "see" themselves in a non-Lebanese and non-Arab environment is a measure of their Westernization. Not the primary circle of personal relations, but the secondary symbolism of psychocultural values, guided their choice.

Another indicator of high empathy is the widespread acceptance of Western music among the Moderns: 56 per cent foreign listeners, as compared to 19 per cent domestic listeners, said that Western music was their preferred radio fare. Taste in music—"the religion of emotions"—often reflects deep affective preferences. A domestic listener declared: "Arabic music and songs . . . make me happy and express what goes on in my heart." (060) "I don't like foreign music," said another. "I think that Arabic music is more fitting for us. It is always soft and dreaming music while foreign music is not what I like." (064) A foreign listener lines up at the opposite pole: "Arab music . . . has no rhythm, no harmony, and nothing at all and the drum is always making the other sound. I hate it." (100) Many foreign listeners criticized Radio Beirut's broadcasts of Western music from its record library as "limited" and "of second quality." One foreign listener described Lebanese who preferred foreign music as "those who mixed more and had more chance to acquire European tastes."

In their devotion to Western music Lebanese Moderns outdid their opposite numbers in all other countries, where there was much resistance to Western music and an overruling preference for the familiar arrangements of sound. Religious affiliation is associated with this profound taste-shift in Lebanon even more closely than education. Among Lebanese with less than a high school education, over 25 per cent Christians compared with 2 per cent Muslims preferred Western music. And Muslims of high education preferred Western music less often than did similarly educated Christians. Domestic listeners prefer Lebanese folk music, Egyptian popular songs and Arabic folksongs of all types. It is less demanding for the little-educated to hear songs in the familiar colloquial language of speech—for them a welcome relief from the classical literary Arabic used in news broadcasts, simplified though it is.

We have just traversed a varied terrain of media behavior, drawing attention mainly to the large and consistent differences between several types of media audience. Recall that these audiences corresponded to our basic typology of modernization (Table 1) and to a hierarchy of social classes (Table 2). We used the audience types because, in Lebanon, the Transitionals are so close to the Moderns on cruder indices. This is itself an important finding. While the Transitionals are not nearly so well-educated as the Moderns, they *are* highly literate (71%) and highly exposed and highly empathic. These attributes combine with their extreme mobility to give Lebanese Transitionals an especially influential role in the further spread of modern ways. Particularly the youthful Transitionals shuttling between city and village, as we have seen, acquire through their direct and mediated experience of the outside world a degree of influence in rural Lebanon that is unparalleled elsewhere in the Middle East. Indeed, these mobile young Transitionals are in process of taking over "opinion leadership" from the traditional rural elite. The 1950 survey provided some data which clarify the inner mechanics of this process.

3. New Opinion Leaders in Rural Lebanon*

The tone of village life in Lebanon is being altered by new *sources* of information and ideas. In the rural communication network, human sources are more important than the media. Villagers get their news, spread it, and interpret it largely by personal means. The historic role of "relay" between isolated village and the wide world was played usually by strangers and often by foreigners. Such people are still important, but as the old isolation yields to rising town-village traffic, the newly-mobile indigenous young men increasingly serve as intermediaries. As they bring in news, so they shape opinion and command respect formerly accorded only the village elders. To gain perspective on this communication revolution, now in progress, we first note the traditional pattern.

The traditional molders of rural opinion were undisputed so long as the village was a self-contained entity, entering into only occasional and irregular contacts with the outside world. Then the individual's widest loyalty was toward the village, especially when it was threatened by such external enemies as rival villages or marauding nomads. In normal times, narrower symbols of loyalty prevailed—family, kin group, the village faction to which one's kin were allied. Relief from economic distress and support in family feuds depended upon the landed patriarchs who headed these village institutions. Additionally, the strong sectarian loyalties of the rural peasantry assured deference and influence to the shaykh, priest or Imam.

Among the Lebanese non-listeners there were 28 illiterate peasants whose interviews were closely analyzed for clues to the changing networks of newsgetting and opinion-forming in the village. In their responses there were few references to traditional

---

*Sections 2 and 3 are based on BASR report "The Radio Audience of Lebanon" by W. N. McPhee and R. B. Meyersohn.

community leaders, and those few references seemed formalistic. One illiterate village blacksmith, when asked if anyone had recently approached him for advice, was startled. "Would any person come to me, a blacksmith, for advice?" he asked. "No, he would go to the Mukhtar or the Priest. I can't advise him. They can." (121) But asked if he had himself gone to them for advice recently, he answered, *"No."* Only one villager ascribed to his Mukhtar a key "relay" position, much in the style of his Balgat counterpart:

[The Mukhtar] holds the guest house open for the villagers. . . . It sometimes happens that we go to the Mukhtar and someone reads the newspaper loudly. . . . We always hear discussions in gatherings at the Mukhtar's. . . . He is a good man and respected and knows how to read. (066)

The other 27 respondents did not mention the traditional opinion-leaders in speaking of the village hierarchy of communication.

Traditional influence in the oral communication network derived from position in the social pyramid. Age in itself conferred high status and was assumed to impart wisdom. Some of the older respondents assume that this relationship still holds. "Time has made me an old man," said a village merchant, "and I know much about everything." (012) "[People always consult me] because I have had long experience," explained another. (201) Some young villagers also confirmed the continuing importance of the elders. One said he asked advice from his father who "is old and knows much." (017) Another said he sought advice on his quarrels with other workers from the older people: "They are more experienced in life and respected by all." (068)

But closer reading of the interviews shows that the influence of the patriarchs declines as village isolation decreases. The old people, it turns out, are consulted mainly on parish affairs—family feuds, farming techniques, personalities, local ventures such as buying land and choosing a wife. Their advice, still valued on such matters, is not sought on problems of the outside world. For they combine local expertise with an extensive range of ignorance. As the Balgati turned from the Chief to the Grocer, a person outside the Traditional hierarchy, when they wanted advice on Ankara, so do the Lebanese villagers turn to the modernizing younger set for instruction on the wider world.

The central fact about these young men is that contact with the mass media builds their prestige and creates their role as opinion leaders. Mobility is at the core of the social changes which elevated them. With growing urbanization and emigration, farm boys no longer waited for their fathers to bequeath them land in order to attain their allotted position in life. They became commuters, urbanites, or emigrants. Their independently acquired wealth, when remitted home, led to a re-evaluation of roles. That this transformation of basic personal relationships has been a painful process is documented by a turn-of-the-century letter found by Afif Tannous in Bishmizzeen. In 1905, three emigré brothers prospering in Australia wrote their old father at home, to whom they had been sending money, and begged him not to transfer to them the deference still due him as their father:

> Two weeks ago, we have sent you a check for fifty pounds. . . . Our dear father, we have to remark about the way you write to us, and that it should not be so. Your letters contain many statements in which you address us and praise us in such a way, as if we were the masters and you the follower. There is no need for this at all, and our financial success should not change the relationship between us. We are your sons and shall always be obedient to you and do all we can to serve you. . . . Write us as father and master, who orders his servants to do their duty towards him.[24]

The new rural elite gained influence only partly because it commanded new wealth. Villagers also learned that traditional authority figures could no longer advocate their interests as effectively as before. As individual gain, long ignored or depreciated by tradition,[25] became a controlling behavioral goal, the power of kin loyalties and leaders declined. Ward politicians and union leaders took the place of priests and kin leaders in the promotion of new social demands. As formal contractual relationships in law often superseded informal understandings known to all through custom, lawyers and politicians replaced the village elders as effective interpreters. Villagers sought guidance among the young men who had access to the political bosses in Beirut, acquaintance with the new legal and financial matters, or substantial funds. The new counselors brought new ways of power with them. As local elections were manipulated in the service of outside politicians, and disputes on national ideology were injected into local feuds, the impact of extra-village interests grew. One villager told his interviewer how a group which met regularly to plot local strategy for a national political party also operated as a source of news and opinion in the village. Another, an active member of the Phalange Party, faithfully read its journal and discussed it among "my Party colleagues with whom I meet almost every night at my village." (029) Union headquarters were mentioned in similar context. For many villagers, the party or union clubroom has come to displace the Mukhtar's guest room as the local communication hub.

The spread of rural education also helped to shape the new elite. Learning is highly valued by the Lebanese. "It is surprising how many sacrifices and privations Lebanese parents are willing to undergo in order to send their children to secondary school."[26] Young men, acquiring education, also gained stature from this common deference for education. Even the Beduin in Lebanon apparently does not share the contempt for learning commonly found among his Jordanian counterparts. The one interviewed said:

> Those who do not read and learn new things are like animals. If that human being doesn't know how to read and write how on earth can he learn about the world? There are many thing to learn. (286)*

Many older villagers dismissed their own opinions as worthless because of their lack of education. A 75-year-old farmer said, "When you ask a person like me, I don't know anything . . . We have many educated young men in the village who will answer your questions very well." (206) Said another older villager: "Am I learned [enough for you] to take my opinion about this? Go to the person who goes to school and let him tell you. What do you want my opinion for?" (162) How different was the situation among young Anatolian villagers who, questioned on a matter of importance would demur: "It is not for us to say, there are older and wiser men who know these things." In contrast, the educated Lebanese youth do not hesitate to take over as their elders cede leadership to them.

An important distinction must be made. Higher education often makes such misfits of rural youngsters that they lose contact with their village environment and exercise little influence there. In his 1939 study of Bishmizzeen, Afif Tannous noted that only 30

---

* Comment by Professor R. Patai: "In evaluating such statements one must take into account the well-known tendency of the traditionally socialized Arab to say what he assumes his questioner wants to hear . . . in the polite turn of conversation this exaggeration ('like animals') perhaps was regarded by him as the right thing to say." (Personal letter.)

of the 212 villagers who had been educated above high school were still living in the village, and all thirty of these were restive and unsatisfied.[27] The 1950 interviews reveal that education still weans some young Lebanese from their village culture. But nowadays, these are more rarely the independent young men, more often the dependent young women. A Shi'i girl, living with her wealthy family in a southern village, said: "To come back from school in Beirut and live in such a place where there is nobody to understand me is very difficult." The greatest problem for people like her, she explained, was "to adapt ourselves with our ideas and habits and opinions derived from our education to our life in Nebatieh with its strict and ignorant people." (009)

The villagers who are "educated out" of the village do not figure as molders of rural opinion. Their story belongs elsewhere. Here we speak of those who do not receive "too much" education. They leave elementary or technical school equipped to learn about the larger world, but still remain in touch with their uneducated elders. Continued access to the mass media—through opportunities by their mobility and skills acquired by their schooling—provides the material for their influence. A young man returning with news is likened to a lord distributing largesse by his illiterate mother:

When my son comes from the city, he feels like a lord among the neighbors because he reads the newspaper in the city, and he always has many new things to tell the people in the village around. (056)

Youth's contact with new kinds of experience impresses the older villagers. "The young men . . . *see a different world* in this cinema," an older said. (308) Another felt that "the men who read newspapers know everything. They sit and talk of things which seem to us *like a strange language*." (185) The youth now perform the ancient function of the caravans, which brought fabulous stories of far-off lands to the village guest room. Said one villager:

Those who read newspapers . . . always have something of great importance to tell. . . . We who do not read the newspapers wait for others to amuse and fascinate us with what is happening in other villages and towns. A friend of ours always tells us amazing and strange stories . . . and he always says that he read this in the newspaper. (063)

The new literates pass on more than bits of information. They are especially valued as explainers of the news, since their minds are considered more capable of coping with the "amazing and strange" occurrences the media report. The villager quoted above felt that newspaper readers:

> . . . understand more than us and their mind is more capable than ours in digesting very difficult news or material read. They understand what the government is doing and what is happening in Damascus or Tripoli. (063)

Many villagers need to have news explained after it is read. The expository style of "things read" is not so readily comprehended by illiterate individuals as the narrative style of "things told." Several villagers cannot grasp news from the mass media directly:

> A shopkeeper here in the village was reading the paper and I stood with them to hear . . . but I can't understand much of what is said or read. I prefer being told rather than listening to things read. (063)
> Maybe [people who don't listen to the radio] don't understand it, like me, I listened once to news [but] did not understand what the talking was because I am illiterate. (286)
> I don't want to listen to the radio. I don't understand it. It's talking and singing. I listened but I didn't understand. (288)

Some villagers cannot follow the simplified form of classical Arabic used in broadcasts and newspapers. Others who could "follow" the language were troubled by the analytic mode of presentation, the unaccustomed categories of discourse, and the impersonality of the mass media. These blocks render such messages unintelligible to persons raised in the oral tradition.* The villager needs a sympathetic personal intermediary to bridge the gap between his traditional communications—colloquial narratives of familiar content told by a visible narrator—and the heavy new demands for empathy by media that report varied events far beyond the range of village experience. The intermediary is likely to be an educated young villager who knows the world of the mass media but has retained enough contact with villagers to "translate" the news into meaningful terms for them.

Many of the respondents identified the types of young villagers who get around: students off at school, tractor operators who go

---

* Professor Patai: "Literary Arabic sounds to the illiterate villager, and even more so to the ears of Beduin, as a foreign tongue. I myself, years ago heard a Beduin say in the lawcourt to the Arab judge who addressed him in literary Arabic: 'O master, don't talk to me in French!' " (Personal letter.)

to the city for repairs, shopkeepers who visit Beirut at regular intervals for supplies, truck and bus drivers who are routed from cities through the countryside.[28] In addition to those whose business keeps them on the move, there are numerous villagers who "make it their business" to get into the city whenever they can. The latter eagerly seek out the media on their jaunts to the city, when they are most likely to see a movie, buy a newspaper, listen to a cafe radio. For the mass media are concentrated in Lebanese cities and the bulk of the population is obliged to seek access there. Most of the 48 movie houses, for example, are urban. The 17 cinemas in Beirut provided about 54 per cent of national seating capacity, and the 10 theaters in Tripoli accounted for another 17 per cent of available seats. The few cinemas in the provinces operate only seasonally, so that a villager usually has to travel to see a film.[29] Thus:

(Do you know what a cinema is?) Yes, I hear about it . . . from the young people who go to Aley and Beirut a lot. (What kind of people are they?) They are drivers, shopowners, and students. We, the old people, have been rarely out of this village. (201)

A friend of mine goes to the movies much more often than I because he has sons in school in Tripoli and he goes there often. He tells me about them. (068)

There are some policemen who go to Tripoli and see the movies and they tell us what they see. (185)

Even newspapers do not automatically reach the village, which depends upon its mobile element to read the papers in town and transmit the news second-hand. Some bring the paper itself to the local coffeehouse, where it can be read aloud to the assembled males. The procedure is illustrated by an illiterate villager:

I heard the Jews were entering Lebanon here from the South so I sent my son to buy the newspaper in Sydon. . . . A teacher from Souk al-Gharb (a large town) came to visit a farmer here. He had a newspaper with him and read a story. All of us asked him to read more. He read everything in the paper. (Why is this not repeated more often?) This man was not from our village and he very few times in a year comes here. (What about other people in town?) The eldest of my sons reads and writes . . . and other people read and write . . . but they hardly ever buy a paper. It does not come to the town. It comes only to subscribers and I don't know any subscriber. (277)

Very few subscribe to newspapers or magazines anywhere in Lebanon, including the cities where they are produced. About 80%

of periodicals were published (as of 1949) in Beirut, the rest in Tripoli, Saida and Zahle. But the post office distributed only about 5 per cent of total circulation, over 90 per cent of all copies being delivered by hand.[30] If the rare subscriber is an obliging teacher or eldest son living in the village, the villagers may have a fairly regular reading of the paper at the local coffeehouse. But usually they depend upon occasional trips of villagers to the city or on urban visitors to the village.

As with the cinema and press, Beirut is the center for production and consumption of radio programs. In 1948, 58 per cent of the 31,000 registered radio receivers were in the capital city wherein live but one-fifth of Lebanon's population. The one family of four or five that boasted its own set usually belonged to the middle or upper urban classes. Most villagers were simply too poor to own radios. An unskilled worker (who earns considerably more than the average peasant) would have to give up nearly two months' earnings to purchase a set.[31] As a village shepherd said:

> Townspeople do listen, but I don't know them. Rich people have radios [but] none around me have radios. (286)

The villager who does own a radio often is socially removed from most of his neighbors. A poor village woman explained how this barrier operated for her, as for the Balgat shepherd:

> Many people have . . . [radios but] I don't know these people. I am poor and don't go to people who don't respect me and treat me well. I mix with people like me, they have no radios. . . . I do not listen to the radio because we have no relations with those rich families. (063)

Most village listeners belong to "secondary audiences" which don't own their sets. Hence, except for the unemployed or underemployed men who regularly frequent the coffeehouses to talk, play *tric-trac* and lend one ear to Arabic music and news in the background, listening tends to be haphazard and irregular. One respondent first heard a radio "while passing in the streets of Tripoli." (286) Another went to Beirut, to the house where her daughter worked, and was astonished at her introduction to the radio: "I thought a man was standing behind it," she avowed. (185) Another was obliged to enter the hospital in a big city, and first heard the radio "while awaiting admittance in the hotel." (226) Many still hear radio only while visiting the city for some special purpose. Since media access is immeasurably easier in the city, we can understand the succinct summary of the villager who explained: "People who go from place to place . . . take the lead in telling us the news." (063) These, nowadays, are the mobile young literates from the villages.

The older people forfeit influence not only because they lack the literacy and mobility of younger men. They also lack the psychic expansiveness. Older villagers do not value empathy and regard the constrictive self-system as a sign of good character. Thus traditional morality often cuts the older people off from contact with Westernizing influences. They vehemently object to the young people's exposure to the cinema, and sometimes even to radio. Thus, in facing the large tensions which divide generations in any transitional society, the elders of rural Lebanon are fighting a rearguard action against what has already happened. They ignore the Koranic injunction that when "systems have passed away in the land" those fare poorly who "deny the messengers."

Two out of three older people expressed some disapproval of movies. Sometimes the explanation was simply that the elders felt awkward at the cinema, since it was the place where youngsters met socially. (188, 206) More often they expressed rejection of "new-fangled" ways by fear that old and accepted standards were being undermined. A 69-year-old Greek Orthodox grocer spoke for his generation in condemning the cinema: "It spoils our youth. It develops in them all these feelings—gambling, drinking, they also follow girls." He was echoed by a pious 71-year-old grain merchant who said: "Movies show films with naked girls . . . with gambling. . . . They teach them how to kiss girls." This respondent begged the interviewer to "please convince my sons that the cinema is bad." (012) Films from abroad, which instruct the young in the freer Western ways of love and courtship, provoke special tensions between generations. We recall the young male respondent who, caught in the throes of a romantic courtship, turned to foreign movies for guidance. Another young Muslim girl acknowledged the tutelary role of such movies:

> When they see a love story full of kissing, the young men or women get so excited as to go directly from the movie to practice what they have seen. (124)

We here leave open the question whether this maiden is testifying to her own responses or those of her peers. In either case, it is clear why older, traditional folk regard the movies as a corrupting influence among the young.

The reactions of a young, educated Lebanese interviewer to a 71-year-old village elder whom he interviewed (308) illuminates the personal meaning of this conflict between generations. The elder yearns for the role of kindly aged adviser to the obedient and respectful young, but instead is relegated to the comic role of a futile and rancorous oldster. "He thought I wanted to get some information from him because he is the oldest man in the place," the young interviewer noted. But this seemed mere pretension, for "his information in some fields was practically nil"—and these fields comprised the whole range of themes and experiences which mattered to the young Modern. The old man succeeded only in boring the interviewer: "All he wanted to talk about was what an important person in the village he was." However, the businesslike interviewer quickly got down to the matters at hand:

(What about the behavior of the Americans in world affairs?) I don't know. All I know about is this village. I can tell you everything that happened here since the Turks were here in the great war. (What do you think of the cinema?) I don't know, I have never been to what you call the cinema. Some of the young men go to it. . . . (Newspapers?) They say the newspaper gives them news about wars and elections. (Do you miss such news?) I don't care about it . . . as I am living here I don't care what happens anywhere else.

Rooted to his village soil, the elder wished to fend off the outside world which, in the shape of his own sons, encroached upon the traditional round of life that gave him security and satisfaction. The interviewer noted that his curses covered "the younger generation" and "the world today" in one and the same breath.

Before people worshipped Allah, now people are worshipping the radio. . . . My son wants to get one into the house and I will not allow him to do that as long as I live . . . it is the work of the devils. . . .

In rejecting even the radio, "the oldest man in the village" personifies an extreme constrictive reaction. More often there is acceptance of radio and press, while movies are condemned as seductive and sinful. An illiterate and destitute Shi'i shoemaker in Saida took this view, though he is as traditional in his way as "the oldest man." The shoemaker was appalled, for example, by the projective questions in the interview. When asked what would be his policies, if he were editor of a newspaper, he reproached the interviewer: "You want to laugh at me, master. The editor of a newspaper. This is the work of one like you." ("With all respect to you," the interviewer insisted, "just suppose you were the editor of a newspaper.") "Suppose the impossible! Change the question, master, change it!" (011)

And change it the interviewer did because, as he noted, the shoemaker was making all kinds of frantic movements with his head and hands. When asked to imagine himself as President of Lebanon, the shoemaker was also visibly distressed. But when assured that "they" would not laugh at him for presumption, he said: "The first thing I will do is find work for everybody. [I would] take the money from those who have it and employ people to work. (What else would you do?) Is not that enough to find work for everybody?" This Traditional looks no farther for himself than finding money "for the bread and olives of my family."

But the same shoemaker acknowledges the importance of media to the status of younger people, when he tells of his desire to buy a radio for his son. The reason is that he longs to see the boy held in the same respect as his Christian rival—a young man whose radio-listening has made him the new neighborhood Wise Man.

[When] the son of our Christian neighbor comes to the shop next to our house . . . everybody there listens to him talking. . . . He talks about the war in Korea as if he were there and he just arrived. I asked him how he got his information and he said from the radio. . . . When my son goes [to the shop] nobody remarks his presence. . . . I wish my son had a radio and could talk about the Korean War like our neighbor's son does.

Although the shoemaker wishes his son to have contact with the radio, he draws limits when it comes to the cinema. Arabic films he can understand. "Of course," he says, they are better than foreign films. "You see people of your own race having the same language and manners as you do. You see somebody having a *nargile* (bubble-pipe) near him. You see Arab coats . . ." Egyptian films levy no tax on the imagination and require no adjustment to new manners, fashions, language or morals. What he finds intolerable is the young people's search for the opposite—their fascination by the strange and new and foreign. The shoemaker frowns upon "those boys that go to American movies . . . they get spoiled."

I have a son that works the whole day; in the evening he goes to the cinema. So now he wants to buy a hat, he wants long trousers, he wants to buy a revolver and I don't know what else.

Nowhere else in the Arab lands have the village youth established themselves in so strong a position *vis-à-vis* their elders. Through their mobility, literacy, media exposure they are taking over the opinion leadership of rural Lebanon on larger public issues. In this phase of modernization, Lebanon is far ahead of its neighbors, among whom the public role of rural youth is not yet an issue. Along with this, in Lebanon, has arisen a modern version of the "problem of women" that is barely visible outside cosmopolitan circles in other Arab countries.

4. Women and the Media

As the modern media arm disputants in the contest between generations, so they equip combatants in the "war between the sexes." Occasional male reformers, like Qasim Amin, have stressed the strategic role of women in Middle Eastern society.[32] These reformers argue that the "relay" functions of women in family and community, their dominance in childraising, put them in a position to retard or encourage modernization. But such arguments have foundered upon the culture of male vanity which is imbedded in traditional lifeways. The basic new impetus has come not from social theory or the small indigenous feminist movement, but from the stream of Western communications. Western movies project upon Arab screens examples of female behavior remarkable by any standards and revolutionary in their impact upon the traditional values of a "male vanity" culture. Says Hourani:

> The process of change is being speeded by one manifestation of Western civilization above all: the film which expresses a way of feminine life, and a conception of the relations between men and women, which are far from those prevalent in the Islamic world.[33]

Radio and print also are important transmitters of the modern images of women. The personal testimony in the interviews shows how they are transforming traditional conceptions of woman's proper roles.

The Arab female figure most frequently portrayed in the West is a pajama-clad denizen of some portly Sultan's harem. This fantastic image does reflect the historic isolation and subordination of women, the sharp division of labor between the sexes, their restriction to the roles of submissive daughter and compliant concubine and obedient wife. At a very tender age it is impressed upon an Arab girl that she must practice rigid self-control. She is taught to internalize her father's fear that she will bring shame upon his house by premarital or extramarital adventures. It is less her soul which is at stake, for this is of relatively small importance, than the good repute of her father. Indeed the Arabic term *'ird*, which derives from the verb to show oneself, has come to mean family honor. A Palestinian Muslim hesitates to send his small daughter as a bride to a strange village, not because of fears for her happiness, but because "she is still so young that she does not understand how to protect our honor among strangers."[34] A brother, as deputy for the father, is obliged all his life to answer for his sister's behavior. To maintain the honor of his house, he must obtain redress for her from others and administer punishment to her for her own transgressions. The single Arabic term for both lord and husband (*ba'al*) tersely illustrates the traditionally asymmetric marriage relationship of the East.

An American teacher in an Arab secondary school, attempting to discipline the boys, found that confining them to an odious dungeon-like basement, without light and full of scorpions, was far less effective than simply addressing them in the feminine form of Arabic. Whereas solitary confinement was met with quiet stoicism and dignity, the latter measure forced them to cringe and beg for an end to the punishment.[35] The masculine-feminine dichotomy is nowhere sharper than in the Arab world, as befits what David Riesman has called a "male vanity culture."

Dress, always an overt differentiator between classes, sects, trades and sexes, has imposed special requirements upon females living under Islam.[36] Segregation of women was reinforced by robes concealing the form and veils concealing the face. These traditional ways have resisted even the power of dictators. Reza Shah forced Iranian women to discard their *chodors*, but many again hid their bodies under the next regime. Atatürk frowned upon, but more wisely never outlawed, the veil—which is still a matter for emotion in Turkey. "I'd like to tear it from their faces," a chic young woman at the University of Ankara told me in 1954, speaking of her veiled elder sisters in the street.

The educational system, deriving from the same perspective as seclusion and veiling, also excluded women from participation in public life. Although ancient Islam boasted great poetesses, learning was wedded by tradition to Koranic study and the Holy Book was considered beyond female capacities. Only the rare highborn woman surmounted social obstacles to the acquisition of the learned arts. Despite the spread of education in recent decades, a large gap remains: even in Turkey 35 per cent males but only 14 per cent females can read and write. These perspectives change slowly. Atatürk created coeducational Village Institutes to train young teachers. But his successors, three decades later, yielded to persistent popular feeling that coeducation stimulated dangerous ideas; hence "separate but equal" facilities for the endangered boys and girls were established.

When Justice Douglas visited Lebanon in 1951, he saw a husband beat, curse and drive off his wife because she had allowed her veil to slip. The man returned later to beg the astonished justice's pardon for the shamefulness of his wife's behavior. But Douglas also attended mixed parties at which gracious, unveiled ladies presided as hostesses with perfect aplomb.[37] The old and new styles still jostle each other, but Arab women have attained a greater amount of freedom in Lebanon than elsewhere. Muslim women are relatively emancipated from the traditional chattel status, and for Christian women conditions were rarely as harsh. Many a rural woman is now *sitt al-bayt* (mistress of the house) in the modern sense rather than a traditional beast of burden. In 1953 educated women exercised the franchise. They moved to their present position through the same process of social change which has transformed the Lebanese village.[38]

Christian women in Lebanon got their start through missionary educational institutions. As early as the 1830's there were two missionary schools exclusively for girls. In 1860, the American School for Girls was founded; in 1921-23 the American University opened its doors to women and gave them access to professional careers. By 1942-43 over half of the students in foreign schools and about one-third in public schools were girls, a sharp contrast with the virtual absence of rural coeducation elsewhere in Arab Asia and its retreat in Turkey.[39] Today there are some Lebanese women in nearly all professions. These form a feminine corps more akin to career women in the West than to the uneducated women of their own country.

With these developments, the "problem of women" emerges in Lebanon on a level of modernity not yet conceivable in other Arab lands. But problems there are. In any society not in imminent danger of collapse, conformity mechanisms tend to be stronger than impulses to deviation. In the Middle East acquiescence remains the dominant response among women, who are often the most stolid guardians of custom and routine. Women more often than men insist upon exaggerated forms of superstitious ritual.[40] Traditional women often oppose the mass media, along with other agencies of the Modern style, most vociferously. An amusing case is the labor crew foreman who, having married a shrew for her wealth and prestige as daughter of a village elder, now complains that she stands between him and the media:

I am afraid to go to the movies. (Why?) My wife doesn't want me to go. (Why?) Because she says that I see girls there and they take away my brains. (Do you go?) Sometimes. (Well, now, what do you really think about the movies?) If you don't tell my wife, I think they're wonderful! (How about the radio? Why don't you listen?) My wife. (How could she tell if you listened?) She says she can smell it! (What would have to happen for you to listen to the radio?) Remove my wife away.

By definition, Traditional women are content to accept the role and status assigned them. They find it natural, or at least comfortable, to defer to the superior talents of men. An old Shiʻa woman explained that God "gave man a more intelligent mind and gave him also supreme power over us." Moreover, as "two women are equal to one man, we must obey them and do what they demand . . . this being the rules of God." This southern villager could not understand why everything was turning "upside-down" in Lebanon. "Here women become men and men women," she complained. She would be happy to go to Saudi Arabia, the citadel of traditional Islam, because there women know their place and men know how to keep them there. She is opposed to women "having opinions" on principle: "Our mothers and grandmothers never cared about the views of the ruling people and what they do, so why should [we] be different?" (063)

The well-trained young interviewer, suppressing her own feminist preferences, contented herself with putting this woman down as "ignorant, narrow-minded, and very simple and naive." But she could not resist adding: "She is submissive and satisfied in her life,

although there are many things to object to." The growing conviction among young and educated women that there are "things
to object to" indexes the diffusion of external standards of comparison and explains the attractions of Western ways to many respondents. The pull of the West is exerted mainly through the
mass media, of which one educated young woman said:

> The articles and broadcasts make us anxious to go and live there
> [USA]. Liberty for women. That is what we listen to in their programs.

The theme of *freedom* was paramount among women exposed to
messages from the West. A young uneducated housewife, bitter
because in her village "we can do nothing in the way of new
without objection or gossip," would move to America if she had
to leave Lebanon. There she felt sure to find "more freedom . . .
I like to live in America where the people are very good and educated with living." (064) The allure of a foreign environment
increases among those who, having formed larger expectations,
feel more deprived by their native milieu. A young girl, chafing
under parental restraints, would like to live in America: "People
there are free in all [ways]," especially women:

> They are free to come and go, to choose the life they want to live.
> They are independent and responsible for themselves with no father or
> mother to count their steps and control their sentences and words. (060)

From Western movies and illustrated magazines there emerges
a picture of glamorous, independent womankind in polar contrast
to the Arab norm of the secluded and subordinated female. The
contrast is perhaps greatest in matters of love-and-marriage. "Our
biggest problems are love problems," explained a young VOA
listener, "people not being allowed to love those they wish to love,
in most cases. Parents here like to run the lives of their children,
even to marriage." (401) The last piece of news heard by a young
Muslim girl concerned a maiden who had committed suicide because she was in love with someone her father rejected. Hollywood
exports fall on fertile soil here. According to one college student,
American movies are not "better than films produced in other
countries but they are only rich in love films." (124) A village
woman reported the tale of a neighbor who moved to Beirut, where
her daughter took to attending the cinema:

> The result was seen when the young girl refused to marry a man her

parents chose and they discovered that she wants to marry the one she loves. All this was because of the ideas and shameful things she saw at the movies.

The romantic girls thwarted by parental control and village gossip are not the only ones to seek a freer environment. The college-educated wife of a professor reveals that women at the social apex also feel the need for more elbow room than the Arab environment affords. (003) The interviewer noted that the professor's wife "is rather popular and has a high status in society." She belongs to the Lebanese Women's Federation, the Advisory Board of A.U.B. Nursery School, the Y. W. C. A., the Arab Women's League. But all this social activity seems to her a poor substitute for professional ambitions ruled out by Arab ideas of proper female careers. This lady, who listens daily to BBC and reads the *Ladies Home Journal,* is aware that occupational mobility is less of a male monopoly in the West. Despite her high status at home she would like to live in America

because in it I can find . . . freedom. It is a country which recognizes the ability . . . and the rights of the women. . . . The woman is considered to be as capable as a man . . . in the sense that she can get any job that she likes.

Other Moderns mentioned the greater opportunities for varied education among Western women, which increase their access to the professions and politics. This is a radical departure from the views of Traditional women, one of whom explained why she did not read the newspapers:

In general most of the material written in newspapers I do not like, because it deals with politics and I don't care to know about it because I hate politics and I don't understand it. I believe it something founded for men and not women. We have many other things to be interested in and to look after than politics. (064)

Two Modern girls, by contrast, mentioned, as their most recent news, the gift of an airplane made by Syrian women to the Syrian army. The event symbolized for them the movement of Arab women from the confines of the home to the political arena of the nation.

America represents a life of fun, luxury, good times for Transitional females. One loves American films because they depict a way of life without a touch of drabness—it is "full of fun." From films and the *Ladies Home Journal,* she has built up a wondrous picture of the United States:

> It is a fantastic country. It has everything in it and it is a very beautiful country. It has beautiful great buildings and is full of zoos and lakes . . . it's a very prosperous country. (124)

America, for the Transitional female, also gives promise of that upward mobility which is so hard to achieve at home. A 24-year-old Armenian shopgirl finds the thought of living in America as satisfying a fantasy as imagining herself at the top of the Beirut social ladder. This girl is disgruntled with her lot: "Girls like me," she says, "who are working and supporting a home and a mother, face many difficulties . . . I have never had enough education." Her craving for good living involves her in a vicarious life supplied by newspapers and movies. She reads only the social page, savoring items "about expensive and flashy social events at homes of big shots or in the upper circles. . . . It feels like window shopping, which I do very often." Films and fashion magazines satisfy this same urge to "window shop" at the upper crust. She would like to live in America because of the picture she has built up from the media:

> From the films we see, and from the novels I read, it seems to me to be a land of plenty. . . . When they show us a film about a family in the slums . . . they had a frigidaire and an oven and a comfortable home. Whereas here a family economically more than modest [does] not own frigidaires. . . . They're all so well-dressed, I know from their fashion magazines. . . . So a simple working girl like me can easily afford to live better than I do, allowing herself more fun and more luxury. (040)

That Lebanese women still feel like a "minority" group was attested by their characteristic way of responding to our questions *first* as women, *then* as Lebanese or Arabs or Christians. For some Modern females, the situation is complicated by ambivalence—they abhor their life in the East but fear they are unsuited for life in the West. One sad young girl (her eyes were red from crying at the start of the interview) had been educated in Beirut but was living with her wealthy family in the only decent house of an impoverished southern village. Despite "all the facilities of living," she seemed to the interviewer "disappointed in life." She was bitter against "the life of woman in the Near East where she is not respected but treated as an animal that has no feeling." This girl's discontent is stimulated by her constant exposure to American communications. "In our country," she says, "wherever we walk we see something American: books, magazines, goods and schools . . . In our school nearly every lecture in Friday's assembly was about America. The documentary films all were about their life there." Her favorite magazines are *Modern Romances* and the *Ladies Home Journal*, but most of all she is attracted to Hollywood films. She considers that "they give us true stories of life with no artificial or altered scenes" and she finds solace in them:

> I go to movies to get many new things about the ways of life in foreign countries . . . their customs, traditions and habits are not like ours in the East. There women are respected and free. Their husbands and relatives treat them with equality and respect while here in the East we are not really treated as human beings. So I find it very pleasant to see such things.

Her favorite movie depicted Ava Gardner's success in turning a respectable man into a gambler. It pleased her because it "shows the influence of women on men's life." But these desires are confined to her fantasy life. Actually, the prospect of living in America was distasteful, for along with freedom would go overwhelming responsibility and insecurity. Several Moderns mentioned the need of American women to support themselves from an early age; also the uncertainties of family life, since "almost all marriages end in divorce." This young girl justified her refusal to imagine living in the United States:

> I am not used to such unlimited freedom which is found in America. Here in Nabatieh we are controlled and ruled by our traditions and customs, so if I have to live outside I must live in a place that is not so different from this because I will not know how to use the freedom which I am not accustomed to.

Some Modern females of this type felt that a more plausible solution for them was Beirut. If an overseas move had to be contemplated, then England (which "is still conservative and traditional") would be more suitable than America or even France.

While the media bring new images, they do not play only a disruptive role in the Lebanese social setting. As the Beduin patriarch who listens only to the Koran and Arab music uses the media to fortify his traditional ways, so radio plays a similar role for some housewives. A village wife, who sometimes resents the narrowness of her milieu and yearns for American freedom, has learned to combine innovational and traditional ways with good grace. She considers radio "the blessing of the twentieth century," for it brightens her day, teaches her useful skills and how to keep happy. Her favorite programs consist of:

Talks and lectures that interest women most of all. Sometimes we have good advice how to care for our children, how to prevent diseases, and how to keep happy. They give us good recipes. This program has many times good stories that teach us a lesson about life. (064)

As the American housewife uses soap operas to fill her day and satisfy her needs, so this young Lebanese woman finds gratification through borrowed experience.[41] The media from abroad are creating a growing market for the Western image of the enlightened and independent woman who enjoys the material amenities, the wider education, employment, deference and marital equality. The attraction is strong, but new desire gestates long before it overcomes the safety of conformism. The personal cost of radical social change leads some potential Moderns to prefer the familiar blend of present comforts and vexations to the hazards of gambling for higher stakes.

So the "problem of women" in Lebanon is posed on a level parallel to its debate in the West—the West of not more than a generation or so ago. As compared with their still submerged position elsewhere in Arab Asia, the rural youth have emerged and the women are emerging in Lebanon. Modernization of the traditional "male vanity culture" brings its own problems but, as we have seen, they are new issues for the Middle East in a distinctly modern formulation.

Such problems can be permitted to emerge in the public forum because Lebanon has developed a relatively stable polity with modern dimensions. It is not ridden by traditionalist fears that public awareness of internal social problems must inevitably undermine the entire structure of authority. Lebanon is not without its political problems, but these have been reduced from the catastrophic proportions that divide other Arab lands to issues that can be managed by rational discussion, negotiation and compromise. We conclude our case study with a brief comment on Lebanese politics.

5. Problems of Modern Governance

Having passed through the dramatic early phases of modernization long ago, Lebanon today suffers only a milder form of the Arab region's political *malaise*. Its postwar *coup d'état* was a bloodless one, led by a social reformer with the cooperation of shopkeepers—not by army officers backed with street mobs, as in Egypt and Syria. Its political atmosphere is freer than elsewhere in the area. However, Lebanon's potentials for a fully participant democracy are still largely unrealized. Great political difficulties are imposed by Lebanon's advanced position in a retrograde area— Westernized at the entry to Arab Asia, modernized at the center of Islamic tradition. Lebanon's division from its neighbors stems from, and in turn reinforces, its internal division. Not powerful enough to impose its leadership on the area, Lebanon must temporize. Unable to resist completely the area's dominant Arab-Islam syndrome, unwilling to abandon its own Christian-modern position, the Lebanese leadership straddles the two value-systems. This tends to widen rather than bridge the ambivalence of ordinary citizens, of which a brilliant Lebanese Christian, Albert Hourani, once wrote:

> To be a Levantine is to live in two worlds or more at once, without belonging to either; to be able to go through the external forms which indicate the possession of a certain nationality, religion or culture, without actually possessing it. It is no longer to have standard values of one's own, not to be able to create but only able to imitate. It is to belong to no community and to possess nothing of one's own. It reveals itself in lostness, pretentiousness, cynicism, and despair.

The result, on the level of national politics, is that Western governmental institutions operate in Middle Eastern style. A partly Europeanized economy operates without modern social controls. There is a chronic lack of the "capacity . . . to dispense with small gains in order later to secure more important ones."[42]

The usual political problems of social change are compounded in Lebanon by its unique religious composition. None of the seven major sects constitutes a majority. The close balance between Christians and Muslims ties internal problems to an unceasing struggle on the level of international politics, between Westward-oriented Christians and Arab-oriented Muslims, between conflicting images of Lebanon as the Christian "foyer" to the Middle East and as the province of an Arab state.[43]

These international considerations are inseparable from internal politics. Only the claim that Lebanon must protect a Christian majority justified, from the start, its independent existence in the face of pan-Arabism. This imposed political institutions based on a numerical Christian predominance by convention (if not in fact) and on the continuation of separatist communal structures. With these institutions, Lebanon *has* safeguarded its independence for a decade and steered between the shoals of world bipolarity. But the external balance is increasingly precarious, due to the rising threat to Christian majority status engendered by the higher Muslim birth rate and by the influx of 130,000 Palestinian refugees. Internally, as Lebanese Moderns complain, the price of the sectarian system also has been high. It has been politically impossible, for example, to authorize an official population census (which would reflect the Muslim increase). This deprives Lebanon of some modern techniques of government. Further, by constitutional provision the religious communities must receive equitable representation in both government and bureaucracy. The highest executive offices, the legislative seats, all levels of administrative position are allocated on a sectarian basis. Despite its limited cadre of competent administrators, only the proper religionist can be picked for a job —a man's denomination takes priority over his capacity.

Sectarianism, authorized by public law and administrative fiat, perpetuates ancient loyalties at the expense of the larger national identification. The clan power of the Druze feudal leaders augments the authority bestowed by the communal system. The widespread tendency of parents to choose their children's schools according to religious affiliation transmits sectarianism through the generations.[44] The Lebanese interviews revealed a similar tendency in media behavior. Choice of a newspaper often was justified solely because its editor belonged to the respondent's sect; hence it gave him news of his own people and alerted him to the sectarian "line" on public issues. The most vitriolic comments usually were directed at editors belonging to rival sects.

This is traditional in the Middle East, where religion has always claimed priority among the secondary symbols of identification. A Middle Easterner related himself to his society by way of his sect, and Muslim doctrine on the *dhimmi* as well as the Ottoman *millet* system accorded cultural and legal authority to recognized sects. "To leave one's sect was to leave one's whole world, and to live without loyalties, the protection of a community, the consciousness of solidarity and the comfort of normality."[45] This profound linkage of personal identity dies hard.

But new loyalties *are* challenging the old. Political parties seek to cross religious lines in their effort to recruit adherents. Labor unions are growing in strength and some are beginning to assert an independent policy.[46] Voluntary associations that bring together civic-minded urban men and women are growing: over a third of the Moderns belong to one or more clubs. The American University of Beirut has been a leader in cutting across ethnic and religious barriers among its heterogeneous student body. The compactness of Lebanon, the good roads and the relatively large number of vehicles facilitate internal travel and thereby gradually attenuate the ancient particularism.[47] But the new identifications of the Moderns constantly encounter the hard political fact that confessionalism still often defines the avenues to power, wealth and enlightenment.

Confessionalism is also associated, especially among Lebanese Moderns, with nepotism, corruption and limitations upon personal freedom. Owing to the power of feudal bosses and confessional leaders, the law is not administered impartially by the police or the judiciary. Nor are personal freedoms assured. Certain urban groups, such as the Beirut taxi drivers, operate with immunity from regulation of any sort.[48] Many Lebanese Moderns gave reasons of this sort for wanting to live in Britain, where the law is applied impartially from "a taxi driver to a Minister." America was chosen by others because of its freedom of expression. The general disaffection, revealed in the 1950 interviews, was to culminate some eighteen months later in Lebanon's "Rosewater Revolution," which displaced President Bishara al-Khuri after a nine-year rule.

The politically-aware had long been disillusioned, since the self-government established by the 1926 Constitution was a mere facade for French control. The low electoral participation in the interwar years reflected this disillusion. From 1922 to 1934, the average number of voters in Beirut, the most politicized section of the nation, came to about 5 per cent of the city's population.[49] This electoral apathy reflected the low level of the interwar party and parliamentary politics. Insofar as their differences went beyond personalities, the parties opposed each other on the issue of Lebanon's future status. The Constitutional and Liberation Blocs campaigned for an independent Lebanon; the National Socialists wanted Lebanon to be absorbed into a unified Syria. Activist youth groups, loosely allied to the political parties, attracted restless extremists who also clashed over the symbols of a Christian or Arab Lebanon.

Judging democracy by its local performance, many Lebanese became skeptical of the supposed benefits of constitutional government. They

began to ask themselves what purpose was served by the existence of a costly Parliament, filled with landowners and lawyers, wasting its time in internecine quarrels and showing no interest in the country's welfare . . . was it not ridiculous, as well as expensive, for so small a region to have so grandiose and complex a constitution?[50]

The nationalist government established in 1943 brought hope of reform. But its leaders had never worked out solutions for Lebanon's internal problems. They suffered the myopic effects of an opposition dealing for years in ideology without policy, exerting influence without responsibility. The good will and support they earned during the fight for independence was soon dissipated.

The government's indifference to social reform derived from its alliance with the wealthy families. Political spokesmen were often landowning lawyers with vested interests against rearrangements in the social system. Furthermore, their regime depended upon the quasi-feudal "strong men" who controlled electoral lists in five of the six national districts and dominated public policy by bribery and violence.[51] Their henchmen intimidated opponents, including overly-critical journalists, and were shielded by a venal judiciary. Corrupt manipulation of public funds did not reach the colossal Egyptian scale, but it was illustrated by a Minister's black-market sale of a canned-beef shipment donated by Argentina for the Palestinian refugees.[52] Constant scandal aroused public indignation and created a crisis in public administration. These signs of an early-Modern political style, whose sources are "envy and the feeling of displacement," Riesman has called "the moralizer-in-retreat."[53]

The "Rosewater Revolution" was largely a strong show of indignation by the Moderns, which paralyzed the cities in September 1952. The shopkeepers closed their shutters. This action, once the

Army decided not to intervene, accomplished the *coup d'état.*
Leadership came from the National Socialist Front, a parliamentary
opposition group, and from newspaper publishers who had persist-
ently defied suspension, imprisonment and fining to denounce
government corruption. The *coup* was interpreted as a step toward
political modernization—"an encouraging sign of the power of
public opinion and its ability to translate itself into action."[54] It
registered a widespread demand for political participation among
Moderns outraged by the inertia of traditional ways.

Some major alterations in the approved political style did follow.
Voting was made compulsory for all males and permissible for
educated women. Over the vociferous opposition of the feudal
leaders, their power was diminished by increasing the five electoral
districts to 33, while the number of seats in the Chamber of Deputies was decreased from 77 to 44.[55] Although marked by some
violence and intimidation, a sign of change was the election of
some Independents who had campaigned on their own rather than
as appendages to the election list of a feudal leader.[56]

But these shifts in political style did not alter the underlying
distribution of power. No permanent organization harnessed the
energy of the oppositionists. The Popular Front was dissolved and
its leader Kemal Jumblat was repudiated by articulate segments of
the elite. (His radical program found no echo except among Communists, who sponsored a rival group using these slogans.)[57] The
paradox of Lebanese politics is suggested by this reform leader's
support—which came not from like-minded modernizers, but from
Druze peasants who automatically voted for Jumblat as their clan
head. The outcome of voting on such premises was that, in 1953,
many old politicians repudiated a scant ten months earlier were
returned to Parliament.[58] What had changed was the legal author-
ization of wider and freer political participation; what remained
the same was the social setting which impairs the efficient operation of modern representative institutions.

At the time of the survey, taken soon after the dissolution of
the customs union with Syria, the country was in a major postwar
economic slump reflected in abnormally high prices and widespread unemployment.[59] Concern with economic issues pervaded the
interviews. Actually, the distribution of wealth exhibits less dis-
parity in Lebanon than elsewhere in the Arab world: smallholders
and tradesmen form an intermediate class between fellahin and

plutocracy; and per capita wealth is high by Middle Eastern standards. But the respondents suffered from "relative deprivation." Constant exposure to modern achievements led them to deprecate their standard of living *vis-à-vis* the West, rather than celebrate it relative to other Eastern countries. Great bitterness was expressed over World War II profiteering, unregulated by government policy, which enriched "some hundreds of merchants, industrialists, entrepreneurs and 'operators' (Brasseurs d'affaires)." While castigating the postwar urban plutocracy, many respondents noted that the middle class, farmers and laborers had experienced an appreciable decline in living standard.

To these conditions the three types responded in their characteristically diverse ways. Traditionals emphasized jobs and bread. A poor illiterate laborer in a clinic said her problem was

> My work—eating—whether I will have enough to get food at the end of the month. Or enough clothes for my mother, my nephew and myself. (031)

Her opinions about international politics favored any state of affairs in which she would "not have to worry about rice and bread any more." Her concern was with subsistence rather than mobility. She felt that

> People with common sense think this way: This is my station and I have to do my work properly. My master's station is above mine and he has his own work to do. We must be content with what God gives us. (031)

In contrast, the Transitionals were more concerned with *living standards*. They have acquired the desires for cash and consumption that spell social mobility. When the local environment does not provide opportunities to match his desires, the genuine Transitional turns his gaze outward and beyond. The key role of the modern West as a reference group for modernizing Lebanese is reflected in the words about America uttered by a Transitional clerk who had been disappointed in his hopes of becoming a lawyer:

> I understand that even if you have a low background, but can prove yourself capable of doing well in a career or profession, you may attain heights I would never dream of obtaining here. (131)

He was echoed by a young law student who wanted to emigrate to America:

American people appreciate every self-made man so that if somebody starts from zero and reaches a high standard of living, nobody
will ever complain about him. (008)

With emigration less easy now than it used to be, frustration is
likely to cause alienation of mobile-minded young men who seek
access to elite status. "A political and social evolution to demagogic
tendencies is much more to be feared," writes Menassa, "since the
majority of intellectuals have seen their living standard lowered."
These demands for greater shares of wealth and security define
the modernizing issue for the Lebanese economy. This is the
familiar issue of "wide divergence between private and social gains
which is a feature of undeveloped countries."[60] The considerable
wealth that now courses through the economy is cornered by the
few instead of diffused among the many. Equally challenging is
the structural imbalance. Limited by size and resources, naturally
an *entrepôt,* Lebanon will always be more a producer of services
than of goods. While Syria exports goods equal in value to 70
percent of its imports, Lebanon exports products worth less than
16 per cent of its imports. An oft-quoted anecdote tells of the
European economist commissioned to survey the Lebanese economy.
After a careful study, he concluded: "I don't know what it is that
you are doing, but whatever it is, keep on doing it." By ordinary
standards, the Lebanese should be bankrupt. But by a fantastic
series of service transactions and invisible exports this "nation of
traders" somehow balances its accounts and makes up annual
deficits.[61]

A long history of such achievements has developed individual
ingenuity aplenty among the Lebanese. They are well aware of
their long lead in modernization over their neighbors. On the day
this is written, a front-page editorial in *L'Orient* of Beirut reviews
UN statistics on Asian food consumption, per capita income, life
expectancy (27 years in India). Concludes the editorialist: "No
Lebanese could say his country was in such a state."[62] The editorialist carefully avoided any direct comparisons with Egypt or Syria,
with Jordan or Iran. This editorial discretion, by now habitual,
illustrates a major source of constriction upon Lebanese modernization in the present and immediate future.

Lebanese modernity is nowadays inhibited by the fresh saliency
given to the Arab-Muslim syndrome among its neighbors. Egypt
and Syria have built their violent and unstable new policies around

this traditionalist symbolism which Lebanon, over modernizing generations, had gone far toward replacing by more relevant issues and more efficacious values. How shall Lebanon, with a population that is officially just under half (and actually just over half) Arab-Muslim, cope with the reinvigorated appeal to these ancient loyalties launched by its massive neighbors?

Since Lebanese modernizers are well aware of the "natural limits" imposed by their own size and resources, they have followed the route of discretion. Not powerful enough to control the Egyptian-Syrian storms, they have sought to ride them out. But this route has given access to a new set of externally imposed "political limits." The dispirited and abortive operation of participant politics within Lebanon, over the past decade, reflects in some measure the jamming of its modernist symbols of national consensus by the traditionalist Arab-Muslim symbols superimposed through Cairo's Voice of the Arabs. These new resonances have diverted many Lebanese Muslims, and deterred many Lebanese Christians, from their previously set course and pace of modernization.

In such ways do politics and communication interact in the living Middle East. The new pan-Arabism has redefined Lebanon's Christian-Muslim problem, which had been headed toward rational and secular solutions of modern inspiration, in such a way as to intimidate the Modernists and encourage the Traditionalists in both parishes. But it is no easy matter to reverse a century of internalized social change by an external campaign through the mass media. Some Lebanese Moderns have come to regard the new pan-Arabism as mainly a strident tone of voice broadcast from Cairo. Recognizing, further, that in the field of public communication the Lebanese have a long historic advantage, these individuals have begun to take heart.

There are signs in the mass media of a new determination, without abandoning discretion, to reactivate Lebanese ingenuity. The editorial in *L'Orient* cited above is an example. That Lebanese, both Christian and Muslim, are considerably better-off than their Middle East neighbors is the focal argument. To retain its force, it must continue to correspond to the observable facts. Lebanon must build its future upon the modernity which is its distinctive achievement, rather than conceal it in the hope that others less favored will not notice. Such a course would have important implications for Lebanese politics and communications.

To reinstate the privacy of modern symbols among the Lebanese population, both Christian and Muslim, requires a more widespread diffusion of political power and responsibility. This, in turn, can be sustained only through a style of public communication that enables more Lebanese to examine their situation candidly, to assess its benefits soberly, and to support the direction of maximum effort required by the private and public welfare. Lebanon's crossroads today illustrates our earlier proposition that no modern society can function efficiently without a modern system of public communication. This locates a critical function in the mass media. Upon its effective performance may hinge the future of Lebanese modernization.

* * *

As of March 1958, when I revisited Lebanon briefly, the situation sketched in the preceding five paragraphs had deepened. The new United Arab Republic posed the familiar problem of Egypto-Syrian "encirclement" in more urgent form for Lebanon—now flanked, on the other side, by the Iraqi-Jordan Federation. The issue was variously phrased: Would Nasser *permit* Lebanon to remain independent? Should Lebanon *wish* to remain independent? The tension generated between external pressures of the Arab-Muslim syndrome and the internal needs of Lebanese modernity was acute.

Where a Muslim majority has long felt deprived by the sectarian system, as in Tripoli and sections of the Beka'a Valley which traverse the road to Damascus, there the call of Arab Nationalism is likely to be heard above the claims of Lebanese nationality. Among Christians and the modernized element of Muslims, who have a stake and a part in their society, the appeal of dependence upon Nasser is likely to fade if the price entails loss of personal participation in an autonomous nation.

In the conversations I heard, anxiety was high and explosions sounded imminent. Where would Lebanon be after the smoke had cleared? Underlying the political discussions of the moment, it seemed to me, was a profound sense that the special Levantine genius would continue to operate best by living in two worlds at once without belonging to either.

VII.

Egypt: The Vicious Circle

> "Our thoughts are an effort to explore within our-
> selves—to discover who we are and what our role is
> to be."
>
> —GAMAL 'ABDUL NASSER

> "It is true that most of our people are still illiterate.
> But politically that counts far less than it did twenty
> years ago. . . . Radio has changed everything. . . .
> Today people in the most remote villages hear of what
> is happening everywhere and form their opinions.
> Leaders cannot govern as they once did. We live in a
> new world."
>
> —NASSER

THE STRUGGLE of modernization has scarred the elite
of every Middle Eastern land, and none more deeply than the
Egyptian. Their frustrations are deeper because their aspirations
are higher and the obstacles greater. The Egyptian elite, after a
half-century of continuous contact with the British, are at home
in the modern world. But the nation for which they speak has
made only marginal approaches to modernity. A population whose
birth rate quickly engulfs every gain of modern technique within
a swollen tide of ancient needs must, as the Red Queen told
Alice, run all it can to stay in the same place. "If you want to
get somewhere else, you must run at least twice as fast as that!"
To break out of the vicious circle of poverty which has been
Egypt's destiny will require herculean efforts over a long, hard
course. Egypt confronts the process of modernization with the
most difficult set of natural obstacles in the Arab region, complicated by a political style that is out of phase with its capacities.
As this situation has heavily politicized public communication in
Egypt, the present chapter deals with communication as a political
instrument in a highly unstable society.

The race for internal growth is impeded by the concurrent search of Egypt's elite for a large place in the world arena. But the reach exceeds the grasp. Elite aspirations often reflect personal anxiety with little regard to political arithmetic. As they respond to the diverse challenges of social change by such grand schemes as the Aswan Dam, so they seek to solve all the problems of national posture at once by such vast dreams as "the Arab nation." When next steps are guided by such distant goals, there is bound to be much stumbling. Hardly any commentator has failed to note the erratic effect upon Egyptian progress of these "illusions of grandeur." One states the case in summary fashion: "The other Middle East countries are far more realistic than Egypt because they do not, like her, consider themselves Great Powers."[1]

The desire to bridge this gap between elite aspirations and national capacities directs the flow of public communication in Egypt. The elite, controlling the sources of communication, shapes their output to convey its own image of the national future. This propensity in Egyptian communication has become especially marked since the survey was made. The seats of power have been taken over by a youthful military junta armed with an apocalyptic vision of Egypt's destiny and their own role in it—"a role in search of a hero," as their leader puts it. President Nasser's autobiography, appropriately titled *Egypt's Liberation,* articulates his personal vision in prophetic style:

> Every people on earth goes through two revolutions; a political revolution by which it wrests the right to govern itself . . . and a social revolution involving the conflict of classes. . . . Peoples preceding us on the path of human progress . . . have not had to face both simultaneously; their revolutions were centuries apart in time. For us, the terrible experience through which our people are going is that we are having both revolutions at the same time.[2]

Linking the goals of popular welfare and national grandeur in this way, in a land inadequately equipped for either, has led to soul-searching and to bold enterprises. The quotations which open this chapter indicate that soul-searching has led Nasser on the quest for a political identity that will fuse the nation and its leader ("who we are and what our role is to be"); his boldest enterprises have originated in his conception of radio as a chosen instrument of national identity. Nasser has sought to cope with his two revolutions simultaneously by means of a unifying "communication revolution."

His success in propagating the symbols of Arab nationalism seems beyond question. The most impressive unifying force among Egyptians and "neutralist" Arabs today is the personality of Nasser as reflected through Cairo's *Voice of the Arabs*. But there is reason to ask whether Nasser, while encouraging popular belief that the dilemma of his twin revolutions is thereby solved, has not slipped through its horns. It may be that each immediate gain will turn into a serious net loss on some later reckoning. This is no prophecy; it is a statement of the conditions of long-run success imposed on Nasser's regime by his own communication strategy. By raising expectations among Egyptians, Nasser has also raised the standards of performance by which his regime is judged. Higher hopes require higher payoffs. But the outlook for conspicuously higher payoffs to the Egyptian population is not bright. The higher their hopes soar—this is the risk—the easier, deeper, wider may be their disappointments. To grasp the full poignancy of this situation, one must see Nasser's vision of the Egyptian future against the stupefying obstacles presented by its current conditions. We begin with the socioeconomic indices of modernization.

1. The Vicious Circle of Poverty

The vital problem of Egypt is plainly visible to the merest tourist. Approaching by air, he perceives how narrow is the green strip of fertile Nile valley by contrast with the vast deserts that roll endlessly away beyond the horizons. Driving in from Cairo airport he passes through suburban Heliopolis, where foreigners and pashas live in villas of surpassing magnificence and modernity. But he brusquely enters the Middle Eastern world as he moves toward the metropolitan center, where a substantial population has no other housing than the city streets. There walk by day and sleep by night men and their little burros, whole families with their belongings in portable bundles appropriate for the needs of urban nomads. The massive and incessant life of the Cairo streets is on a 24-hour daily basis. Caravans arrive at dawn from distant places; several hours later, but before getting very far into the city, they are caught up by limousines speeding in

from Heliopolis or crossing the river from Zamalek. Camels stall
Cadillacs as the human mass afoot dominates the roads and regulates the tempo.

The initial predicament is set by a simple statistic: over 20
million people are living on 6 million acres of land—a population
density of 1,198 persons per square mile of habitable land as compared with 27 in Turkey and 44 in the United States. Pestilence
regularly decimates the surplus population. If its birthrate is
among the world's highest (averaging over 40 per thousand), so
are its deathrates. Infant mortality soon reduces the number of
children to feed by *half*: one out of every four children born dies
during its first year and another before it is five years old. The
demographer finds that "one of the most striking summary comparisons is the age by which one-fourth of the original cohort are
dead. . . . 1.1 years in Egypt . . . 51.5 years in the United States
(whites)." The average Egyptian's life expectancy at birth is just
half that of a white American: 30.2 years as against 60.6 years. In
the continuous flow of new life, few survive and those not for
long.[3]

The lifeways and deathways of a traditional society tend to
become interlocked in a vicious circle of poverty.[4] Escape from
the circle is extremely difficult, since piecemeal efforts often make
things worse in the long run. For example, the ancient system of
basin irrigation was superseded during the late 19th century by
perennial irrigation based on modern methods of dam- and barrage-
construction. Distributing the Nile waters over the cultivated
lands in this way enabled Egyptians to produce two crops instead
of one each year, at sustained high yields per acre. But the innovation also caused a rise in the water table and a consequent
increase of *bilharzia,* one of the endemic diseases which sap
vitality and shorten life among the fellahin. Even the survivors suffered ultimately from the imported new technology. In the next
half-century, while cultivated land increased by only 12%, the
population of Egypt increased by 96.8%. Despite increased productivity, there was a "serious drop in real income per head of
rural population."[5]

The lesson of perennial irrigation is not without relevance to
the project for a High Dam at Aswan. Public interest abroad has
been confined to the political question—under whose auspices?
But the essential question is rather: Will the project figure in a

larger design to propel Egypt, finally, into a growth phase; or will it stand as a solitary monument to the present ruling junta? Some competent observers have concluded that, alone, the Aswan Dam will not pierce a durable pinhole in the self-sealing circle of agrarian poverty.[6] Only with substantial support on its industrial flanks can the Dam spearhead a major breakthrough into the modern world. With this giant step would be needed rising urbanization, industrialization, and per capita income. The Egyptian record on these indices is not encouraging.

During the past half-century no urbanization policy was visible. From 1897 to 1937 there was only minimal movement, and what there was went to the six capital cities (Cairo, Alexandria, Port Said, Suez, Ismailia and Damietta). These increased by 3.8%, while all provincial cities together increased by only 0.4%. Such haphazard movement, which gave scant relief to the overburdened fertile strip, occurred while population density was *doubling*. During the next decade an astonishing leap (19%) increased population by over 3 million, giving Egypt in 1947 a total of about 20 million, while infant mortality decreased by almost 20% and life-expectancy showed a corresponding increase of about 8 years.[7]

These happy signs, for another society, might have spelled disaster for Egypt. Increasing prosperity with decreasing pestilence deprived Egypt of the twin institutions which, historically, had stabilized its vicious circle of poverty. More of this sort of "progress" could have been catastrophic. With more people surviving infancy and living longer, even Father Nile would at this rate have been quickly outpaced. But the prosperity was transitory, for it derived from war-inflated world prices on agricultural commodities. When the bubble burst, no real program was available (or ever produced) for deploying idle farmers into urban jobs.

During the past decades, rural population finally did start moving, but it was simply jettisoned into an already overflowing city. While total population was increasing by 20%, Cairo increased by over 60%. During 1937-1947 the population increase of Cairo alone was greater than the increase of the 20 largest towns combined.[8] In such displacement, new bodies are simply agglutinated to a floating urban mass, converting their old indolence into a new aimlessness. The ancient metropolis has not the social capacity to absorb them as participants, and these urbanized nomads increase the nation's explosive rather than productive potential. This tragedy of waste leaves unused the absorptive capacity of towns, in which, under a rational and comprehensive development policy, the location of new industries, new schools, new markets, new media would figure as items in an array. Such a policy, as exhibited in Turkey and Lebanon, modernizes a society over decades and generations. No country has yet shown how this can be accomplished in a hurry.

How *have* Egyptians been getting their living and how much of a living have they been getting? Over half of the labor force remains in the agricultural sector, with mobility only at the very top and bottom of the occupational scale. The increases in "personal services" and "undefined and unproductive" occupations doubtless represent the huge growth of floating population. While this surplus languishes on the lower periphery of productive life, the "middle sectors" which distinguish modern society register only marginal gains. Over the two decades in which modern transport and communications made their most spectacular advances elsewhere, Egyptian employment in this sector lost ground. The commercial sector barely held its own. The crucial industrial sector registered gains that are pitiful by comparison with the need, growing less than the "elite" sector of public services and professions.

We shall soon look in detail at this disproportionate bulge in the elite formations. Here we note the failure of the middle sectors to provide channels of access for the continually swelling mass. As the industrial sector absorbed but *one* new worker for every *ten* surplus persons who constituted its potential labor force, the other nine (already ejected from the land) simply increase the non-productive floating population. Having neither productive jobs nor expendable cash, they do not "participate" in economic life.

Even the one in ten who has been "gainfully employed," as this term is understood in Egypt, functions only nominally as a "consumer." The average weekly wage of industrial workers during the postwar period has been 133 P.T. (piastres), or about $5.40, with little significant gain throughout the decade. Between 1945-1951, the average annual income increased in the industrial sector from 95 L.E. (Egyptian Lira) to 98 L.E., while the average in the agricultural sector declined from 48 L.E. to 46 L.E. Says Issawi: "In effect, nearly three-quarters of the whole population are not a market for industrial products."[9]

The "bulges" continue to swell at the top and the bottom of Egyptian society. The "average family" cannot expect better quarters than were reported in the 1938 Survey of Poverty, while there are only 113,000 people engaged in the construction industries. Nor can a market economy develop where few ever have spare cash. On the land, too, ownership is heavily concentrated in a relatively few hands. Two million own less than one feddan and over a half-million own less than five feddans; together these account for some 95% of all landowners.[10] While legally protected from expropriation since the British Five-Feddan Law, little has been done to increase their productivity.[11] Instead, agricultural disparities tend to accelerate and become more acute by comparison with other sectors, as in the figures in Table 1 worked out by Issawi.[12]

Table 1—Income Differentials

Occupation	Average Income
Agricultural Laborer	10 L. E.
Industrial Worker	26 L. E.
Minister	2,500 L. E.
Bank Chairman	3,000 L. E.

We have stressed the enormity of the bulge in the lower depths. Not less significant, for the long run, is the corresponding bulge in the elite levels. That almost as many men are employed in the bureaucracy and professions as in the whole industrial sector is a serious anti-growth mechanism in any economy. That the public service-professional sector has grown almost twice as fast as the industrial sector, in the past two decades, indicates that things have been going from bad to worse.

The way out of the vicious circle requires a coordinated program of productive investments located, as Nurkse indicates, to achieve a general rise in income that will be distributed in reasonable proportions between consumption and reinvestment.[13] Such growth would have to reverse Egyptian trends in the distribution of population, work, and wealth, which have produced a society in very poor shape. Whereas the typical modern society resembles a clock, which is most massive around the middle, Egyptian society is shaped rather like an hour-glass, bulging at both ends and with hardly any middle at all. An hourglass, too, looks quite stable until the very instant when it performs the only movement of which it is capable—an extreme flip-flop, usually accompanied by a hissing sound. The figure is exaggerated, but it does suggest the explosive potential of the Egypt which Nasser inherited.

How, under these conditions, were the Egyptian people disposed toward Nasser's dilemma of "the two revolutions"? It is never certain, in advance, how impoverished people will respond to the conflicting symbols of NATION and CLASS. Highly traditionalized people often are nonresponsive. Their identifications are firmly localized in family and community. The effort to incorporate such larger entities as Class or Nation within their personal identity seems irrelevant or impossible. On what psychic soil did Nasser's more complex strategy of fusing the Class-Nation symbols fall?

2. The Revolutionary Symbolisms:
NATION and CLASS*

THE 1951 survey provides some information about the Egyptian communication arena on the eve of the Revolution. Even before Nasser launched the official quest for a usable identity, Egyptian respondents aligned themselves along the axis of political identification. The choice between national and class symbols, whereby each respondent defined his public identity, indicated where he was likely to stand on most issues confronting his country. Indeed, the way each respondent positioned himself with respect to the symbols of nationalism usually revealed which of the great public issues came to his attention at all.

Nationalist agitation throughout the land had succeeded, over several generations, in diffusing among Egyptians of all classes some measure of "national consciousness." As the symbols of nationalism are highly ambiguous, meaning very different things to different men, such consensus provided only minimum guarantees of a common will on specific issues of public policy. There was little dissent among respondents from the proposition that

---

* This section is based on the BASR report "Climates of Opinion in Egypt" by P. L. Kendall and B. B. Ringer. See also P. L. Kendall, "The Ambivalent Character of Nationalism Among Egyptian Professionals," *Public Opinion Quarterly* (Spring 1956).

Egypt should be independent and its corollary that the British occupation should, somehow, vanish. But the sociology of this limited dissent is an important clue to the political meaning of Egyptian attitudes, as is the varying saliency and intensity of the assent. The tonality of assent ranged from an upper extreme of feeling that nothing in the world could be more urgent than Egyptian independence to a lower extreme of tolerant indifference. Persons ranged at the different levels of this scale were found to differ correspondingly on most essential questions of personal position and public posture.

To deal with the sociological distribution of these attitudes, respondents were classified on a different basis than in preceding case studies. Whereas our Turkish respondents had been classified initially by the range of their opinions, and Lebanese respondents by their radio-listening habits, the Egyptian respondents were sorted by their jobs. As this proved useful in differentiating responses to the symbols of CLASS and NATION, the 262 respondents (out of 331) whose jobs were known and classifiable are presented in the four large occupational categories: Professional, White Collar, Workers, Farmers. This produced remarkably regular differences, also, on the indices of modernization in our basic typology. The cross-tabulations in Table 2 show the differences of education and status between groups.

Table 2—Education and Status

EDUCATIONAL LEVEL	Professional	White Collar	Worker	Farmer
Illiterate	—	3%	45%	58%
Elementary School	1%	11	48	40
High School	22	60	7	2
College & University	77	26	—	—
	100%	100%	100%	100%
SOCIOECONOMIC STATUS				
Destitute	—	—	9	25
Poor	7	3	74	44
Modest	63	79	16	23
Well Off	26	18	1	8
Rich	4	—	—	—
	100%	100%	100%	100%
Total Respondents	(110)	(35)	(69)	(48)

As one descends the scale from educated and better-off Professionals to illiterate and impoverished Farmers, as in Table 3, the groups also become more homogeneously rural and Muslim.

Table 3—Residence and Religion

	% Living in Rural Areas	% Muslims
Professional	20	75
White Collar	12	79
Worker	38	98
Farmer	100	96

These groups make a close fit to our general typology of Moderns, Transitionals and Traditionals. The Professionals—urban, educated, relatively well-off, and with a substantial admixture of non-Muslims (mainly Copts, Greeks, Armenians and Jews)—represent the elite Modern sector of Egyptian society. The White Collar group clusters at the upper limit of the Transitional type, as defined in Chapter II, and the Workers aggregate closer to its lower limit. The Farmers provide, as always, the solid corps of Traditionals. (The data on media participation, reported in Section 3 below, further show the close connection between occupational groups and modernization types.)

The divergent attitudes characteristic of each group are strikingly illustrated by the subtle, yet profound, variants of the one attitude common to all groups—hostility toward the British, then still in Egypt. The keynote among the Professionals was extreme ambivalence, an unruly coexistence of love and hate toward the British. Oriented toward the West by their education, whence they have derived their conceptions of the good society, they suffer from a sense of rejection by the West. Many feel driven, in self-defense, to turn their rage against the erstwhile object of affection. From high expectations crushed seems to come their sense of extreme deprivation. More often than other respondents, the Professionals justify their hostility in terms of Britain's "unfulfilled promises." (171) This phrase of a young engineer was echoed in many versions. A woman doctor complained that: "Although Britain preaches that she deals with Egypt on an equal and friendly basis, she does the contrary." (156) The nagging sense of inferiority that underlies much of this ambivalent hostility was expressed by a teacher of social studies: "England has no confidence in us. That is why they want to keep an army in Egypt." (065)

Hostility was regularly infused with grudging admiration and wistful envy. These ambivalent feelings toward Britain underlay what the preliminary analysis of our data characterized as "impotent and shallow" manifestations of nationalism. The Egyptian elite, as Miss Kendall concluded, "have not developed a real nationalistic movement largely because the countries which they admire most and therefore want to emulate are, at the same time, those which they hate most."

Among White Collar respondents, the expression of Anglophobia took a quite different form. Hardly touched by the Western standards which the Professionals acquired through schooling and travel, the White Collar group exhibited little ambivalence. (We note in passing that 27% of the Professionals had travelled outside of Egypt, mainly in the West, as compared with 6% of the White Collar people.) Their hostility toward Britain was uncomplicated and direct. When asked for their judgment of British behavior in world affairs, 22% of the Professionals expressed mixed (partly favorable) opinions as compared with 6% of the White Collar respondents. This difference is noteworthy on the one issue which found virtual unanimity in principle among Egyptians.

These differences involved more than a tone of voice, as was shown by responses to the question of what should be done about getting rid of the British. The Professionals were embarrassed and evasive, reticent and uncertain. Many of them said that nothing could be done. Others looked, despite their fervent nationalism, for help outside Egypt—to the United Nations, to the United States, to Britain herself. A poignant expression of ambivalence was the wistful hope that the British sense of "fair play" would one day convince them voluntarily to leave Egypt for the Egyptians. White Collar recommendations, by contrast, were simple, direct, active, even violent: "I would drive the British away" (087); "I would boycott the English economically" (051); "Importing arms from any country except England and America . . . not supplying the British troops in Egypt with daily purchases." (323) One respondent, asked what he would do about this if he were head of the government, responded with a comprehensive program of direct action:

I would do the following things: (1) cut the political and economical relations between us and Britain; (2) absolutely not cooperate with the forces in the [Suez] Canal Zone . . . ; (3) strengthen the Egyptian army by buying weapons . . . ; (4) if a world war arises, we can stab *from the back;* (5) strengthen relations with all nations of the Eastern camp. (269)

An interesting aspect of White Collar activism compared with Professional reticence is that the latter group expressed far more eloquent and intense concern about getting rid of the British. When asked "What would you say is the biggest problem that Egypt as a nation faces today?," the Professionals alone among the four groups named the British occupation more frequently than all the issues of social reform combined. Yet, fewer of them responded in these terms to a subsequent question: "Suppose that you were made head of the government. What are some of the things you would do?" By collating the answers to these questions, we can see whether each respondent's *program* for Egypt was directly related or not to his own prior definition of Egypt's biggest *problem*. This was done with a Professional subgroup of 34 respondents, evenly divided between those identifying British Occupation rather than something else (mainly Social Reform) as Egypt's main problem. The results are shown in Table 4.

Table 4—Problems and Programs

My Program as Head of Government Would Be	EGYPT'S MAIN PROBLEM IS:	
	British Occupation	Social Reform
Directly Related	5	13
Not Directly Related	12	4
	17	17

This evasiveness on Britain among Professionals contrasts with the uncomplicated White Collar responses to the same questions. Fewer of them worry so intensely about the British, but those who do exhibit no anxiety about dealing with them. That is, proportionately fewer White Collar respondents named British Occupation as Egypt's biggest problem; but among those who did, 8 out of 9 subsequently proposed vigorous programs directly related to solving this problem.

Two nuances characterized the aspirations of the Professionals, as of the Egyptian elite more generally—and these contrapuntal themes we shall describe more fully as the "Nasser syndrome." One was the interlocked desire to be respected by, and disengaged from, the Western world. This conjunction of desires to be simultaneously engaged and disengaged often leads, in the arena of world politics, to the evasion of current choices. It explains why the Professionals, who wanted Egypt's independence, were unable to endorse such direct action formulae as "Kick the British out!"

The other nuance was a sense of guilt which, among moraliz-ing intellectuals, often accompanies the rule of pride. On this point my subsequent interviews, in 1954, were very clear. There was little dissent among the Egyptian elite from the proposition that Britain's home democracy is far more admirable than her world empire. Or from the corollary proposition that the great need for developing a democratic Egypt is not necessarily answered, but may only be evaded, by a policy of global adventurism. Of those who identified Social Reform as Egypt's greatest need, some later evaded this issue by stressing national greatness in their pro-grammatic proposals. There was an uneasy feeling among the elite that imperial reveries might be an unworthy sort of self-indulgence at the expense of their impoverished and needy countrymen. Per-haps no problem that confronted Nasser was so profoundly com-plex as this uneasy guilt over the fusion of CLASS and NATION symbols. Nasser reports, in his autobiography, that this incapaci-tated substantial segments of the Egyptian elite from effective action.

The Egyptian farmer, historically, conforms to the picture of Traditional man—"shut in no less *by its habits* than by its villages," writes Habib-Ayrout about the fellahin.[14] The fellah is bound to his soil by the same constrictive round of life as peasants elsewhere. His symbols of identity have been confined to work, family, mosque, village; his wisdom has been the ancient lore transmitted through time by the tales of father to son, by the training of mother to daughter. The Arab Conquest, which imposed Islam upon the fellahin, once brought the world to them. This codified the unknown world; then, leaving its deposit behind, the wave receded and the villagers continued their ways much as they had done since ancient time. Of the newer secondary symbols of political identity, they heard little and remembered less. Father Ayrout, a Catholic missionary who worked long years among them, writes: "Patriotism and nationality mean no more to the fellahin than the ideas of cooperation, public interest, or civic pride."

Yet, Egyptian Farmers are not so completely contained within their parochial universe as rural people in other Middle Eastern lands. One explanation is their history. Egypt is the oldest con-tinuous folk-nation in the world. While the greatest part of its history has been spent under foreign occupation (indeed partly because of this) the indigenous folk long since acquired the sense of being "one people." This sense of a proto-national community is not found among the Christians of Lebanon, the Druzes of Syria, the newly-commingled migrants of Jordan, the Kurds of Turkey, or the fierce autonomous tribesmen of Iran. The proud theme of Coptic (Christian) spokesmen that they are the original Egyptian stock is received respectfully in Egypt.

Another, perhaps more important, explanation of the strong national bonds that link rural Egypt to the urban centers is economic. The creation and control of irrigation channels, allocating the Nile waters which are the life-blood of rural Egypt, has long been in the hands of government agents, tying the men on the land to the men from the cities. Cotton is the basis of the Egyptian economy. Its distribution has been handled by the cotton factors, the shippers of Alexandria, and other urban visitors, upon whom the Farmers have learned to depend for the means and rewards of their productive labors. These visitations have brought the outer world, continuously over the past decades, into the attention frame of Egyptian villagers. They have learned that the rewards from their cotton crop, sold for cash in the world market, fluctuate according to the vagaries of circumstance far beyond the confines of their village. In every rural community I visited during 1954, some persons had mastered the idea of a fluctuating world market and explained its local significance to their fellows. Recognition is fairly widespread that the immediate welfare of each Farmer is contingent, beyond weather and water, upon distant events in the world arena of price and power.

Their interest in what happens to the cotton market thus pierces the shell of Traditional isolationism and extends their horizons beyond the village limits. It directs their attention especially to the activity of their national leaders, who function as their principal intermediaries and agents in the vast and remote world upon which their daily bread depends. At the time of my visit, no international event had been more clearly registered in the consciousness of rural Egyptians than the recent Soviet purchase of their surplus stocks of cotton. (Nor was Washington's almost simultaneous decision to sell its cotton surplus on the world market, in competition with Egypt's current crop, likely to pass unnoticed.) The Soviet purchase boosted Nasser's stock throughout rural Egypt, much as the postwar decline of world cotton prices undermined rural support for the regime of King Farouk. The future of cotton, which links the Egyptian hinterland to the wide world, thus bears directly upon the future shape of Egyptian nationalism. So a perception of their national identity exists among the fellahin; its potential force for social consensus at the level of national policy is great.

Among the fellahin, however, the new aspiration toward an Egypt great in its own right and freely competitive with its former overlords takes a primitive form. Their Anglophobia is neither the halting ambivalence of the Professionals nor the ready activism of the White Collar people, but an intensely personal rejection of a remote Other (non-Self) on the level of moral judgment, without any clear definition of problem or implication of program. In interview after interview among the Farmers occurs the same thematic sentence: "The English are our enemies." (007, 015, 099, 175, etc.) The penetration into the collective fellahin conscience of the equation *Inglesi*-Evil is expressed by one destitute Farmer, unhappy over his lot, who expanded the routine formula: "They are our enemies. People say that they are the roots of all the evils." (126)

The personalization of public issues is a characteristic mode of Traditional men. This is illustrated by the very substantial majority of Farmers who flatly refused when asked whether they would be willing to live in England. (Only five of the 61 Farmers interviewed said they would be willing.) The rationale of refusal included the fear of the new and strange which we have found among Traditionals in every land. Many added, however, the dimension of physical fear. One would not live among the British "because they shed our blood with their guns" (224); another "because they hate Egyptians and because they are cruel." (099)

Whereas most ambivalent Professionals who would not live in England (and many of them *would*) revealed a fear of not being accepted as social equals, the ego-constrictive Farmers spoke rather of fear for their personal safety. Threatened deprivation of dignity creates anxiety only among those who have or seek it; such preoccupations seem quite remote from the needs of the Farmers. They fear from living among the British not social inferiority, which is their accustomed lot, but rather (lacking the Professionals' acquaintance with British traditions of fair play and justice at home) the physical destruction which traditionally resolves personal enmities in their familiar world. Their nationalism is shaped by the inherited framework of Traditional values.

As we turn to the Workers, the climate of opinion undergoes another significant transformation. In this group appears the clash, long familiar in the Western world, between the competing symbolisms of NATION and CLASS. Much of modern history has been written in terms of this conflict; in those Western nations which remain underdeveloped by twentieth century standards, such as Spain and Italy, the competition between these symbolisms still shapes the course of political life. In Egypt, where the quest for a usable political identity is recent, the symbols of Class have just emerged and are barely visible in a political vocabulary dominated by the resonant symbols of Nation. As Egypt moves toward modernity, the class-conflicts that mark a social revolution (to which Nasser alluded) are likely to find more frequent and intense expression in the surface of political life. At this point Nasser's "crisis of the millstones"—the conflicting demands posed by class and national interest—may no longer be met by adroit use of the mass media.

Among the 69 persons classified as Workers, 19 were urban factory workers whose jobs subject them to the modern industrial discipline. The views expressed by these 19 Workers, which forecast their reaction to Nasser's New Way, provide clues to the shape of Egypt's future. Most striking is the non-saliency of nationalist sentiments as compared with Professional, White Collar, and Farmer respondents. Of the 19, only four considered the achievement of nationalist goals to be the biggest problem facing Egypt. They express far greater concern with social reform—the problems of livelihood confronting themselves and their fellow-workers—than with the need for Egyptian independence. Unlike the Farmers, who objectively are more impoverished than they, the Workers give priority to the problems of their nascent class over the problems of their newborn nation.

These priorities can be understood in terms of their life-situation. Workers in Egyptian society today are exposed to the full impact of modern insecurity. They are subject to the fluctuating labor requirements of an economy still far from a modern "growth phase," in which the modern theory that widespread distribution of purchasing power is the essential solvent of prosperity seems as yet irrelevant. Secured by nothing more substantial than the day's earnings from an uncertain job, there is no mystery in their paramount concern with their daily lot. "I am threatened to be expelled," says one such worker, "at any moment the owner of the factory wants." (313) Another respondent, employed in a weaving factory, speaks more comprehensively in the name of his class:

> Workers are very poor indeed. They cannot save any money. If he or one of the family falls ill, he cannot call the assistance of a doctor. Nobody knows what comes with the morrow. The worker is always worried about his future, and his present is very unhappy. He cannot look after his family, wife and children as he should. (117)

Not only the day's contentment, but also the morrow's security —this is the characteristic concern of the urban worker. He acquires a higher level of needs and wants, inevitably, as he moves from the relative stability of village life to the urban division of labor on a cash basis. On the farm, subsistence requirements usually can be met; living among kin and community, help is forthcoming at times of need. In the city, where each nuclear family is a self-contained economic unit, even ministration to the sick is done by a licensed doctor and must be paid for. The migrant learns to place the higher urban value upon security as he puts behind him the communalism of the village.

The familiar process of secularization accompanies urbanization in Egypt as elsewhere. While almost all of the Farmers interviewed visit their village mosque daily, the Workers have ruptured this Traditional bond. None goes to the mosque daily; three out of four go only once a week or less; one out of four never goes at all—behavior unheard of among the Farmers. With the replacement of old pieties by new secularism goes the replacement of old acquiescence by new desires. The urban worker quickly learns the thoughtways of the consumer. By far the most discontented of the four groups (over half declaring themselves "very unhappy"), the Workers are disturbed by the discrepancy between their desires and their resources. One says he is unhappy "because I am poor and have no money to enjoy myself." (072) Another "because I want to live a good life and have not sufficient money. I have a big family." (191)

The Workers are Transitionals, showing the impact of modern desires. But they may be outrunning their social context. "Enjoy myself" and "Live a good life"—these are phrases appropriate to the consumer of abundance in a highly productive and widely participant society. On the lips of workers in Egypt, where scarcity rules, these phrases may augur a time of troubles ahead. They bespeak desires that will not easily be satisfied. So long as a poor man laments his lot we are in the Traditional universe symbolized by Scriptural glorification of poverty and castigation of wealth. ("Sooner shall a camel pass through the eye of a needle . . ." etc.) Once many poor men phrase their common complaints against poverty in terms of their joint concerns as workers, then we are abruptly in the modern world of Class consciousness.

This is a significant feature of the Egyptian Worker's attitude toward the symbols of nationality. He is less interested in the common identity as Egyptian which he shares with all his countrymen than in the common identity as Worker which he shares with a more homogeneous segment among them. The future of Egypt will be different because many an urban worker has acquired the image of himself as Worker. The symbols of Nation now confront a much more potent adversary than the British—namely, the symbols of Class. This is Nasser's "crisis of the millstones"—his predicament of managing simultaneously the symbols of social revolution and national revolution.

On the side of political attitudes, it is clear that Nasser tackled a difficult problem when he decided that the sharply stratified Egyptians must reach minimum agreement on a national ideology in order to sustain an effective capacity for national action. But there were also important technical problems: Were means available for the rapid diffusion of a comprehensive secondary symbolism? Assuming that Nasser could define a political identity that would unify the cloven strata of living Egyptians, which media could he use to reach which groups, and how use them to best advantage? The 1951 survey dealt with matters relevant to these media problems, as they stood when Nasser came to face them.

3. The Media and the Revolutions

In general, the patterns of media participation in 1951 reflected the sociological and attitudinal differences that have just been reviewed. As expected, Professionals were most participant and Farmers least participant. But our interest centers on the early-Transitional group of Workers. The mass media, in modernizing societies, are most influential in shaping the lives of people newly located in the sectors of maximum transition. This involves the chicken-and-egg relationship we have already described: those who are modernizing tend to be more accessible to the media; media participation, in turn, teaches them modernity. The new urban Workers are such a group in Egypt today. Pervasive illiteracy reduces their newspaper consumption, but despite this they participate in radio and movies almost as fully as the upper social groups.

Table 5—High Consumers of Radio and Movies

	Professional	White Collar	Workers	Farmers
Listen to radio *daily*	89%	82%	78%	42%
See movies *weekly*	46	50	45	8

From the media the Workers learn how to look at their new social role, and in the media they seek out clues and confirmations for their preferred perceptions of the world around them.

One Worker, having acquired a vivid sense of his class-identity, made this his standard for judging the media. Thus he disliked *al-Ahram* because it was read by "other people" and adds: "I never see a worker reading *al-Ahram*. Workers read *al-'Assas* and sometimes *al-Misri*." His preference for *al-'Assas* was not unrelated to this paper's friendly attitude toward working-class activities:

It gives the correct news. And it happened that they published about our strike in our factory in *al-Misri*, but it was not correct. But *al-'Assas* published the strike in details. We made our strike because nine of our fellows were dismissed. *Al-Misri* did not mention this reason. But *al-'Assas* mentioned this reason. *Al-'Assas* is not afraid of the government and gives the correct news. (117)

On the same basis—that the radio ignored his factory's strike while *al-'Assas* covered it fully—he concluded that "the newspapers are more important" than radio. The interviewer, struck by his class-consciousness on most issues, commented: "He is very enthusiastic and is always speaking about the workers and their strength and their strikes."

Many Workers nourish their sense of class consciousness with themes of class solidarity drawn from the media. Some demand more such nourishment. One mechanic, when asked what he would do if he were editor of a newspaper, declared that he would promote unionization. He would "support all those who want the true improvement of the working class, the trade union movement." (095) A shop worker, as editor, would "write supporting the increase of payment for laborers and poor people." (110) A machinist would, if manager of a radio station, shape its programs into a Voice of the Workers:

> I would increase the numbers of talks which is particularly about laborers and their problems. I would suggest what treatment is necessary to solve their problems. I would ask the capitalists to listen to the complaints of laborers and then treat it accordingly; that is to decrease the number of hours of daily work and their wages to be increased. I would ask the government to ask the owners of factories to teach their laborers arts of industry which they work without having some knowledge about. (313)

This intense relationship to the media among the Workers is rather special; its meaning is conveyed more fully when contrasted with media behavior among the other groups. An important question for radio behavior is, who owns the sets? The data show large gaps between the groups: 80% of the Professionals and White Collars own sets, as compared with 30% of the Workers and 15% of the Farmers. (As the sample was deliberately controlled to over-represent radio-listeners, no extrapolation to the general population is possible; these figures are useful only for comparing groups within the sample.) Listening habits vary, of course, with radio ownership. Over 80% in the two upper groups, owning their private sets, usually listen at home. But 56% Workers and 65% Farmers go elsewhere to listen—a friend's home or, in most cases, a coffeehouse. One obvious result of this is that most Professionals (66%) and White Collars (74%) plan their listening ahead; whereas few of the Workers (29%) are able to do this. In view of this, the proportion of *regular* listeners among the Workers is extremely high: 78% listen daily.

What do they listen to? News reports rank high with all listeners. Notably, it is most often the favorite program among Farmers—chosen by 57% of listeners in this group, about 25% more than among Professionals and Workers. This is doubtless related to the inaccessibility of other news media among Farmers: illiteracy deprives them of ready access to newspapers and magazines; newsreels are extremely rare in their rural world. Another factor appears to be the less inhibited pleasure which Farmers take in the highly emotive content of Egyptian news broadcasts. Egyptian State Broadcasting (E.S.B.) operates on the basis that news-without-views is a waste of radio time. All its newscasts are heavily charged with vibrant opinions, calculated to keep nationalist sentiment in a continuous state of high excitation. Such programs are well liked by Farmers and by White Collar respondents (47% of whom call news their favorite program), the groups whose nationalist sentiments, as we have seen, are uncomplicated by competing symbolisms. The Professionals, involved in their complex ambivalence toward the West, do not take unalloyed pleasure in E.S.B.'s shrill campaigns to stimulate mass emotion. The Workers, with their strong competing allegiance to the emergent symbols of class-conflict, are less interested in the univocal nationalism of E.S.B.

Other differences in program preferences are worth noting. Interests and tastes are most varied among the Professionals, and the range narrows steadily in each group down to the Farmers. The latter approach unanimity in assigning top preference to a single type of program—89% prefer Koran readings to all other broadcasts, as compared with 64% Worker, 38% White Collar, and 28% Professional listeners. The steady decrease is one neat indicator of progressive secularization. It should be read together with the finding, already reported, that none of the Workers attends services at the mosque (while nearly all the Farmers do go daily). The Workers, it appears, can take the Koran as "living literature" and leave it as theology.

Another relevant datum is awareness of foreign broadcasts. The rule that international listening indexes transitionalism—specifically, from parochial toward cosmopolitan perspectives—is reconfirmed by the figures in Table 6, obtained when respondents were asked to identify the foreign stations that can be heard in Egypt.

Table 6—Awareness of Foreign Broadcasts

	Professional	White Collar	Workers	Farmers
England (BBC)	94%	91%	42%	17%
United States	56	49	10	6
France and Monte Carlo	42	31	10	2
Arab League Countries	43	51	32	17
Cyprus (Near East)	38	43	28	19
Russia and Satellites	23	29	3	2
Don't know	2	—	26	67

The BBC *présence* is widely felt among the respondents. But awareness of all Western broadcasts declines steadily as we move down the status scale. Conversely, awareness of Middle East stations (Arab League and Cyprus) increases relatively as awareness of the West declines. The most striking difference, of course, is the proportion of ignorance in each group. As compared with virtually complete information at the top, and preponderant awareness among the Workers, two out of three Farmers are simply not aware at all that a world network exists.

These distributions were confirmed by a subsequent "double check" question, which asked respondents to identify foreign countries that broadcast in Arabic, and by a question about each respondent's own habits. The latter showed that over 70% of the two upper groups listen to foreign broadcasts, as compared with 36% Workers and 17% Farmers. The world-involved Professionals also declare themselves to be quite regular foreign listeners: about a third listen "almost every day" and another half "two to three days a week." They give the palm of preference to BBC, followed by Cyprus—which is a "gray" British station, neither affirming nor denying its British control but simply avoiding the question.

The differential impact of the media is further clarified by data on the movies. The first question was who goes to the movies and how often? Table 7 shows the answers.

Table 7—Movie Attendance

Attend Movies:	Professional	White Collar	Workers	Farmers
Once or more a week	46%	50%	45%	9%
Once or twice a month	43	29	36	54
Less than four times a year	11	21	19	37
	100%	100%	100%	100%

Many of those Workers who have neither enough literacy to read newspapers, nor enough cash to buy a radio, can get fairly regular access to the movies. It is the Farmers who are most sharply cut off from regular participation in the vast expansive universe of the movies. (We recall again that the sample was controlled to over-represent media-participation; overall rural movie attendance is much lower than in this particular sample.)

The world of movies, however, is not the same for all spectators—and its impact involves more than frequency of exposure. What types of films a person sees may matter more than how often he sees them. When each respondent named the country whose films he liked best, the interesting distribution in Table 8 was obtained.

Table 8—Nationality of Preferred Films

Prefer films Produced by:	Professional	White Collar	Workers	Farmers
United States	68%	76%	40%	15%
Great Britain	18	12	2	—
Egypt	20	21	60	85
Other	6	3	6	5

The upper groups express overwhelming preference for Western products, to which the Farmers are relatively indifferent. The converse applies on preference for Egyptian films, which draw preponderant approval among the Farmers but only a minority vote among the Uppers. The Workers in the characteristic manner of early Transitionals, were more evenly divided—with an edge of preference for the local product. It is doubtful that these differences can be ascribed to pure judgments of film technique. What separates the groups, more likely, is their responsiveness to the divergent contents of Western and local films. Many Farmers and some Workers find in Egyptian movies a more familiar world of faces and landscapes, people and problems. They invariably contain a heavy freight of Traditional morality, and when Good triumphs over Evil it does so in Koranic and easily comprehensible categories.

The Uppers are more profoundly involved with the modern lifeways exhibited in films from the West; the problems that grip their interest, and the triumphs of virtue that satisfy their sense of justice, occur in terms more remote from traditional Koranic preoccupations. A nuance worth noting, in this connection, is that the distinction between British and American films is virtually confined to the Uppers—and that preference for the British product is most frequent among Professionals. These few people learned to state the problems of modern life in a British formulation, and they remain intensely responsive to the British dramatization of modern lifeways.

These differences in media behavior indicated discontinuities of Egyptian sentiment which correspond to the class cleavages. The Westernized sensibility of the elite differentiated them brusquely from the mass of their compatriots. It also divided the elite internally and reduced its capacity for joint action. The disjunction was sharpest at that point where, in a communication revolution, reciprocity counts heavily—i.e., the relations between men of knowledge and men of power. Social and economic trends in Egypt had reinforced, over generations, the psychic gap.

In particular, the torment of desires that exceed capacities, while new to the political section of Egypt's elite, had long been familiar for the intelligentsia. Leadership in the search for an intellectual accommodation of Islam to modernity was assumed by Egypt long before it claimed the title to political premiership (which, indeed, it has not yet firmly won). For generations it was distinctively the Egyptian intellectual who sought a rationale of social change appropriate to the Arab-Islam setting. The interior evolution of their quest presents fascinating problems in the sociology of knowledge that would repay close study.[15] As our present interest centers upon the political function of intellectuals, we may summarily note that the condition of an efficient elite—namely, good working relations between those who *know* and those who *decide* —had not been met. For one thing, on the judgment of leading Islamists, the analytic quality of Egyptian social theory was rather mediocre, hence its prescriptions tended to be superficial.[16] Expositions of modernity ran to exhortation, and the defense of tradition ran to apologetics. The programs they advocated were derived mainly from the ambiguous implications of high doctrinal controversy and their instrumental value for the rulers was slight.

For another thing, the vast overproduction of intellectuals had debased honor without increasing influence. The proportion of university graduates to total population, for example, was eleven times greater in Egypt than in Britain.[17] This produced unemployed intellectuals, almost invariably an index and agent of social troubles. In 1937 jobless Baccalaureats were estimated at 7,500 and unemployed graduates of Higher Schools at 3,500. The postwar proportion of unemployment was even higher in a university population which had grown nearly ten times greater than it was two decades ago.[18]

This excess of university students creates a massive pressure upon government jobs, for "the Arab who can read and write resolutely refuses to work on the land. He insists on living in a large city—the capital if possible—and he seeks above all else a job in a government office."[19] For status reasons, an Egyptian with any degree of education is likely to seek a public post. This produces a situation rather the reverse of what happens in a modern society. Professor Berger writes:

> When an Egyptian goes to the post office or police station or even railroad ticket office, he is almost certain to meet government officials who earn more than he does and who are better educated. In the West the situation is more likely to be just the opposite. The mere fact that he can read and write places even the lowliest clerk above the vast mass of the illiterate population.[20]

Even the swollen Egyptian bureaucracy cannot absorb the growing population of new literates and literati. Secondary-school graduates push for the lesser posts; college graduates find fewer openings. Only a tiny proportion of 1948-1952 college graduates found government employment. (See Table 8.)

Table 9—College Graduates in State Employment[21]

Profession	1948-1952 Graduates	State-Employed
Lawyers	2,713	—
Liberal Arts	1,895	278
Doctors	1,450	430
Polytechnicians	336	—
Pharmacists	277	120
Commerce	260	—
Agriculture	153	70
Dentists	50	33
Total	7,134	931

Those who did not get government jobs often found no gainful work elsewhere. A striking example, in this agricultural economy, is the inability of even the relatively few agronomists to find non-governmental employment. A careful postwar survey concluded: "At present the supply of technically trained advanced students of agriculture exceeds the demands for their services on big agricultural projects or in agricultural companies."[22] So potent is the prestige attached to a university degree among the literate that many thousands prefer to expend the time, money, effort—and endure the subsequent deprivations of unemployment and underemployment—rather than settle for the free technical education offered by the Ministry of Education in over a dozen specialized schools. Despite the waiver of military service and other inducements, attendance at those free technical schools has lagged relative to university growth. Their total enrollment was 5,449 in the year ending 1934; 7,905 in 1946; and 9,658 in 1952.[23]

Here, again, the middle range of technical aspiration and achievement remains undermanned while the nonproductive bulge swells toward the upper limits of professional status. Table 10 shows the rate of increase, in the decade preceding our Egyptian survey, among the occupations we classified as professional.

Table 10—Growth of Professional Class[24]

	1937	1947	Increase
Men of religion	51,000	52,400	2.7%
Schoolteachers	35,300	52,000	47.3
Engineers	8,400	15,800	88.1
Physicians and Dentists	3,700	6,300	70.3
Lawyers	3,400	4,700	38.2
Chemists and Pharmacists	1,200	1,600	33.3
Writers and Journalists	1,200	8,200	583.3

Within the pattern of overall increase, the sharpest contrast is between the two main occupations which initiate ideas and diffuse symbols—the "men of religion" show the lowest rate of increase, whereas the rate is highest among the "writers and journalists." Linked with the latter is the substantial increase of teachers, a process which has accelerated with the recent fivefold increase in Normal school enrollment: from 3,875 in 1940 to 19,961 in 1952. The postwar teaching corps has been increased, too, by the recruitment of engineers and others unable to find work in their professions.[25] The traditional founts of sacred symbolism are being overtaken by the newer disseminators of secular knowledge, but the modernizers have fewer places to go in the larger society.

Here is a root of the dilemma which confronts the Egyptian intelligentsia. Oriented toward secular modernity, they find themselves torn by the imposed need to define Egypt's course in terms acceptable to traditional Islam. This produces aggrieved defensiveness and ambivalence, which, by engaging the self in indecisive debates and inconsistent decisions, reduces their efficiency. Ambivalence is the more disorienting where political identity is struggling to attain precedence among the secondary symbols of self-reference (e.g., race and religion). As Nation is a key symbol in the political array, ambivalent nationalism tends to produce indecisiveness or a spurious show of conviction at the level of top policy. This showed throughout the 1951 interviews with Professionals. There was little consensus on what to do or who should do it, but instead a striking lack of self-confidence and self-reliance. They looked outward for help—often to the same Western world against which, on other grounds, they invoked the routine slogans of petulant self-indulgence.

The lack of a self-starting intelligentsia, providing the initiative needed by all vigorous new nationalisms, was a severe handicap to Nasser. In particular, the direction of Egyptian mass media had to be entrusted to loyal members of the junta rather than men with professional skills and experience. This complicated the problem of public communication for the junta in rather profound ways. The record of their first three years is an important chapter in the evolution of public communication in the Middle East.

4. Politics and Psyche in The Vicious Circle

Political leadership in any society needs a base in some social class, from which it can recruit its cadres. The modern West established a base in the mobile, continuously self-reconstituting middle classes. The military junta in Egypt has sought to create some such base rapidly. The Western model has not been feasible so far, but neither has the Soviet model. Proletarian democracy is hardly viable in a society lacking a proletariat: the Workers in the Egyptian sample bear the marks of genuine proletarians, but they are few in number. Nor is agrarian democracy: the impoverished, illiterate fellahin take more strength from the leadership than they can give and each effort to align this inert mass for political action is fraught with great risks. This is another version of Nasser's "crisis of the millstones." Every leadership seeking to modernize a traditional society rapidly faces this dilemma—in Egypt the distance between the horns is widened by the extraordinary gap between pretension and performance, between claims and capacities.

This gap led the Egyptian intelligentsia into extremist alarums and concealments which suggest, in Professor E. A. Speiser's phrase, "the nervousness of one whistling in the dark."[26] Uncertainty as to their identity, their function, their future obscured clear vision of themselves in the future world and increased their remoteness from the Egyptian masses. Their ambivalence foreshadowed the zigzag course of Egyptian policy since the military coup of July 23, 1952. When the original interviews were made, the Free Officers (*Zubat al-Ahrar*) were a clandestine organization of quite junior officers who mainly produced some muted echoes of the nationalist clamor. Now they rule Egypt as the Revolutionary Command Council (R.C.C.). They have brought Egypt's problems to a dramatic focus at the center of the world arena. But their course has been erratic, their goal remains undefined, and their future path obscure.

The junta's course has been zigzag largely because the difficulties of modernizing Egypt are real; perhaps no other Arab land represents quite so unfavorable a net ratio of population to resources. But they lacked clarity on an important question that preceded any program: which set of problems ought to have priority—their own need for a stable elite to bolster their national leadership, or rapid movement toward the Good Society promised as the fruit of independence? Before their revolution, the junta had perceived national independence and social justice as reciprocal functions. Once in power, they learned that the two were badly out of phase. Their attention fluctuated from one to the other, and their policies were improvised responses to unavoidable pressures.

The shifts in the junta's policy are exhibited in the autobiographical accounts published by their two successive chiefs—General Naguib and Colonel Nasser. These leaders, like their contemporaries, acquired early familiarity with the conflicts experienced by persons who observe their ancient world being flooded with new and impotent desires. Nasser writes of his school years:

Waves of thoughts and ideas came over us while we were not yet developed enough to evaluate them. We were still living mentally in the captivity of the 13th century. . . . Our minds tried to catch up with the caravan of human progress, although we were five centuries or more behind. The pace was fearful and the journey was exhausting.[27]

The goal was modernity on the Western model, designed in Britain. This shaped the junta's quest for a usable political identity in the early phase. But it *assumed* an inevitable correlation between the national and social revolutions. The Egyptian nation was to find itself by driving the foreigner out and bringing the good life in. The equation was simultaneous. Nationalism meant a free and equal homeland—free of the British and equal for the Egyptians.

Hence, their focus of attention was domestic. Events outside

Egypt seemed unreal; only the homeland was vivid and present. Even the 1948 war against Israel bears, in Nasser's account, the extraordinary title: "Egypt Was the Center of Our Dreams." It begins with this remarkable sentence, considering Israel's current role as devil in Egyptian imagery: "When I now try to recall the details of our experience in Palestine, I find a curious thing: we were fighting in Palestine, but our dreams were centered in Egypt." (p. 21)

The junta, in that early phase, conceived their revolutionary role in Robin Hood terms. Armed with the long bow of primitive Marxism, they would equalize the homeland by taking from the rich and giving to the poor. But they soon learned that their brave new land reform, while high-minded, was conceived in innocence. With a maximum of one million acres for potential development, of which but 5,000 acres are actually under cultivation, such an enterprise as the Liberation (*Tahrir*) Province is notable mainly for its heuristic intent. Dr. Warriner, a sympathetic expert, concluded: "No reform, even if it went much further than the present measure, could provide land for all in this congested country, or could increase employment in agriculture."[28]

As the staggering burden of real needs was borne in on them, the R.C.C. began to feel oppressed by their slow progress and sought other solutions elsewhere. The focus of effort shifted from home economics to world politics, and the junta acquired a new official vision of the future. This entailed a reallocation of ideological priorities and the communication revolution in Egypt took a new turn. The historic shift, personified by the two main actors in the drama, can be summarized in three phases: Naguib primacy, transition, Nasser control.

Phase 1: The Naguib Technique—Vox Populi. The issue between Naguib and Nasser turned, indeed, upon the process which is the theme of this chapter—the use of public communication as an instrument of social change. The conflict is dramatized in their respective autobiographical reflections on the revolution. Naguib summarized the case thus:

I shall not enumerate my specific differences with the Council here. It is enough, I think, for me to say that most of them revolved around what Abd el Nasser has called the "philosophy" of the revolution. Perhaps, since neither of us are philosophers, it would be better to call it the "psychology" of the revolution. Abd el Nasser believed, with all the bravado of a man of thirty-six, that we could afford to alienate every segment of Egyptian public opinion, if necessary, in order to achieve our goals. I believed, with all the prudence of a man of fifty-three, that we would need as much popular support as we could possibly retain. . . . It remains for the course of history to determine which of us was right.[29]

Naguib hinged the long-term success of the revolution, from the start, to popular acceptance. In these terms he explains why the junior officers sought his leadership before attempting the coup:

> I was known to every man in the Army and could count on its support; my reputation was above reproach; and my personality was such as to appeal to the Egyptian people. (p. 33)

It was his function to win them "the popular following necessary to succeed." (p. 14)

The management of public communication can be decisive for the style of modern governance. Naguib and Nasser disagreed, fundamentally, on who constituted the relevant public and what was the proper scope of their participation.

Naguib

I did my best to make it a persuasive rather than a coercive dictatorship. . . . I travelled throughout the country listening patiently to everyone's complaints. I encouraged people to petition the Government to redress their grievances and I personally saw to it that thousands of grievances were redressed. I spoke to the people in their own language, and in my speeches, most of which were extemporaneous, I confined myself to the use of simple phrases and expressions that they could understand. That no attempt has yet been made on my life, I think, is proof that my approach to the Egyptian people was correct. (pp. 191-192)

Nasser

We were deluged with petitions and complaints by the thousand and hundreds of thousands. . . . There was a confirmed individual egotism. The word "I" was on every tongue. . . . I realized that [our task] would be accomplished at the expense of popularity. We had to be blunt, outspoken, armed with reason whenever we addressed the people. Our predecessors were skilled in deluding people and telling them what they liked to hear. How easy it is to appeal to people's emotions and how difficult to appeal to their reason. . . . We could have smothered the public with resounding words compounded of delusion and fancy. . . . But was this the mission with which Fate had entrusted us? (pp. 35, 36, 72-73)

A governing body cannot long endure with its public face chronically divided between a smile and a scowl. Naguib was retired and replaced by Nasser. But the populace was disturbed and their demonstrations, doubtless abetted by the Communists and Muslim Brothers, who foresaw ampler scope for themselves under Naguib's tolerance than under Nasser's austerity, impelled the junta to restore him. But the differences were profound, not easily reconciled, and the restoration was short-lived. Again Naguib was retired and Nasser advanced. The official R.C.C. statement of the issue was broadcast by the Minister of National Guidance, Major Salah Salem, on February 26, 1954, over E.S.B. This is a revealing document on the use of mass media. Dealing with the "psychological crises from which Naguib continued to suffer," the statement said:

When I assumed the post of Director of the E.S.B. in October last in order to reorganize it I had to face tragedies every day. For the President . . . used to contact E.S.B. officials . . . to give them direct orders to repeat broadcasts of his speeches several times. Even the news bulletin could not be broadcast before it was checked by him and before he personally recorded his contacts, visits and meetings.

During his trip to Nubia he used to give direct orders to the Deputy Director of the E.S.B. and other officials to change the programmes and to repeat the speeches delivered by him there several times, so much so that the public had become disgusted and abstained from switching on their radio sets. This was contradictory to the orders issued by me to the chiefs of sections in the E.S.B. not to make any changes in the programmes except in certain serious cases. These chiefs often complained to him that they were at a loss as to which order they should obey. Two senior officials of the E.S.B. had to feign illness in order to avoid the consequences of such contradictory orders.

One day in December last when I was facing the Sudanese election campaign alone I felt near a nervous breakdown as a result of Naguib's contradictory orders from Nubia and his insistence on punishing officials who failed to carry them out to the letter, although most of such orders could not possibly be carried out for material and technical reasons.

I remember, for example, on the Prophet's Birthday he asked me to repeat three broadcasts, of which one lasted for 76 minutes, the second 30 minutes, and the third 45 minutes. This was the day on which we had to broadcast the Propet's birthday celebrations. I gave orders for two of his broadcasts to be postponed to the next day. The same evening, however, the Deputy Director of the E.S.B. received a telegram from General Naguib demanding punishment of those who had not obeyed his orders.

One day, I could stand this state of affairs no longer and went along to tell my comrades on the Revolutionary Council all about them. They asked me to keep on trying to improve the E.S.B. As this did not solve my problems I finished up by going along to the Military jail at Bab al-Hadid and asking for a cell where my friends found me in the evening and called on me to stand up to the situation.

As I had control of the press, I recall too that General Naguib used to send delegates to the newspapers and ask them to publish photographs, statements and special articles. Any editor, reporter or official can confirm my statement.

Very often I was obliged to censor certain of his statements which contradicted decisions taken by the Revolutionary Council. One day I had to suppress the title of an article which he sent to *al-Ahram* for publication on the front page. This was an article by John Gunther entitled "The Smiling Dictator of Egypt."

He telephoned me and insisted that this title appear. I tried in vain to dissuade him as we could not permit a newspaper to call Naguib a dictator at the very moment that Churchill was making the same charge in the Commons. He refused and I had to ask the Editor-in-Chief of *al-Ahram* to publish the article as it had been sent by General Naguib.

I defy any Editor or reporter to mention any one member of the Revolutionary Council who has asked for his photograph or a special article to be published.

The chief editor of *al-Ahram* even got into touch with the Chief Censor and said that he could not as a patriot publish a statement that Naguib was a dictator. I told him to do as he was ordered by the President. . . .

You ask why we made him into a symbol of confidence and to this I reply that we never wished to create symbols as in the olden days. No member of the Revolutionary Council is permitted to praise any of his colleagues. Some of them were even angry with me when they were praised in the press. Personally I am convinced that the public was wrong, for it should never place all its hopes in any one person, but should concentrate on principles only.[30]

Phase 2: Transition—What Price Persuasion? Nasser and his youthful colleagues were deeply shaken by the implications of Naguib's bid for mass popularity. In words begin responsibilities; a communication network implies a power structure. The democratic use of power requires communication from below as well as from above. Discussion and decision tend, in a participant society, to implicate each other. It is unnecessary to persuade those whose views can be assumed or ignored; it can be fatal to ignore or coerce those whose consent must be gained. Naguib's courtship of the *vox populi* implied a politics of mass participation which seemed dangerous to the R.C.C. To Nasser, the masses that had "come in endless droves" through the revolutionary breach already appeared "dark and ominous."

Nasser preferred the military image of an orderly "advance" led by a vanguard and followed by masses that would "fall in behind in serried ranks." The principle of a "smiling dictatorship" was more risky than the impersonal politics of a proper "chain of command." The Egyptian masses were not "ready" for mass participation, hence a politics of persuasion was premature. Nasser's account of his disillusionment by the Egyptian mass is candid:

> Before July 23rd, I had imagined that the whole nation was ready and prepared, waiting for nothing but a vanguard to lead the charge against the battlements, whereupon it would fall in behind in serried ranks, ready for the sacred advance towards the great objective. . . . but how different is the reality from the dream! The masses that came were disunited, divided groups of stragglers. The sacred advance was stalled, and the picture that emerged on that day looked dark and ominous; it boded danger. . . . We were not yet ready. So we set about seeking the views of leaders of opinion and the experience of those who were experienced. Unfortunately we were not able to obtain very much. (pp. 32-34)

In turning from the mass to seek "the views of leaders of opinion," the R.C.C. shifted its priority to the formation of a usable elite. In good military fashion, they sought to recruit the cadres which could then train the line regiments. Their task was to create a fresh coalition out of aggressive elements in the old elite and the newer group of Transitionals. They turned first to the radical intellectuals —the symbol-manipulators who can give direction to the forward movement of a revolutionary program. Since the orthodox intelligentsia often will not or cannot fill this role, revolutionary leadership usually turns to the secular intellectuals located at more "mobile" positions in the universities or mass media. But we have seen how ambivalent the secular intelligentsia of Egypt had become; and the literature of political sociology suggests how treacherous their political alliances in any country can be.[31] Nasser experienced the symptoms at first hand:

> I remember visiting once one of our universities where I called the professors together and sat with them in order to benefit from their scholastic experience. Many of them spoke before me and at great length. It was unfortunate that none of them advanced any ideas; instead, each confined himself to advancing himself to me, pointing out his unique fitness for making miracles. Each of them kept glancing at me with the look of one who preferred me to all the treasures of earth and heaven. (p. 37)

His sense of deception by the fawning professors was matched in other elite circles, among which he singles out for special mention "large landholders . . . the politicians of the old regime . . . many government officials." (pp. 74-75) This deprived him of any solid base among the existing elites of enlightenment, wealth and power. So Nasser came to the crucial decision that, faced with masses whose deeds could be "dark and ominous" and without an efficient elite to count on, his mission "would be accomplished at the expense of popularity."

Small wonder, then, that Nasser, a Puritanical man with exacting moral standards, should have formed his Revolutionary Command Council exclusively with fellow Army officers of equal dedication:

> The situation demanded the existence of a force set in one cohesive framework, far removed from the conflict between individuals and classes, and drawn from the heart of the people: a force composed of men able to trust each other; a force with enough material strength at its disposal to guarantee a swift and decisive action. These conditions could be met only by the Army. (p. 42)

But a scowling dictatorship is not necessarily more efficient, and is probably less durable, than a smiling dictatorship. To run a revolution takes more than an austere mien; and other than military perspectives are needed to run a civil society. Atatürk had symbolized this by changing his public portrait from military uniform to white tie and tails. More recent military *coups d'état* in the Arab area—the prewar seven in Iraq (1936-1941) and the postwar four in Syria (1949-1952)—have also shown that recruitment from a broader social base soon becomes essential. Professor Majid Khadduri, keen student of the military role, suggests why:

> At best the reform program of the military was eclectic; it included various ideas and proposals that had become popular among the people, but these were never integrated or worked out by specialists as to the ways and means of carrying them out. Thus in Egypt, the army has been advocating land reform by limiting landownership to a legal maximum of 200 acres and encouraging small holdings; but in advocating this appealing program, which has become very popular among the masses, the military do not seem to realize that improving the economic condition of the nation would be dependent on new means of increasing agricultural production for an already overpopulated country rather than on redistributing the land among a larger number of people.[32]

Confronted with apparently insuperable short-term problems of social organization and economic development at home, Nasser overleaped them to stake the Egyptian future upon his skill at long-term play in the world political game. He shifted public attention from land-reform to Czechoslovak arms and Suez tolls. Thereafter, he no longer detailed the program for an Egypt of social justice but sketched the portrait for an Egypt of surpassing greatness.

Naguib had chosen, for the closing theme of his book, this sentence:

> The revolt of the Arab peoples, after all, is but a belated reflection of the revolt of the Western peoples that began with the revolutions in the United States and France. . . . the sort of federation that I envision would begin like Benelux and end like Switzerland. (pp. 273, 262)

For Nasser this has become a parochial view of the Egyptian future. In *his* current aspirations, Egypt figures as the patron spirit of a nascent Africa, as the vital center of an Arab circle, as the prime ministry of an Islamic World Parliament. His vision has wandered far from the homeland. As his sketch of the Egyptian future closes, Nasser's new reveries are playing political arithmetic with

> the 80 million Muslims in Indonesia, and the 50 million in China, and the millions in Malaya, Siam, and Burma, and the nearly 100 million in the Middle East, and the 40 million in the Soviet Union, together with the other millions in far-flung parts of the world—when I consider these hundreds of millions united by a single creed, I emerge with a sense of the tremendous possibilities which we might realize through the co-operation of all these Muslims. (p. 113)

What had happened to Nasser?

Phase 3: The Nasser Syndrome. The shift from home democracy to global imperialism appears at first to be an aberration. This sort of talk from a man of modest mien does not seem serious. For the Muslim millions of the world are no more "united by a single creed" than, say, the Catholics of Mongolia and the Baptists of Mississippi. But there is psychic meaning in political visions, even when aberrant.

Nasser has gone the way of total politization—the distinctive mark of totalitarianism in our century. Wielding inadequate power to enact rapidly their grand designs, such leaders have yoked all values to their quest for more power. Nasser has perceived how the "dark and ominous" mass, which so depressed him when it had to be served, can be made to serve him—and through him, so runs the rationale, ultimately serve its own "higher ends." Such thinking has come to seem a viable political strategy in the era of mass communications. Now it appears feasible to shape mass emotion to a large political purpose. Nasser's new communication strategy shows in the burst of activity given, under his guidance, to the "Voice of the Arabs" and to the "Arab News Agency." Also in his new readiness to exploit, politically, the pieties of the pilgrimage to Mecca:

> Journalists of the world should hasten to cover the Pilgrimage, not because it is a traditional ritual affording interesting reports for the reading public, but because of its function as a periodic political conference in which the envoys of the Islamic states . . . lay down in this Islamic world-parliament the broad lines of their national policies and their pledges of mutual cooperation from one year to another. (p. 112)

Utter politization underlies such efforts to fuse modern parliamentarianism with the ancient theocracy of Islam in a global fantasy. It suggests why a once austere leader, contemptuous of public opinion, is beguiled by chimera that will attract the "journalists of the world." More than political calculation is at work here. The naive candor of Nasser's "philosophy" stems from the conviction that his vision is clever—and righteous. He seems, at times, to be still fighting the battle of his youth: to show the hated imperialist from the West that he is just as strong and much more virtuous than his conqueror. He writes:

> Sometimes when I re-read the pages of our history, I feel a tearing grief . . . we were the victims of a tyrannous feudalism which did nothing for us except suck the lifeblood from our veins. Nay, even worse—it robbed us of all sense of strength and honor. It left in the depths of our souls a complex which we will have to fight for a long time to overcome. (p. 63)

This is the sense of shame before their conquerors which has scarred the Egyptian leaders and marred their conception of right role and proper place. Naguib, a simpler person than Nasser, speaks of the same "complex" somewhat more bluntly:

> I was ashamed of the low esteem in which Egyptians were held by Britons and other foreigners, and I was determined to show our cynical rulers that something could and would be done about it. (pp. 19-20)

These statements explicate the feelings so widespread among the intelligentsia interviewed in 1951—viz., the schoolteacher who, although he believed "England is the greatest country," would nevertheless "feel ashamed [to live there] because they would look at me as a master looks at his slave."

The difference is that Nasser makes Egyptian policy, and the year is 1958. The battle for independence is done and won. The British Empire is gone—from Cairo, from Suez, and now even from the Sudan. To persist in shaping the world to the ambivalent imagery of youth, among ex-colonials as among ex-imperialists, may in the long run serve pathology better than policy. Seeking to compensate the fantasy life for damages inflicted in a no longer relevant past obscures the lines to a realistic political future. The new Constitution, announced by Nasser on January 16, 1956, documents the excesses of ambivalent nationalism. It proclaims Egypt to be an Islamic and Arab state under a republican and democratic form of government. But this combination of all desirable identities is, at the moment, sheer fantasy. To proclaim Egypt a democratic republic ignores, but does not alter, the fact that it is a military dictatorship. To proclaim Egypt formally an Arab nation (for the first time in history) leaves unaltered the fact that Egyptians are ethnically *not* Arabs. To proclaim that "the Arab nation" now "extends from the Atlantic Ocean to the Persian Gulf" overlooks current reality in order to prophesy a massive rearrangement of the present facts of life.

Whether this is "rational prophecy," of the sort described by Max Weber, remains to be seen. But we shall be better prepared for observation by understanding the psychopolitical model which the "Nasser syndrome" seeks to diffuse. Ambivalence is still the recurrent theme in the unfinished script of the Egyptian drama. But release through aggression is the approved new posture defined by Colonel Nasser. His role on the world stage provides the living model to his countrymen. Only optimists in the West interpret his seizure of Suez, for example, in such petty terms as canal tolls. The press and radio of Egypt, as indeed of all Arab lands, celebrate a more basic meaning—exalting the Self by humiliating the West. Nasser is aware, however, that avenging past nightmares can become a dangerous self-indulgence. Hence he speaks of:

the crisis of the millstones—a revolution which obliges us to unite in one phalanx and *forget the past,* and another revolution which demands that we restore lost dignity to our moral values by *not forgetting the past.* . . . One revolution makes it obligatory that we unite and *love one another;* the other brings dissension upon us against our desires, causing us to *hate each other.* (pp. 44, 41)

Ambivalent affect and erratic policy will continue, probably, until Egyptians agree to do one effectively—to forget or not forget, to love or hate—instead of struggling to do both simultaneously. Meanwhile, Nasser has accepted total engagement with the "dark and ominous" mass and has undertaken to cope with the heavy emotional requirements of mass communication. Now, no longer hesitant to acknowledge his dictatorship, he often smiles in public.

5. Whither the Communication Revolution?

Nasser, then, has converted his earlier view that Egyptian society was not "ready" for mass participation into a more daring hypothesis—that he can use the mass media to achieve national consensus *without* unduly raising public demands for full participation. This feat hinges upon effective control of the media, along with all other channels of access to the Egyptian mass. He has not unlimited freedom of action, but moves within what he has called "the scope of our necessities." As empirical limits, three aspects of the current communication network merit special attention: (1) the disproportionate growth of "production" over "consumption" in the mass media; (2) the erratic penetration of the media beyond the urban elite sector; (3) the counteractive effects among the mass population of messages diffused through traditional oral networks by non-Nasser sources.

We noted earlier the extraordinary increase of "writers and journalists" recorded in the Egyptian census during 1937-1947. Even when treated with the prudence required by all Egyptian statistics, the trend is clear and has continued. It has not been paralleled by the expansion of media participation. The surplus of producers over consumers is great and growing, as indexed by the wiespread unemployment or foreign employment among "symbol specialists."

The national capacity to consume mediated messages is determined by three attributes of the potential audience: residence, cash, literacy. The initial obstacle is sheer physical access—where people live, in a transport-poor land, usually determines whether they are reached at all by media products. When overcome, the question of economic access arises. The mass media usually prosper only where a large number of people have at least small amounts of surplus cash—enough left over from the requirements of daily bread to buy a newspaper, a cinema ticket, a radio. We have seen that these conditions for growth of a mass audience are poor and relatively worsening in Egypt. But even a spectacular growth of cash customers in town and country would not be enough. For the third precondition—which may be called psychocultural access—must also be met.

The tool that provides psychocultural access to the media is literacy. In 1950 (the year to which most of our media data refer) a UNESCO report estimated the Egyptian population over seven years old to be 90% illiterate; in 1956, on a more favorable basis for estimation, the proportion was still about 82% illiterate.[33] Despite ambitious plans, the development of free elementary schools has not been paced to the growing needs, as Issawi points out, partly for fear of aggravating the rural exodus.[34] Those with physical access and surplus cash, but not a usable literacy, tend to remain outside the media network. Conversely, those with literacy, even when living in rural poverty, exert themselves to gain access. The new literates constitute the corps of restless Transitionals that may remake Egypt and the Middle East in the next decades. Literacy is their tool, mobility their method and the participant life their goal.

For while literacy as a tool equips people only to consume print, in the deeper sense acquisition of literacy transforms a person. He acquires some of that capacity to move from particular to general, from concrete to abstract, which is standard in modern communications. Mastery of the logical conventions of grammar and syntax, which print imposes upon routinely-acquired speech, is a long step in this direction. Thus, the illiterate Lebanese villager who found even *"listening* to things read" on the radio difficult, and preferred "being told" in the colloquial narrative of the oral tradition. An illiterate Egyptian villager explained why he learns less even from radio and movies than those who can read: "They see something I do not see, know about many things I do not know. [*What things?*] More about the world." (104) This is why literacy usually increases consumption of all media, the centripetal tendency we have observed in all lands. While literacy is essential only for print, everywhere it correlates highly with exposure to other media as well. The newspaper-readers tend to be also the radio-listeners and the movie-goers. How, faced with an illiterate population, have the Egyptian media fared?

The output of printed matter seems large, but collation of relevant figures corrects the impression of a thriving industry. UNESCO reported that in 1950 there were 55 daily and approximately 200 weekly newspapers in production. But only 26 dailies were in Arabic, the majority serving foreigners. Over half were published in Cairo, 20 in Alexandria, and the remainder in three governorates. No daily newspaper was produced in all of Egypt outside these five capital cities. Moreover, total circulation was only 350,000 copies, averaging 17 copies daily per thousand inhabitants as compared with 624 in Britain.[35] The difference between production and consumption of books was even more striking. Twenty publishing houses produced about 500 books per year; but "unsold books pile up and inactive stocks impede the development of publishing." There were only 2½ million books in all Egyptian libraries combined—about half of the number in the New York Public Library alone.[36]

The situation was similar in the other media. Radio has been, since 1947, a government operation called Egyptian State Broadcasting (under the Ministry of Social Affairs). Equipped with five medium-wave and one 10 KW transmitters, E.S.B. had a total transmitting power of 81.1 KW. But there were only 288,000 licensed radio receivers in all of Egypt, averaging 12 per thousand inhabitants as compared with 610 in the United States. Similarly, 40 film companies produced 40-50 feature films each year, but the annual paid attendance of 42 million averaged about 2 attendances per capita as compared with 22 in the United States.[37]

Media consumption was not only inadequate relative to production but sharply skewed relative to population sectors. Mainly confined to the great cities, the distribution of radio sets is shown in Table 11. Cairo had almost half of all the radio sets in the country, Alexandria had more sets than all the rest of Lower Egypt, and the

Table 11—Radio Ownership (1951)[38]

Area	Permits	Contraventions*	Total
Cairo	103,322	24,000	127,322
Alexandria	55,404	15,000	70,404
Lower Egypt	56,622	10,500	67,122
Upper Egypt	18,782	4,800	23,582
Total	234,130	54,300	288,430

* Radio-owners are required to obtain permits by payment of fees. Contraventions are detected violations. Doubtless, some "illegal radios" remain undetected.

vast rural expanse of Upper Egypt averaged but three sets per thousand people. Consumption of print and film was equally concentrated in the great urban centers. As compared with 226 urban cinemas seating about 200,000, there were but 28 mobile units in the rural areas and their annual attendance averaged out to *one film per year for every three persons.*[39]

Under the regime of Nasser there has been substantial media growth shown by UNESCO figures for 1950 and 1956 in Table 12.

Table 12—Growth of Media Consumption[40]

	1950	1956
Total Daily Circulation	350,000	500,000
Total Licensed Receivers	238,000	405,000
Total Cinema Attendance	42,000,000	86,000,000

Radio and film have grown most. With slow reduction of illiteracy, new recruits have gained access mainly through non-printed media. Press circulation also increased, but not—when increased sales among non-Egyptians (e.g., Palestinian refugees) are computed—in proportion to the growth of literate population.

The press, too, has been rigidly homogenized. Formerly cosmopolitan and free-wheeling, newspaper output has been brought under central directive. The foreign press, under Nasser, was cut (even before Suez) to one-fourth its former size—French dailies from 13 to five, Greek dailies from seven to two, while the two Armenian and two English dailies have disappeared. The major new daily is *al-Goumhouria,* published directly under the auspices of Nasser's Liberation Rally. The Arab News Agency, formerly controlled by the Hulton Press Organization in London, has become a supplementary voice of Cairo throughout the Middle East. Recent media growth, then, reflects mainly the increased ambitions of Cairo as a message center in the world network. Media development has gone the way of general development projects. After a brave start toward building home audiences, the media were diverted to adventures abroad in support of the new globalism of Egyptian policy. The E.S.B. transmitters, which still reach only a fraction of their potential audience at home, nevertheless have been so deployed as to blanket the Middle East. The programming schedule gives top priority to its role as spokesman for the Afro-

Muslim areas. E.S.B. now broadcasts in French, English, Greek, Italian, Spanish, Portuguese, Hebrew, Turkish, Persian, Urdu, Indonesian and Swahili.[41]

A major instrument of Cairo's drive for political leadership is E.S.B.'s Voice of the Arabs (*Saut al-Arab*), which broadcasts over short and medium wave five hours daily in a modern form of literary Arabic that can be heard from Algeria to Uganda, from Iraq to the remote shaykhdoms at the southern tip of Arabia. In these broadcasts away from the homeland, E.S.B. lets itself go. Despite Nasser's public remorse over domestic blood-letting, the Voice of the Arabs became a major relay in the chain-reaction of assassination and mob violence through the area. So blatant were its calls for murder in North Africa, and so weighty the evidence that tied E.S.B. to a secret espionage and terrorist apparatus, that the Quai d'Orsay followed many futile protests by restricting French exports of military materiel to Egypt. Subsequently, the Voice of the Arabs received major credit for inciting the riots which toppled two governments and prevented Jordan's adherence to the Baghdad Pact (MEDO). The *New York Times* dispatch on these events stated:

> Jordanian and Western observers alike noted one outstanding thing about these riots: they broke out almost simultaneously in towns and villages throughout a country where roads and communications are most primitive. Political leaders in 'Amman and Jerusalem said they had no contact with people of remote sections of the country, but that those people had been listening to the Voice of the Arabs' reports about demonstrations in the capital and had followed suit.[42]

Outside the Arab area, E.S.B. articulates the reveries of a Cairo-centered world sketched in Nasser's "philosophy of the revolution." In Urdu, official language of Pakistan, and in Indonesian it resonates his theme of Islamic World Power. In Swahili (E.S.B. now broadcasts in more African languages than BBC) it propagates, with the tongue of many million Africans, Nasser's plan for an Egypt-centered continent. Thus, on October 13, 1955:

> The Mau Mau revolt, in which white arms defeated black courage, must be revived, not only in Kenya but in the entire continent and must go on until Africa belongs to the Africans.[43]

The highly differentiated operations of E.S.B. abroad are described by the psychological warfare specialist Edmond Taylor. In its broadcasts to Ethiopia:

Radio Cairo has adopted at least four different propaganda lines for various Moslem enclaves within Ethiopia, whose dominant class, comprising about one-half of the population, is Coptic Christian. To Ogaden, returned to Ethiopia by Britain in 1955, Cairo broadcasts that the British sold the region out to the Ethiopians (it had always been part of Ethiopia until the Italian invasion) and urges separation. To Harrar, which happens to be the native land of the Emperor himself, Cairo likewise advocates a breaking away from Ethiopia. Eritreans hear appeals to join the Arab League, since this is the only part of Ethiopia where some of the Moslems are also Arabs. And Radio Cairo encourages the detachment of the southern part of Ethiopia, populated by Somalis, by promoting the cause of Greater Somaliland, which would make one unit out of French Somaliland, British Somaliland, Somalia and the Ethiopian Somali country.

Here Nasser strikes at another African country *already* confided to Africans, for Somalia is the former Italian Somaliland, for which the United Nations decreed independence. If all these campaigns succeeded, the disjointed sections of Ethiopia which would remain should be prey for any country interested in gaining control over the sources of the Blue Nile.[44]

These excursions are directed by a junta which early learned that, at home, words breed responsibilities. Hence, it reserved for dissemination abroad the words that shape desire and incite action. To its own restive rural population E.S.B. spoke less thunderously, in another accent and vocabulary, of the tasks of construction and the building of a Good Society.

But the withholding of words also had consequences. In the first period after Naguib's replacement by Nasser, the rural communication void was filled by messages diffused through traditional channels of oral communication. Nasser's early distaste for the politics of *vox populi* put his government at a disadvantage *vis-à-vis* the extremist factions. The Muslim Brothers and the Communists were well organized to sustain informal oral networks among both proletariat and peasantry. Nor did vigorous security action cut these networks. Despite Nasser's stringent measures, the *London Times* reported on September 23, 1954: "Communist leaflets continue to circulate, Communist doctrines are popular in university circles and the organization, with some 7,000 members, seems to remain in being."[45]

Both Communists and *Ikhwan* actively recruited, among the unemployed surplus of college graduates, cadres capable of diffusing throughout Egypt a uniform set of messages. Despite their divergent sources, these messages have tended to produce one common political effect: namely, to make more difficult the rule of moderation among the elite by constant agitation for extremist solutions among the masses. Thus, while E.S.B. stirred popular restlessness abroad, the home territory remained exposed to agitation by potential counter-elites. Nasser, worried, sought to recoup his position by approaching *vox populi* directly. His own broadcasts, now frequent, mark a radical innovation in public style by using the vernacular tongue known as "Egyptian Arabic."[46] He has also "popularized" his philosophy by giving the "national revolution" an excessive, and possibly crippling, lead over the "social revolution."

This involved a basic revision of his own historical formula— to stake Egypt's role on pan-Arabism and pan-Islam elevated traditional symbols to the global level without clarifying any modern goals. To declare Egypt, historically tolerant of minorities, now a Muslim nation unleashed the violent xenophobia of fanatics while silencing the voices of modern rationality. In the junta's own weekly *al-Tahrir* ("Liberation"), the editorial of April 10, 1956 read: "Every Egyptian is proud to be a Goebbels. Britain was able to defeat one Goebbels, but it will never prevail over the innumerable Goebbels who have emerged in Egypt now." This has seemed to some observers, including very many Egyptians, a retrograde version of modernity. Writes Professor von Grunebaum: "The more closely Islam identifies church and state, the more it will be forced to build a 'modern' house on fictitious traditionalist foundations."[47]

Within the Egyptian tradition there are usable clues for an elite seeking both interior reconstruction and external dignity. But their effective instrumentation requires an unabashedly secular elite, open to new aspirants. Instead, Nasser has chosen to rule with a military clique, which appeases revolutionary-reactionary fanaticism while moving toward a totalitarian model of mass society. Here upward mobility does not reward excellence in the varied productive roles needed for modernization, but is preempted by those skilled in mobilizing mass enthusiasm for the central power. The elite does not embody before the public those values which all may emulate; it survives by spreading the belief that only mass enthusiasm for the current Leader can avenge the terrible past and speed future felicity. Among the paradoxical re-

sults of such a strategy is this: the elite soon becomes captive to
the mass. Edmond Taylor has vividly sketched this process at work
in Egypt today:

> Educated Arabs, whether they are steeped in the lofty traditions
> of their own culture or oriented towards the West, shy away from the
> mongrel pattern of Nasser's leadership even when they are passionately
> dedicated to the cause of Arab unity, and many of them fear or hate
> him in their hearts. The *fellah* and the desert nomad care nothing for
> Nasser one way or the other. But to the gutter-barbarians of the teem-
> ing Near Eastern or African slums and to the uprooted, muddle-minded,
> inferiority-obsessed young Arab intellectuals who are torn between East
> and West, Nasser—at least since the Canal coup (in Egypt he was
> a curiously unpopular dictator before that)—has become the perfect,
> irreproachable, untouchable champion of Arabism against the world.
> So strong is the pressure of the invisible mob that Nasser has conjured
> up in all the Arab countries, that even his critics and his enemies, know-
> ing themselves to be his future victims, now feel obliged to applaud or
> uphold him in public. This increases his prestige with the masses, which
> in turn increases the mob pressure on the Arab elite, and this unpre-
> dictable political chain reaction, unless it is somehow halted in the near
> future, seems likely to vaporize every stable, independent Arab authority
> outside of Egypt.[48]

6. Which Way Is Forward?

In "vaporizing" all other authority, can authority in Egypt
itself remain stable? Can the course Nasser has set reach its goals,
on his terms, under his leadership? The failures elsewhere to construct a stable governance on such terms—Iran under Mossadegh,
for example—show that the case is difficult. How durable is public
support organized by displacing hatred against an external enemy
—Britain, the West, the Baghdad Pact, Israel? The rich imagery
of invective against Israel ("thorn in our flesh," "bone in our
throat") suggests that this hostility can be sustained a long while
by the mass media. But the basic wants for a better life among
Egyptians are little supplied by such transitory satisfactions. The
signs of long-term instability, visible before Suez, are still present.

The dedicated band who made the revolution and formed the
R.C.C. has already been decomposed. General Naguib is gone—
under house arrest for years. Major Salah Salem, original junta
spokesman, is gone—publisher of a tame Cairo newspaper. So is
former Vice-Premier Gamal Salem. Shortly after seizure of the

Canal, when huge Nasser portraits began to appear everywhere, Gamal Salem remarked to a newsman: "There is only one thing on which I agree with the Communists. I am against the personality cult." This comment was suppressed by the censor and shortly thereafter he was dismissed. A coincidence, perhaps, but Gamal Salem no longer makes his voice heard in the ruling council.

Decimation of the leadership occurs, as we have seen, against the background of an incapacitated elite. This elite still lives spiritually in the Western world, whence derive its main ideas of the good life in a participant society. But it lives physically in the Middle Eastern world of massive inequality, widespread illiteracy, prevailing destitution, early death, and the constrictive power of traditionalism. Highly involved in the symbols of national aspiration, these persons find no guidance in Koranic fundamentalism. Nor is the Nasser way their way. The modern world imposes new problems and makes available new solutions. Psychic displacement of the elite between the ancient world of piety and the modern world of ingenuity is possibly the most fundamental problem of stable governance in Egypt.

A third area of instability is the failure to develop a program that may bring the rural mass to a decent level of life. The real difficulties, which seem almost insurmountable within the theoretical framework of classical market economics, were not obviated when Nasser turned from them, after a brave start, to global politics. While no easy solution is ready at hand, it is clear that possible ways out of the vicious circle of poverty are not necessarily advanced by giving the peasantry a spurious "public voice" before it has acquired a real "social stake."

The Egyptian mass is willy-nilly being shaken out of its traditional routines. The rule of cotton has, over the past few generations, spread awareness of interdependence with the wide world. Concentration upon an external enemy has diffused a minimum sense of common nationality. Their position as the new media "targets" has brought the outer world into an acute focus of their attention and exposed them to an unfamiliar range of expectations and demands. Through their accustomed oral network come the new agitators, both Communist and *Ikhwan*, polarizing sentiment around ostensibly conflicting long-run goals but with the common short-run effect of crystallizing restless discontent. Traditional passivity is replaced by a new activism. Thus the Egyptian mass gets under way, and the classic question acquires a new urgency: which way?

A fourth main area of crucial policy decisions concerns industrial development. There is little hope for a satisfying future without some suitable adaptation of modern technique. Cities, factories, markets are indispensable under the rule of modern living. This requires, in behavioral terms, a population equipped for production and consumption—a population quite different in its style of life from the rural folk who planted cotton seeds before the rich waters of the Nile arrived and picked cotton puffs when they receded. Needed are people who, among other things, read and write, tell time, change underwear, and go to the movies. These are the people who make things sold to others and buy things made by others. A key role is played by the industrial workers, whose routines of daily life become decisive for those other segments that work in shops and offices, schools and hospitals, transport and communications. Working class standards define the contours of the urban-industrial sector and ultimately of the society as a whole. The future of Egypt hinges, in this sense, upon the future of its industrial workers.

Among the Workers, three common attributes stand out as especially noteworthy: (1) their high mobility; (2) their political alienation; (3) their social utopianism. In contrast to the Farmers, still rooted in their familiar soil (albeit with a new eye on the larger world which buys their cotton), the Workers have already acquired some psychic mobility. They are prepared to imagine themselves in strange and unfamiliar environments. Perhaps our most striking single datum is the readiness exhibited by Workers to leave Egypt and live in a foreign country. Their attenuated nationalism is the reciprocal of their growing sense of class—they will live in any country that responds to their new demands for a more secure life at a higher level of well-being. Despite the universal Anglophobia around them, several Workers declared themselves quite ready to live in Britain. One asked only: "Could I educate my children and get medical treatment for them freely?" Another put the point sharply: "I am in favor with any person who helps me. If the British people provide me with money and find a job for me, I will certainly love them."(072)

Many would choose to live in the United States for the same reasons. Says one: "Workers are well paid there and can live a good life like big employees in Egypt." (191) Another: "It is an industrial, big nation. A worker like me can find work there with a suitable wage and limited hours." (313) A third says wistfully: "Is it, as we hear, a magnificent life?" Other Workers would just as soon go to Russia. One tells why: "It makes no difference between the rich and the poor but everyone according to his cleverness. It is a great city where you find the equality and I would like to live there." (213). The essential point, that national symbols are subordinate to class demands, is contained in another Worker's response: "I can't choose any exact country to live in. I am ready to go anywhere if there is work for me there. I am sure I can work in any country." (245)

One Egyptian interviewer, struck by this new class-consciousness, summarized what *he* had learned from the survey by insisting that "the worker is becoming a man who must be respected and appreciated." As this small class grows and develops an "organizational weapon," its power becomes a multiple of its size. As their influence grows in the streets, factories and market places, so their potency increases in the political arena. Seeing a large gap between what they want and what they get, the Workers look to government as the source of new social policy. This and any future government, confining its attention to the easier terrain of international maneuver, will sooner or later be forced to recognize that a potentially powerful class at home keeps its gaze firmly riveted on the primacy of social reform.

The rural mass moves in the same direction, though its pace is slower and its organizational gains less cumulative. A distinctive feature of Communist and *Ikhwan* agitprop strategy is the effort to conjoin proletarians and fellahin in a single apparatus of mass action. Nasser's success in making himself the Number One Voice of Arab Islam has, at least temporarily, stalled their advance. But no evidence indicates that their leaders have been converted or silenced. Rather, these counter-elites remain an autonomous force in being. The junta can neutralize their appeal only by adopting their special revolutionary-reactionary syndrome of populist, anti-capitalist, "integral nationalist" symbols. But the junta can hardly rally, under such banners, the new middle class of secular intellectuals, rational entrepreneurs, efficient managers, liberal landowners —the class that must first be created in order to be "represented." The old symbols impede policies that would activate new enterprises. For the junta, preoccupied with its ideological flanks, neglects its main line of advance. Professor Gibb has lucidly summarized the situation:

Inevitably, as the nationalist leaders felt mass support slipping away they made ever more violent efforts to regain it by continuing to harp on the continued presence of European forces or enterprises or controls, or on the hidden hand of Western diplomacy and on Western support of Zionism. When accused of neglecting social issues, they insisted that those were secondary and controversial, and must not disrupt the nation's united determination to achieve its national aims. However genuinely the politicians desired national independence, they did not know what to do with it. Concentrating on its negative aspect as freedom from interference and without positive program, *they could only try to fill the void of policy by propaganda.*[49]

The current leadership thus finds itself in a position where, confronting long-run social problems of extreme difficulty, it has sought to operate with a short-run communication strategy. Such a political posture is inherently unstable. Pan-Arabism and Pan-Islam abroad, however skillful, are not likely ultimately to solve class-conflicts at home. This is the dilemma of Egyptian governance and thereby hangs its future.

* * *

While I was in Cairo, in March 1958, Nasser returned from his first visit to Syria as President of the new United Arab Republic. The streets of Cairo were jubilant for days before and after his return. From dawn till midnight the young enthusiasts, jammed into requisitioned trucks, trolleys and busses, coursed through the streets of Cairo incessantly chanting *"Ya Gamal!"* In one government department, as I sat in the director's office, a clamorous concert arose in the corridor outside his door. His employees wanted the morning off to go and welcome home the President—who had, in fact, been home three days already. The Egyptian workday for government employees ends at 2 P.M. Said the director drily: "Isn't it curious that they are always moved by these patriotic urges in the morning?"

There are circuses aplenty in Egypt nowadays. There is also bread. The government has used much of its precious foreign exchange for wheat purchases that assure the supply of bread at nominal prices kept low by official subsidy.

Bread and circuses sustain the sort of high morale that keeps

the streets resonant with chants of *"Ya Gamal!"* But high morale
does not automatically solve the crucial problems of growth and
governance in Egypt. It tends, sometimes, to complicate matters.
The Director whose corridor had been taken over by demonstrators considered himself victimized by mass morale. As he explained, at a subsequent sociable meeting, his department was
charged with producing an urgently-required report for the planning agencies. If he let the demonstrators go, as they had demanded on three successive days, the work would not be done
in time and he would be charged with inefficiency. If he did *not*
let them go, they would not work properly out of spite and he
would additionally be charged with lack of patriotism.

Such dilemmas occur regularly among bureaucrats, teachers,
journalists and professional men—people charged with rational
tasks in an environment pervaded by the irrational compulsions of
mass morale. This is the cost to rational social institutions of the
high morale gained by charismatic personal leadership. The more
effective the charisma, usually, the higher the cost.

Nasser must now cope with these problems raised by his great
personal success. Of that success, since Suez and the United Arab
Republic, no observer can any longer doubt. On my travels around
Egypt, Syria, Lebanon in the spring of 1958, the presence of
Nasser was palpable everywhere. Those who did not love him
feared him. But none ignored him.

Charisma is a great power in an area still respectful of tradition but newly desirous of modern gains. Such power can be used
for good or ill by the man who wields it. Nasser's place in history
remains to be defined—for the real work of modernization lies
before, not behind, him. But already, it is clear, the Middle East
will never be the same as it was before Nasser rose. He has shaped
and diffused a new image of self-and-society in Egypt and the
area. If he cannot satisfy its requirements, this image may prove
his undoing. But the image itself will remain.

VIII.

Syria: The Lures of Extremism

> "The serious threat . . . is the existence within our own personal attitudes and within our own institutions of conditions which have given a victory to external authority, discipline, uniformity and dependence. . . ."
>
> —JOHN DEWEY

> "Military service is the best means for training the soul so that it can face hardships."
>
> —SYRIAN SCHOOLTEACHER

IN AN AREA rocked by explosive politics, Syria is a case study of political instability. A merchant-landlord oligarchy, long in control of the nation's wealth and power, latterly has been challenged by an army officer class. Under variant ideological amalgams of Nationalism, Arabism, and Islam, the competing groups have sought to rally a popular following. But the gulf between the few and the many has been too deep for steady traffic. A long history of mass indifference, alike to oligarchic governance and counter-elite contentiousness, is reinforced by a traditional communication system. Peasant and worker remain nonparticipant in the political dramas enacted at or near the social apex.

Political challenge in Syria comes not from the deprived masses, but from the alliance between young army officers and the radical intelligentsia of the "new middle class." The interviews with young bureaucrats, lawyers, teachers and students documented their disaffection and their groping for dangerous solutions. Claiming elite status by virtue of their education and modernity but feeling cheated by the immobile traditional "system," these men merge their personal frustrations with national grievances in ways that undermine stable government without producing durable changes.

The existing tensions are aggravated by the governing elite's short-sighted communication strategy: pronouncements are made that raise expectations which cannot be met. The resulting turmoil of postwar politics has produced no less than six military *coups d'état*. The growing mobilization of intellectuals in the Communist movement, which up to now has not shown its strength openly, augurs a stormy future.

The chronic inability of Syrian governments to maintain themselves in power signalizes the social schism. Challenged by an articulate new class, the traditional institutions deteriorate while the incorporation of more satisfying ways lags. In the absence of minimal social stability, the chances of efficient government are reduced. Conversely, when government's persuasive and coercive functions are ineffectively executed, there is little chance of social stability and less of stable growth. This is a reciprocal relationship akin to Egypt's "vicious circle." In Syria the circularity is neither so deep nor so comprehensive as in Egypt, but it is compounded of an underdeveloped economy and underparticipant population. A glance at the Syrian economy indicates some of the heavy limitations which such a social setting imposes on the policy scope of the national center.

1. The Social Setting of Political Instability

A modernizing economy requires an evolving division of labor. This develops an urban-rural market network which enables an increasing number of people to earn and spend cash in exchange for a variety of goods. Syria has no occupational census and labor force estimates vary widely. The approximations are that about 70% of Syrians get their living directly from agriculture and 1% (under 40,000) work in factories, half of these in textiles. The Beduin still outnumber the industrial labor force.[1]

Some postwar industries were established in textiles, cement, and food processing—the major "natural" industries—but the irrigated area for agriculture almost doubled. The continuing primacy of agriculture as a ready channel for enterprise indicates that postwar industrial growth already has strained its short tether. An International Bank team concluded that the new factories may already be overequipped, that business growth can continue only if accompanied by a large development program in the other sectors. But there are large impediments. One is the slow rate of capital formation in the rudimentary monetary and banking system. Savings do not enter the capital market, but are hoarded or invested directly, thereby limiting credit institutions. The lack of natural resources (mineral and oil deposits, energy sources, natural ports) combines with lack of skilled labor, technicians, managers to impede industrial development.

The agrarian economy goes with the traditional social setting. A condition of modernization is mobility. But, in Syria, obsolete transport confines mobility to a narrow population belt along the Western frontier. Remnants of the old Berlin-to-Baghdad and Hijaz railways do not serve contemporary traffic flows, providing only .67 railway route kilometers per 100 square kilometers as compared to 4.50 in Lebanon. Road systems do not compensate for this lack; dry weather roads (completely impassable during the winter rains) in 1948 totaled only 8 kilometers compared to Lebanon's 43 per 100 square kilometers. Moreover, Syria's 12 passenger cars per 1,000 population compared with 77 in Lebanon. There is no good link between the grain-cotton producing Northeast and the exporting-distributing Northwest.

Another condition of modernization is rising per capita income distribution. But, despite the doubling of real national income since 1939, average per capita income in Syria is only $123—half that of Lebanon.[2] The great majority of Syrian fellahin live at subsistence levels, outside the national market, and consume much of their produce directly. Two-thirds own no land, but sharecrop large estates, turning over 50-80 per cent of their crops to landlords, tractor owners, and irrigation pump proprietors. Indebtedness ties them to the land as it did the medieval European serf. Stricken with malaria, trachoma, and intestinal infection, they live in mud huts which are often shared with animals. The peasant smallholders have no better living standard, and usually sharecrop additional plots to survive. Hardest is the lot of the landless laborers, who live on a starvation wage: "They can only eat enough in harvest time, and in winter must subsist on maize, bread and grass."[3]

Syrian institutions interact to keep the peasantry submerged. The tenure system affords no security. Further, as subsistence agriculture is a bad risk for bankers and credit institutions are poor, the peasants must rely on merchants, landowners and professional moneylenders for loans at exhorbitant rates. There is little incentive to increase fellahin productivity since the landlords automatically take a larger share. Marketing and transport facilities are so rudimentary that distribution must be handled by middlemen, who deprive the individual peasant of gain from his increased output. Public finance does nothing to rectify the situation. Taxation is extremely regressive. All marketed produce is taxed at a fixed rate of 7%. Syria has nothing to match Lebanon's rural property tax based on income derived from cultivation of the land. Only 10% of government revenue is derived from income and property taxes of all kinds; most government funds come from customs duties and excise taxes, mainly on articles of popular consumption.

Agricultural expansion is feasible. Compared with other Arab countries, Syria has a favorable man-land ratio: one hectare of cultivated land for each inhabitant, or 8 to 9 times as much as Egypt. Cultivable land now uncultivated could accommodate more than double Syria's present farm population. But this remains potential, for, under present methods of cultivation, the land does not now support even its present population. Hence, in the past two decades, peasants have deserted the land to compete for scarce urban jobs. They bypass nearby towns and go to the six large cities, which account for a third of the population. Particularly in Aleppo and Damascus, where nearly one out of four Syrians live, they swarm into slums that blight the Old City and its shanty-town outskirts. The postwar urban building boom went into high-cost European-style housing far beyond the range of displaced peasants. As the wretched overcrowded conditions spread, periodic riots by urban workers demand that government restrict further influx from the villages.

To break the vicious circle, some industrialization will be required. The International Bank Mission estimated that, under favorable circumstances, Syria will have to create at least 20-25,000 new industrial jobs (a 50% increase) during the next six years, just "to keep its industrial labor market in reasonable balance." But this is again a circular problem, for it cannot be tackled until the rural standard is raised: first, to decelerate movement off the land; and second, to support industrial expansion. With modernization also must come the changing lifeways styled by public communication. Here, too, the Syrian means are feeble.

Our exploration in global statistics (chapter II) showed that the institutions of modernity are systemic. Charles Issawi, also with an eye on the Middle East, points out that the 17 currently operative democracies in the world include the 15 nations with the highest per capita income and the most equitable distribution of wealth.[4] Only such nations sustain a modern communication system which interweaves elite and mass perspectives into a national consensus. Syrian poverty and illiteracy limit media development, thereby impeding growth of a vital national center and a participant citizenry. Government awareness of these connections has stimulated efforts to develop a national radio network, but policy has not been effective enough to dominate economics.

In 1949, when the average per capita income was $100, a radio cost an average of $135. Only the rich Damascenes and Aleppans could afford a set.[5] About 50,000 sets (including an estimated 5,000 unlicensed sets) were in use—one for every 60 inhabitants. Collective listening facilities increased some audiences beyond the usual coffeehouse sets. Many Syrian schools and villages have radio loudspeakers for their central meeting places. But national poverty and disorganization hamper the government aim of extending radios to all schools and villages. The limiting factors include inadequate rural electrification, lack of technicians, transport difficulties (which prevent frequent battery recharging), and shortage of hard currency to finance import of equipment. Poverty limits the producing center as well as the receiving periphery. During our survey, four transmitters had been in operation from one to three years, but as yet provided daytime reception only within a radius of 30 to 50 kilometers from the capital and Aleppo.

For many Syrian radio listeners, as a result, London was closer than Damascus. A judge living in the large town of Hama could not hear Damascus as well as Cyprus and BBC. Unlike the British, he said, the Arabs

don't pay much attention and money to have a respectable station. Also the station is not strong enough to be heard well even in Syria. . . . It needs money which the government is not ready to pay. (015)

Many intellectuals were sensitive to the dangers of a domestic communication vacuum, which foreign powers would be eager to fill. Said a wealthy young lawyer from Homs:

In our country we need a good [radio] station . . . so that people don't depend on foreign stations. Because nationalism is feeble in our country we have to build up our means of propaganda and make people enthusiastic about our culture and not depend on the West. (019)

To shore up "feeble" nationalist sentiment and lessen reliance on the West are familiar objectives. But their implementation requires a media system evolved within a matrix of general economic growth.

Similar limitations are shown by Syrian cinema. Damascus and Aleppo account for about half of all cinemas and two-thirds of all seating capacity. Cinema attendance averages about once a year per capita. About 80% of feature films are imported from Western countries (60% from the United States). The single Syrian studio, even with the help of Lebanese capital, produced but one full-length film and a few documentaries as of 1950. Facilities are lacking for subtitling in Arabic or "dubbing" the sound track. This must be done in the country of origin or in Cairo. Foreign films must therefore be *read* to be understood, or the Syrian must adjust to the strange sounds of Egyptian colloquial. Accordingly, Syrian respondents of all classes were less favorably disposed to movies than any other Arabs.

The press also reflects poverty. Syria, with its threefold population, produces far fewer papers than Lebanon. None achieves national circulation and they are held in low esteem by those who are reached. The press run of dailies ranges from 400 to 3,000 copies, "the latter being a maximum under normal conditions. Only in outstanding circumstances, such as a political crisis, do some papers sell as many as 6,000 copies in one day."[6] Impeding growth of a healthy press is the small market of literates—only 30% claim literacy. Recent efforts to expand education can bring an appreciable increment of newspaper readers only very slowly. For, where child labor is commonplace and education (particularly for girls) is devalued, there is great wastage in the educational system. Up to 40% of elementary school pupils leave school before completing their course and never attain "permanent functional literacy"—defined as the ability to read a newspaper and write a simple letter. To achieve this level, it has been estimated, five to eight years of elementary schooling are required.[7] Since mastery of classical Arabic is virtually a new language for Arab children—so great is the gap between written script and colloquial tongue—a sustained training period is essential.

The linguistic problem has special relevance to newspaper consumption. A high-school graduate and municipal clerk said that he did not read *Barq al-Shamal* because "I am not sufficiently strong in Arabic so as to understand it." (207) Though far more educated than most Syrians, he is still a limited consumer of the native press. Those with but a few years of elementary school cannot master enough of their language to understand newspapers.

The limited public capacity to consume messages reinforces the national disunity which has plagued Syria before and since independence. A subsistence farm economy breeds the poverty, the illiteracy, the constrictive psyche of the Traditional—a cluster, we have seen, which predisposes people to remain within the familiar channels of local leadership and to feel alien toward the national center. The absence of consensus between elite and population opens the way to counter-elite formations of the type which unstabilize Syrian politics today. In the next section we shall deal with the counter-elite of "young effendis" who play such a powerful role in Syrian life. To conclude this review of the social setting which produced them, we here look at the governing elite.

The very concept of a Syrian elite requires qualification. The native elite did not exercise sustained authoritative power before 1946; from 1949 to 1958 it was displaced by military dictatorship. During the Mandate, uneasy cooperation between nationalist leaders and the French was regularly punctuated by open rebellion, passive resistance, boycotts on the Syrian side; martial law, constitutional suspension, and bombardment of civilians on the French side. Unable to loosen the French grip, the elite stood by impotently while parts of Muslim Syria were annexed to Lebanon, autonomous areas within the Syrian mandate were established, and Alexandretta was ceded to Turkey. Meanwhile, the French Parliament refused to ratify the 1936 treaty which granted self-rule within the context of an alliance. Only after the British wartime occupation could independence be asserted. Syria, then, had no effective native leadership on the international level until 1946.[8]

In the domestic context, there was a continuous native leadership of sorts. Members or adjuncts of the Syrian plutocracy became self-constituted leaders, under French tutelage, and used their political leverage to entrench their oligarchic interests. Effective power had long been wielded by an elite of "city notables," who derived their wealth from large landholdings which they rarely saw. This class interlapped with the professional class—trained in the law and medical schools of Constantinople, Beirut or Europe —and the wealthy merchants. Many landowners were descendants of the Ottoman elite, which had become a tax-farming class after the original military basis of Ottoman feudalism had deteriorated.[9] The rentiers were peculiarly rapacious; none of the interest in actual cultivation found among the European landed gentry moderated their profit-seeking. Amidst the comforts of urban life, they dabbled in commerce, sent their sons to professional schools, and learned to play the complex game of Arab politics.

The Mandate strengthened their power. Since "the French relied on the collaboration of the wealthy upper class, that is, on the landowners, [they] could make no fundamental reforms in the land system."[10] Various French land reform measures were abortive: e.g., the attempt to extend rural credit. Other virtuous efforts miscarried: e.g., large-scale irrigation that produced more water than was needed in some places and not enough elsewhere. Such basic reforms as secular village education and land tenure reform were barely attempted. Other measures, modifying the protective Ottoman code, buttressed the landlord's position over against the sharecropping tenants: e.g., *waqf* properties formerly held inalienable were sold to businessmen and landowners; the right of ownership after ten years' cultivation, which had put some land in peasant hands, was abrogated. Nor did the urban workers fare better. In 1939, the French opposed labor legislation before the Mandate Commission because "local industrial circles fear the serious consequences which may follow a sudden change in regional tradition and customs if new social legislation is introduced to regulate conditions of labor, child and women labor, and workmen's compensation." The Mandatory did not wish "a servile imitation of the schemes in force in Western industrial countries. . . . Before social laws are issued and the workers are given weapons against their employers . . . the handicrafts should be protected and raised once more to an honored place."[11]

The wealth of the landlord-merchant elite was thus increased by Mandatory policy, while their aspirations for power were constantly thwarted. The French played the classic game of divisiveness. Every internal minority—linguistic, ethnic, regional, religious or nomadic—was encouraged to develop its own case. This deprived the elite core of Damascus nationalists of a constituency in the land. Undermining any potential national center was a policy developed by the Ottomans, who "maintained their authority by exploiting the rivalry of sects and class."[12] The French relied primarily on territorial division, cutting up the Syrian mandate into autonomous sections and reducing the projected Arab state to a small land-locked enclave around Damascus. But political patronage and educational policy also figured as divisive techniques. The particularism of Druzes, 'Alawis and other minorities, strengthened by the Mandatory policy, continued to plague Damascus even after formal unity and independence had been achieved.

National control by the Damascus center also is weakened by the nomad challenge to organized government which has perennially divided the Middle East. Damascus claims that it has reduced the proportion of nomads in the total population from 13% to 3% in 25 years.[13] But restricting their movements is only a start. A new set of thoughtways must develop before the Beduin can be integrated into national life; and a workable relation between farmers and nomads must still be found in the regions too dry to support agriculture. The human transformations needed to make a citizen out of a Beduin are suggested by one respondent:

> Though I have a Syrian passport—still I don't feel I am so. We Beduin are used to a different life and we are primarily loyal to our Amir. We follow him to death and we have 70,000 men with rifles and some machine guns. We can shake the desert if we want. (005)

The lack of widespread national participation in central government shows in the low "circulation of the elite." The original core of landowning nationalists has exhibited amazing homogeneity and longevity. Although postwar authority has had to be shared with exogenous army officers and with assorted extremists of the Right and Left, the same names keep recurring in Syrian parliamentary life. A biographical analysis of about 75 deputies and ministers in the 1936 Chamber of Deputies (the first had been elected in 1932) is still a pertinent guide to the current wielders of power.[14] The elite status of this group is shown by its educational attainment. Fully one-third had professional degrees acquired in France, Switzerland, Damascus and, less frequently, Constantinople and Cairo. Over half had completed secondary studies of some kind, only four reporting no education. That many were able to travel abroad for their education indicates their access to wealth. Of every five deputies in 1936, three were middle-aged (between 37 and 58), one was under 37 and one was over 58. The great majority were Sunni Muslim. The largest occupational group were the landowners. Next were the ex-Ottoman functionaries, many of whom had been displaced by French administrators. Then came 9 lawyers, 6 doctors and 7 merchants (of whom 3 were also landowners). There were no journalists or literary men, engineers or teachers. The deputies had experienced an eventful military and political past. About half had been exiled, imprisoned or forced to flee the country during the Mandatory regime. "Many," Signora Vacca notes, "are stories of administrative and military careers broken by the advent of the Mandate." Twenty deputies had fought as officers on the Ottoman side in World War I. Only six had fought to preserve Faysal's regime from the French, but more had participated as irregulars in the 1925 revolt. Many had been members of the Syrian Congress of 1919-1920, which pressed the claims of Arab nationalism upon the Paris Peace Conference.

A recent analysis of the thirty key political personalities in Syrian politics (excluding army politicians) showed much the same configuration.[15] Many old names recurred, and continuity was indicated by age: 18 were over fifty and 12 were over sixty years of age. Again, landowners, lawyers, and old Nationalist fighters predominated. Personnel makes policy—and it has been aptly said that the Nationalist Bloc, in gaining independence, removed "the only plank in the party's political platform."[16] In internal matters, the national leaders were extremely conservative, resolutely opposed to any program of reform. Although underpopulated Syria was a promising area for Arab refugee settlement, and though impressive American aid would have made refugee integration a great step forward in economic modernization, this proved absolutely unacceptable to the Syrians. Later, in the same spirit, they rejected Point IV aid. The prospect of economic development held no charm for those who feared they might lose power by diffusing wealth.

Only education received vigorous expansion—in one postwar decade showing twelvefold increase in educational expenditure.[17] But activism here was oriented to immediate indulgence of national pride rather than long-term growth. The policy was designed for radical excision of French culture from Syria even if, in the process, the ostensible patient might suffer a severe setback. The language issue was central. The government of Faysal, among its first acts, had declared Arabic to be the sole medium of national communication.[18] Subsequently the French ousted Faysal, and established their language in all state schools and law courts along with Arabic. (They showed some restraint by starting French instruction only in the fourth grade, by which time the Lebanese pupil already used French with some facility.) In 1944, while French troops were still in control of Syria, the newly constituted Nationalist Government abolished the teaching of French in elementary schools and brought pressure upon private schools to do the same. Its aim was to de-Europeanize the state school system and to undermine the foreign schools. Although Syria's only foreign institution of higher education was the American junior college in Aleppo, she had been second only to Lebanon among Arab countries in postwar foreign and private school enrollment. By 1951-1952, with the elementary school population about doubled, the proportion in nongovernment schools had dropped from 40% to 19%[19] This radical rearrangement had been abetted by popular nationalism. When the French bombarded Damascus in 1945, Syrians responded by boycotting all French schools, which then accounted for 83% of the foreign school enrollment. The government then forced all to close and, by 1947, had permitted only seven to reopen.

The survey, five years later, revealed the continuing intensity of this sentiment. A taxi driver declared he would close all foreign schools if he were head of the government. Reason: "We are through with foreigners . . . we don't want any more of them . . . foreign schools teach us not to be patriotic." (227). Capitalizing on such sentiments, the government jettisoned the foreign school system. Standards in public schools were lowered to allow for accelerated expansion. Foreign language study was discouraged, thus depriving Syria of needed Western skills among its citizens.

Such subordination of rationality to pride is common among people frustrated by their status in the modern world and nostalgic for the glories of their Golden Age. Syrian leaders, along with the whole educated class, are occasionally victimized by their own self-congratulatory reading of history. Damascus, which reached the height of its power and culture over a milennium ago, was the proud capital of an empire that extended from the Atlantic coast to the Indus River deep in Central Asia. Muhammad hesitated to enter the city because he wished to set foot in paradise but once.[20] The modern heirs of this past glory had faced the humiliation of being classified as a backward people by descendents of those who had been barbarians at the time of the Ummayyads. The Syrians, in the words of the Mandatory instrument, were "not yet able to stand by themselves under the strenuous conditions of the modern world," and hence their well-being and progress formed "a sacred trust of civilization." The erasure of these rankling words became an overpowering aim. But the elite's obsessional concern with its own status symbols provided no relief for the prevailing poverty and ignorance in its social setting. The rise of an urban counter-elite, which has shaken the old leadership, is abundantly evident today. The 1951 survey provided some illuminating data on this corps of "Young Effendis."

2. The Young Effendis:
From Personal Frustration to Political Extremism

The Turkish elite under Atatürk rapidly integrated the educated urban young men into the new national life, so that the stratum which earlier had supplied elite Ottomans now produced new-style Turks. The design of Turkish modernization built institutions that would incorporate newly participant elements. The Republic thus adapted Ottoman administrative wisdom, which assured political stability by incorporating those who might form the opposition. In Syria, by contrast, the old elite excluded new aspirants and thereby engendered a counter-elite within its own social class. The ruling group paid no heed to the "young effendis"; now they form an active corps which does not recognize the authority of the old national leaders. This has led to a jurisdictional struggle for power which is relatively unproductive of national welfare. Indeed, no long-term policy of modernization can be operated while conflict rages over who will make and who will manage such a policy. (Appendix B reports an independent distribution of modern attributes, which can be compared with the political typology in Table 3.)

The young effendis have been able to challenge the old nationalists so effectively because they occupy a strategic new terrain between the apolitical mass and the ruling oligarchy. This is the terrain of public communication and they occupy it by their location in the sociological middle. In Damascus and Aleppo "a middle class of functionaries and employees has been growing up since 1948. . . . Their flats, between the splendor of the rich quarter and the huddle of the *suq*, are being built in quantities and their

new, middle-class way of life is based on European standards."[21]
These young men are turning away from the Nationalist Bloc to
the radical parties which made their appearance in the November
1949 elections—the Arab Socialist Party, the Resurrection Party,
the Syrian National Socialist Party, the Muslim Socialist Front.
Alternately, they became undercover communist supporters. This
group also supplies new recruits to the army officer corps, which
has been involved in all the postwar political crises. Professor
Khadduri writes:

> Not infrequently high school teachers and lawyers, dissatisfied with
> their professions or believing their ambitions can better be attained in
> the army, enter military schools and resume their public careers in the
> military service.[22]

The course of postwar politics in Syria already has been in-
fluenced by these restless young men who seek status through the
counter-elites. Their influence is likely to grow, for they have shown
their capacity to convert social instability into political crises. The
economics of underdevelopment impels them toward radical ideas.
The number of educated young aspirants for social mobility is
increasing at a much faster rate than the capacity of Syrian institutions to absorb them satisfactorily. Higher education is no longer
the privilege of a small upper class. From 1923 (the first year
diplomas were issued) to 1950 there were 3,334 graduates of the
Syrian University; the number of graduates in 1950-51 alone was
553, fully one-sixth the number of all previous graduates. In 1952-
53, there were 2,580 students enrolled.[23]

Recent development in industry and agriculture has created
shortages of agronomists, engineers, and a range of professional
skills which Syria has been unable to produce at home or to educate abroad. But the educational system continues to produce a
surplus of lawyers and doctors. (The doctors are not surplus to
the country's health needs, but almost all remain in the large cities
and engage in strenuous competition there.) Until 1950, over half
of all university graduates were lawyers. That year, about 600
students who otherwise would have entered the Damascus Law
Faculty were drawn into the newly opened School of Arts, drop-
ping the proportion of law students to one-third of the total. In
all likelihood, however, the Arts graduates are looking for the same
kind of job as the lawyers—a white-collar sinecure in government.
Outside the bureaucracy, there is little opportunity to utilize the

skills acquired by legal or humanistic training. These educated young Syrians predominated in our sample of Moderns, of whom 86% were men, 60% under 30 (only 2% over 50), and 42% Christian (as compared with 14% Christians in the total population). As elsewhere, Syrian Christians are more urban, better educated, and of higher socioeconomic status than the Sunni Muslim majority.[24]

These Moderns live a Western-style life in the manner of the wealthy elite, albeit on a more modest scale. They eat beefsteak and macaroni rather than *burghul* and *shish kebab*; the men wear Western clothes and their women go unveiled (or wear head scarves as a gesture to tradition); their apartments are equipped with Western-style furniture.[25] They pursue the same leisure activities which characterize the Modern style elsewhere, with some minor differences. Fewer spend their leisure in reading or sports. They listen to the radio more than other Moderns. Their musical tastes are more traditional, showing greater fondness for native folk songs and popular tunes than any other Arab Moderns. Only 14%, as compared to 47% Lebanese Moderns, enjoy Western music. Only 15% consider religion of no importance. Only one out of five never attends mosque or church, the lowest proportion of non-attenders among all Moderns (though they attend less *frequently* than Egyptians).

Although more traditional in these ways than other Moderns, they clearly belong to the Westernized stratum of Syria. Those forced to live among peasants feel themselves cut off from the civilized orbit. Thus a village high school teacher complained that "his environment is not high . . . his surroundings were illiterate people that he could hardly communicate with." Although his "salary can hardly cover his expenses," he felt so constricted by village life that he constantly spent "a lot of money" in Aleppo "seeking luxury." (143) A wealthy young judge in the Hama district also stressed the gap between the Moderns and the mass. He found it almost impossible to administer Western legal codes among people used to the rule of custom or of the Koran. The judge said he was unhappy "because I am educated among ignorant people. They can't understand me and I can't do according to their mentality. . . . By myself I can't do anything because it is a huge task to educate a whole nation." (015) The theme of noncommunication between educated and ignorant recurred with great frequency.

Even in a relatively large town like Latakia, the Modern feels isolated. One young landowner, an A.U.B. graduate in political science, said his greatest problem was "how to adapt my environment to myself." He had "passed quite a time in foreign schools and universities. My way of living now is far different. But my environment does not understand this and believes that if, for instance, I listen to classical music it is to show them that I like Western things, not because I really like it—they think it is pretension only." But Arabic music, he declares, has "a bad effect on my nerves. I simply detest it." (210) Thinking of themselves as a true elite, these young Moderns are all the more disgruntled with their own lot and with Syrian politics, neither of which they can control. A thirty-year-old, college-educated secretary was described as "too ambitious" by the interviewer, who suspected his "great confidence in himself and in his talents that will enable him to become once upon a time one of the outstanding personalities in his country." Although this young man occupied a "respectable position," he was discontented because he lacked the income and deference that he believed his education and talents warranted. "Though I am working very hard," he says, "I hardly could secure a decent life. . . . If one has the money, he can do whatever he likes [such as] buy a car, have a better house." (171)

Young bureaucrats appear especially disaffected by the current distribution of wealth and power. Middle East bureaucracy often is "the haven and catch-all for a large portion of the mediocre, partially educated, and less aggressive aspirants for an easy and prestigeful position among the white-collar class."[26] Those more able persons who do get a government job soon feel victimized by an unfair system. Pay is low; advancement depends on favoritism; inefficiency and corruption create a frustrating atmosphere. The International Bank Survey described Syrian bureaucracy as "understaffed in the upper ranks of the service and overstaffed in the lower ranks," since 80% of government employees are concentrated in the three lowest grades of the service.[27]

The bureaucrats and other professionals belong to the ranks of the "spiritually unemployed." Like the frustrated young intellectuals *manqués* who sparked the Nazi movement—which appealed to many restless Syrians—they are not employed in jobs which make them proud or content, and suffer from *seelige Arbeitslosigkeit* (spiritual unemployment). One such young man told the interviewer that he was "not satisfied with his job. He wants to work in Damascus, and he believes that he deserves a higher salary than what he is receiving at present." (040) A 24-year-old junior clerk, in Damascus, is unhappy "because of my bad financial condition and the environment I am living in which I do not like. ... The jobs we can obtain are very limited." (310) Another bureaucrat "is not content with his position because he was not promoted." He says: "I ought to have better backing. Those from good families and who have many people in government get promoted easily. ... It is unfortunate but this is the case everywhere." (012)

Pervasive discontent among ambitious young men indicates a highly immobile elite structure. The junior clerk, when asked what he could do to solve his own and Syria's problems, replied: "I can't do much because nobody will help me and I am all alone." (310) He called "the selfishness of the people and the favoritism that exists in our government" Syria's greatest problem. A senior government clerk, age 27, appeared to have reached a dead end at that age. "He looks useless," the interviewer wrote, "fed up with life, and very weary about his future." His main problem was "the way I get paid, because it is not enough for our standards of living." Asked if he could do anything about this, he answered: "No, because whatever I have to say or do no one would listen. I would only give a bad impression about myself." (130)

Frustration in their private careers was paralleled by despair over the nation's political problems. The young effendis were preoccupied by government weakness; among all classes concern with government instability was greater in Syria than elsewhere. During our survey, early in 1951, Colonel Shishakli had not yet assumed direct personal control of the government. After his *coup d'état* in 1949 he chose to rule through Parliament, allowing the Populist *Sha'ab* Party to organize the Cabinet. Never a majority, the Populists led an extremely unstable coalition, always subject to Army pressure and veto power, until December 1951. In our interviews many respondents reported with pleasure, as their most recent news, that a new Cabinet had finally been presented after a long crisis. But none had illusions that the situation was at all stable; disgust with government was widespread. A well-to-do A.U.B. student declared sweepingly:

I object to everything . . . the present regime of government . . . the army governing Syria . . . the present distribution of incomes, and to the whole way of life which the Syrian people are leading. We need a deep evolution. (044)

Despair often focused upon the press, then under arbitrary control by the military dictatorship. Syrian Moderns were least satisfied among all Arabs with their native press. About 75% preferred that newspapers rather than radio stations be closed down, and 85% of these said that radio is more truthful. Syrian papers, fiercely competitive for a small reading public, cannot depend on circulation revenue for their existence but must resort to a variety of secret or party funds or to blackmail. It was this lack of integrity that most offended the educated respondents. The Hama judge complained: "Editors are not loyal to their conscience . . . they are bribed to give news. We do not have a free press yet." (015) A wealthy A.U.B. graduate, head of a school in Homs, attributed to government the low estate of the press:

The newspapers don't dare mention the facts, because they are afraid of the government. The Press is not free and the people are dead. [Do you have an example?] They would praise a man while he is robbing the people. . . . They talked of Sharabati [Minister of Defense] as if he was the most patriotic and he proved to be the most unreliable and even a thief. This situation is pathetic. . . . When the press is under pressure and the people are ignorant it will have a bad influence. . . . (036)

When it came to specifying remedial measures, the young effendis spoke with less assurance. Some felt powerless, even in imagination, to change the course of the national crisis. Many seemed unable even to define the nature of the problems confronting them. A higher proportion here than elsewhere (indeed a majority of all three types) could give no reason for their inability to solve the nation's problems. Further, Syrians were the most prone among all Arab Moderns to present isolate personal solutions to national problems. A third of them suggested programs that envisaged no support from any existing social group, a perspective that ties in with the proclivity for personal dictatorship expressed by several respondents. The lack of a coherent image of a desirable national future led some to sullen passivity: "Just wait for justice to happen" (179); "Sit and wait what the result will be." (178) Others offered a wild array of prescriptions with little bearing on the problem they had mentioned. A 25-year-old graduate of Aleppo College, who said that Syria's greatest problem is "disorder," would adopt the following program if he were head of government:

> I will build grand theatres.
> I will make parks and gardens.
> I will fight the Jews. (160)

The most prevalent response among the young effendis was advocacy of force and strong moral support for violent dictatorship. The inadequacy of Syrian republicanism had no more poignant testimony than the longing of the most Westernized and enlightened elements for its termination. A schoolteacher, 26 years old and an A.U.B. graduate, described Syria's main problem as "a government that is not permanent." As head of the government: "First I would only make strict laws and reduce the number of parties, renew the laws and *last of all be a dictator.*" (074) A Homs lawyer, who favored social reform, felt that "the whole system of government" was wrong:

> The only way I can do something is to *become a dictator.* A large enlightened minority must take hold of the situation by force. . . . I will aim at the support of the army . . . break down unemployment by opening agricultural projects . . . or else we will stay another 100 years dragging. (019)

The sense that a strong man is needed has diffused through other sects and classes. A retired army sergeant, an uneducated fellow of 60, said that as head of government:

> I would blow up all the government and have a new one that would respect the people and fear God. [How would you do that?] *I would act as a dictator* and educate the people to work for their good. I am not educated and so don't know what is good and what is not. Yet I respect laws and expect the government to respect me. (018)

A retired government official, a rich Catholic who spent three years in Brazil and speaks French and Portuguese, declared: "All the bad things . . . will be corrected by *making a dictator* for a week." (052) A Maronite teacher-priest, who considered Islam the greatest problem of Syria, was resentful that a Christian could not become President. As head of state, "I will cut all relations with the other Arab countries, except Lebanon. I will act according to my own will, because *I believe in dictatorship.*" (008) A 30-

year-old member of the Muslim Brotherhood, still in secondary
school and hopeful of attending law school, called "weak and
despotic government" Syria's greatest problem. As head of state:

> I would have a sword and kill all those in the big chairs in the
> government now. . . . Once I have done that I could *set up a dictator-
> ship* and strike with an iron hand on all who dare move—that is how
> our people understand—and then I would start improvement. (006)

A young housewife said: "It is necessary to have a strong hand
here . . . a *hand of iron* to redress the people and make them ful-
fill their duty." (193) Finally, a Catholic doctor, worried about
"bad government and army control" would "bring back the real
democratic rules and stop the government from taking the bread
of the poor and encouraging the rich to become richer still."
Asked how he would do that, he said: *"If I am head I can just
order."* (053)

The longing for stability underlies the desire for dictatorship
among the young effendis. Middle Easterners many centuries ago
decided that tyrannical government is preferable to no government. They followed Caliphs, even those lacking the spiritual
qualities required for a Defender of the Law, so long as they
were strong. Since the breakdown of the Arab Caliphate, the area
has been plagued by political chaos; frequent interregnums; in-
vasions by Crusaders, Mamluks, Tatars, and Europeans; widespread economic disintegration and population displacements.[28]
In its first 184 years as an Ottoman city, Damascus witnessed no
less than 133 *walis,* of whom only 33 held the office as long as
two years.[29] There is strong historical tradition for the preference
of despotism over instability.

At the time of the survey, the recent defeat by Israel still
rankled and the current government crisis persisted. Thoughts of
violence and dictatorial solutions provided an extropunitive displacement of affect—projecting blame for the troubled domestic
scene onto foreign enemies. Western imperialists, Israel, other Arab
States were the objects of hostility even among young Moderns
who had defined Syria's major problem as internal instability and
corruption. Militarism was strongly advocated by young effendis
with a sense of frustration. If he were head of the government,
a 30-year-old schoolteacher said:

> I will make military service obligatory. . . . Military service is

the best means for training the soul, so that it can face hardships. This is point number one in my program. (040)

Many young intellectuals who gave priority to military might had, aside from this, neither articulate ideas nor concrete programs for Syria's future. But some carried their displaced affect to extremist programs of a quite specific order. Another teacher, a 27-year-old Damascene, declared himself to be frustrated by the dearth of opportunities in Syria. He was unhappy "because I have wanted to get a better education, but have not been able to do so." But Syria's main problem, he said later, was to liberate Palestine from the Jews. He would be willing "to fight in the Army— either live or die." If he were President, he would carry out a "complete rearmament of our army on a very large scale—even if we have to buy the arms from the devil since America is not selling us." (311) Likewise, the lawyer from Hama would "strengthen the Army by alloting 75% of the budget for it. Make an extraordinary tax on rich people for the army. Make a secret treaty with Russia against American interference. . . . I will use a diabolical policy like that of the West." (212)

The young effendis were not uniformly anti-Western. Some, like the Egyptian Moderns, exhibited a characteristic ambivalence, in which desire to emulate and need to reject the West uneasily coexist. In their personal lives, they self-consciously imitate the Western style and some ingenuously admit its tutelage. A "progressive" young government clerk said:

When we see the lives of people in the West, and then compare it with our own lives, we find that we still have a long way to go before attaining their level. The movies are . . . like a teacher to us, who tells us what to do and what not. (310)

Many, however, must belittle the Other in order to esteem the Self. One young teacher, unhappy with his job, his residence, his modest income, nevertheless advocated military expansion rather than economic improvement for Syria. National duty and personal desire contest within him. Syria's "lack of political, social and spiritual unity" depresses him; by contrast, "the U.S. is a rich country in everything. The average worker there owns a motor-car. . . . I wish I could live there." He then caught himself and added: "I mean I wish I was born an American. Because, being a Syrian, I feel that it is my duty to remain in my country. Unless I help her, I will not feel that I am very happy."

Ambivalence requires that this desire to emulate be counter-balanced by a sign of rejection—even a vicarious rejection. Accordingly, this teacher eagerly consumes anti-Western communications. His favorite newspapers "speak nothing in favor of the European countries. [How do you feel about it?] I feel a sort of mental satisfaction, or call it if you wish spiritual satisfaction." He prefers Egyptian films for the same reason. His favorite film depicted a Westernized villager who "is very straightforward while his cousin, who wears native clothes, is still shy and backward in his manners. You see a contrast there between the East and the West." The modern fellow's sister, educated in the city and returned to her village against her will, is persuaded by her brother to marry her old-fashioned cousin. "In the films of Yousef Wihbi," the teacher explains, "the East always wins over the West. . . . I feel a kind of satisfaction." (040)

A Syrian Tito: Preliminary Sketch. The ambivalent young effendi driven to extremism is a major Syrian figure. His final portrait is not yet drawn. But a preliminary sketch emerges from the 1951 interview with a government clerk, 25 years old, a Damascus Sunni living in modest circumstances (246). When asked his main personal problem, he replied with an explicitness that bespoke frequent brooding upon his bad luck:

> In the first place I could not finish my studies, then I could not get a position I desired, and thirdly, I could not bring my girl back with me [back from Paris], and lastly my financial condition is not very helpful.

His sequence of abortive starts recalls the "uncompleted life activities" that characterized the life-histories of those young neo-intellectuals who became the "armed bohemians" of the Nazi elite.[30] His dissatisfactions were sharpened by his two years of engineering study in France, which terminated because he lacked funds. Back in Syria, he soon found company among the footloose young effendis who, lacking productive and satisfying uses for their abilities and aspirations, spend their time merging fantasies of personal desire and national policy. Their problem, as he put it, is "thinking about their future—that is, the uncertainty of knowing what our future is to bring." The prevalence of revery in this young man's life, the dissociation from his current time-place situation, is signified by the total absence of institutional ties to his society. He belongs to no social groups, considers religion of no importance, and can find no Arab girl he would care to marry. He would like to go back to France, but cannot afford it. Although he calls America a "cheap democracy," he would go there "on condition I become an American."

Frustrated in their personal careers, many young effendis tend to seek power and glory through political maneuver. This young bureaucrat, however, apparently combines the usual grandiose desires for political power with a real position of personal influence among his peers. According to the interviewer, he is the "recognized head of his quite large group of young men who are about to form a party . . . having as slogan Arabism above everything else." This "opinion leader" thus describes his own program: "I would like to make Syria a really socialistic state, and try to approach Russia, in order to get rid of the influence of the Western powers—in other words I would make a second Yugoslavia of Syria and would be its Tito." Like many respondents of this type whom we have quoted, his view of democracy in a "socialistic state" requires uniform acquiescence to *his* beliefs rather than a free exchange of competing ideas. To instill "the proper public attitude" is Syria's greatest need: "We should give the public the proper political and social attitude, by educating them and showing them the right attitude."

The counter-elite orientation guides the media behavior of this young man and his followers. His preferred newspaper is *al-Nasr,* which, he says, is read "by the government officials in particular and the middle class in general. Because it gives us the latest changes in government positions and does not write too much about our so-called aristocracy." His autobiography is externalized in his proto-communist program: "to evenly distribute the national wealth in the country." He believes that Russian propaganda is doing an excellent job, that Russia is successful in world affairs "and will continue to be so, until these social differences which exist in our countries are done away with . . . their system of life is one where everybody gets equal shares, and people want this life today."

Although he overtly repudiates the ruling elite, he shares their outlook in many respects. Second only to redistribution of wealth is his desire to "strengthen the Arab cause, in general to build up a new Arab world, renewing its past glories." The interviewer notes that "although he likes foreigners, and in particular the French, he still believes in drifting away from Western influence." In part this is a reaction against a world which is perceived as indifferent (or hostile): "We cannot depend on any country to help us, for all of them have imperialist motives regarding us." It is intelligible also as a step in the search for a national identity. Here the would-be Tito exhibits symptoms of the "Nasser syndrome." If he were head of a radio station he would not worry about the domestic audience. "I believe we have enough things for the local population to listen to," he remarks, disregarding the vast communication vacuum in which a majority of his compatriots live. He would rather pursue foreign adventures, by stressing overseas broadcasts: "[We] should not neglect to inform foreign countries of our presence, and give them our news and ideas just as they give us theirs."

Such disaffected young men, with little hope of advancement under the present social order, provide the counter-elite cadres of political extremism. They accent the incoherence, instability, and confusion which prevail in the Syrian political scene. As their ideology is a displacement of personal desires onto public issues, with minimal analytic content, any demagogic appeal that promises self-advancement is likely to elicit a response among them, whether from the extreme Right or Left. Their special combination of Leftist populism and Rightist nationalism has become a useful instrument of popular agitation throughout the Arab arena. The once dissonant themes of nationalist dictatorship and populist socialism now are orchestrated by the young effendis as the New Harmony.

Few among these challengers of existing institutions invoke the symbols of a more participant, more democratic social order. In their eyes, democracy has been discredited in Syria. The young men want to be dictators, whether as head of a Communist satellite, a Military cabal, a Fascist party, or a National Socialist state. They begin by displacing their personal frustrations onto political objects; they continue by constructing extremist ideologies of the national welfare; and they end by tying national aspirations to the shifting of world politics. Hence the paradox that those who claim to promote national welfare often wind up by seeking foreign adventures which are likely to impede the course of Syrian modernization. Even the Syrian Tito, starting from the desire for an autonomous national policy independent of foreign entanglements, comes to the same end. Syrians apparently have come to see their national future as inevitably tied to world politics. Many, indeed, have hitched their wagon to one of the bipolar stars.

The young effendis have played a role in this process. Ranging themselves as a counter-elite, they reduced the chances of stable central government by embracing a strategy of oppositionism. This obliged them—once they had projected their domestic frustrations into the world arena—to oppose the foreign policy of the government they had rejected. The obvious opposite of official pro-Westernism was a radical pro-Russianism. Some of the young effendis were uneasy about this bipolarity—an ambivalence rooted in a taste for Western culture and branching into Syrian variants of Titoism. Others associated the "primitive Bolshevism" of their predilection for violence and dictatorship with the current ideology of the U.S.S.R. As the young effendis occupy key posts in Syrian public communication—as teachers, journalists, civil servants, lawyers and judges—their ideas get a wide hearing. Pro-Russian sentiment has become highly visible in Syria during the years since the survey was made. But the data contain some clues to the pattern of diffusion. To these we now turn.

3. A Typology of Political Attitudes*

The attitudes of the young effendis indicated that pro-Russian sentiment would not be located in simple socioeconomic packages. This was demonstrated by classifying all respondents who expressed pro-Russian attitudes according to their economic status, as in Table 1. Clearly, as many "well-off" as "destitute" respondents ex-

Table 1—Pro-Russian Attitudes

Rich	31%
Well-off	44
Modest	30
Poor	25
Destitute	45

* This section is based on the 1952 BASR report "Syrian Attitudes Toward America and Russia" by W. N. McPhee and R. B. Meyersohn. The account here given is highly condensed in anticipation of a fuller report by the authors.

pressed pro-Russian attitudes, and "poor" respondents least of all. Moreover, the tone and content of the utterances ranged from simple sentiment to doctrinaire dogmatism.

To deal adequately with these responses required a more comprehensive context of political attitudes. Five questions asked in the interviews had consistently provided, as we saw in preceding chapters, a useful guide to the respondent's political posture. These were:

1. What is the biggest problem that people in the same circumstances as yourself face in life?
2. Is there anything that you as an individual can do to solve this problem?
3. What would you say is the biggest problem that Syria as a nation faces today?
4. What do you think people in the same circumstances as yourself can do to help solve this problem?
5. Suppose you were made head of the government, what are some of the things you would do?

A qualitative analysis was made of responses to this battery of questions. Respondents were classified first as Right or Left—according to the type of problems which were salient to them. Right respondents were concerned mainly with problems of the *national posture;* Left respondents gave priority to problems of *social reform.* Each group was then subdivided into three ranks of extremism, and respondents were classified by the degree of violence they proposed for solving the problems they had named. For example, all Left respondents worried about the inequitable distribution of wealth—but a mild Reformer would "pass an income tax" whereas an extreme Revolutionary would "hang the landlords!" Similarly, all Right respondents were concerned with national prestige—but a mild Conservative proposed new elections whereas an extreme Nationalist demanded violence ("Kill the the foreigners!" or "War against Israel").

This produced six types of political attitudes cross-classified by content and by intensity. A seventh type of respondent saw public problems only in a personal light, like Traditionals everywhere in the Middle East, and these were classified as Apolitical. On this typology, 251 Syrian respondents distributed as shown in Table 2.

Table 2—Political Types

Revolutionary Left	6
Middle Left	40
Reform Left	45
Apoliticals	38
Conservative Right	47
Middle Right	44
Nationalist Right	31
Total	251

In studying these figures, the reader must recall our oft-repeated caution that no extrapolation can be made from such distributions to the national distribution of pro-Communist or other political attitudes in Syria today. We are dealing only with the distribution of attributes within the controlled sample of political types. This gives us a "profile" for each type. Where differences are clear-cut, one may infer that such a "profile" will tend to be associated with persons of each political type throughout Syria.

Table 3 shows the distribution of relevant social attributes among the political types and links them with our basic typology of modernization. The Apoliticals correspond most closely to the Traditionals in our basic typology. They show the largest profile of rural, illiterate, destitute and nonparticipant persons among the political types. They discuss the issues facing Syria in the constrictive style of Traditionals. A housewife said: "I know only about my town and about Homs, but I don't know about the country." A village grocer retorted crisply: "It [Syria's problems] is none of my business. For whom do you take me? Please stop such stupid questions." (269) A male hairdresser, unable to generalize from his personal unhappiness to the class struggle, is "very unhappy" because "I am illiterate and so can understand nothing about life. Another thing that makes me unhappy is my inability to teach my only son, and I can't find the way how to do this." He is baffled by public problems. Asked what he would do as head of the government, the hairdresser replied: "This can't be. . . . I wouldn't know what to do. Even the greatest philosopher can't answer this." (029)

The Transitionals, in Syria, produce the political types of the extremist Right and the Middle Left. They include fewer illiterate, destitute and nonparticipant persons than the Apoliticals, but rather more than the other types. An interesting reversal occurs on place of residence. The Nationalist Right is mainly rural; the Middle Left mainly urban. As these depressed social groups move out of the classic apolitical stance of Traditionals, the direction they take is conditioned by their immediate environment. The rural peasant tends to adhere to the Right symbolism of national posture, while the urban laborer is more attracted to the social class symbolism of the Left. That the Transitional group splits in this way may follow from Syria's past political instability—the cleavage within the elite and the consequent lack of a unifying, consensus-creating national center.

The cleavage within the elite is reflected in the fairly even distribution of Modern attributes between the more moderate elements on both the Left and Right. The profiles exhibited by respondents classified as Conservative Right and Reform Left are more like each other than like any others. (The Middle Right are so close as to be grouped sociologically with the Conservative Right; the Revolutionary Left, with only six members, must be discussed separately.) These moderate respondents are the least illiterate and most educated, the least destitute and most well-off.

Table 3—Social Attributes of Political Types*

| | POLITICAL TYPES | | | | | | |
| | LEFT | | | APOLITICALS | RIGHT | | |
SOCIAL ATTRIBUTES	Revolu-tionary	Mid-dle	Re-form		Conserva-tive	Mid-dle	Nation-alist
Place of Residence							
Urban	50%	67%	42%	38%	55%	50%	35%
Rural	50	33	58	62	45	50	65
Education							
Illiterate	0	31	13	58	9	16	39
Elementary School	50	43	38	34	25	27	32
High School	17	8	27	5	41	25	16
College	33	18	22	3	25	32	13
Socioeconomic Status							
Poor or Destitute	33	62	24	60	18	25	35
Modest	50	23	44	26	42	43	42
Well-off or Rich	17	15	32	14	40	32	23
Media Participation							
Read Newspapers	83	45	87	18	87	66	49
See Movies	83	47	73	48	72	68	58
Hear Radio	67	57	84	50	72	73	68

* Appendix B presents an independent reclassification of the Syrian respondents according to the Empathy Index used in the basic typology of modernization. The results show the close correspondence with this political typology.

They are by far the most participant in all three media of news-papers, movies, radio. What unifies these people of similar back-ground is their personal style of moderation; what divides them is the secondary symbolism of ideology.

When the moderate elite of a nation is split by doctrinal dis-sensus, its public forum tends to be invaded by extremist symbols from both sides. Only six representatives of the Revolutionary Left appeared in the 1951 sample of 251 respondents. (This proves nothing whatsoever about the size of the Syrian C.P. then or now: political *affiliations* were not investigated; no special effort was made to sample C.P. *members*; these are usually reluctant, in any case, to be interviewed under non-Party auspices.) Their socio-logical profile merely conforms to the analyses, published else-where by official political observers, that Syrian Communism is promoted mainly by a middle class intelligentsia: the Soviet ex-pert, Mrs. L. M. Vatolina, cites "journalists, writers, artists, law-yers" as key figures; the U. S. Congressional investigating committee concluded that "active Communists come mainly from the middle class, in a few instances from the well-to-do."[31] What the six cases show, beyond this, is that both urban and rural Revolutionary Left-ists are literate (the only type with no illiteracy) and extremely high media participants.

This, however, may be the nub of the story. The suggestive value of these few cases lies in the unanimity of their opinions and the intensity with which they are expressed. If ideological extremism is invading the Syrian political arena, and if media participation is a channel for diffusing its symbols, then these six cases may illustrate how this process operates.

This gives us the more comprehensive context needed to ex-amine pro-Russian attitudes in the sample. Respondents were classi-fied as pro-Russian or pro-American according to the answers they gave when asked their views on the policies and peoples of these two countries. The ratio of pro-Russians to pro-Americans was then tabulated in Table 4 for each of the seven political types.

Several features of this distribution are noteworthy. In every type there is some division of opinion—except that the six Revo-lutionaries are unanimous. In every divided type the pro-Ameri-cans outnumber the pro-Russians except among the Nationalists. Even the Middle Left is relatively less pro-Russian than the Ex-treme Right. Hence, if a line were drawn connecting the pro-

Russian bars for each type, the result would approximate a U-shaped curve. (Note that the Nationalist Right included the most non-respondents on these questions. If their unexpressed attitudes reflect the same ratio as between expressed attitudes, the U-shaped curve would be more distinct.) Recent studies have shown that a U-shaped curve is often a sign of current instability and incipient change in the attitude so distributed. When the extremes converge upon the middle from both sides, the middle is likely to shift its ground—particularly when, as in the present case, the middle is characterized by moderate measures and the extremes by violence. The hindsight of 1958 indicates that pro-Russianism has, in fact, spread since the survey was made. What do the interviews of 1951 reveal about the role of the extremists?

Table 4—Pro-Russians and Pro-Americans

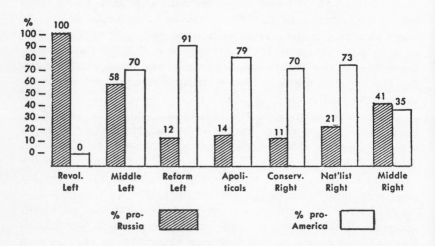

NOTE: Percentages were computed by dividing the number of respondents expressing favorable attitudes by the total number expressing any attitudes.

Taking the extreme Right first, the Nationalistic type was composed of 31 respondents. Table 3 showed them to be mainly poor, illiterate farmers. Additional data showed that 84% are Muslims, most of them devout, who live in relative isolation from urban contacts. These people come closest to fitting the stereotype of "xenophobic Arab." They exhibit extreme hostility and aggressiveness toward all foreigners. In the aftermath of the Palestine defeat this was focused on Israel, but included the Western powers as well. A farm account-keeper, as head of the government would "unite all the Arabs and endeavor to get Britain and its Jewish crooks out of all Arab lands because they are corrupting our lives." (155) A woman, who named "war with the Jews" as Syria's biggest problem, called for a war that would restore the national honor:

It is not difficult because with courage and patriotism nothing is difficult. . . . [We can help by] encouraging people to enroll . . . to enlist in the Army . . . by showing them the beauty of a glorious death. (193)

Another woman would "hate [to live in America] as I hate hell . . . because they brought us the Jews here." (278) A farmer, asked where he would live if he had to leave Syria, answered: "A million curses on these and their country, these Jews, these low, uncivilized people. To live there would be hell for any Arab." (103)

Such resentment against the West led to pro-Russian attitudes among Nationalistic respondents aware of the bipolarity in world politics and determined to make *it* serve *their* ends. This readiness to take extreme, and even violent, measures occurred among those who expressed Nationalistic ideology with maximum intensity. Since they gave undisputed priority to Nationalistic goals, they were ready to subordinate even doctrinal disputes with communism to achieve these goals. This accounted for their pro-Russian sentiments, which were animated less by admiration for the USSR than by animosity toward the West. Following the old Arab adage of tribal politics—the enemy of my enemy is my friend —the extreme Nationalists supported the idea of a Syrian alliance with the Soviets. Some, mainly Arab refugees from Palestine, even endorsed the idea of a Communist regime in Damascus. (The question occurs, in passing, who spread these ideas and how?) One such refugee stated this extreme position concisely: "I will fight the Americans who ruined my country and the best way to fight them is to have this regime of Communism spread everywhere." (193) Through such a dialectic, some extreme Rightists found themselves in accord with all extreme Leftists on a general pro-Russian sentiment.

The extreme Leftists, however, arrived at their attitude by quite another dialectic. Among the Revolutionaries, specific pro-Russian orientation and general ideology are equivalent. The six respondents of this type included four professionals (two lawyers and two government clerks), a shopkeeper and a carpetweaver. As the attitudes of radical intellectuals are more familiar, we look more closely at the two others. The carpetweaver said: "We live like animals and see nothing but the loom and poverty." (022) Unlike the Apolitical hairdresser, who was unhappy that he could not educate his son but had no idea what could be done about it, the carpetweaver sees the solution of personal misery in terms of class conflict. Asked the standard final question, what he thought of such interviews as this, his hostility erupted at the well-dressed and highly-educated young interviewer: "Why should *you* go to the Universities and study, while *my* children start working at ten years of age?" This man is not only unhappy and aware that others are better off, but he is prepared—at least verbally—to do something about it: "When the need comes, I will rise up and with as many as possible, change the government and have a fair rule for everyone." The symbolism of Class rather than Nation consistently motivates the carpetweaver. He would live in Russia because:

I would choose any country where I am treated and have equal rights as anybody else. I would choose Russia, because there each is given all facilities of life and insurance of the family and illness and is treated in all ways like the most important men.

Similarly, the small shopkeeper says that Syria's problem is "Poverty, my poverty and the poverty of my community, with nobody to care." (013) He, like the carpetweaver, differs from others who complain of personal deprivations by his intense involvement and violent prescriptions. The shopkeeper would "hang all those who have been ruling in the last ten years and take their lands and distribute them among the needy." He would live in Russia because:

I prefer to live any place where the proletariat class is ruling . . . because it is then democratic and the majority is ruling . . . and there are no poor people.

The Communist representation of the world has reached these men. They see Russia as an egalitarian social system, and America as a class society which oppresses the poor: "[America] is a country where a few live at the expense of 130 million people, so I don't want to be one of these poor victims." When they criticize American foreign policy they use the Communist slogans of anti-imperialism, not the anti-Israel slogans of the Rightists.

The impact of class symbols diffused by such forthright and vigorous spokesmen of embattled poverty as the carpetweaver and shopkeeper can be great. In each type, there are some respondents who express pro-Russian attitudes. On the Left, this is often an aggrieved proletarian or artisan who has begun to seek political solutions for his personal problems. In such cases the idea that there is a Russian balm for Syrian hurts is clearly defined. But a similar idea has appeared also among the impoverished workers and peasants of the Right. Said one pro-Russian hotel worker of the Nationalistic type: "Russia is good for the poor like me. Everyone finds work there and can live. It is far away, but if one is taken there, he can work." (295) A peasant woman of the same political type said:

> I think I heard of this country . . . a man told us there was a country called Russia who helped the poor, where there are no rich people. . . . I hear this country helped the poor, so I love her because she feels with us. (194)

We note that the hotel worker, though a Nationalist, speaks "for the poor like me." The peasant woman mentions that "a man told us . . ." Who was "the man"? Who were "us"?

For "telling" such people through the traditional channels of oral communication, the articulate carpetweaver and shopkeeper make excellent relays. Moreover, as Table 3 showed, media participation has spread among the political types. Only the Apoliticals fail to show a majority of participants in all three media. Elsewhere, media participation and political involvement have grown together. This has transformed the situation as of 1924, on which Professor Hitti has provided expert testimony: "The Syrian is the man without a country *par excellence*. His patriotism takes the form of love for family and sect [and] has no political aspects. . . . Radicalism has no votaries among this people. Very few of them interest themselves in politics." A generation later politization has increased and, abetted by the media, both nationalist and radical symbols have their votaries.

Whether they are turning Right or Left, the Apolitical ranks seem to be thinning. The process is slow because few established parties have recruited them. Even the Communists and the *Ba'ath* have believed, in Hourani's words, that fellahin and laborers "are too unenlightened to have much effective sense of grievance or capacity for political or economic combination."[32] This estimate doubtless *has been* right, but the data show that the situation is changing. Although some Traditionals stolidly accept their deprivation, others are being stirred out of their ancient lethargy and are caught up in the new ideological currents. As yet, political attitudes do not appear to have formalized into political organizations. The *types* reported here, in any case, do not correspond with *party* affiliations. The types represent, rather, a fund of latent political sentiments which remain to be articulated in political action. The prospects, judged from the record of the past decade, are not bright for those who prefer modernization through rational planning rather than violent change.

4. The Politics of Insecurity

Syria's odyssey in the decade since independence exemplifies the degeneration of politics into violence. Although parliamentary government was formally interrupted for only three years, at no time did the Chamber of Deputies have much weight in the actual process of decision. A series of external struggles provided the substance of the parliamentary shadow play. The struggle between forces seeking to align Syria with Egypt or with Iraq was primary; its other face was the Great Power competition for Middle East influence. Interlocked were the complex plots to draw blood-revenge from Israel in a "second round"; the conflict between landlord-merchant elite and army reformers for domestic control; and the increasingly complicated competition between parties, factions, and extremist groups of the Right and Left. Minimum stability has been imposed through government by *coups d'état*. Lacking a unified elite to administer it, or a genuine constituency to be administered, national power became the object of palace politics amid popular apathy. The public role was played by staged demonstrations instead of voluntary participation. This led to the violent consequences described by Professor Lasswell in general terms:

> Where means of peaceful influencing are not at hand, and deprivations are widespread, attempts at enforcing accountability are likely to end in coercion, whether in the form of assassination, uprising, sabotage, or civil disobedience.[33]

The decade passed through three phases—breakdown of civil government; military rule with interludes of civilian cooperation;

restoration of the *ancien régime* with the cue-giving military hovering in the wings. As in Iran, open destruction of the constitutional facade made representative government, when restored, even more precarious than it had been. Syria, after the spate of military dictatorships, was ruled by an old elite more discredited than ever. Huge social sores had been made visible to the public eye, thenceforth to be less passively accepted. Extremist attitudes flourished. The current (1958) scene reflects the ascendancy of extremism. To see how Syria got where it is, we summarize the three phases of the past decade.

Phase 1: Breakdown of Civil Government. The Arab defeat in Palestine catalyzed military revolutions in both Syria and Egypt—where elite corruption and conservatism had already alienated the politically aware. A basic error of propaganda strategy compounded the effects of the Palestine war. The Syrian press never reported Arab reversals, but confidently predicted the speedy liquidation of Israel.[34] The public was completely unprepared when the Arab defeat could no longer be suppressed, particularly as hundreds of thousands of Palestinian refugees poured in from the south. When a propaganda strategy of deception is caught up by reality, the boomerang can be disastrous.[35]

The March 1949 *coup d'état* of Colonel Husni al-Za'im sought to vindicate the army's role in Palestine, placing the onus for defeat on civilian venality.[36] A further aim was to forestall a plan for merger with Iraq that distraught President Shukri al-Kuwatli, faced with town riots and parliamentary crises, favored. The army's assertion of power met with popular approval and the enthusiastic backing of the disaffected intelligentsia.[37] But before the year was out, both Za'im and his successor had been removed and executed. A third military dictator, Colonel Adib Shishakli, stepped up to interpret the "irresistible will of the people" until such time as they had acquired sufficient "political sophistication" to be "entrusted with power."[38]

Phase 2: The Army in Control. The longest and most significant postwar military regime was that of Colonel Shishakli, who ruled from spring 1949 until February 1954. His regime reflected the ardent nationalism, the vaguely-articulated reformism, the deep-rooted authoritarianism of the young effendis—whom it pleased by launching an excoriating attack on the displaced elite. Its major policy statements (issued by his front-man, General Fawzi Selo) denounced the old politicians as "hardhearted oppressors" who had "pampered the whims and desires of factious groups and parties . . . making the winning of a cheap popularity their only motive and not caring in the least for the terrible price that had to be paid."[39] The Army was pledged to "work for the transformation of Syria into a modern and progressive country in which there shall be no master and no slave but absolute justice and assured freedom."[40]

Between the vision and the achievement of an apocalypse lie many pitfalls, particularly if speed is essential and planning is inept. The tempo of social change in Syria has always been leisurely—e.g., the cadastral survey for land reform was started in 1923; thirty years later it was half completed.[41] Said Shishakli: "Our reform needs to be done quickly." Out of his offices poured hundreds of reform decrees that quickly transformed Syria—on paper. No sense of historical sequence guided this regime. A plan to engage a Spanish musician, to elevate the musical taste of Syrians, jostled decrees abolishing parties and regulating the civil service.[42] No knowledge of governing technique tempered the belief (which our interviews found prevalent among the Syrian intelligentsia) that reform can be *decreed* by a military dictator.

Shishakli's proposed reforms threatened to destroy utterly the landlord-merchant oligarchy. Plans to distribute among landless fellahin the state domain held illegally by powerful landowners, to impose a progressive income tax, and to organize agricultural credit—all these decreed simultaneously—caused landowners and others fearful of radical change to close ranks in opposition. Against this show of unity, Shishakli lacked the communication resources to mobilize effective support by persuasion when coercion alone was no longer enough to save him and his program. Although dubbed the Syrian Atatürk by impressionable foreign observers, Shishakli failed to emulate the Turkish dictator in communication techniques. Professor Khadduri has observed:

[Arab army leaders] failed to understand that the Kemalist regime was not established· overnight, by entrusting power to the military, but that Kemal from the beginning made it clear to his fellow army officers that they had to choose between the army and politics. He launched his social reforms in the formative period by democratic methods, spending endless hours in trying to persuade his opponents, displaying patience and tolerance rarely to be found among statesmen with a military background.[43]

Atatürk, who did not hesitate to use force when tactically necessary, knew how to use argument, propaganda, education and speeches (his six-day speech to the Grand National Assembly in 1927 was only an extension of his usual procedure). Shishakli had little thought for the "endless hours" needed to persuade political waverers and opponents. He approached the public rarely and "only under formal circumstances surrounded by the panoply of the Army."[44] Seeking to exercise absolute power without accepting popular responsibility, he failed on both counts. To avoid the taint of personal aggrandizement (which had contributed to Za'im's downfall) he represented himself as the "neutral pivot" in a society ridden by dissension—requiring the support of all moderates and reserving to himself only the ultimate sanction. But the logic of politics finally forced him to manifest his power overtly by dissolving Parliament, abolishing parties (except for his Arab Liberation Movement) and revising the Constitution. Like his two predecessors, he reinforced Syrian disillusion with Western institutions by cynically manipulating the forms of free government.

At the time of the interviews, Shishakli had not yet dissolved Parliament. But our respondents correctly assumed that the army, not the politicians, were in control and already there was resentment. By "gangster techniques" he was eliminating rivals and creating an atmosphere of fear and uncertainty (of which, after a score of assassination attempts, he was as much victim as creator).[45] An interviewer in northern Syria wrote:

I heard that after I had finished this interview rumors started to go around that I belong to F.B.I. looking for Communists. Others said I want to take their sons to Korea. The atmosphere is not calm at all in this area. . . . Although I had explained the matter and purpose of the interview, yet people were very skeptical about it. And any time the name of any big power or the name of their government is mentioned, you feel that they are not at ease and give short, dry answers. This is the attitude I met with most of the non-educated class. (271)

In Damascus, reportedly riddled by petty spies and informers, such feelings were also widespread among the educated interviewees.

Like Nasser, Shishakli longed for "serried ranks" as he led Syria toward his version of the future. Instead, faced with chaotic opposition from a volatile people, his increasing repressions only stiffened resistance. Students, refugees and workers staged recurrent mob demonstrations; civil servants struck for higher pay; the parties, the press, the landlord associations and the Muslim Brethren sought to undermine his position. Nationalist gestures —such as rejection of foreign aid—failed to placate the articulate sections of the public. Finally, Damascus lawyers, Homs students, and Druze tribesmen (acting separately) prepared the way for the Army revolt that overthrew Shishakli.[46]

Phase 3: The Aftermath. After Shishakli was deposed (and his constitution, party and collaborators eliminated) the old power elite resumed control, first under 89-year-old Hashim Atassi, then with Shukri al-Kuwatli in the Presidency he had held five years earlier. The post-Shishakli period has been characterized by feverish alignments in the Arab and bipolar arenas. Presidential elections, assassinations of notables, massings of demonstrators have occurred in an atmosphere of xenophobic insecurity and governmental instability.

Communist growth was one of the unwitting accomplishments of the Shishakli regime. In the 1954 elections (the fairest ever held) decay of the two older parties was evident in their failure to win more than 45 out of 142 seats. Independent deputies, tending to be neutralist in foreign policy and obstructionist in domestic politics, were in the majority. The radical parties, gaining support among the officer corps, scored impressively with 16% of the seats. The most portentous result was the election of the head of the Communist Party, the first official Communist deputy in the Arab world and "one of the most forceful and influential members of the Chamber."[47] This stimulated the persistent infiltration of Communists into radical parties and army officer circles; it helped to spread an array of front organizations "for practically all academic professions, writers, artists, women and youth organizations." A Soviet expert considers Syria as the Arab country most likely to go Communist by means of an internal coup.[48]

Intellectuals provide the backbone of Communist organization. Since the Syrian bourgeoisie is regarded as a necessary (although unreliable) ally at the present stage of Communist development, class-struggle themes are muted and nationalist goals emphasized. This encourages disillusioned young effendis, including the army officers, to seek Communist comfort for their despair with contemporary Syria. The Communist Party, the best organized party in Syria today, indoctrinates the educated groups through four dailies and a host of other publications. These groups become its oral relay for wider diffusion of the Communist message.[49]

The future of Syrian politics hinges on the Communist campaign to broaden its social base. In the past, traditional peasants and laborers were bypassed by the Marxist effendis. A 1951 report to the Central party command said:

Nearly 75% of [Party] activity, whether in propaganda, organizing or daily work, has been confined to petty bourgeois elements in cities and villages on the one hand and selected workers on the other. . . . But the broad masses of workers and fellahin have received hardly any attention.[50]

The tactical necessity of bourgeois participation, it continued, must not obscure the ultimate aim of "mass organizations of a peasant character, i.e., composed of the peasants themselves." The psychic hurdles confronting Syrian Communists were illustrated:

Our comrades in certain rural districts misunderstood, and when they were told to strive to organize mass movements . . . of fellahin under the name of "The Salvation of the Fellah," they began to constitute in the city a committee of intellectuals . . . and called it "The Committee for the Salvation of the Fellah." They did not understand that the main aim of fellah organization is to organize the fellahin themselves and attract their broad masses to the struggle for their demands against the feudalists and the government.

Communist success in mobilizing the hitherto apolitical masses remains problematic. In 1951, disbelief in the fellahin's capacity to enter the political arena was common among Syrian intellectuals. One respondent, a rich 24-year-old A.U.B. graduate, summarized his experience in the *Ba'ath* party, which has backed radical land reform and recruited peasants, in these words:

The people who should revolt against the land-tenure system are illiterate and don't know anything about the conditions under which they are living. They do not have any idea about social, political and economic equality. They take everything as being the will of God. (044)

The interviews with these Traditionals suggest, as we showed earlier, that their historic nonparticipation has been changing rapidly. It was natural that the urban intelligentsia, who rarely mingle with the fellahin and unskilled laborers, should in 1951 have underestimated the extent to which political issues have diffused among the masses. Responsible leaders of radical parties are not likely to make this error today. In the current situation, extremists can take heart.

*   *   *

In March 1958, when I revisited Syria, the United Arab Republic was newly installed and Syrian extremism had taken another turn under Egyptian guidance. Nasser's official brand of Arab Nationalism was in command and the leader of Syrian Communism, Khalid Bakdash, had departed hastily for Moscow, where he remains. A prominent banker in Damascus told me: "So long as it's only politics that's involved, the new setup is fine. We must be careful not to attempt any brusque changes in the economics of our countries. After all, the Egyptians are not very intelligent in these matters. Their economy must be run by the central government; ours flourishes under private management. If we do not try to change things too fast, the new Union may work out."

An important merchant said: "We could do with a little less politics in Syria for a while. Maybe now the students will go to their classes at the University occasionally and normal commerce will become possible." A Christian university coed told me, as I was leaving Damascus: "I hate it here; I'd rather be in Beirut. A woman is so restricted here. Nothing is changed by this new politics."

A transitory visitor could hardly agree that "nothing" had changed. What remained the same was the problem of maintaining tempo and balance in the changes everywhere visibly occurring. Could Nasser solve the thorny problems of Syrian extremism—could he provide mobility for the young effendis while maintaining stability in the society?—this was the great question. He had clearly, since 1957, improved the odds by ranging Syrian extremism within a more unified cadre behind a stronger leader. The new question was: Would they stay there?

IX.

Jordan: One State with Two Peoples

"Who taught you tender Bible tales
Of honey-lands, of milk and wine?
Of happy, peaceful Palestine?
Of Jordan's holy harvest vales?"
—JOAQUIN MILLER

"Look at the Palestinians. They listened to the radio
and God destroyed them."
—A TRANSJORDANIAN

JORDAN is an ancient world, a pre-Biblical world of which the psalmist wrote: "The sea saw that, and fled; Jordan was driven back." (*Psalms CXIV.3*) Jordan was still "back," with Arabia and The Yemen, in a desert universe when the interviewers made their rounds in 1951. Jordan did not share the problems imposed upon her neighbors by the modern world; Jordan's problems had been imposed upon her by *them*. While their neighbors puzzled over the problems of shaping an Arab-Muslim syndrome into an instrument of Middle East policy, Jordanians were puzzled by their neighbors. Transjordanian tribesmen could not grasp the "Arab-Muslim" idea: *what else* was there? The "Middle East" idea was no easier: *where else* was there? Even the idea of "neighbors" meant, in their normal usage, only the nearest tribe or the next village.

This desert fief suddenly found itself cast in the role of a modern nation, and the role had to be played under conditions of extraordinary difficulty. The defeat by Israel had brought over 800,000 Palestinians into Jordan, trebling the population within its new borders. About half of this new population (400,000) lived in the West Bank area once earmarked as part of the state of Arab Palestine. Another 475,000 were listed on UNRWA rolls as refugees from Israel; these dispersed themselves over the East Bank areas —about 30% in camps, 32% in villages, and 38% in towns.[1] With this influx, ancient Transjordan abruptly entered the modern world as the turbulent Hashemite Kingdom of Jordan.

The more numerous and advanced Palestinian population, superimposed upon a backward people in a terrain whose poor resources were virtually unmapped, raised problems which might be capable of solution, but neither compelling plans nor adequate means were ready at hand. How could economic viability be created among this mixed mass? How could some measure of political stability be maintained? A long-range policy sequence, sustained over a period of years, would be required to work out reasonable solutions. Meanwhile, getting a start was impeded by the acute problem of "culture contact" between two peoples who, while both Arab and Muslim, were foreign and hostile to each other. The urban Palestinians regarded the desert Transjordanians as unspeakably backward, and were regarded in turn as impious and effete products of the degenerate city. One Beduin whose ignorance of the world outside the desert was total, when asked by the interviewer what he would like to know about foreign countries, responded: "Do they live like us or like 'Amman?'"

1. "Culture Contact":
The Setting of Social Change

Jordan's population is two-thirds Palestinian, but 94% of its territory is Transjordanian. These proportions suggest the challenge of integration that faces the new nation. The task of "Jordanizing" is beset with difficulty and doubt, since a historical as well as a geologic divide has long separated the East and West Banks (formerly Transjordan and Palestine respectively). Narrower "Palestinian" and wider "Arab" identities continue to rival Jordanian allegiance. Jordan, lacking an autonomous tradition, having existed always as a fief under Syrian, Egyptian or Ottoman rule, has no magnetic symbolism for Palestinians. "At no time in the Arab period," writes Professor Hitti, "did it achieve distinction in any realm of endeavor."[2] The establishment of Transjordan (originally included in the Palestine mandate) as a separate entity in 1923 was dictated not by indigenous need but by French and British jockeying for Middle East power. Its borders, said some Arab nationalists, "violated every known law of physical and human demarcation."[3] Although the principality achieved political stability under Amir 'Abdullah, and even formal independence of Britain in 1946-48, culturally it remained a vassal of the surrounding Arab countries. Its films, broadcasts, and printed matter, its music and other forms of folk art, were imported from Cairo, Damascus and Beirut.[4] The few Transjordanians who sought higher education went to other Arab or to Western centers. The educated elite—government officials, the professional class, and indeed the monarch himself—were imported from the neighboring states. Disgruntled nationalists since the 1930's moved from Damascus, Jerusalem, Beirut and Cairo to 'Amman, which became known as the Mecca of Arab Nationalism. Their ranks were augmented by Palestinians invited into the administration by the British.[5]

This thin elite layer did not touch the static society of fellahin and nomads that made up mandatory Transjordan, whose relative insulation from change was structured and certified by its ecology. East of the Hijaz Railway the sod gives way to the sand that surfaces four-fifths of the land. A 1944 estimate classified half the population as camel-breeding Beduin or as goat and sheep-raising semi-nomads.[6] Even among the settled population, also of nomadic stock, tribal tradition remains stronger than elsewhere in the Fertile Crescent. Social institutions were unaltered by British governance—with the major exception of measures taken to ensure public safety and order, particularly from Beduin marauding. While antiquated Ottoman codes were gradually being replaced by modern legislation on the British models of common law and equity across the Jordan River in Palestine, here they remained in force.[7] While the Palestinian struggle continuously pushed both Jews and Arabs in the direction of modernization, Transjordan remained untouched by social changes. Indigenous opposition to 'Abdullah's benevolent autocracy and the firm paternalism of British administrators was nearly nonexistent. The hardy Communists and labor organizers who ventured to set up shop in Transjordan, invariably agents from the surrounding countries, made little headway before the merger of 1948-50.[8]

In production of literates and urbanites Transjordan lagged behind its neighbors—rather deliberately. "Social stability was prized above education," noted the RIIA survey.[9] After two decades of British rule, schools enrolled about 28% of school-age children—as compared to 52% of Palestine Arabs. The pupils were mainly town boys, minority children were much more numerous than Sunni Arabs, and the nomadic boys were hardly reached at all. No more than 20% of the population lived in the four towns of 10,000 or more, and even these settlements comprised rural people to a considerable extent.[10] Compartmentalized into tight "quarters," the towns functioned "as if they were a number of villages bordering upon one another."[11] A working class hardly existed, apart from the small cadres trained as pipeline workers for the Iraq Petroleum Company or as aides to the British armed forces.

Jordan is an impoverished land. Primary is the shortage of water. People cluster in the arable area: 56% live on the crowded West Bank (6% of the total area), raising density per square kilometer to 580 compared with 107 in East Jordan.[12] In ratio of population to cropped area, Jordan is "one of the most densely settled of the agrarian countries." Present methods of cultivation are extremely extensive, with little investment of capital and labor, and with land left fallow every three years.[13] But to intensify and rationalize cultivation is a long-term process, and it is immediate absorption that poses the crucial political problems. With good reason, some respondents considered that lack of natural resources had permanently decided the country's fate. Beyond scarce land and water, the mineral base for industry is also lacking. The 153 establishments existing in 1950 were mainly in the handicraft stage, employing just a few persons. Plans for new industries (cement plant, petroleum refinery, textile plant, tannery, soap factories) were inactivated by lack of capital, poverty of the domestic market, difficulty of access to external markets and political instability. Foreign specialists regard a development program as exceedingly difficult; to many Jordanians the prospects are utterly hopeless.[14]

Into this traditional environment surged the Palestinian refugees, among Arab peoples second to none in degree of modernity. Before partition, 30 to 40% of the 1.3 million Palestine Arabs were urbanized.[15] A large labor force had developed in the great centers of Haifa, Jaffa and Jerusalem, during the 1930's and subsequent war years. Over 25,000 Arab industrial workers had been organized into the more than 30 unions active before partition.[16] Villagers constantly swelled the urban corps, pulled by job opportunities, pushed by growing population pressure on the land (the Palestinian Muslims had the highest known birth rate in the world, 54/1000). Hence "possibly 50% of the earners" among the Palestinians had some acquaintance with nonfarming occupations.[17]

Jordan alone among the Arab states gave the Palestinians citizenship and the right to work, but it could not provide an economic basis for re-establishing their lives. The refugees continued, year after year, to be indigestible. Initially, the international community assumed responsibility for feeding and sheltering destitute newcomers, and well-to-do refugees brought assets that doubled the total Jordanian money supply (currency plus bank deposits). A building boom started which still impresses the cursory traveler through 'Amman with a sense of growth and excitement. But these beneficial short-range effects have not altered the long-range prognosis. Despite large international expenditures, the absorptive capacity of Jordan has barely risen during these past few years.

But if the refugees have not raised economic supply, they have significantly increased political demands. Traditional evasiveness by the elite is hard to maintain. Demands for accountability are growing in a society which hitherto provided no channels for popular participation. A poor, illiterate farmer—who has learned to listen to international broadcasts—told his interviewer about Jordan's great national problems: "We do not have good roads, modern machines for agriculture, doctors, clinics and clean water." Then he added: "Every day I hear of new plans but never saw them in action." (126)

To determine the internal proportions of the Jordan sample, we sorted all interviewees into the Modern, Transitional and Traditional categories of our basic typology of modernization. The results, given in Table 1, show a consistently greater modernity of refugee Palestinians over indigenous Jordanians. The refugees are proportionately better educated, more urban, more active media consumers, and more widely empathic than the nonrefugees. A profound shock which the refugees applied to Jordanian polity was their capacity to consume and manipulate public communication. On media behavior, 65% of the refugees, compared to 50% of the nonrefugees, were "high" scorers on the Exposure Index. This index is based on frequency of newspaper reading, radio listening and movie going. The range is from zero (no exposure to any media) to 12 (daily exposure to newspaper and radio, and weekly attendance at the cinema). Scores over 7 were scored "high"; under 7 "low." Since Refugees were usually destitute new arrivals, and Nonrefugees include Palestinians who retained their homes on the West Bank, the difference between Palestinians and Transjordanians are greater in actuality than shown by the division of the sample in Table 1.

Table 1—Modernity: Refugees and Nonrefugees

	No.	% of Refugees in Each Type	% of Type Composed of Refugees	No.	% of Nonrefugees in Each Type	% of Type Composed of Nonrefugees
Traditionals	29	22	30	68	43	70
Transitionals	24	18	48	26	17	52
Moderns	63	48	54	53	34	46
Unclassified	15	12	60	10	6	40
Totals	131	100	—	157	100	—

NOTE: If "Refugees" and "Nonrefugees" were sorted into "Palestinians" and "Jordanians," the proportion of Palestinian Moderns would probably be about 20% higher than the 54% for Refugees.

Widespread social changes resulted from the commingling of the two groups. Among these are high unemployment (officially estimated at one-fourth of the male labor force), widespread underemployment in the towns and on the land, and the sharp drop in wage levels. The rapid growth of towns is another example. Today, Jordan is at least 35% urbanized.[18] The West Bank towns swelled with the influx of refugees from coastal Palestine. But the East Bank towns have grown as well—notably the astonishing expansion of 'Amman from a town of 30,000 (in which 37% of dwellings were temporary structures, tents and caves in 1952) to a metropolis of 200,000. Of the new 'Amman residents 75-80,000 are refugees, but the majority are indigenous rural migrants.[19]

Variations of town life in Jordan are striking. The two genuine cities are 'Amman and Arab Jerusalem. A few West Bank towns resemble the modern Lebanese pattern. Christian Ramallah, for example, has the highest literacy in Jordan (80-85%); many of its youth study abroad; many commute to work in Jerusalem; there are seven welfare agencies, good housing, and two movie theatres. At the other end of the scale is Karak, on the fringe of the Eastern desert, where the single street offers few urban amenities, and the settled tribes easily maintain their traditions and clan loyalties.

In general, "the Jordanian town appears a straight-laced, sober, and dull place which has lost much of the simple beauty and charm of the village without either gaining the conveniences, advantages, enticements or acquiring the vices of the city."[20]

Media development also reflects the poverty of Jordanian resources and the difficulty of balanced growth. In 1951 Jordan had 17 cinemas (10 of these in 'Amman and Jerusalem) with a total seating capacity of 8,000 or about six seats per thousand inhabitants. In 1953-54, UNESCO reported 24 cinemas (six of them open-air, functioning only during the summer) with seats for 12,000, raising the capacity per thousand to nine. Despite its efforts at growth, Jordan is still considerably behind every other country in our survey: e.g., Lebanon, with the same population, had 30,000 seats in 60 cinemas. The 700 films shown annually are all imported—45% from the United States, 30% from Egypt and 15% from England.[21]

Radio, likewise, is growing but still limited. Before 1949 there was no broadcasting service in the country. Jordan acquired the important transmitter at Ramallah during the war with Israel (although its studios, located in Jerusalem's New City, were taken over by Israel). The interviews were made in 1951, before the new transmitter was established in 'Amman, when only Ramallah was functioning with a broadcast schedule limited to eight hours daily. This effectively left the field to interested foreign powers, notably Cairo's Voice of the Arabs (after the 1952 *coup* in Egypt), which with increasing boldness sought to replace British by Egyptian predominance in Jordan. The 'Amman station was designed for defense against this insistent and effective propaganda campaign. Before 1948, there were only 2,000 licensed receivers in Jordan—or five per thousand persons. The most recent estimate is 14,000 receivers, or 10 per thousand—but, despite the doubling, still the lowest Arab figure in the survey. Some villages and refugee camps are now equipped with loudspeakers for communal listening, but private sets generally are found in the larger towns. About one-third of all sets are in 'Amman, another 11% in Jerusalem. This distribution reflects the refugee situation; many of them had to abandon radios in flight and cannot afford new ones.[22]

Among mass media, the press reaches the largest audience, averaging 12 dailies per thousand persons. In our sample, which overrepresented urban literate males, an extremely high 44% read dailies. Palestinians, as expected, were more devoted to the press than Transjordanians. While almost half the nonrefugees never read a paper, only a quarter of the Palestinians go without printed news; about half claim to read a newspaper daily and the others several times weekly. By its Palestine annexation, Jordan fell heir to some of the oldest and most respected papers in the Arab world. *Falastin*, founded in 1911, and *al-Difaʿa*, founded in 1933, transferred their offices from Jaffa to the Old City of Jerusalem. In 1944 ʿAmman housed one weekly, which actually appeared intermittently (a daily produced in 1939 had meanwhile folded), and the merger stimulated publication of a daily. But in 1950 the Jerusalem press still accounted for most of the daily circulation. In the press, as in radio and cinema, Jordanian dependence upon Egypt, Syria and Lebanon (as well as the West) is evident. The Amman office of Egypt's Arab News Agency is its principal source of news; foreign broadcasts are monitored for the balance of the articles. Literate Jordanians still prefer newspapers, magazines and books from the more advanced Arab countries to the local product. *Roza al-Yusuf*, a sensational Egyptian weekly, "has the largest circulation . . . and has been nicknamed the 'School of Politics' in Jordan."[23]

Before 1948, the small knots of political malcontents could express their dissent only in radical sheets published abroad.[24] With acquisition of the Palestine papers, whose editors were consumed by a burning irredentist issue and hostility to the Jordanian elite, political journalism took a new turn. ʿAbdullah retaliated by suspending and banning newspapers, punishing editors and correspondents, under cover of the most restrictive press laws, as of 1951-52, in all the Arab countries. Application for a newspaper license could be arbitrarily rejected even though all legal requirements were met; administrative suspension was used, with terms unlimited by law.[25] The International Press Institute reported that censorship was very severe for local correspondents and stringers, "incalculable but not very stringent" for foreign correspondents.[26] But foreign publications were subject to censorship. At the height of his bitter struggle with the Arab League in 1949, ʿAbdullah banned six Egyptian newspapers from his territory.[27]

Censorship led editors to abandon or reduce editorials. Instead, their views figured in selection and slanting of news reports. It was sometimes hard to distinguish between reporting of what ought to be and what was. Thus, a wishful surmise reporting Israel's cession of Ramleh, Lydda, and Jaffa was published as a fact. Likewise, the refugee's hopes for repatriation were fanned with false information. Such tactics prompted a well-to-do social worker to declare that papers "poison people's minds and mislead public opinion." (106) Similarly, a college-educated refugee stated that if he were editor of a newspaper

> I'll suggest to publish the news correctly as they receive it and not to deceive the public for the purpose of more sales. (050, Administrative Officer in Chamber of Commeree)

But some Jordanians valued the partisan press, preferring concurrent opinion to distasteful information, even if distorted news was a by-product. A young refugee restaurant owner, educated at the American University of Beirut, said:

> The people are as a majority ignorant and they need someone to explain and show them what to do. . . . The government is despotic and so if the editor is bold it needs him badly so as to awaken those that still have a little consciousness in the government and maybe some good will come out some day. (015)

Many advocates of a crusading press were Palestinians, long accustomed to newspapers active in political struggles against the mandatory regime. When rumors had 'Abdullah signing a separate peace with Israel, a violent press campaign was credited with reversing the king's policy. One respondent, "a very important officer in the Ministry of Education," stated:

> When the people thought that the King wanted to conclude peace with the Jews and the editorial appeared the next morning the people were so enraged that the cabinet had to resign. . . . It is very pleasing to see the people force their way through in that way. (014)

Jordanian politics, since this official was interviewed, has witnessed the increasing potency of popular demonstrations against established authority, led by organized extremist blocs. Before the merger, 'Abdullah ruled arbitrarily and any check on his power derived less from public opinion than from British representatives in 'Amman. Provisions for representative government were ignored. It was impossible even to bribe one's way into office against the royal will. Colonel F. G. Peake, former head of the Arab Legion, recalled a defeated candidate in the 1926 elections "complaining bitterly that he had given over £400 to the voters and yet failed to get elected. I knew but could not tell him, that he never would be elected until he brought his political views into line with those of the Government in power."[28]

Since then, the 'Amman government has been steadily infiltrated by the highly-politicized Palestinians. Their long frustration by diplomacy and intra-Arab factionalism developed their contempt for governmental authority, their divisiveness, their skill in opposition. By applying these techniques to Jordanian politics, they undermined the old power arrangements. The interviews, made a few months before King 'Abdullah was assassinated by an adherent of al-Husayni (the former Mufti of Jerusalem), reflected the deep Palestinian hostility toward the Hashemite monarchy. A Jaffa-born government auditor, who considered "the King's interference in public affairs" as Jordan's gravest problem, said:

> If I were made head of government, I would put an end to the King's interference. He is a King and he has no rights to interfere in every administrative measure by the Parliament. (201)

'Abdullah's efforts to integrate the Palestinians into the domestic government were impeded by his favoritism toward the anti-Husaynis (the pro-British Nashashibi and Tuqan clans in particular), by his friendliness toward the West, and by his willingness to come to terms with Israel.[29] Assigned one-half the seats in Parliament, the dissident Palestinians clamored for full proportional representation. Shortly after the survey, the Palestinian deputies precipitated a parliamentary crisis when they demanded that the Cabinet be made responsible to Parliament rather than the King (a demand met in the 1952 Constitution promulgated after 'Abdullah's death). They further demanded revision of the budget, of which 65% went for the army and police, 20% for maintenance of the royal household.[30]

The Palestinians relentlessly pushed Jordan toward extremism *vis-à-vis* the West and Israel, and toward mob rule at home. Their radical politics reflected their widespread disbelief in the possibility of lawful change. This showed when respondents were asked: "Is there anything people like you can do to solve the biggest problem the nation as a whole faces?" Palestinians said "No" much more frequently than native Jordanians—more than twice as often on questions of this type. Since legal action seemed to them ineffectual, the Palestinians placed correspondingly heavier reliance on the use of force. In answering questions as to what should be done about the various public problems they had named, they tended much more frequently to endorse violent solutions. Of those who named Israel as a problem, 34% refugees compared with 13% nonrefugees spontaneously advocated military action against Israel. As propensities toward extremism are focused by Israel, it is important that, when asked to identify the greatest problem facing Jordan, large proportions of all respondents named Israel. To permit comparison with the other Arab countries, Table 2 reports these results in our basic typological categories.

Table 2—Priority of "Palestine Problem"

	Traditionals	Transitionals	Moderns
Egypt	2%	7%	3%
Lebanon	5	—	3
Syria	19	28	17
Jordan	45	56	53
Refugees*	76%	63%	57%
Nonrefugees*	32	50	47

* If these groups were recoded as "Palestinians" and "Jordanians" the differences between them would probably be increased by 20%. The high Syrian figures, relative to Egypt and Lebanon, also reflect the presence of Palestinian refugees.

Advocates of violence included many white collar Palestinians of the sort who, in a settled social system, usually tend to be bulwarks of law and order. For example, one college-educated young bank accountant declared that if he were head of the government: "I would march on Palestine and do not care whether I will be the loser or the victor." (251) A 34-year-old college-educated history teacher said that if he headed the government: "I would fight Israel and would subjugate the Jews as Nebuchadnezzar and Senecharib did in the past and I tell you the day shall come when this shall take place." (146) Other questions further revealed, among Palestinians, the most intense bitterness against the British and the most frequent endorsement of violence.

The pressure generated by these intense Palestinians forced the government to grant them increased political participation. In 1954 two opposition parties received recognition, though they "represented not real political groupings, but the private instruments of individual politicians," and the Communist-led National Front (*al-Jubha al-Wataniyya*) emerged openly.[31] Joining with crypto-Communist groups and National Socialists, they organized urban election riots in the course of which American and British government buildings were fired and sacked. Although the government retained power by rigging the election, the explosions of popular sentiment evoked by the episode undermined its authority.[32] The relatively free elections of October 1956 reflected the government's uneasy respect for "public opinion" in action.

Not only internal issues, but the large questions of foreign policy that agitated Jordan after the merger, came to be decided by street mobs. The December 1955 riots against Jordan's accession to the Baghdad Pact capped the trend. Communists and refugees joined in organizing demonstrations that used the slogans of Cairo's Voice of the Arabs (e.g., describing the Pact as a British-Zionist plot to sell out Jordan to the Jews) and in the process nearly produced a *coup d'état*. Two governments resigned and only the intervention of the Arab Legion quieted the disturbances.[33] A major victory of the extremist Palestinians followed soon after, when the British head of the Legion was unceremoniously booted out and his place taken by a young Palestinian officer with marked Egyptian sympathies. Subsequently King Husayn, making decisive use of the loyalty and troops of the Beduin chieftains, has handed the pro-Soviet, pro-Cairo extremists a sharp defeat. But the balance is precarious and the drama is far from completed. Excursions, alarms, reversals lie ahead.

For, here as elsewhere in the Middle East, popular discontent and growing anti-Westernism have nourished the Communist movement. The Jordan Communist Party has continuously gained adherents and fellow-travelers. The government's policy of treating liberals as harshly as Communists has encouraged cooperation between the two groups. Led by the settled Palestinians, not merely the embittered refugees in the camps, the intelligentsia provided leadership and core membership. These cadres, particularly large in the old strongholds of Palestinian Communism (Jerusalem, Bethlehem and Nablus), quickly established themselves among professional men in Jordan. "Teachers, physicians, and lawyers were approached and cells established in the upper forms of secondary schools, and these became the backbone of the party."[34] Most of them were nonrefugees and fairly well-off financially—e.g., they never figured on the relief rolls of UNRWA.[35]

So much for the impact of the Palestinians upon the political scene in Jordan. How did the highly visible changes centered in 'Amman enter into the lives of Jordanians of different type and station? To deal with this question, respondents were sorted according to the four principal locales of Jordanian life: desert, village, town, city. The four groups were constituted as follows: 26 desert Beduin, 12 village Farmers, 55 town Enterprisers, 29 city Elite.* These groups differed consistently on the four indices of the basic typology—urbanization, literacy, media participation, empathy—which together represent the degree of modernity in a person's style of life.

The desert Beduin were, of course, a group lacking all the attributes of modernity (aside from one literate). The village Farmers, with little or no education, were smallholders working their own parcels of land. (It is noteworthy that this small group, with only 12 members, positioned itself consistently between Beduin and Enterprisers on all tests of modernization.) The town Enterprisers are middle-class business people, almost half with high school education. The Elite includes the college-educated upper-middle and upper classes.

Between these four groups there are strikingly large and regular differences of attitude and outlook. We shall deal with these by way of their communication behavior. The next sections of this chapter take each group in turn. Here we present some comparative data to clarify the scope of differences between them. As the Beduin are illiterate and the Elite are college-educated, naturally there is a huge difference between their levels of information about the world. The other two groups position themselves with remarkable consistency between these extremes. When asked to identify the Secretary-General of the United Nations, for example, no Beduin —but all Elite except one—could name Trygve Lie. The proportions responding correctly were: 0 Beduin, 17% Farmers, 73% Enterprisers, 97% Elite. Such differences reflect their interest in, and access to, news of the larger world. When asked to tell the interviewer the last news item they had heard—a question we have found illuminating in previous chapters—their responses distributed as shown in Table 3. Family and local news, which preempts the attention of most Beduin, drops sharply among rurals and falls off to insignificance among Enterprisers and Elite. Conversely, international news, non-existent among Beduin, composes nine out of ten items recalled by the Elite. Interest in news is related, we have

---

* The discussion of these four groups throughout this chapter is based on the 1951 BASR report "Communication and Public Opinion in Jordan" by J. M. Stycos.

Table 3—Recall of News Items

	Beduin	Farmers	Enterprisers	Elite
Family or Local News	68%	20%	2%	0%
National News	16	25	22	9
International News	0	50	70	91
Other	16	5	6	0
Total	100	100	100	100

seen, to the availability of media. *How* people get their news conditions *what* news they get. Respondents learned the news items they had recalled through the channels shown in Table 4.

Table 4—Sources of Recalled News

	Beduin	Farmers	Enterprisers	Elite
Word of Mouth	100%	50%	26%	15%
Radio	0	42	49	36
Newspaper	0	8	25	49
Total	100	100	100	100

These figures illustrate the historic shift from oral to media networks. Word-of-mouth is the exclusive channel of Beduin news, which consists mainly of family or local items. Use of the media increases directly as one climbs the social scale, and with the range of news interest expands. The newspaper shows a steady increase in use, while radio shows a characteristic decline (relative to newspapers) among the Elite—reflecting the preference frequently found among educated people for acquiring intelligence through the eye rather than the ear. These differences in source of recalled items were confirmed as general differences in media exposure by responses to this set of questions: "Do you listen to the radio? Read the newspaper? Attend the cinema? Do you know which foreign stations can be heard in Jordan? Do you hear foreign broadcasts?"

Table 5—Exposure to Media

	Beduin	Farmers	Enterprisers	Elite
Listen to Radio	0	58%	80%	97%
Read Newspaper	0	25	63	93
Attend Cinema	0	25	58	83
Know of Broadcasts by				
Britain	0	42	69	97
America	0	25	27	62
Russia	0	17	22	59
Hear Foreign Broadcasts	0	28	57	72

Awareness and exposure to the media increased consistently with rising rank in the social structure. The top position of BBC among international broadcasters was once again confirmed by these data. Noteworthy are: (1) the general awareness of BBC among the Elite; (2) the extraordinarily high proportions of Elite and Enterprisers who claim actually to listen; and (3) the relatively small differences in awareness, among all classes, of American and Russian broadcasts. (This last point suggests the equal-indifference to the bipolar centers which, though shocking to many Westerners, is a major component of political attitudes among the growing corps of newly-participant Arabs.)

What do the different groups like to hear on radio?

Table 6—Favorite Radio Programs

	Beduin	Farmers	Enterprisers	Elite
News	0	71%	90%	64%
Koran	0	71	14	4
Arabic music	0	57	57	42
Western music	0	0	14	68

News and music are popular with all three groups. Fewer of the Elite, who prefer newspapers, favor news broadcasts. Western music is heard, where at all, almost uniquely by the Elite. While 71% of Farmers prefer the Koran, this item is insignificant among Enterprisers and Elite. The differences summarized in the preceding tables express in statistical frequencies the bare bones of profound contrasts in lifestyles. These group contrasts are the meat of the story. We begin with the Beduin.

2. The Constrictive World of the Beduin

As Jordan is the most impoverished land in the Fertile Crescent, so the Beduin are its most depressed element. The trend of recent decades has worsened the nomadic way of life in Jordan.[36] The British extended the area of settlement and the fellahin's land was protected from Beduin herds. Newer trade and communications undermined the market for animal products, basis of the nomadic economy. Increasing control by the central government all but eliminated the raiding that had provided the tribes with excitement, pride and sustenance.

The continuous deterioration of Beduin society forced many into agriculture or into semi-nomadism, based on goat and sheep-raising in limited districts rather than camel-breeding over large areas. The true Beduin—camel-raisers belonging to one of the noble tribes—numbered only 40,000 in the 1940's compared to 120,000 semi-nomads (out of a total population of 340,000). As few interviews were made in the southern and eastern desert areas, most of the Beduin sample are semi-nomadic. But they differ enough from villagers and townfolk to be called Beduin—since the sample ranges from a nomad woman, attached to a wandering tribe which subsists only on camel products, to a dweller in a permanent camp near a village "so he is supposed to know more and therefore he wears trousers under his garments." (194)

The condition of the Beduin elicited the pity of more than one interviewer. Their poverty was softened only by their unquestioning acceptance of it. Beduin responses revealed a fatalistic resignation to their lot: "I am satisfied with what God gives me, and that is enough." (917) "I am living thanks to God, and everything I want is here so I am happy." (188) Also characteristic of the Beduin was the total unawareness of the world outside their immediate environment. Geographic isolation, poverty, illiteracy have circumscribed interest in affairs beyond "our tents and our camels" and excluded them from the network of modern communication. The media have wanton ways, however, and intrude where they have not been invited. Even among the Beduin, as will appear, they have insinuated some of that restlessness which augurs change on the social horizon. But meanwhile, the dominant tonality of Beduin life still resounds, in the interviews, through classic themes.

The Tribal Focus: The mark of the Beduin is his complete absorption into tribal life. The tribe and its parts—sub-tribe, section, family—are the primary objects of personal loyalty. Tribal affiliation is the source of safety and, conversely, expulsion from the tribe for some grievous offense is the gravest sentence. Law and morality are also defined in tribal terms, for only a rare central government could effectively mete out social sanctions among the nomads. Personal allegiance to any larger social unit has been historically an expedient mode of material gain for the tribe. Beduin shaykhs were adept at playing off one ruler against another. But within the tribe, the shaykh was in principle only the first among peers. This has stimulated the theory of "Beduin democracy," though "fraternal anarchism" may more accurately describe their attitude toward public authority. This feeling shows in their responses:

> We Beduins don't have prime ministers and we don't like them. [Why?] We are free and have no ruler but God. (197)
> Nobody is head here and we don't want prime ministers. [Why?] We are all brothers and have no need for foreign heads. (151)

Attachment to the tribe is evident in the consistent Beduin refusal to imagine living in a different land. Imagination was constricted by primary identification not with place—for the Beduin lacks the peasant's devotion to his particular piece of land—but with *tribe*. Said one: "I will never leave this country because I will not think of becoming a foreigner to my tribe and their camp." (151) And the interviewer pointed out:

> Beduins believe that having to travel far from one's country and relatives and friends is a curse that descends from the forefathers to the child.

The conditions under which travel becomes plausible for Beduin is movement of the intact tribe *en masse* to another grazing area—a far cry from personal mobility:

> I will go to any land where there is enough food for our tribe and the cattle provided they accept all of us. [Which country would you think of?] I don't care.

Disdain for Civilization: "Beduin" is a word of contempt among educated Arabs. But the Beduin regard themselves as the elite of the human race and commonly refer to themselves as "thoroughbreds." Camel and sword are the marks of valor and virility; the aristocrat is by definition a fighter. The corollary is Beduin disdain for the "civilized" world, which connotes soft living and femininity.[37] Attitudes toward the mass media are intertwined with these feelings, for the media are symbols of the city:

> We Beduin don't need the cinema. . . . Those who go are not real men. They are useless and have lost all value of morals. (120)
> Movies spoil men. . . . Those who go get a very bad character and

are no more men. But if you don't go you are a man in all senses of the word. (087)

By God our hair tents to us are better than a kingly castle. What care we for your movies? (160)

Those who go [to the cinema] are town people and all of them are bad. (194)

The Beduin, with a diffuse but sure sense of his own lifestyle, associates literacy and the participant society. Reading connotes politics and the evils of urban government:

Those who read are politicians and trouble seekers. If you don't read you are far away from trouble and the government. (150)

We don't have prime ministers and nobody rules us like these girlish city folk. We rule ourselves. . . . The effendis who read are all hypocrites. They all want to be politicians. We want to live peacefully and away from politics. (90)

City people in 'Amman are liars and cheats. (79)

Ignorance of the Modern World: Aversion to the modern world is paralleled by a large ignorance regarding it. "God knows" was a frequent response to questions about the West, Russia, and the mass media. After his interview, one middle-aged Beduin complained: "All the questions were bad. [Why?] Because I couldn't answer them. You should have asked me about hyenas and I will tell you." (186) Another said: "I can tell you about camels and the wild beasts of the wilderness, but your interview was uninteresting and talking about strange things." (188)

Many Beduin became irritated by the interview because their specialized knowledge of desert and camel lore (there are about 600 words in the Beduin lexicon for the beast), and their fantastic memory for genealogies and tribal exploits, remained untapped. Instead, only their ignorance (appalling to the city-bred Jordanians who interviewed them) was revealed. Of 26 Beduin, 15 had never heard of the United States, and the others had only the most innocent notions:

The U.S.? What is it? Where is it? (186)

Where is their country exactly, and do they live like us or like 'Amman? (079)

The U.S. is a land, always dark and cold and behind the sea. It is full of beasts. (183)

The U.S. is a very far and cold country and they sleep all winter and have lots of ice. How many days walking distance is it from here? (150)

Concerning Russia there was almost equal ignorance: 12 had never heard of it, and the others were vague. The one literate Beduin, a desert patrol guard, told the interviewer that he had been instructed by his superior to hate all Russians and to jail anyone who praised them, but he had no idea why. A few did not like Russia because it had a different religion—Communism.

Knowledge of mass media was restricted: nine had never heard of movies, three of radio, and three of newspapers:

A radio? What is this thing you are asking me about? Is it an important place or man? (151)

Radio? Walahee! [My God!] I have never heard such things before. How do you know about all these things. . . . I am listening to riddles from your mouth. (188)

[Do you know what a movie is?] No by the Great God, what is that. . . . [Respondent showed great amazement and listened attentively while I explained shortly what a movie is.] (160)

Ignorance of the outside world is socially acceptable in the Beduin community. A man is not expected to have opinions on large matters which, according to his neighbors, do not concern him. To mind one's own business is estimable and the Beduin contents himself with a narrow range of opinion and experience.

[Are there any sort of news that you don't care to hear about at all?] Yes. We don't like to hear about war in far away countries. When Beduins start a fight among themselves, they never bother other people about it. So why should we bother about what other countries have to go through whether in war or peace? (160)

I am interested in news about my household and my camel because these are my life and my link with this world. I don't care for anything else because what is outside my concern I am not supposed to care for. (118)

All I need to know is here in this tribe and that is enough. . . . My business is only what happens in the tribe. Do you expect me to worry my head over what is going on outside our camp? We have enough news and activity here and we don't like to mingle it with the outside. (079)

At the most, external "news" concerns what happens in other Beduin camps. Beyond the Beduin world lies the obscure domain of irrelevance and iniquity. A person too curious about this domain would be suspected of unBeduin activities.

The Oral Network: Constricted range is shown in Beduin recall of the last piece of news they received. The concrete local event predominates in all cases, viz:

My neighbor slaughtered his wife. . . . I felt she deserved it because she was scandalizing him by looking at other men, and sometimes smiling at them. (184)

Others mentioned camels not producing milk, relatives getting married, locusts ravaging the pastures. For such news, traditionally the staple of oral systems, relatives and friends continue to be the only satisfactory purveyors of information: "From my friends, my brother and my cousin I get to know everything in my tribe from A to Z." (001)

For outside news, the Beduin also depends mainly on known persons who can be "faced and placed," such as tribesmen returning from trips with gossip. The media reach him only through the "two-step flow"—occasional visitors, such as travellers and merchants, serving as oral relays of information that originated in the media.[38] One shepherd, relatively more settled than the true nomads, gets his news with some regularity "from friends or relatives who take frequent visits to 'Amman, perhaps once a month. They are usually merchants from the nearby village or on a passing drive." (155) A Beduin woman gets her news rather more sporadically: "From people like yourself. We see someone with a paper in his hand. We ask him to tell us what is going on in the world and they do." (160)

News is usually exchanged for tribal hospitality. Travelers are welcomed to the tent of the shaykh—social center of the encampment. While the shaykh "pounds coffee" the vistor brings tales of the outer world. Here Beduin form their images of the outside —e.g., one who "learned" that England is cold and poor from a passing Amman merchant. (087) But even such contact is rare:

You must be a missionary because nobody talks to us except an old English woman who tells me of a shepherd boy long ago called David and how he became a king because he believed in Jesus.

Another source of ideas about the world is the oral literature. As medieval troubadors carried information around a largely illiterate world, so itinerant poets and storytellers are news-bringers at the Beduin campfire. Their subjects are war, camels, horses, and women, in that order of importance. Beduin, whose love for language and passion for heroic legend enliven their otherwise barren culture, prefer current events cast in this traditional mold.[39] One Beduin woman derived her opinions of British policy in

Jordan and her choice of country for emigration wholly from such sources:

> Our men say that our kind loves the English people. In weddings and evenings of joy, most of our men sing for the victory of the English. . . .
> [Where would you like to live if for some reason you had to move from Jordan?] By God I don't know. The Arabs say al-Yemen is a good place. They think it is the rich and fertile country. Old poetry says that al-Yemen is the Garden of Eden where every living thing lives comfortably and happily. (160)

Opinion, as well as information, is locally derived. The shaykh is considered the authoritative source of correct ideas. Although the shaykh must respect the views of tribal elders, he occupies the seat of judgment. He is expected to have opinions, as others are not, since he is responsible for the tribe's external relations. It is his duty to be the repository of correct views, which the rank-and-file of the tribe may use if they feel the need. Note how these views converge in one response:

> [In your community who is the one whose thoughts are most highly respected?] My uncle the Sheikh. He is tall, old and respectable. He sits on his pillow all day long in his own tent and people of the tribe come around for advice. [Why is he a leader?] He is the eldest in the family and the people of the tribe go for the advice of the eldest.[Why?] Don't you know the common saying, "who is one day older in age is one year older in knowledge." Our respect is according to age, for experience counts a lot with us.
> We like to rest our heads from such responsibilities [as government]. We eat our daily bread, thank our God and are satisfied and happy. Our Sheikh alone may worry about that because that is his business. (160)

The shaykh and elders "speak for" the tribe. An interviewer noted that a venerable member of a tribal council was "quite proud because I chose him, thinking that as he answers he represents his tribe." (090) These elders, who display surprising knowledge of even their distant desert brethren are regarded as "the true bearers of desert tradition and history."[40] The respect due them constrained one interviewer, who was too embarrassed to pose some of the scheduled questions. He could not ask one elder "To whom do you go for advice?" because it would be an affront to suggest that such a leader should have to go to anyone else for advice. Another interviewer found it difficult to ask a Beduin leader what he would like to know about Saudi Arabia, because "asking this question to a person with the mentality of the respondent and his age and he living next to that country would be quite insulting."

Since tribal leaders control the dissemination of news and views in the Beduin community, *their* attitudes are important. One such leader, with pretensions to chieftainship, is described by the interviewer as follows:

> Thirty-three years old, he is of noble descent and is greatly honored and admired in his tribe. He wears rich, clean clothes and has very sharp eyes and features with a little beard. He owns many tents and cattle. He has a shrewd and fearful personality and is very strict and hard to his servants, yet they like him. (187)

This impressive person turns out to be little different in outlook from his tribesmen, and distinctive mainly by the resonant confidence with which he articulates traditional convictions. With regard to communications, he feels that newspapers are "uninteresting and unnecessary for life" because "the papers have nothing to offer me . . . our news are in our camp and needn't be written in a paper . . . I am only interested in news about my people." Toward radio his attitude is the same. He would not even like to listen to one "because it is unimportant in my life." Where, then, does he get his news? Not only does he fail to mention sources outside his own tribe, but he cites intratribal sources stemming only from *his own clan*: "I get to know it from my people. From my brothers and cousins and all the other members of my family."

When asked about his last two pieces of news, the response illustrated both his parochial range and his high aspirations: "Our chieftain is dying" and "He wants me to marry his daughter . . . I don't like his daughter but she is rich and, therefore, I might marry her." Regarding foreign powers, however, he showed two interesting differences from Beduin of lower status. When asked what country he would choose if he could not live in Jordan, he soared beyond the habitual self-constriction of most Beduin: "America. Because they are rich. If I go there I can open a ranch and keep thousands of sheep and horses and there is lots of fertility and pasture for them there." His final comment foreshadows the Beduin future. He asked the interviewer: "Is this information going to a school?" The interviewer replied "Yes, why?" The future chieftain said "I want to send my children to a school." *Sic Transit!*

Rejection of the Media: To people who have barely heard of the mass media, the notion that these modern contrivances might be introduced into the tribe is regarded with horror. Such innovations are beyond their understanding and many hastened to dissociate themselves from the diabolical strangeness of radio and movies:

There must be something bad about this that [allows you to] listen to voices in the air. (186)

Radio? By God if I see one I will destroy it. This is from the devil. [What do you miss by not listening?] You are mocking me. Why did you ask me that? You know I hate a radio and it is evil. (090)

That, the cinema? Oh God forbid! It is the working of the devil. . . . To go to such things that are the inspiration of demons are terrible. Oh no, then one would be tormented by the fire of hell. (021)

Superstition finds "evidence" quickly, since the Traditionalist logic forbids no *post hoc propter hoc.* Just as Beduin attribute rain to their incantations to the Rainmaker, so they connect media exposure and subsequent evil:

Those who go to the movies beat their wives. The devil gets into them. I know of one who has gone to the city and then he was seduced to go to the cinema and when he came back he started being on bad terms and beating his wife. (150)

Those who listen are full of evil and God's curse comes upon them. *Look at the Palestinians. They listened to the radio and God destroyed them.* We don't want this trouble here. (090)

Newspapers are rejected, not because they terrify the imagination, but because they have unpleasant connotations of government and urbanism, and because they lack utility for the Beduin. For example:

It writes nothing for us; only for the townspeople . . . papers don't write what we want. [What do we want?] We want God's mercy and a good crop this year. (090)

I will not lose if I don't read a paper, because papers don't write for us. (154)

I can't read or write, yet I don't regret it, because I don't like to read papers. They are uninteresting to me. . . . Papers don't put things about our life here in the camp. [How do you know that?] The last time my cousin, who is in the army and knows how to read, read me one and it had no news about us. . . . Those who read papers do so because it writes about their affairs and they have to read in order to know. (001)

Piercing the Isolate's Armor: Where are the modernizing elements within this tradition-bound community? Our theory enjoins us to seek those who are becoming outwardly-oriented through exposure to modern media. Do the Beduin youth take the avantgarde role? Here the lines of demarcation are not so clear as in settled communities. Beduin youth are still kept in line by patriarchal authority:

Cinema is bad and has nothing good to offer to me. [How do you know that?] That is what my father tells me and I believe him. . . . I don't know a radio. But I heard our elder telling us it is an evil device and dangerous for our character. [What else?] What he says I believe and I do. (187)

There are some counter-indications. Even among Beduin, younger people are more prone to resent and resist traditional values. The "young boys" were often described as knowledgeable about the outside world. They were expected, for example, to identify overhead planes as British or American. They also showed more interest in radio and movies. An old Beduin declared: "I personally will not . . . listen [to the radio] but some of the young men in the camp would like to listen." (083)

But innovations do not come easily to the Beduin, even among the young. A 17-year-old shepherd, chafing at camp life, declared himself "fairly unhappy . . . because we are not free to do what we want in this camp. [Like what?] Go to cinemas and listen to radios." This lad saw an American movie once and has been restless ever since. He keenly misses the opportunity to watch "good things" such as "beautiful girls, horses, and very nice fighting between Indians and white men." If he had to leave Jordan he unhesitatingly would choose America "because they have beautiful girls and lovely cars and a thousand and one things. [How do you know that?] I saw it in the cinema once." His question about the United States is, "Do they still have Red Indians with feathers growing from their heads?"

Although this boy felt that he was losing nothing by his illiteracy, and wouldn't care to learn to read and write, he hoped to save enough to buy a radio: "Only it has to be very small and very easy to conceal so that I will not meet the disapproval of my father." (001) Another shepherd said: "I like to listen to the radio but I can't. [Why?] Because I have no electricity and our elders don't like the presence of a radio in the camp." (079) The only literate Beduin commented:

> We don't listen here because there is no electricity. I think that is the main cause although some people might tell you the Chief doesn't allow it. I know you could get one. (189)

The main characteristic of the deviant younger men is some previous exposure to the media and contact with foreigners from the West. Two shepherd boys illustrate the effects of such contact. One has a cousin who worked for the Americans when Aramco laid its pipeline from Dhahran to Saida. Assured by his cousin that the Americans were "good and rich," the shepherd admires them and watches for their planes flying overhead. He regrets that he does not have a chance to listen to the radio, and blames it on the camp elders. The other shepherd worked in the British army kitchens during World War II, and still gets news from merchant relatives who visit 'Amman. He expressed great interest in reading the papers (he claims, dubiously, that he can read), but no newspapers reach his tribe. News to him, unlike his tribesman, means also national and international news. His contact with the West has pierced the constrictive shell of the traditional style:

> [What do you think you miss by not knowing what the newspapers have to say?] You lose news about what is going on in the world and in our country . . . quite important is foreign affairs and what the government is doing. [Why?] Because this although indirectly is responsible for my life as an individual and a nation. (155)

He also misses radio and believes that people who listen "enjoy themselves and have a better fun in life." He has more information than others. Not only does he know that the United Nations meets in America, but he defines it as "an international organization that helps to relieve people that are badly in need." Unlike most other Beduin, who are happy despite their lot, this shepherd boy rates himself as "fairly unhappy" ("because I don't get a good standard for my life"). Like the Grocer in Balgat, he suffers the relative deprivation of those learning to aspire for "better things" without the means of getting them. Modernization starts here.

These first stirrings among the young Beduin represent the motivations which set traditional men into motion and activate the modernizing sequence. Among the villagers, to whom we now turn, we see the process actually under way.

3. The Village Farmers

As half the current Jordan population lives off the land, the rural cultivator is an important type. Unfortunately, the sample included only 12 farmers. Nearly all of these own their land, and hence are better off than most; hence, atypically, most of them own a radio set; the others, who might own a radio, live in non-electrified villages where battery sets are unavailable. From this small and unrepresentative group we can make no generalizations about the farming population of Jordan as a whole. Nonetheless, their responses do illustrate some aspects of change in rural Jordan.

The world of the farmers is far removed from that of the Beduin. Better off financially, they have the means and opportunities to gain wider exposure to the world. Whereas illiteracy is the rule among Beduin, four of the 12 Farmers attended high school. Proximity and trade with larger towns also expose the Villager more directly to the ways of his urban compatriots. *They* form the reference group by which the Farmer appraises *his* lot. This may explain, by the mechanism of "relative deprivation," why the Farmers are less content than Beduin, who *have* less in fact. Whereas most of the Beduin described themselves as "very happy," only three of the 12 Farmers did so. This occurred, in previous case studies, among Transitionals vacillating between traditional and modern perspectives. No longer isolates, narcotized by fatalistic passivity, the Farmers are not yet full participants. Whereas the Beduin, stunned when asked what they would do as head of the government, responded mainly by silence, the Farmers divided between passivity and specific responses of this type:

I would make projects and let the people work. Open roads and make schools and government buildings. (103)
I will import many tractors and distribute them among the villages to be used for deep plowing . . . I shall send missions to America to learn the modern ways used in agriculture. (223)

In questions requiring place-transference, rather than role-transference, the Farmers again divided between constriction and mobility. Whereas hardly any Beduin could imagine living elsewhere than in the Jordan desert, seven Farmers empathized readily: three chose other Muslim countries, two chose the United States, and one chose Russia. Even those who would not move did not simply react with horror, like the Beduin, but explained their views cogently:

The United States is too rich and improved. I will not be able to catch up with them, being a simple farmer. (86)

I would prefer to stay in my country, because I like to stay where I was born. *I am not ready to be maltreated or disqualified in other countries.* I can't bear any insult from any person young or old, otherwise I will have to make a quarrel. . . . I hear that America is a beautiful and rich country, nevertheless I don't risk going there, because its habits, traditions, way of living and language are all unknown to me, and I am sure that they are different than ours. (211)

My parents and grandparents are buried in this country so it is impossible for me to leave it. (223)

The Farmers know more of world affairs than the nomads but less than the urbanites. Only two could identify the UN Secretary General, but nine had some idea as to where the UN met, and all but one gave a roughly satisfactory definition of its purpose. Their rising level of information reflects their slowly growing preoccupation with the media. Of the 12 Farmers, only four read a paper (or have it read to them) and only four go to movies. The survey deliberately over-sampled radio listeners, but it is interesting that among the eight regular listeners only two read newspapers and none sees movies. Ordinarily, radio-listeners also tend to be heavy consumers of other media. To see whether this deviation reflected only the unavailability of other media, the Farmers' responses to questions on *interest* in the media were reviewed. Why radio wins more acceptance is clarified by an educated well-off landowner:

Papers are nonsense. They are big lies. . . . I gain very much by not reading them. I will not have a chance to know what lies are found in the papers. Those who read the paper are government employees and merchants. Other people use it for wrapping, or they just look at pictures if there are any. (211)

Several reject newspapers on principle, because print brings them into unwanted contact with the larger society. Newspapers connote government, which in turn evokes anxiety about taxes and conscription and land records. Jordanians have an aversion to contact with civil authority, the product of hard experience with unsatisfactory government.

Cinema is rejected for different reasons. Religious scruples are involved here by the Islamic injunction against image-making, which fosters anxiety about deviation from traditional moral standards:

> I only hear of the movies. All those who go there are devils because it is magic against the laws of religion. (115)
> Movies are detrimental and spoiling for the conduct in general of the people . . . people who don't go are far wiser and better off. They cling to their old customs and habits. They never have any tendency to change their present situation. (218)

Older people usually are horrified at the possible effects of movies upon the young. One rich old Farmer combined this fear with a frank interest in the forbidden delights for himself:

> [Do you remember any film which attracted your attention?] Yes, that of Hajer Hamdi. She was very enticing and fascinating to such an extent that I felt very much excited. . . . Films are very detrimental to young and unmarried people, especially young girls. It is really a shame for a girl to see such films because she will try to find somebody with whom she will be able to try the experience. . . . Movies are good for persons like me. I can spend a very nice time. I feel that I have seen something about which I can tell my friends. (223)

Such fear of sexual laxity often underlies rejection of the movies. No traditional Arab could bear to have his honor sullied by a wayward woman in his family; he would be obliged to take drastic steps in revenge. The dread of involvement through "plays dealing with love affairs" is expressed thus:

> There might be a person who acts as a lover and speaks love words. So one of the chaps [of the village] will carry these words to one of his neighboring girls, thus creating trouble and bloodshed. (216)

Radio is less menacing, since it is possible to select broadcasts in which the modern world does not intrude beyond the tolerance of the traditional environment. The Farmer is a religious man (eight of 12 considered religion "very important" and attended services every week) and religious programs provide the rationale for the acceptance of radio:

> At the beginning I considered the radio to be against our religion and the devil is in it, but when I heard the Koran on it I changed my idea and considered it my best friend. I can hear besides the Koran

the talks in the Mosques and many religious sayings besides music. (115)

The Sheikh reads the words of God and the prophet in a very melodious voice for which on hearing I can't help stopping myself from submitting all thanks for the Almighty God who has bestowed such beautiful and effective sayings on us. [Are there any days of the week that you are more likely to listen?] Fridays. There is a special prayer program rebroadcast from the Mosque of Omar in Jerusalem, very often the King prays there. I heard his voice asking blessings from God. (216)

Once initial doubts are dispelled, radio becomes a valued friend. It brings the Koran and sermons, then the beloved Arab songs, into the home. In gratitude, some farmers endow their sets with human properties, thus "incorporating" the strange new mechanical device into their familiar world by the traditional empathic process of anthropomorphism. It is noteworthy that three of the 12 farmers used similar expressions to three different interviewers:

Radio is a very good friend at home who is very loyal and useful. I consider it my best friend. (115)

It is my best companion. (144)

Radio is the best friend at home. You can order him any time to stop talking without him being angry or disappointed. . . . (216)

Further insight on media behavior is gained when listening Farmers are differentiated according to the size of the arena within which their news-interest is confined. The interest of some listeners evaporates at the limits of the local community; with others it extends to the borders of the nation; still others are interested in the wider world. When these three types of listeners are classified respectively as Locals, Nationals, and Cosmopolitans, they show clusters of common attributes that are congruent with our more general typology of Traditionals, Transitionals, and Moderns.

Locals: These Farmers, otherwise quite divergent, show no interest in affairs outside their immediate community:

I am most interested in my own community because such things are very important. I know what is happening nearby, who was married, who has died, how many babies were born, the market prices and all such news which have a direct effect on my everyday life. (216)

Listen to news? Never. I am not interested because I don't want to buy worry. (86)

This group includes a relatively rich landowner and *Mukhtar,* described by the interviewer as follows:

He is the only person who owns a radio and believes that he is the cleverest in his village. . . . He is a little conceited and does not like to take advice from others. His only reference is the Koran and religious sayings. . . . he is very respectable and religious.

As a youth this landowner attended *kuttab,* where he learned laboriously to decipher the Koran, but reading modern newspaper Arabic is a skill he did not acquire. He neither likes nor understands news of any kind: "News are of no interest to me and that is why I live a peaceful life because we are far from false civilization and its troubles." His disinterest in the outside world is justified by religious principles. He has excluded the West from his ken because it is infidel. Thus, he would not dream of going West because "the women sit with men bareheaded and without sleeves on their arms and their skirts are very short." If forced to leave Jordan, he might migrate to Saudi Arabia, but his questions indicate that even the Land of the Prophet may no longer be holy enough: "Is it true that they have alcoholic drinks in Jidda? Is it true that the king allowed foreigners to enter Mecca?" It seems natural that the media would not appeal to such a man. Yet he describes the radio as his "best friend," for the manifest reason that it supplies him with Koran readings and mosque sermons. Monopoly radio ownership also bolsters his preeminent position in the village, as it did for the Chief of Balgat. It is an augury of social change when such traditional opinion-leaders sense that, to maintain their position, they must equip themselves with the new techniques of opinion-formation. But restricting the new by partial incorporation also transforms the old. The traditional opinion leader who has "incorporated" radio is a different man than he was before, and his conversion accelerates changes in the community for which he speaks.

Nationals: Several farmers who mentioned news among their favorite programs are early-Transitionals. They prefer national to local news, but they do not care about foreign news:

[What are you least interested in on the radio?] Foreign news. They are news of far away events that have no effect on us here. (85)

Foreign news is only for foreigners. They care for their business and so we care for ours. Why should I worry what happens in Europe or America? For example, when I live here, what can I do if I hear their news? Nothing, so I will be just losing my time on something useless. (216)

I don't like to hear the foreign news. . . . BBC foreign news are so boring and monotonous that you can't tolerate hearing it. I simply close the radio for I don't want to discharge the battery on non-sense. (218)

The latter, a rich, literate landowner, not only rejects foreign news, but also dislikes "educational talks and plays . . . You only hear imaginary things which you can't get anything out of." (218) He discharges his battery only on worthwhile fare—agricultural programs for practical farming advice, Koran readings and Arabic music beamed from Egypt. Though literate, he does not read newspapers and regards movies as "superfluous and unnecessary." Even his concern with national news is related to personal interest: "Because I am a landowner and I like to be always aware of taxes imposed and levied on properties." (218) Another literate land-owner elaborates this view:

I am most interested in what the government is doing. This con-cerns me most. I shall be able to estimate my net proceeds, when I know how much I have to pay rent for the land, how much for the government. I shall be conversant with the prices of the market as compared to that of the government. This will help me not to be cheated. (223)

Their interest broadens beyond the national arena only on major events concerning Pan-Arabism. Several National listeners mentioned French activity in North Africa with intense feeling because it touched the Arab-Muslim components of the extended self. Foreign news, not involving these symbols of identification, usually is dismissed. For example, one Farmer, keenly interested in Morocco, was unconcerned by news of the Korean War: "I only listen and feel nothing special about it. They are fighting; let them do so until they get tired. Who cares?" (144)

Cosmopolitans: Among the Farmers only two, both Palestinians, exhibited a range of news interests that encompassed the foreign world. As an important graft on Jordanian growth, bearing seeds of the future, their views merit examination. One of these, working a farm with his parents and sisters in a village near Irbid is de-scribed by the interviewer as "the type of scientific farmer not plentiful in the country and bound to be a leading person in that field." He goes to the movies only infrequently, but reads a news-paper every day:

Newspapers are very effective on the mentality of the public. They tell them about politics and what the government is doing. . . . I would like to have a newspaper that helps the farmers and the peasants in improving their living conditions. [Why?] Because our country is agricultural in the first place. (145)

His media preferences show a Transitional configuration. The parts of the newspaper which interest him most are "proverbs, translations and local news"; also his two favorite radio programs are news from Jerusalem and local news. While he regards radio as a medium for education, he dislikes listening to "silly talk and long, repeating speeches." Although aware that Britain, America, Russia, Turkey and France broadcast in Arabic, he listens to them "rarely" because:

They only put propaganda in Arabic. I care to put on Arabic programs so that my people at home can share with me in having entertainment.

But the last two pieces of news he recalled were about the Chinese intervention in Korea and the "disgusting" actions of the French in Morocco. His reaction to the former was only casual because "we have no interest in the Far East." Though aware of the world, his interest does not really go beyond an interest in agricultural information.

A somewhat deeper involvement with the world at large is exhibited by the other Palestinian (239), who comes from an authentic cosmopolitan background. An educated Orthodox Christian, who speaks English and French very well, he was born and raised in Cairo. "His social role," comments the interviewer, "is limited to that of a gentleman farmer who tries to teach the peasant around him a few things." His personal style is illustrated by his vigorous hatred for Britain, by his confidence in his own judgments of public issues, and by his readiness to assume responsibility:

[As head of government] I'll never allow a Britisher to interfere. I will be a second Atatürk, deal with people in a severe way, but it will get you somewhere. Teach people to be independent.

[As editor of a newspaper] I would run a commentator paper, on all that the government (damn them) does.

He reads the paper every day, and formerly was a faithful radio listener. Asked under what conditions he would resume listening, he replied:

I would have to persuade the municipality of Bethlehem to spread an electric cable to my farm, and then I would have to buy a radio to replace the battery set I sold.

As a Palestinian he does not identify with Jordan as yet. Asked to describe Jordanians, he instead talks of Palestinians and calls them "courageous and misled." Although he calls Americans "crooks and liars" for their Palestine policy, he would love to live in the United States: "It suits my farming work and a large, spacious country that gives the chance to carry on any agricultural scheme." Newspapers are good in his eyes:

They enlighten to new phases in life. . . . They write about recent discoveries and lectures by important people. They use small maps and war news, the latest being Korea, to illustrate the attacks and retreats of a war.

Broad interests and empathic capacity are occasionally circumscribed, however, by traces of the parochial outlook. Often, he relates international news to his immediate local interests in order to justify his sense of their importance:

I like it [foreign news] because it shows me where I stand in the world. From it I will know what is happening. . . . [For example] the division of Syria and Lebanon. That affected our farm a bit because the price of our vegetables went up. The newspaper wrote about it, and I knew what was going to happen.

But there is a definite strain of disinterested "cosmopolitanism," of interest in events "on their own terms." He reads five foreign publications (English, French and American) which are quite varied: *Better Homes and Gardens, Dairy Farming, Home Notes, Woman and Home,* and *L'Illustration.*

4. The Town Enterprisers

The shopkeepers and government clerks who compose this group represent the growing class of newly articulate people in Jordan. They have left traditionalism far behind and are now situated just above or below the fine line of Modernity. Most have had elementary or high school education; their opinions indicate a good, though unsophisticated, knowledge of world affairs; they are well acquainted with press, film and radio. Almost half are Palestinians in moderate circumstances, with good education, and claim to speak some English. To compare those living in larger towns with those in more rural settings, the 55 Enterprisers were divided into two groups. Table 7 compares the rural and urban Enterprisers.

Table 7—Rural and Urban Enterprisers Compared

Education	Rural	Urban
Almost none	28%	19%
Elementary	28	35
High School	44	46
College	—	—
Total	100%	100%
Socioeconomic Status		
Destitute	5%	5%
Poor	34	19
Modest	56	54
Well Off	5	22
Rich	—	—
Total	100%	100%
Communication Habits		
Listen to Radio	84%	79%
Read Newspapers	55	67
Attend Motion Pictures	50	62
Number of Respondents	(18)	(37)

The relatively small differences indicate that occupational mobility is the key attribute—an individual tends to modernize if he makes his living in a typically urban occupation, even though he actually resides in the countryside. The urban Enterpriser is somewhat more educated and media-participant than his rural counterpart—but this may reflect only greater availability of papers and movies. Before turning to the modal profile of the Enterpriser, we glance at the deviant case of an illiterate tinker (80). A man who *looks backward,* remaining close to the Beduin or Farmer mentality, the Tinker shows the large gap that must be crossed to reach the typical Enterpriser's level of modernity.

The Tinker exhibits strong proprietary feeling toward local news. His occupation requires passing contacts with a great number and variety of people in the urban manner. His handling of information so acquired qualifies him as an informal "opinion leader" in his community. The interviewer noted:

Although a tinker he looks more like a boss in his neighborhood and practices lots of authority . . . he had an air of confidence and a superior self complex. . . . He could worthily be claimed a dictator in his kingdom.

The Tinker operates as a highly traditional "relay" in an oral network. Both his inputs of information and his outputs of opinion are strictly parochial. In explaining how he gets his news, the Tinker's extreme localism leads him to regard persons outside his village as foreigners:

> Usually our imam carries most of the news to me. [What does he tell you?] Oh different things like the other day he told me that my uncle married his only daughter to a foreigner from the other village. . . . I felt disappointed because . . . he must have kept her for his family and village men.

His attitudes toward news are those of traditional man:

> This [local news] is my only interest. I get to know what is happening in my village—who is marrying who and who has died. [I am least interested in] foreign news. Because it is not my country so why must I know about its news? I really don't care what happens to them. Let the foreigners kill each other. Why must I worry?

He is exposed to none of the mass media and considers that he loses little by this, since movies and newspapers are for the rich. Toward the radio, he is somewhat more favorable:

> I would like to have one because I like to listen to some programs. . . . Oh, like the Koran and music. . . . Give me a radio and the cost for running it and I will listen to anything you want.

His conceptions of the outside world represent the extreme limit of ignorance in the entrepreneurial group. On Russia, for example,

> I don't know much about this country. It is mysterious to me because no one hears nothing about it. . . . Russia is very backward and it is all cold jungles where beasts and very bad war-like tribes kill each other. They tell me that it is 150 degrees below zero there.

The Tinker has hardly more information than his Traditional compatriots, but he has many more opinions. It is his readiness to express views on a variety of issues that puts him over the lower limit of Transitionalism.

The modal profile of the Enterprisers exhibits a much more modern array of attitudes than the Tinker's, particularly with respect to news, views, and the media. As compared with Farmers, who regard radio as a living thing, Enterprisers hardly ever refer to radio in animistic terms. They view it instrumentally, in the modern manner, as a channel which supplies entertainment and education. When asked, "What do you think of the radio?" Enterprisers responded in these terms and with no references to radio as a source of religious edification. Radio is good merely because it is interesting; it requires no rationale in terms of higher morality as among the Farmers. Even the newspaper is seen in this light. A print-seller, living in an area without newspapers, bemoaned the entertainment he missed and looked to radio with a kind of desperation:

> The radio is the only entertainment left for me, because I miss the newspapers. So to keep interested in what is going on I must have the radio or else I will break down and die. (55)

Circumstances oblige several Enterprisers, living in areas isolated from the principal towns where newspaper delivery is non-existent or erratic, to rely heavily upon radio for their news. Said one:

> I do not get newspapers here and people hardly leave the village, the roads are no good and we are out from the rest of the kingdom: so you can see why we do not read papers here. . . . I miss a lot but it is not my fault. We are living like animals. There is nothing but work, food and sleep. (215)

Illiteracy among the entrepreneurial group also contributes to the popularity of radio news: "Here is my newspaper [pointing to his radio]. I can't read but I can hear so I don't miss a single bulletin." (055) This is an important characteristic of the Enterprisers. Illiterates in more traditional groups tend to deprecate the radio. Beduin, and even radio-listening Farmers, rate "word of mouth" as their most important source of news. Enterprisers rely mainly upon the media for their information, as in Table 8, but with interesting differences between rural and urban persons.

Table 8—Principal Sources of News

	Rural	Urban
Radio	72%	65%
Newspaper	39	54
Word of Mouth	34	19

The rurals rely upon word of mouth more than the urbans; but they rely much more heavily upon radio—somewhat more, indeed, than do the urbans.

Some *literate* Enterprisers also prefer radio, condemning newspapers as agencies used to dupe the masses:

I don't think I lose anything by not reading the papers because I don't find much interest in them. The papers are full of untruthful news in order to betray many of the simple people like me. . . . I like very much to hear the radio. (225)

Two other literates echoed this view with added arguments—that newspapers only copy and distort news that is heard *sooner and cheaper* on the radio. Both trust radio, but maintain that newspapers rework radio news to their own designs:

All our papers are censored and do not write things correct. They get most of their news from the radio. Why should I poison my mind by reading such false news? . . . Why should I pay money to read news when I could get them from the radio? (214)

One of my friends who works at *al-Urdun* newspapers told me that they take domestic news from the coffee houses, official communiques from the radio and all the rest from their own fabrications. (219)

The Enterprisers are clearly "news conscious." When asked to name their favorite radio program, 90% gave top priority to news (as compared with 14% for Koran readings). What kind of news are they interested in and why? When asked to tell the last news items they had received, the Beduin exclusively and the Farmers mainly recalled family and local news. By contrast, over half the items recalled by Enterprisers were international, and an additional 15% of items concerned Jordan-Israel relations. On this point, in Table 9, there were interesting differences between the rural and urban subgroups. Rural interest in family and

Table 9—Last Item of News

	Rural	Urban
Family or local news	23%	2%
National	20	22
International	50	70
Other	7	6
Total	100%	100%

local news virtually disappears among the urbans, who put their attention mainly on international items. Many urban respondents say they listen to international news just "to be well informed" or because it "is good to listen to the news." Such attitudes toward "the news" and toward the desirability of being "well-informed" become manifest, in the Middle East, among the Transitionals. Often this occurs only because the individual's occupation encourages it. In such cases, interest in foreign news is related to immediate economic utility—the perspective of the petit bourgeois, whose main concern in life is his shop. Anything which impinges upon it will attract his interest; anything else tends to be irrelevant. Several small Enterprisers reveal this perspective. A goldsmith is concerned with gold:

> I like to hear foreign news, because to a certain extent these news have a relation to my work. The price of gold is higher than it was before the war in Korea. . . . I care for news about wars or any other changes in the international affairs because such news have a direct connection with my work. If I don't follow the news daily I can't work; I will be losing a lot in difference of price only. (199)

Similarly, a grocer says "the war in Korea affects the market in the village." A cereal agent explains:

> I care for the foreign news so that if a war is going to happen I shall have to guard against it by taking care of my expenses and all other matters which will be regarded as extravagant. (153)

A tailor is concerned with government economic policies:

> It has direct effect on me. Anything that the government does, whether in putting more taxes or giving licenses to import goods and all other things, will cast a beam of light as to whether I shall charge people or not. (104)

A driver is interested in the potential advantages of war for himself:

> I am most interested in foreign news because I am very anxious to get a war. Because then I can work for more pay. The British army will come . . . they will employ me for more pay and that is good. (91)

A barber is concerned with the increasing prices of imports:

> I like to hear the foreign news. Of course nowadays the most important news are about the Korean war. All the markets of the world are affected. All prices went higher since the Korean war. All the articles which were imported from the various countries have stopped now. (200)

As one goes down this roster, it seems increasingly likely that these respondents are playing the thoroughly modern game of finding "practical" reasons to "rationalize" their preferences. That international prices should concern a goldsmith seems plausible; with a barber rather less so. But the "reality" of these views is less relevant than that the Enterprisers have begun to perceive connections between their personal concerns and the larger universe of events. This is not cosmopolitanism, but an intermediate step from localism to a wider arena. That this step occurs in the Cold War epoch tends to link it with the political issues which nowadays dominate the wider arena.

Enterprisers who listened to international radio tended to divide, on the question of preferences, into two groups: those favoring Arabic broadcasts from Cairo as against British broadcasts from London. These groups differed in more than a simple matter of taste. A striking difference was the greater interest in and knowledge of international affairs possessed by BBC listeners. For example, all but one BBC listener correctly identified Trygve Lie, whereas less than half of the others could do so. In recalling news items, twice as many BBC listeners referred to international events. Among BBC listeners the distinctly modern type of news interest becomes quite manifest—the interest in *news for its own sake*. Such persons sometimes identify more intensely with the world than with their country. Thus a wholesale grocer:

What happens in our country is insignificant as compared to the foreign world. What does it affect the world if we had not rain this Winter? But it affects them if Russia has overwhelmed Korea and occupied it. (172)

This attitude begins to appear among respondents who heard BBC at all in the past month; it is highly developed among those listeners who heard BBC most often in the past month (and hence may be considered BBC veterans). Three such "veterans" rank at the top of the media-consumption scale. All three have a good knowledge of English, two speak French, and two read such foreign publications as *Life, The Spectator, Picture Post* and *Reader's Digest*. Their psychic posture is illustrated by their detached, analytic comments on these magazines. One such, comparing *Life* and *Spectator*, finds that the latter's "arguments are more sound and reasonable. It is more scientific and original." (169)

The owner of a stone quarry, asked to compare *Picture Post* and *Reader's Digest* with newspapers published in Jordan says:

> The difference is almost equal to the distance between Mercury and the earth. Foreign writers are specialized, better paid; therefore they can afford to improve their qualifications; thereby they have productive ability of a much higher standard. (013)

These respondents feel that they "belong" in the larger world as participants, and consider it important to "know what is going on." They articulate modern reasons for their interest in foreign news. One feels the obligation to know; another stresses the enjoyment of knowing.

> I am following the news of the war in Korea. I don't know why, but I find myself interested to follow such news very closely. It doesn't affect me directly, but I am indirectly affected, for if they have an effect on the country's situation then I will be affected in the same manner. (169)
> The world is getting so near together that one enjoys knowing things from here and there. (013)

This is a long step toward the Modern perspective which, in Jordan, we find mainly among the group we have designated Elite.

5. The Cosmopolitan Elite

As the most self-confident and activist group, the Elite exhibit the participant style of modern man. Twice as many Elite as Enterprisers (and three times more than Farmers) declared that the individual *can* do something to solve the biggest personal problems that he faces. But *vis-à-vis* the West, the Elite are relatively insecure. This shows in their frequent description of Britons or Americans as cold and snobbish; many of them feel personally rejected as well as politically dominated. The fear of being misunderstood by the West runs through some interviews. A young lawyer, born in Jaffa and living in 'Amman, 26 years old and described as having an aristocratic bearing,

> was very particular in stressing to write full details—word by word—of what he said. "But why?" I asked him. He said, "I like that the Americans will have a correct idea about the Arabs. Not all the Arabs are Beduin. There are many who are educated and have valuable thoughts and ideas." (222)

Another young refugee in 'Amman, a rich company executive aged 30, made the following reply when asked what he thought about the interview:

Americans can tell how far behind them is the rest of the world. Because they think that they are superior in every field, they look down on all the other races. (203)

The thread of ambivalence toward the West, so profound among the Egyptian and Syrian elite, also runs through the Jordan responses. But extreme oscillations between admiration and aversion occasionally are reduced to equilibrium in a well-ordered personality. Thus, a college-educated restaurant owner, aged 30, said:

I would like my countrymen to know how to *choose the good things* about western civilization for in my opinion this is a very important stage . . . there is a tendency towards imitating the Westerners in *everything* they do. (015)

The most salient Elite characteristic is its Palestinian background. These respondents were interviewed less than a year after formal unification of the East and West Banks into one nation. Psychic displacement was indicated by their responses to the interviewer's request for adjectives to describe "Jordanians." Some refused. Some substituted "Arabs" and others "Palestinians." Still others, less discreet, applied to Jordanians such adjectives as "stupid," "rash," "ignorant," "lazy," "in need of medical aid," "obedient and simple"—clearly implying that these descriptions applied not to themselves, but to the backward people in whose midst they unhappily were settled. This Palestinian influx was the latest accretion to what was already an "external elite." Transjordanian officialdom had been "recruited" earlier, under the British mandate, from surrounding areas. A careful observer in the mid-1930's concluded that most government officials, teachers and professionals in the Amirate were imported. The educated Palestinians naturally found Jordan lacking in the civilized amenities to which they had grown accustomed in Haifa or Jaffa. They resented the lack of freedom in politics and the press. They were appalled by prevailing standards of literacy and health. And they were preoccupied with problems external to those of Jordan.

The media judgments of the Elite illustrate their discontent. Practically none of the refugees had anything good to say about Jordan's leading paper, *al-Urdun*, which was cited as least liked, and often in terms of contempt. Although it provided the only detailed account of daily government operations in 'Amman, almost all Elite respondents of Palestinian origin read instead *al-Difa'a* or *Falastin*, published in Jerusalem, which focused on matters of interest to refugees and reflected more familiar viewpoints. The rare approval of any Jordan paper by the Elite went to *al-Mithaq*, for reasons explained by a refugee lawyer:

> I like its dissatisfaction with the prevailing situation in the Arab countries on the whole, particularly Jordan, and especially the political aspects of it. [What else?] They also discuss political and social injustices in Jordan. (222)

This 'Amman weekly was the organ of the opposition National Front, legalized in 1950. Its daily complaints column proved so popular, however, that it was closed down in March 1951.[41]

Elite dissatisfaction with life in Jordan was evident also in their low opinion of local radio. They turned rather to foreign broadcasts. Of 15 BBC and VOA listeners among the Elite, only four approved the local station; the others took a tone of disdain. Even apart from political issues, the foreign listeners considered its broadcasts too parochial for their broad interests:

> I feel it is limited. Too localized. (175)
> It is quite elementary. (203)
> I don't think too highly of them. No variety. (105)

This group represented, of course, the peak of Jordanian exposure to mass media. Of its 29 members, all but one listened to the radio; all but two read a paper; all but five attended the cinema. All attended college and practically all lived in the major cities, 'Amman and Jerusalem. While the group included a poet and a Member of Parliament, more typical occupations were the professions (lawyers, doctors, teachers) and government officials.

As we would expect, despite its anti-Western politics, this was the most Westernized group in the sample. All but two spoke English fluently; indeed one woman was so Westernized that she could read Arabic only with difficulty. Half of the group had traveled in Europe; 23 of them read such publications as *The New York Times*, *Time Magazine*, *Ladies Home Journal*, *Colliers* and *Vogue*. Striking evidence of modernization was their strong preference for Western music, in both the jazz and classical modes. The M. P. said only: "The music of the local stations is *not* applicable to the taste of the educated classes." (012) A high civil servant explained the cosmopolitan demand for variety more fully:

The musical programs [from Turkey] are varied every night. They have a different series with a different tempo. One night they have a very nice selection of Turkish and Greek tangos. They are really very pathetic and sensational. Another night they have hot music, jazz and swing. This is also very enthusiating. On another occasion they have an excellent series of Spanish guitars. Very often they have classical music —music of Beethoven and Schubert. (203)

To most of the Elite, the mass media are an indispensable instrument of modern civilization, serving a deep personal need. Among these respondents, resistance to the movies on religious grounds disappeared and their function in modern living was stressed:

Movies are the best means of showing a nation's culture and art through a tangible and visible way. (026)
It can be very good, useful, psychologically and morally. (106)
They are very necessary for life. (050)

A wealthy young architect summed up these views with a tribute to movies as purveyors of insight, as teachers of the modern style:

Movies are the best means of communicating a people's culture and civilization to the other parts of the world. It is a mirror of a country's advance in life. . . . Movies are one of the modern means of entertainment which is quite indispensable as a part of our daily life. I couldn't imagine how flat life would be without the movies. It has become very essential that everybody should go to movies and learn many things about the secrets of life. One usually pays much money to learn a new thing about life. In the movies such a lesson costs very cheaply. (176)

Newspapers, too, were seen by several Elite respondents as not merely useful but essential:

In general they are a necessity in life. Every educated man should read at least one newspaper daily. (146)
Papers are the best means of communication, for conveying a nation's ideas and movements in any part of the world to another part. (166)
Newspapers are necessary for the community. (050)
Every one of us like and should know about his neighbors and up till now the newspaper is the best way that can give us all this. (015)

This feeling for the value of the media reached its peak with radio. More than any other medium, radio gave this Elite instantaneous access upon demand to the larger world with which they identify:

> Radio? Wonderful. . . . A school in its own. Takes one all round the world in one sitting. (106)
> Radio is very essential. No one can stay without hearing a radio once or twice a day.
> Radio is a necessity in life because during this age of speed one must know everything as soon as it takes place, otherwise he is outdated. (050)

The *quality* of media interest among the Elite was distinctively Modern. A majority registered the news-for-its-own-sake attitude, which, among the Enterprisers, had been exhibited only by the BBC listeners. Some have learned to handle news at the peak of modern style, in which world politics is perceived as a game. Thus a Palestinian pharmacist:

> [I listen to the news about Korea] just to know who is winning and to pass time as if watching a football game. (102)

But this uninhibited modernism of Palestinians reflecting their own recent liberation was less easy for those who had grown up in an older traditional environment. Such persons, though they had learned much that was new, had perhaps not wholly unlearned the awesome old wisdom which motivated some Transjordanians to say: "Look at the Palestinians. They listened to the radio and God destroyed them." For older persons among the Palestinians, it was not quite so obvious that God speaks wrathfully through the radio. But one was beset by doubts and dilemmas. What, after all, about the movies?

We began this review of the modernizing impact wrought by the Palestinian influx by sorting respondents according to the four principal *milieux* of Jordanian life: desert, village, town, city. Within each group there are consistencies of similarity; between the groups there are regularities of difference. Bearing especially on questions about the mass media, these similarities and differences trace the course of modernization in Jordan. But as a modern society evolves, a traditional society passes. What of this story in Jordan? To tell this story in the same way would require another chapter repeating the same data in a different setting. This would try, unduly, even the most patient reader. Perhaps the outlines for such a chapter can be suggested by a single case.

The Questioning Qadi. The passing of traditional society in Jordan is suggested in the responses given by one old Palestinian, an influential member of the Muslim clergy. Wise and patient, responsive to the demands made upon him by the world, this established elder dramatizes the tensions which modernization engenders in an educated person committed to traditional ways. This 63-year-old, white-bearded *Qadi* (judge), appareled in the flowing robes proper to his profession, occupies a position in Jerusalem such that "when people address him they take all care to do that with every respect and they listen carefully when he talks." (011) A wealthy man, formerly owner of vast orange groves in Palestine, he studied Islamic law at Istanbul in pre-1914 days. He represents the top stratum of religious leadership, commanding respect from all classes, and exempt from the scorn that one young college-educated refugee had expressed: "You see, most of our sheikhs and those that pretend to be religious leaders are laymen and they do not represent the thought of the educated class." (050) Our judge falls into a different category. Among his steady stream of house visitors are not only ordinary folk seeking advice on such matters as the propriety of taking a second wife, but government officials and prosperous merchants asking his opinion on problems of food supply in the event of world war.

In contrast to the secularized leaders who are cut off from the more religious masses, the *Qadi* has a ready-made channel of influence with the population. An important Islamic journal has complained that religious leaders waste their opportunities to mold public opinion:

> The sermons and speeches that one hears . . . expiate on heresies, sins, the life after death, its pleasures and torments, corruption and laxity of sexual morals to the exclusion of all such topics as have a direct bearing on the social, economic, and political well-being of the Muslim community.[42]

Few religious leaders are equipped to guide Islamic youth over the spiritual crisis arising from their need to harmonize conflicting values. The *Qadi*, however, is cognizant of his role as influential arbiter between the old and the new. He cites as his greatest personal problem: "How to form an idea and an attitude toward this changing civilization."

He is influential because he is grounded in tradition and speaks

in the accustomed categories of thought, yet he is aware and informed on modern problems. His intellectual lineage is that articulated by Muhammad 'Abduh, Mufti of Egypt during Lord Cromer's
administration and prototype of the Muslim seeking reform within
an Islamic framework:

> To attempt reform by means of a culture of philosophy that is not
> religious in character would require the erection of a new structure,
> for which neither material nor workmen are available. If the religion of
> Muslims can work these ends and has their confidence, why seek for
> other means?[43]

The judge accepts this rationale, but he is no longer so confident as 'Abduh was that it can work. He was pleased, for example,
that he had been able to serve nationalist ends by theological
means. With "a smile of satisfaction and reward" he described
his role "when the government thought of applying the inheritance
tax . . . we opposed it and we succeeded in our efforts and we told
them it is against Islamic law and tradition . . . I feel that I did
my duty towards my country because then we were under the
British mandate and all the tax would go out of the hands and
benefit of my countrymen." (The implication is that, under an
independent Arab regime, equal theological force could be applied
toward the opposite end.) But the *Qadi* is not completely happy
with the need to justify all activities in terms of religion. For
Islamic tradition is often at odds with the processes and products
of modern civilization.

Hence, it is not surprising that the judge's basic ambivalence
between Islam and the West is most apparent in his reflections
on the media. He has a radio and he listens both to news broadcasts and to Koran readings; he is indeed among the rare Elite
respondents (14%) who mention the latter. His comments reveal
a desire to defend radio as an instrument for fostering *both* traditional and modern values:

> To tell the truth, one gets mixed up from the many things he wants
> to impart to the public. [I would give more] religious talks in order to
> turn the people from being too materialistic. We can dwell on the verse
> from the Koran: "Material things are not eternal." Moreover, one can
> give talks over the radio and instruct the people about . . . literature
> and health.

Newspapers should perform a similar function. The judge feels that they serve a didactic purpose, that they are means of communication of thought between highly educated writers—such as those on *Falastin*—and the rest of the population. If he were editor, he would run a party paper that "would lead to progress—education and the raising of social standards."

But it is with regard to the cinema that the conflict is most apparent. The *Qadi* is not a movie-goer, though he is bemused by the cinema. He once saw a movie, twenty years earlier, and apologizes by explaining that he was compelled to go for occupational reasons:

> You see, I personally do not feel like it, but I have a position which many look to as a religious authority. . . . You see, I had to know what a cinema looks like as many people talked of it and I believe as a Judge of legislation I should know about new things.

The professional obligation, however, in the end turns out to constrict an intense personal interest. The *Qadi* is a prisoner of the tradition which he feels obliged to represent. Confiding in the interviewer (because the latter was a friend of his son and a Christian), the *Qadi* admitted that he feels restrained by the conventional Muslim norms which his followers expect him to uphold. His personal dilemma involves those public choices between Mecca and mechanization which are crucial for the Middle East elites, particularly those who wish to gain modernity without losing the traditional Arab-Muslim syndrome:

> Although I do not know why and how it came to be as such, but traditionally people are used to look at us—people in religious clothing—as carriers of the flag of tradition. In their own way of thinking about us they rule for us, through time and tradition, the line we should follow. . . . Frankly, I see no harm to see a good and well made film. Take, for instance, the film of *The Thief of Baghdad*. My son says it invoked in him the feeling of hope towards the glory of the Arab Caliphs. When he was telling me about it, I also remembered the greatness of the Abbassid Caliphs. . . . [I went to the movies] twenty years ago, doing so with the saying, "to know something is better than ignorance about it."

But he has not gone back since.

On the Margins

X.

Iran: In a Bipolar World

> "Never did reformer take
> Passion's way,
> But that both worlds he must stake
> In the play."
>
> —SAADI

GEOGRAPHY set Iran's destiny as a gambit in contests among great nations—"Persia Among The Powers." Says one historian: "The modern era for Persia may be considered to have opened with the rise of Russia and the pursuing by Peter the Great of policies aimed at extending Russian rule to the Persian Gulf."[1] If one starts from the first Russian war in 1804, under the reign of Fath Ali Shah, the modern era in Iran is designed by the criss-cross of Russian ambitions and Western counterpoints.[2] Iran's internal evolution has been cut to the pattern of her external dependence, following the move-and-check sequence played across the Iranian plateau by the great powers. Iranian modernization today still follows the leads of external power.

1. Iran Between the Powers

The historic lines drawn in the contest between Imperial Russia and Imperial Britain still shape the Iranian role. But today the political arena is global, Russia is Soviet, and the Western spearhead is in Washington. The familiar stakes of Persian geography have been augmented by the flow of Iranian oil. This heightened interplay as subject and object of global politics explains why Iran has so seldom, in the cold war era, been far outside the spotlight of world attention. The current interaction between external stakes in Persian oil and geography with the internal process of social change in Iran merits consideration.

Warm Waters and Crude Oil: Russia's historic search for warm waters inevitably took the southerly direction. Contained in the north by frozen Arctic seas, in the east by Siberian wastes, in the west by the ramparts of modern Europe, the course of Russian empire led southward to the Mediterranean or the Indian Ocean. Effectively blocked from passage to the former through the Turkish Straits, she only prized more highly the alternative route through the Persian Gulf.

Britain's interest in denying Russia access to the Mediterranean and the Gulf followed from her permanent, almost obsessional, concern with the imperial Lifeline. The Gulf was used merely as a way-station between British Channel and Indian Ocean, but it figured also as essential link in an alternate Tigris-Euphrates route of egress from the Mediterranean—should Suez and the Red Sea ever fall. So powerfully did the Lifeline image work upon British geopolitical thinking that inalienable control of the Persian Gulf became a fixed condition of imperial policy.

A century of war and diplomacy aimed at Russia went to maintain British primacy. The main concession to Russian ambition was acquiescence in the conversion of the Caspian Sea into a Russian lake. But Soviet policy, while welcoming the Caspian fisheries, never renounced the larger design of Russian imperialism. When the Soviets joined with the Nazis to carve out a Eurasian "new order," Secret Protocol No. 1 of the Four-Power Agreement signed on November 26, 1940 began: "The Soviet Union declares that its territorial aspirations center south of [its] national territory in the direction of the Indian Ocean."[3] The postwar Azerbaijan maneuver, the tours of Bulganin-Krushchev and Mikoyan-Saburov, signify that the USSR has not renounced the traditional goals of Russian expansionism. But the old stakes have grown more weighty. Soviet presence in the Persian Gulf today endangers more than the British Lifeline. It gives the Soviets access to Asia Minor and North Africa; and therewith the posture for an envelopment action against the whole of Western Europe. That is why the American purse and power have now become available when British primacy has faltered.

Moreover, the modern West has become an oil civilization. Without the lubricants derived from petroleum, the wheels of Western life would grind to a halt. Mobility is the condition of modern enterprise and oil is prerequisite to movement. Some equivalent of a Berlin-to-Baghdad lifeline has become essential for every industrial nation of the modern West—e.g., the calamity which befell the Nazi *Luftwaffe* in World War II was not unrelated to the failure of the *Drang nach Osten*. This is not likely to change until some distant day when nuclear energy has replaced oil as the major means of mobility. Hence, there was consternation in the West when Dr. Mossadegh nationalized the Anglo-Iranian Oil Company (AIOC) in March 1951, forced its British operators from Iran, and thereby halted its daily flow of 700,000 barrels at a critical phase in Western rearmament. Domestic production in the U. S. and in Kuwait, Saudi Arabia, and Iraq was accelerated so rapidly that 1951 world production exceeded the previous year's by 460 million barrels. Thus the West reinsured itself against extreme dependence on Iranian oil.

But the West still needed the Iranian buffer to Soviet penetration of the Persian Gulf, which could compromise Western access to its other and possibly irreplaceable oil sources. Oil and geography thus conjoined as strategic necessities in a bipolar world. Stated concisely: "Any optimistic outlook for the free world rests on the availability to the NATO nations of adequate supplies of petroleum at all times and under any circumstances."[4] The oil image has become the nightmare of Free World policy as once the Lifeline image was of British policy. But there are genuinely new elements in the old game, which may prove decisive for social change in Iran.

New Bottles—New Wine? It was a Persian poet who pointed out that old wine may be poured in new bottles. The old geopolitical stakes in Iran have received a new bipolar packaging. What effect have these external rearrangements upon the internal processes of Iranian life?

While Russian designs still supply a central theme of Iranian politics, Russian policy today is armed with the specifically Soviet instrument of a world Communist movement operating in each country according to Soviet requirements. The *Tudeh* Party is a genuinely new ingredient in Iran's world posture. Through its organization ancient grievances and new demands in the internal life of Iran can be channeled into a position of maximum leverage on issues of world policy. The collaboration of the *Tudeh* with Dr. Mossadegh in driving out the AIOC was a potent expression of this new force.

The classic counterpoint to fear of Russian ambitions has always been, for Iranian diplomacy, reliance upon some protector in the West. The usual big brother was Britain, but there was room for maneuver. In 1808, with Britain and Russia jointly engaged by Napoleonic maneuvers, Persia joined France in a campaign aimed at both—directly at Russia and also (with Napoleonic wile) at Britain in India. A century later, as Britain seemed ready to concede Tsarist supremacy in northern Iran for Russian support against the Triple Alliance, the diplomats at Tehran turned from "Perfidious Albion" to Berlin for protection against their ancient Russian enemy.

In the traditional game, then, "the West" was composed of highly competitive nations among whom, as one protector deserted her to seek Russian favor, Persia could choose another. The rules of the game have changed under the discipline of bipolarity. The Baghdad Pact raises Iranian balance-of-power politics to a global level. As the European nations no longer compete against each other with Russia as a balancing power, but rather form a Western bloc coordinated against a Soviet bloc, Tehran is likewise obliged to deal with "the West" as its protector. The terrain has expanded, while Iran's space for maneuver has shrunk. What changes of political style have accompanied this new structure of the world arena?

One type of change, under the rule of bipolarity, is the effort to eliminate the cruder forms of profiteering developed under the old imperialism. Before it was expropriated the AIOC provided the British government, which owned a 52% interest, with its greatest single source of revenue and was regarded as a pork barrel. The American government, deriving no part of its revenue from Iranian oil, regarded the issue as a powder keg. American intervention in the dispute led to an agreement which gave the Iranian government a far larger share in oil revenue than it had previously enjoyed. This represented a shift from colonial to cold war perspectives, from economic to political goals, from coercive to persuasive means.[5]

The impact of this new Great Power style is visible in recent Soviet practice as well. The Irano-Soviet Fisheries Company provided over the past quarter-century as rapacious a model of imperialist economics as the AOIC, with a measure of chicanery added. The Fisheries Convention of 1927 provided for equal shares of world proceeds from Soviet marketing of caviar bred by Caspian sturgeon in Iran's territorial waters. The USSR ignored its stipulation for a rotating director, chief accountant, and chief engineer. By keeping these posts in Russian hands, the USSR managed to keep the profits in the same place. Whereas Iranian sources computed the Company's annual earnings at about $2 million, the actual sums received by the Iranian government annually averaged about $25,000 (1/40 of the amount due).[6] Recent negotiations sponsored by the USSR suggest that the Soviets too have reconsidered whether this game is worth the candle. As the primacy of politics over economics is acknowledged, $1 million a year more or less comes to seem relatively trivial. The solicitude for genuine friendliness among the Iranian population, rather than mere acquiescence by its government, is quite new. As late as 1943, the allied Big Three felt free to hold their momentous conference in Tehran without the invitation, or indeed the prior knowledge, of Iranian officials.[7] Today such behavior might seem bad form.

Some new wine there doubtless is in these new bottles. The Baghdad Pact's MEDO—Middle East Defense Organization—is a case. Whatever its military value (and current depreciations may be as excessive as were earlier expectations), MEDO does possess psychic dignity. Unlike the regional security foreshadowed in the Sa'dabad Pact of 1937, it brings great powers of the West into reciprocally-binding arrangements with the regional powers. Hence, whatever its impact upon Soviet designs or the Cairo calculus, the impulse underlying MEDO is likely to reshape the social structure of its participants. How much of the new wine of national autonomy can Iran take?

The Insecurity Elite: Aspirations toward autonomy are quickly raised, but the lifeways of dependence die hard. In a land habituated to defining itself in terms of those outside powers which, at any given moment, threaten or protect it, there develops a chronic instability. This diffuses certain traits of insecurity, which have cumulated in an Iran immobilized by a closed elite through many centuries. A recent monograph on the Iranian economy concludes:

The background is insecurity: the insecurity of the landlord against the caprice of the government, insecurity in the face of attack by hostile elements, whether internal factions or foreign invasion, and the insecurity of the cultivator *vis-à-vis* the landowner and others. The law was not backed by a predominant and impartial force; effective power therefore rested with whoever wielded the greatest force and, in the absence of control by the law, the exercise of this force depended almost entirely on personal caprice. Insecurity is no less the keynote at the present day than in the past.[8]

Chronic insecurity breeds distrust. Government becomes a game of intrigue played by those who can pay the stakes. An elite forms with no claim to power but its purse—the machinery of Iranian politics being, according to Miss Lambton, "the relatively large sums of money which are at the disposal of the privileged classes."[9] Politics by bribery among the few usually implies politics by blackmail against the many. The Iranian peasantry, cowed by ignorance and fear, has traditionally maintained a stolid indifference regarding maneuvers in Tehran.

A frequent outcome, in nonparticipant social systems governed by a closed elite reliant upon intrigue and coercion, is the widespread diffusion of mendacity as an acceptable mode of self-defense against the mighty. Every army has some such phrase as "to lie like a trooper" and every autocracy has tended to produce a similar code among its subject peoples.[10] In the Ottoman Empire there flourished the code of *ketman,* whereby people spared themselves difficulties over their beliefs by simply disavowing them at appropriate moments.[11] The Persian Empire, home-based on Shi'ite Muslims in a non-Shi'ite world, long ago developed the comparable doctrine of *taqiyeh* or dissimulation. This permits a Shi'ite, in danger by reason of his religion, to pretend that he is a Sunni, a Christian, or a Jew as best serves his needs of self-defense. One American authority has moderately observed: "The ramifications of this practice extend beyond religion."[12] While Western discussions of *taqiyeh* have produced a net surplus of moral indignation over careful description, the pervasiveness of mendacity is acknowledged by Persians.[13] *Taqiyeh* has even been conventionalized to deal with superior force on the level of top policy negotiations:

> In view of Russian strength and Iranian weakness, the latter government . . . was compelled often to resort to almost every known form of evasion in dealing with issues, which originated in Moscow. Apparent naiveté, circumlocution, dilatoriness, specious argument, misunderstanding—these and numerous other techniques were employed by Iranian officials.[14]

Widespread mendacity as a mode of self-defense against a chronically insecure environment makes for a highly unstable self-system. Indeed the Persians are, according to Professor Frye, a "people of extremes" and a basic condition of modernization is to remedy "the Persian's lack of confidence in his fellow man."[15] Professor Hoskins notes the political relevance of "the character and behavior of the Iranian peoples, who are as given to extremes in temperament as their habitat is full of contrasts."[16] The extremist temperament leads to extremist politics, in which violence and the frenzy of mobs play a role. This makes conduct of a moderate policy exceedingly difficult, particularly within the limited margins for maneuver left by current world politics. No longer can Tehran, when Britain and Russia seem ready to lay Iran on the sacrificial altar of their joint convenience, counterpoint by *ad hoc* arrangements with France or Germany. "East" and "West" are now solid blocs. Tehran has been obliged to make a net choice between the two world constellations.

When domestic violence adjudicates world issues, the politics of the mob requires systematic supervision. Certain social formations take over the distinctive function of mediating messages, including calls to action, between elite and mass. Added to the traditional relay chains of bazaar merchants and itinerant peddlers are the modern message centers manned by the new-style intelligentsia in government, education, mass communication. Preoccupied with the play of power, they claim in return larger shares in the process of decision than a closed elite in a non-growth economy can accommodate. Those deprived of what they consider their due, under the rule of things-as-they-are, often turn from the course of moderation to stake their chances (having nothing to lose but their claims) on extremist action. Operating against the center from both extremes of the political spectrum, these extremists limit the scope of moderate governance. By maintaining mob rule in the streets, they can reduce any government to counter-violence or impotence. One horn of this dilemma is Hajji Baba's ancient formula: "Our kings must be drinkers of blood and slayers of men to be held in estimation by their subjects and surrounding nations." The other horn is surrender.

This cycle of Iranian politics was exhibited in the great postwar crisis symbolized by Mossadegh. By coalescing the extremist factions around his leadership, backing the slogans of radicalism with the techniques of assassination and mob violence, Dr. Mossadegh was able to destroy a moderate government, force the Shah into flight, and install himself in power. As the inherent instability of governance by violence in turn undermined his own controls, Iran tottered on the bipolar verge. The balance was restored only by a vigorous coup organized by the army. Violence countered violence. The rule of terror—not of principle or policy—decided the course of events.

The survey of Iranian attitudes was made at a propitious moment. Iranian extremism had long focused on the AIOC. Passage of the oil nationalization bill in March 1951, and the overt display of British resistance to it, had raised to fever pitch the anti-British sentiment common to all varieties of political extremism in Iran. The Nationalist interest in driving out the foreign overlords was obvious; the Communist (*Tudeh*) interest followed logically from its permanent alliance with the USSR. United behind Mossadegh, who incorporated the stirring symbolism of independence in a strategy of violence that released ancient hatreds and repressions, political extremism took control of Iran. In the crucial months of this crisis—May to July 1951—the interviews were collected. They provide a rare gallery of political self-portraits, painted at a moment when cumulative tensions had reached a critical phase.

2. The Struggle at Home

Underlying the chronic tensions of Iran, as of other Middle East lands, is the great gap between aspirations and capabilities. The desires for national independence, social justice, personal pride of place—these have been stirred among Iranians by the same gusts of ideology that have dispersed the symbols of modernity over all the lands of the earth. A "backward land" becomes an "underdeveloped country" when these winds of doctrine have inseminated a substantial portion of its population with the aspiration toward a modern style of life for themselves and their fellows.

Slow Starts and Extremist Goals: A modern society must know enough about itself to plan its probable future course in terms of trends from the past to the present—social science being, in this sense, a distinctive "feedback" mechanism required for modern governance. Iran does not know the distribution of its population, nor even its approximate total size. Population estimates range from 15 to 20 million—with a consensus around the median figure of 17-18 million.[17] This population occupies a total area of 628,000 square miles, a territory larger than all of western Europe. As no official census has ever been taken, estimates of population density are partial and unreliable. But Iran clearly is not over-populated, with density averaging about 27 per square mile over total area and (excluding desert) about 41 for inhabited areas. Density varies from a high 70-95 in the Caspian provinces to less than five in the southern regions.[18] Nor is there any early prospect of overpopulation. While actual rates of fertility, mortality, and morbidity are unknown, the birth rate has been estimated at 30/1000, which is low for the Middle East. With infant mortality estimated as high as 500/1000 live births, and average rural life expectancy at 27 years, net natural increase is relatively slow.[19]

Population distribution shows little regional mobility or ur-banization. There are over 40,000 villages in Iran housing about 60% of the population, with another 10% living in migratory tribes. The 30% of townspeople are about equally divided between smaller towns, cities over 50,000 and Tehran. Rural resettlement during the past decade has been mainly toward larger cities. The popu-lation of Tehran alone doubled, in the period 1940-1950, to over one million.[20] These urban migrants, in Iran as in Egypt, encounter unemployment, undercompensation, and the miserable conditions of slum life. For there are few signs of a growth phase in the Iranian economy. Without industrial expansion, the movement of discontented and deprived thousands to cities augurs not economic growth but political instability.

The ecology of Iran provides optimum conditions for the prev-alence of extremism. The population is dispersed around the vast desert, in villages isolated by inadequate or nonexistent commu-nications. They remain locked in the ancient round of daily life, eking from their old soil with their antique tools (some antedating the Christian era) their immemorial produce. Regarding the new world stage, on which their national drama now unfolds, they are uninformed and uninvolved.

A striking result of the survey, made at fever pitch of the most profound crisis which has racked postwar Iran, is that a sub-stantial proportion of the population was unaware and even unin-terested. When the interviewers asked about the most important problem facing them and the nation, they responded in the man-ner of Traditionals in all places and times. Their concerns were not the nationalization of AIOC and expulsion of the British, nor the contest between Dr. Mossadegh and the Shah, nor the future alignment of Iran within the Soviet or Western worlds. Salient were the familiar concerns of the daily round—ranging from major problems of survival (health and livelihood) to trivial details of family life.

Sharply contrasted with this remote and inarticulate mass was the small group whose personal involvement with the national crisis was profound. These persons cared deeply about public affairs, vibrating to the day's headlines with the intense affectivity of a farmer hearing news of his sick calf or a mother of her soldier-son. When asked what were their main private and public problems, these Moderns could scarcely differentiate between them, so deeply had they incorporated the symbols of political identity. By contrast with the apathetic mass, these highly-involved persons expressed an urgent need to impart to others their concern with public issues, a compulsion to "do something about it." This agitational disposition among a small frustrated corps is a distinctive mark of revolutionary extremism, just as the less intensive mode of "participation" by a massive contented electorate is a mark of democratic moderation. The mark of extremism is highly visible in Iran.

Non-Growth and Counter-Elite Formation: In each Middle Eastern land, we have seen, the political drama is played by a small cast of characters with the mass as chorus. As the wheel of social change turns, new aspirants come forward eager for a role downstage center. How the traditional elite will handle these aspiring young is a key question for the changing social structure: will they be incorporated in new sub-elites or alienated into counter-elite formation?

Incorporation is no easy task in a non-growth economy. Iran develops few of those constantly growing and changing occupational roles which embody young men in the elite structure. The clergy, the military, the bureaucracy—all these are charges on the public treasury, already overburdened and scarcely capable of expansion. The teaching corps is pitifully inadequate, but unlikely to multiply opportunities until Iran develops a modernizing economy in which literacy is an essential skill. Without an expanding business sector, there is little room for the lawyer and accountant, for the specialist in industrial management or labor relations, for the insurance broker or the investment manager, for the account executive or the public relations counsel. Advertising is stillborn and the mass media abortive. Where, in Iran, is "the man in the gray flannel suit"? Whatever his unpopularity among Westerners wearied by opinion brokers, in Iran he would be a more useful stimulus to modernization than the agitational intellectual in a hairshirt of vivid hue.

Given its limited absorptive capacity, Iran suffers from an overproduction of intellectuals. In a society about 90% illiterate, several thousand young persons go through the classical routines of higher education each year. Learning no skills that can be productively employed, these collegians seek outlets in the symbol-manipulating arts toward which their humanistic studies have oriented them. Their effort supplies a poignant instance of usable training rendered useless by its social environment—newspapers without readers that last a week or a month, film companies that never produce a film. The mass media, as distinctive index of the Participant Society, flourish only where the mass has sufficient skill in literacy, sufficient motivation to share "borrowed experience," sufficient cash to consume the mediated product. In Iran the mass media are anemic and with them, annually, die a thousand hopes.

Meanwhile Iranian higher education continues to overproduce intellectuals as noted in this ironic comment:

> The existing school system has been relatively successful in accomplishing the aims of its founders three-quarters of a century ago, which were to produce a distinguished intellectual elite and to establish an instrument by which the thoughts and actions of the common people might be efficiently manipulated.[21]

A decade later, while "the secondary schools have produced graduates who apparently are not fitted for anything but to continue their schooling or to enter teaching," the collegiate population continues to rise. In the two-year period after 1946, a 50% increase brought the number of university students to 6,525. Adding to these another 2,000 abroad for higher education, one perceives that young intellectuals are being produced in quantities far exceeding Iran's capacity to consume.

Identifying the Extremists: All dressed up with no place to go, these frustrated young men go looking for excitement. It is they who form the hard core of political extremism in Iran today. This was indicated by the 1951 survey and confirmed by subsequent interviews which the author conducted in Tehran four years later. The political extremists were consistently the most Modern group in the Iranian sample. As in the other countries, so in Iran. The higher a respondent ranked on the scale of media behavior the more likely he was also urban, educated, well-off, and highly empathic. Controlled sampling had apportioned five men for each woman, three radio listeners for each non-listener, two urban for each rural resident; over half were relatively well-off by Iranian standards. But even among this preponderantly Modern sample, the Extremists differentiated themselves as a relatively homogeneous group.

The whole sample was classified along a continuum of political attitudes, located first by orientation as Left-Center-Right and then by intensity as low-moderate-extreme. Each person was classified by his response to these four questions:

(1) What would you say is the biggest problem that Iran as a nation faces today?

(2) What can people like yourself do to solve this problem?

(3) Suppose you could suggest anything you wanted to our government—what are some of the things you would tell them?

(4) What is the biggest problem that people in the same circumstances of life as you face? What can you do about solving it?

Responses were differentiated by the key symbols around which they were organized: Person, Class, Nation. Those responding in purely personal terms were classified as Apolitical. Respondents who defined problems in terms of Class—e.g., poverty, illiteracy, feudalism—and proposed solutions requiring social reform were classified as Left. Those preoccupied with problems of National aspiration requiring national action were classified as Right.

As in Syria, classification was based on the complete problem-solution sequence. Of two respondents naming "poverty" as the main problem, the one proposing to solve it by redistributing wealth was classified Left, the other solving it by "kicking out the foreigners" was classified Right. Similarly, if the problem was "disunity," the one proposing to solve it by "punishing the landlords" was sorted Left; if his solution was "strengthen the Army" he was marked Right. Attitudes toward the symbol NATION were usually consistent and decisive: the Left emphasized national obligations to the people, the Right individual responsibility to the nation.

Respondents both Left and Right were then sorted into three levels of intensity indexed by: (1) personal involvement in public problems; (2) violence of proposed solutions to these problems. All respondents had been asked whether they considered themselves happy or unhappy—and why. Those who specified public problems as reasons for their unhappiness were classified as more involved, others who cited only family or other personal problems as less involved. Those who proposed such solutions as "hanging the landlords" or "overthrowing the government" were classified as more violent; others as less violent. The extremist Revolutionary Left was *both* involved and violent; the Middle Left was *either* involved or violent but not both; the Reform Left was *neither*.

To determine intensity among Right respondents, who were mainly preoccupied with National problems, a variant of this index was used. A respondent was considered involved if he expressed willingness to undergo personal deprivations for the achievement of national goals; if not he was considered less involved. Violence was indexed by the advocacy of aggressiveness against foreigners. A person who wanted to "destroy Britain" was classified as violent; one who merely wanted to "defend Iran against Britain" was not. The extreme Nationalistic Right was *both* involved and violent; the Middle Right was *either* but not both; the Conservative Right was *neither*. In this typology of political attitudes respondents distributed as shown in Table 1.

The Apolitical group represents the passive uninvolved mass of Iranians; the moderate groups on both sides include the tradi-

Table 1—Distribution of Political Types

Political Type	% of Respondents	No. of Cases
Revolutionary Left	12%	29
Middle Left	14	33
Reform Left	18	42
Apolitical	7	16
Conservative Right	29	69
Middle Right	10	22
Nationalistic Right	10	23
	100%	234

tional elite that has governed Iran over past decades; the extremists represent those newer formations that in Iran, as in the Arab lands, are using their access to the mass to challenge the traditional elites. The latter form those potential counter-elites whose influence upon the mass may be decisive for the duration, tempo, and balance of the modernizing processes at work in the area. This is why, despite their small numbers and lack of statistical significance, the data on extremism may clarify the interplay of communication and social change in shaping Iranian lifeways.

3. The Structure of Iranian Extremism*

The ideologies of Iranian extremists present themselves as sharply opposed. They espouse different causes, command different layers of loyalties, and appeal to different sets of sentiments. The *Tudeh* Party, a lightly camouflaged Communist movement which speaks for the Revolutionary Left, and the extremely nationalistic Pan-Iranian Party regard each other as mortal enemies. Underlying the symbolic divergence of the party ideologies, however, there is a remarkably similar sociology of party ideologists. The recruitment and composition of leadership at these schismatic extremes appear to follow the same process.

Sociology of Extremism: At both ends of the political continuum, Extremists register consistently higher on the sociological indices of the Participant style. Thus, while the sample was 20% female, the Extremists are exclusively male. Further, while the sample contained equal numbers over and under thirty years old, a disproportionate share of the younger persons are Extremists. It is no news that younger men tend more frequently than their elders of either sex toward extreme political positions. In Iran they move toward both extremes, and are mainly recruited from the same sociological environment as the ruling elite. A stable social structure, operating under a consensual elite, would absorb many of these vigorous young men into governance rather than alienate them into counter-elite extremism.

Consider urbanism, the index which makes the profound initial

---

* This section is based on the 1952 BASR report "The Political Extremes in Iran," by B. B. Ringer and D. L. Sills. See also their "Political Extremists in Iran," *Public Opinion Quarterly* (Winter 1952-53). (As 18 cases were added after these reports appeared, there are differences in percentages, usually minor.)

cleavage between elite and mass in Iran as elsewhere. By comparison with the Apoliticals, as in Table 2, both varieties of extremism are highly urban.

Table 2—Urbanism

	Extreme Left	Apolitical	Extreme Right
Those in *urban* areas now who were:			
raised in urban areas	73%	37%	73%
raised in rural areas	16	13	18
Those in *rural* areas now who were:			
raised in urban areas	0	13	0
raised in rural areas	11	37	9

At both extremes three of every four were raised and still live in cities, as compared with one of three Apoliticals. Whereas 13% of the latter raised in a city have since moved to the country, not a single Extremist at either end has forsaken urban for rural pleasures. Clearly, the Extremists are urban.

Consider education, the next great cleaver between elite and mass in the Middle East. When differentiated at the point of effective literacy—the passage from elementary into secondary school—the results are shown in Table 3.

Table 3—Education

	LEFT			APOLITICAL	RIGHT		
Education	Extreme	Middle	Moderate		Moderate	Middle	Extreme
Elementary or less	39%	59%	53%	81%	56%	27%	25%
Secondary or higher	61	41	47	19	44	73	75

The Right is better educated than the Left. But the progression away from both sides of the Apolitical Center is more striking. What the Extremists have in common, compared with current elite as well as the mass, is that they are better educated. Consider, in Table 4, the index of socioeconomic status (SES).

Table 4—SES

	LEFT			APOLITICAL	RIGHT		
SES	Extreme	Middle	Moderate		Moderate	Middle	Extreme
Poor	6%	18%	12%	57%	17%	14%	9%
Moderate	78	65	55	36	68	71	82
Well off	16	17	33	7	15	14	9

Poverty prevails only among the Apolitical mass. The politically-involved respondents are better-off. Their lot improves as they move toward the extremes—up to a certain point. A lower proportion of Extremists than others is in the poor group, but the highest proportion is in the moderate (not wealthy) group. The data obviate the conventional assumption that the Extremists are simply the "have-nots," suggesting rather that they are the "want-mores." They oppose the current "system" not because they have no stake in it but because, on a range of social values, they want more than they get.

Illustrative are Extremist responses to the question whether they were happy about their lot in life. As unhappiness had been used to classify Left Extremists, in this analysis the Extreme Left is unhappy by definition. Distribution of responses on the Right demonstrate, in Table 5, a comparable prevalence of unhappiness among the Extremists.

Table 5—Happiness on the Right

	Apolitical	Moderate Right	Middle Right	Extreme Right
Happy	61%	56%	57%	29%
Unhappy	39	44	43	71

What makes the Extremists so much unhappier than their fellows is that they "want more" and believe they deserve more—i.e., that the society has not done as well by them as it should. While they have more education than the ruling group, for example, they have less money. Far from poverty themselves, they talk about the poor while their eyes are on the rich. This produces the phenomenon of "relative deprivation," whereby a person's discontent with his lot is set by the standard to which he aspires. His expectations determine whether a person feels that life has indulged or deprived him.

To check this attitude, each respondent's spontaneous references to economic matters were sorted into two categories: descriptive and deprivational. A doctor talking without affect about public health programs, a farmer about the relation of weather to crops, a business man about the costs of production—all such were classified as descriptive references. Counted as deprivational were statements reflecting the individual's dissatisfaction with his share of the national wealth. Included were general references to the economic status quo which indicated personal frustration—e.g., poverty, unemployment, economic insecurity. Where deprivational outnumbered descriptive statements by 5 to 1, the respondent was classified as highly deprivational, with results shown in Table 6.

Table 6—High Deprivation

Extreme Left	Middle Left	Moderate Left	Moderate Right	Middle Right	Extreme Right
80%	45%	29%	33%	36%	66%

While the saliency of deprivation is more frequent on the Left than the Right, there is a clear progression toward the extremes at both ends. This common attitude underlies their common posture toward the national community. This posture we call *alienation* and its widespread occurrence among Iranian Extremists on both sides merits consideration.

Psychology of Extremism—Alienation: Counter-elites typically dissociate themselves from the governing elite and its institutions. "We or they" is the classic rhetoric of dissociation. It symbolizes the counter-elite's partial or total transfer of participation from the current institutions of governance to competitive institutions under their own management—secret societies, clandestine networks of communication, illegal political parties (or legal parties controlled by a covert apparatus). If their withdrawal into covert institutions is successful, the counter-elite then uses these bases to re-enter the arena of public participation for the purpose of subversion.

In Iran, the 1951 survey showed this subversion process in operation. While it is no part of our purpose to study political organization, the interviews do reveal pervasive dissociation from current institutional life among Extremists. In the next section we shall describe the ideological formulas invoked to justify their alienated posture. Here we note only the frequent occurrence of its psychic manifestation, namely dissociation from the major institutionalized orbits of social life. An Index of Social Dissociation, using the following items, provided the relevant data:

1. *Lack of family ties.* Those single at normal age-range for marriage; also those divorced, separated, or widowed, who have not remarried.
2. *Lack of religious ties.* Those who state that religion is of little or no importance, and rarely or never attend the mosque.

3. *Limitation of friendship ties.* Those who prefer to have few friends rather than many.
4. *Individualistic recreational patterns.* Those who prefer solitary rather than interactional recreations (e.g., visiting, conversation).

When respondents having more than two of these attributes were scored as highly dissociated, the distribution in Table 7 was obtained.

Table 7—High Dissociation

	LEFT		APOLITICAL	RIGHT		
Extreme	Middle	Moderate		Moderate	Middle	Extreme
75%	45%	38%	13%	28%	41%	51%

Dissociation from the institutional structure, among Extremists, paralleled its dissociation from the prevailing value-system. Very striking, for example, was the extent of Extremist withdrawal from religious participation. As Shi'ites, Iranian intellectuals historically have shown a special religious concern. Withdrawal from the community of religious practice and sentiment is a profound matter. Hence it is noteworthy that most Extremists score low on an index of religious involvement. In their responses to the question how important they considered religion to be in their daily life, and the saliency of their spontaneous reference to religion, respondents showing high religious involvement are grouped in Table 8.

Table 8—High Religious Involvement

	LEFT		APOLITICAL	RIGHT		
Extreme	Middle	Moderate		Moderate	Middle	Extreme
29%	37%	51%	44%	60%	33%	33%

A further test of alienation was made by constructing a general index of traditional reference. This classified and counted each respondent's spontaneous reference to traditional symbols—e.g., family, locale, religion, ethnic group—in discussing his views on public policy. Fully twice as many at both extremes, compared with the politicals, made *no* such traditional references whatsoever.

Extremist alienation from Iranian tradition is modulated by their acquisition of more expansive perspectives. An index of social horizons was constructed by noting the number and variety of "reference groups" which each respondent mentioned spontaneously. The assumption underlying this index is that a person who refers exclusively to a few familiar groups (family, community, nation) thereby exhibits narrower horizons of social contact than another whose discourse goes beyond these to include other, less traditional reference groups (class and mass, great powers and small, parties and politicians, etc.). Scoring the number and variety of their reference groups gave the distribution in Table 9 of respondents exhibiting broad social horizons.

Table 9—Broad Social Horizons

| | LEFT | | APOLITICAL | | RIGHT | |
Extreme	Middle	Moderate		Moderate	Middle	Extreme
55%	33%	26%	0%	26%	38%	54%

This suggests that detachment from the governing institutions and dissociation from elite perspectives has not confined the Extremist within a narrow circle of purely personal activities and interests. On the contrary, withdrawal from the traditional governing symbolism has been accompanied by displacement of affect onto a new set of symbols. The outcome has been not privatization, but extreme politization—with the flow of political activity running in separatist counter-elite channels.

This was suggested by the broader social horizons among Extremists than their more moderate compatriots. But it was not conclusive, since social horizon so defined could be achieved by a social isolate, who might "interact" heavily in his fantasy life but experience few real contacts in his daily round. The question was whether Extremists really interacted so much more with others in their daily lives, as their broader social horizons indicated. To check the Participant Style in actual behavior, an index of social interaction was constructed on the basis of these three questions:

(1) Has anyone come to you for advice recently?
(2) Have you yourself gone to anyone for advice recently?
(3) Did you talk to anybody about this [news item]?

Persons answering yes to two of these questions were scored as socially active in Table 10.

Iranian Extremists, despite alienation from governing institutions and perspectives, are actively engaged with their fellows.

Table 10—Social Interaction

	LEFT		APOLITICAL		RIGHT	
Extreme	Middle	Moderate		Moderate	Middle	Extreme
45%	33%	12%	6%	20%	34%	46%

Indeed, this appears to be closely related to their political commitment. To test whether this was so, respondents were divided by education, which provides skills and opportunities that foster contact among people. If only the better-educated persons in the sample scored high on interaction, then no new relationship had been estiblashed. Table 11 shows respondents scoring high on interaction.

Table 11—Social Interaction by Education and Political Type

	LEFT			APOLITICAL	RIGHT		
High Interaction With	Extreme	Middle	Moderate		Moderate	Middle	Extreme
High Education	60%	36%	21%	0%	33%	46%	55%
Low Education	30	31	5	6	11	17	35

Two findings emerge from this distribution. First, as expected, well-educated people tend to be more interactive than poorly-educated people. Second, and more significant, the relationship between high interaction and political extremism exists *regardless of educational level.* Even among the poorly-educated, Extremists are more actively engaged with their fellows than Moderates. It is not possible, from these data, to draw any chicken-or-egg conclusion: that interactivity breeds extremism or vice versa. We can conclude that the two "go together" and, whatever their psycho-genetic relationship, tend to reinforce each other.

The importance of this finding is highlighted by a final test, designed to see whether high alienation (as scored on the earlier index of social dissociation) in fact occurred among the same persons as high interaction. If not, then we could not properly speak of an "extremist syndrome," but only of the high frequency of two special traits among different individuals who happened to share extremist political views. Cross-tabulating the two indices produced the distribution in Table 12. The association between the two traits, as we move toward the extremes, is very striking. There seems to emerge a clear "extremist syndrome"—an underlying psychic structure of political extremism in Iran which combines high dissociation from institutions and ideologies with a high degree of interaction among people.

This syndrome is important for public communication because it is the classic posture of the revolutionary agitator. Alienated from the governing system, he goes forth among his fellows to preach a new faith and gain loyalties for a new power. This mission is performed by persons who have mastered the New Word, and when political extremism enters this phase in any society it usually comes under the management of the alienated intelligentsia. In later phases of the quest for power the revolutionary movement is dominated by persons skilled in organizing techniques; but during the earlier phase of recruitment by propagation, leadership goes to those trained in the manipulation of symbols.

Table 12—Dissociation and Interaction

	LEFT			APOLITICAL	RIGHT		
	Extreme	Middle	Moderate		Moderate	Middle	Extreme
Persons with *high* dissociation showing high interaction	67%	42%	6%	0%	26%	50%	57%
Persons with *low* dissociation showing high interaction	0	27	16	7	18	31	17

This requires a corps habituated to the skills and channels of the old elite—living and working in circumstances that provide the time and opportunities needed for prop-agit work; educated enough to formulate and diffuse the new ideologies. The Iranian Extremists, who are mainly urban, professional, moderately well-off, and well-educated, meet these sociological requirements. They manifest also the main psychological requirements—that they be sufficiently alienated from the old elite's perspectives and practices to develop their own code, and sufficiently interactive with their fellows to spread the new gospel through the society. The Extremists thus exhibit the characteristics that define radical opinion leaders. That a majority of Extremists appear to be potential leaders does not, of course, mean that a majority of Iran's potential leaders are Extremists. But if such a leader is detached from existing institutions (alienation), is receptive to new ideas (rejects traditional for broader social horizons), is skilled in presenting these ideas to others (highly educated), and is in regular contact with his fellows (highly interactive)—then this type of leader is found most frequently, in Iran, among the political Extremists.

The survey reveals, then, the existence of a maturing Iranian counter-elite. As the sampling was originally controlled for other purposes, and the number of Extremists relatively small, the data permit neither inferences as to the present size of this revolutionary corps nor extrapolations as to its growth-potential. What the findings do show is that the logical structure of a revolutionary counter-elite is already in being, and that its internal struggle for power is inevitably linked to the bipolar external conflict between Communist and Free Worlds. At this point the Extremists diverge sharply in matters of ideology—the cleavage reflecting in miniature the bipolar division in the outer world, with the usual quota of qualifications imposed by local conditions.

In such a situation, where rival propagators of revolutionary symbols are locked in ideological conflict, the questions that interest students of communication concern content, technique, conditions of sucess. What are the rivals selling? With what sales technique? What market conditions favor the ones over the others? We examine these questions in turn, starting with the competing commodities—the rivalrous ideologies.

The Ideologies of Extremism: The function of ideology is exceedingly complex. It requires clinical data of an order quite different from that obtained by survey methods to make a complete evaluation of the interaction between the public and private faces of any person. But our results do contain some findings of considerable suggestive value.

How ideology modifies perspective is illustrated by the divergent images of their own countrymen held by the two extremes of Iranian political sentiment. All respondents were asked what words they would use to describe the people of Iran. A composite description of an Iranian, as viewed by Left Extremists, presents us with a poor, talented, intelligent, broad-minded, hospitable laborer. As perceived by Right Extremists, he is patriotic, brave, patient, faithful, chivalrous, intelligent, hospitable. Aside from the consensus on intelligence and hospitality, the Extremists are talking about two consistently different sorts of person. The differences recall our historical distinction between a traditional "courage culture" and a modernizing "ingenuity culture."

The main line of ideological cleavage ran along the axis of

CLASS *versus* NATION symbolism. The nationalist Right, in the summer of 1951, was mainly preoccupied with expropriation of the AIOC, thereby putting the British in their place and restoring to Iran the glories of full national sovereignty. Their comments on this specific issue provide a profile of their posture. The greatest problem facing the nation is "the oil nationalization law," said one university teacher, and "to nationalize its oil, Iran will suffer death against any aggression" (072).

The vocabulary of violent action against foreigners pervaded the solutions to this problem offered by the extremist Right. Some emphasized that the responsibility for such action rested with the government, which "should kick all foreigners from Iran" (172) or "should oust the foreigners and cut their hands from Iran" (175). Others stressed the need for popular action: "[We must] cut the English hands from Iran" (092) and "get the pirates out of Iran" (021). Still others invoked joint action by elite and mass—e.g., the government should "let all the people fight for oil nationalization." (070)

Rightist attention was focused upon national aspiration and action, with no consideration of possible class deviations from the common goal. They simply assumed popular consensus behind the symbols of national will. One government employee sought direct action by the whole population: "All should be united and participate in demonstrations against the usurper oil company." (192) Another civil servant, who considered himself a "holy warrior," said simply: "There is nothing above shedding blood for the nation, for which all Iranians are ready." He had no doubts about the universal readiness to struggle:

All the people of Iran are of a single, united opinion. Fifteen million Iranians long for the day to sacrifice themselves for their country. The solution can be achieved merely by blood-letting. (134)

This statement epitomizes the ideology of the Nationalistic Right. Expressed here is the supremacy of national goals, the mystique of national unity—an image of the big body politic in which no class-sentiment can compromise the universal desire to sacrifice oneself upon the altar of national aspiration. Furious indeed are these Right Extremists against all who permit personal or class desires to obstruct the course of national destiny. They call upon the government "to punish internal traitors" (175)—for dissensus, in their eyes, can only be treason. And they would "hang all the country-sellers in one morning." (134)

On the Rightist verdict, the trees of Iran would be well populated. For Leftist ideology, while enthusiastic about nationalization and expropriating the British, locates these items in a different battle order. On the Extreme Right, the goal is national sovereignty and the means is a unified national will; on the Extreme Left, the goal is a classless society and the instrument is class-struggle. Hence, even when the Extremists agree in identifying Iran's problems, they quickly diverge over appropriate solutions. The Left regarded nationalization of AIOC as but one step among several required to create a just society—and not necessarily the most important step. In discussing this issue, the Left quickly generalized its solution: "We should nationalize our industry, dividing the lands which rich people would turn over to the government." (106)

The same divergence appears when Extremists discuss poverty, the other great commonly-recognized problem. The Rightists perceive this as "the economic plight of Iran" and solve it by expropriating foreigners. The Leftists perceive it as "the suffering poor" due to class inequality and exploitation, and solve it with a class conception of Iranian society. "We should," they say:

—"remove class discrimination by distributing the land among the peasants." (097)
—"give the right of every class to its own, so that the toilers would get their own, and the capitalists would not ask for more." (032)
—"take the idle money of the capitalists and exploit the mines in order to solve our problems." (061)

From these different perspectives on such common problems as oil and poverty follow conflicting systems of loyalty, patterns of organization, courses of action. The Right seeks national unity in the struggle, to the point of bloodshed, directed primarily toward the expulsion of Britain. Says one Extremist physician: "I wish to see some day the British Isles completely overrun by water, and not an Englishman living on the earth." (092) Says another Rightist, a civil servant: "If we could get the oil profits, we could solve all our problems." (074)

The Leftists waste no affection on Britain, but they locate her on a different psychopolitical map of the world—not as personal enemy of all Iranians, but as political symbol of decadent imperialism: "Britain likes to have the whole world as her colonies; she has colonizing policies in Iran" (188); "She wants to perpetuate her colonizing policy in the world." (147) The Leftists consider that colonialism maintains itself by alliance with the indigenous elite. Accordingly, they regard "national unity" against the British as a diversionary tactic (except, for the *Tudeh* Party, when this coincides with the requirements of Soviet foreign policy). Instead they urge a clean break with existing institutions, and advocate a struggle in which the blood that will be shed is Iranian blood.

Equally armed with their conflicting ideologies, equally equipped by temperament and training for public agitation, it remains for the Extremists on both sides to position their internal struggle with respect to the world bipolarity.

4. Bipolarity and International Communication

Most significant, for the general purpose of this study, is the manner in which international communication complicates or reinforces the bipolar postures inside Iran. One process is illustrated by a student, an articulate extremist of the Left, who dislikes certain Tehran newspapers because their editors "work for a group of parasites and are servants of obnoxious imperialism." He prefers to get his news from Radio Moscow which exposes "the ominous policies of stockholders, bankers, and brokers." These broadcasts reinforce the ideology of the Revolutionary Left: "It wakes the nation up, so we are not deceived by the pro-foreigners, parasites, and the subservient ruling class of Iran." (147)

On the Right, the relationship between internal and external polarities is complicated by the special hostility toward Britain. Hence, the line of international communication from the West to the non-Communist population is less direct than that from Moscow to the Iranian Left. One government supervisor explains that he does not like BBC programs "because they emphasize the service which they believe they have rendered Iran, although in their 150 years of dominance they have done nothing except ruin the entire political, social, moral, and economic structure of the country." (162)

An additional complication derives from the subtle differentiation in Rightist ideology between the beloved nation and the detested elite—between the abiding state and the current government. It is difficult to formulate this distinction clearly and persuasively, except in the name of some recognizable counter-elite formation. Thus, the Leftists can make clear, when they seek to subvert the ruling elite, that they propose to install their own governance in the form of the *Tudeh* Party or some other recognizable agency of revolution. The Right Extremists, on the other hand, oppose to the solid substance of the current elite mainly the incorporeal symbolism of the nation—its mission, primacy, unity. The Leftist advantage shows in their attitudes toward external communications.

Bipolarity and Extremism: Frequently respondents were unable to draw from their domestic political posture a definite choice between the bipolarized superpowers.* While a substantial number of Leftists were not univocally pro-Russian, this was more marked among Rightists who were not pro-American. But here an extraordinarily interesting difference appeared: deviants from the American side were mainly Right extremists; deviants from the Russian side were mainly Left moderates.

This suggests a major modification of the conventional assumption that pro-Americanism is Rightist and pro-Sovietism is Leftist. The more exact formulation would be that pro-Sovietism goes with extremism, pro-Americanism with moderation. We shall examine the full implications of this finding in section 6 of this chapter. Here we present the data on which it is based. The seven political types were regrouped according to the intensity of their political convictions—respondents on the extreme Left and Right combined as "extremists," middle Left and Right as "middle range," Reform Left and Conservative Right as "moderates." These groups were then cross-tabulated into the categories pro-Russian, pro-American, Neutral. The distribution in Table 3 was obtained.

Table 13—Bipolarity by Political Intensity

	Pro-Russian	Pro-American	Neutral
Extremists	40%	7%	4%
Middle Range	28	25	24
Moderates	28	66	55
Apoliticals	4	2	17
Totals	100% (28)	100% (94)	100% (75)

* This section is based on the 1952 BASR report "Partisanship and Communication Behavior in Iran" by B. B. Ringer.

The pro-Russians are more likely to be Extremists, whereas two of every three pro-Americans are Moderates. The more intense political involvement of the pro-Russians goes with the fact that they are a younger, better-educated, more active group. Compared with the pro-Americans, 13% more pro-Russians are under 30 years old, 23% more have had higher education, and 8% more score higher on the index of social interaction.

By contrast, the pro-Americans are more numerous in the sample. Of 157 who expressed judgments on *both peoples*, 70% scored as pro-Americans compared with 36% pro-Russians. On judgments of the *two governments*, the margin was narrower but still substantial: of 110 respondents, 50% were favorable to the U.S. government, only 29% to the Soviet government. (That the survey was American-sponsored, even though Iranians did all the interviewing, probably biased these results.)

But the most striking feature in the attitudinal map of Iranian bipolarity is the huge zone of nondifferentiation. Many Iranians assign equal-values to both poles. This finding emerged when the joint judgments of respondents on both American and Russian peoples and governments were cross-tabulated in Table 14.

Table 14—The Zone of Neutralization (Equal Values)

Attitudes* toward Americans	Attitudes* toward Russians			
	Favorable	Ambivalent	Indifferent	Unfavorable
Favorable	3	15	2	23
Ambivalent	10	19	3	44
Indifferent	0	1	21	8
Unfavorable	10	5	2	35

* Respondents disapproving *neither* people nor governments are classified as favorable; those disapproving *both* are unfavorable; those disapproving *either* but not both are ambivalent; those expressing *no* judgment are indifferent.

We have given the actual numbers above, rather than percentages, for the persons in several of these categories may be regrouped with others to illustrate various points. For example, all 95 respondents (47% of sample) *above* the diagonal line were counted as pro-American on the view that each person in this position exhibits a less hostile view of the USA than of the USSR. On this view the 28 Iranians (14%) *below* the line are classed as pro-Russian; and the substantial 78 respondents (39%) *on* the diagonal are classed as Neutrals.

We note further that the process of equal-valuation does not lead to the theme "bless you all" but rather to "a plague on both houses." Only three respondents were equally favorable to both poles; over ten times as many were equally *unfavorable*. Moreover, hostility toward one pole does not imply a real preference for the other. Thus, 52 of the respondents unfavorable toward Russia are ambivalent (partially unfavorable) or merely indifferent toward America. If we consider these Iranians as effectively neutralized by the bipolarizing process, then the proportion of genuine Neutrals rises to 64% of the respondents—and this in a relatively dynamic and participant sample of the total Iranian population.

Why are they hostile toward Russia? Some see the cold war as a new name for the ancient geopolitical game: "Russia wants to lock us up behind the Iron Curtain. She wants to get to the Persian Gulf and develop her strategic position." (134) Others still think of money rather than strategy: "Russia wants the whole world to become Communist. She has the same thought about Iran, besides she has some financial interests in Iran." (009) Still others, recalling past cases where the Powers were quick to solve their differences over Iran by dividing the cake, see the current bipolarity as a new version of great-power conspiracy: "The Russians want to divide Iran between England and themselves." (037)

Why are they hostile toward America? Here, be it noted, hostility is less widespread and more qualified—it is the U.S. policy, not the American nation, that draws fire. But the feeling is intense, and underpinned by a sense of deception. American performance has somehow not squared with Iranian expectations: "it has not fulfilled its promises" (007); "it has given many compliments [talked too much] but has not shown any effective action" (006); "she doesn't do what she says." (011) Beyond this, America in a bipolar world has behaved just like every other Great Power—handling Iran as just another strategic pawn on her global chessboard. Thus: "America is thinking of its benefit all the time in any country. It wants to make Iran a military base, but it wasn't successful yet." (070) Or, more generally: "America works for its own benefits. It pretends to be a friend of Iran, but its purpose is finding some influence in Iran." (061)

The sense of deception became acute during the AIOC crisis: "Recently America has interfered against us and for the British in the oil dispute—that is why all the people dislike America."

(026) But its effects upon pro-American sentiment appear to be less profound than one might suppose. At the height of the crisis, the interviewees were asked: "Has your attitude changed any during the past year toward the U.S.?" Those who responded affirmatively were then asked: "Would you say you felt more or less favorable toward the U.S. today than you did a year ago? Why?" The same questions were asked regarding Russia, with results shown in Table 15.

Table 15—Attitude Changes During Oil Crisis

	Pro-Russians	Pro-Americans
More favorable to own side	68%	15%
Less favorable to own side	8	25
No change	24	60
	100% (25)	100% (70)

The most striking change was the proportion of pro-Russians who declared that they had become even more pro-Russian. Given the dialectical attitude of Communists toward public statements, the relatively low evaluation of objectivity among Iranians, and the difficulty anyone has in self-appraisal, this is a type of declaration that must be interpreted with considerable reserve. Even so, only one of four pro-Americans declared himself less favorable to America. Other evidence shows that American influence remained strong enough, through the crisis, to modify unfavorable attitudes toward the British. The reserve of good will which enabled pro-Americanism, though shaken, to survive even the oil crisis was formulated by one high school teacher:

Americans in general are freedom-loving people and at the same time are prospered by conditions in their own country. Thus, their policies toward other countries, including Iran, are favorable. But I am worried that probably in a few cases they have joined Britain to take steps against foreign countries. This, however, is not proved to me yet. (024)

The lesson of the oil crisis is significant for our study. Pro-Americanism did not founder, but it faltered and was slightly weakened. Pro-Sovietism, even with reserves made for purposeful mendacity, apparently gained a massive consolidation among its adherents. This was largely a communication process—for most Iranians had little direct knowledge of events, but judged the issue by "what they were told" through the mass media and through their informal networks of oral communication.

In these circumstances, it is important to understand why the bipolar allegiances of so many respondents were effectively neutralized. An important element is that the pro-Americans, while more numerous than the pro-Russians, are more Moderate. They take their political convictions more lightly, are more subject to the seizures of ambivalence, and are more likely to weaken in the presence of crisis. The pro-Russians, on the contrary, are Extremists whose personal involvement with their political ideology is very intense. In a crisis situation, they consolidate their gains. History, they feel, is on their side. And, sociologically, they are better equipped to act as the agents of a historical destiny. They are younger and better-educated; they take a broader view of Iran's role in the world arena. Perhaps more important, they are more active among their fellows—giving and seeking advice, discussing the news. The pro-Russians, in short, have gained a superior position astride the Iranian communication networks, and this is likely to influence the future shape of Iranian society. Consider the facts.

The Bipolarization of Media Behavior: Each respondent was asked a set of questions about his radio-listening habits: (1) Did he listen at all? (2) How often? (3) By plan or at random? The answers are distributed in Table 16.

Table 16—Radio-Listening by Bipolarity[22]

	Pro-Russians	Pro-Americans	Neutrals
Radio listeners	93%	78%	56%
Daily listeners	87	79	29
Planned listeners	55	45	39

More pro-Russians listen at all; of the listeners more pro-Russians listen daily and more plan their listening.

What do they listen to? An important index is source: where messages come from, in the bipolar world, often determines their contents. Knowledge of international broadcasting indicates ideological sophistication—i.e., awareness of the interplay of interests and ideologies in the world arena. The pro-Russians are way ahead in ability to identify international broadcasts that can be heard in Iran as shown in Table 17.

Many more pro-Russians know every major foreign station and all the minor stations grouped under "Other." Not only do more of them know Radio Moscow—but also BBC and VOA, broadcasts from India (voice of Asian Neutralism), from Pakistan (ally of MEDO), from Cairo (adversary of MEDO). Sophistication is not confined to a few pro-Russians but is spread uniformly among them. Whereas over half of the Neutrals and a fourth of the pro-Americans could identify no foreign stations, only one of 25 pro-Russians was so uninformed.

Table 17—Awareness of International Broadcasts

	Pro-Russians	Pro-Americans	Neutrals
Russia	96%	55%	43%
England	88	61	40
India	84	71	40
Pakistan	76	46	35
United States	68	55	38
Arab Countries	24	15	11
France	16	7	5
Other	60	32	21
Don't know	4	25	54
Average per Respondent	5.1	3.4	2.3

The pro-Russians match their extensive information with intensive partisanship. Asked which was their favorite foreign station, 83% named Radio Moscow and a few named India—that was all. By contrast, 71% of the low-intensity pro-Americans named India, while BBC and VOA were poor "also rans" for most of them. The non-differentiating Neutrals mainly preferred India of course; while a few liked BBC and VOA, rather more liked Radio Moscow.

While the others listen apolitically and rather aimlessly, the pro-Russians put their superior knowledge of international broadcasting to the service of their political bias. As in air warfare a priority mission is to knock out the enemy's means of reprisal, so the pro-Russians have concentrated on "poisoning" rival sources of information in the war of the airwaves. Says one: "The domestic radio is for a small portion of the people, but Moscow radio is for everybody" (184). Says another: "England broadcasts for propaganda but the Russians want to acquaint Iranians with the world situation." (180) Still another says: "The United States broadcasts for propaganda purposes. But the Russians," he adds with the privileged logic of the propagandist, *"only for changing the people's ideas."* (187) As with radio-listening, Table 18 shows, so with newspaper reading. More pro-Russians read the newspapers at all. Among those who do, more read their paper daily and they

Table 18—Newspaper Reading by Bipolarity

	Pro-Russians	Pro-Americans	Neutrals
Reads newspaper at all	89%	78%	49%
Reads a paper daily	76	51	40
Reads three or more papers	78	48	44

read more papers. None reads only one paper and few read only two papers, whereas most of the others are content with one or two papers. The pro-Russians also read more types of news; they show more interest in *all* parts of the newspaper and particularly political items (editorials, national and foreign news) as in Table 19.

Table 19—Preferred Parts of Newspaper

Most interested in:	Pro-Russians	Pro-Americans	Neutrals
Foreign news	88%	73%	64%
Domestic news	88	84	85.
Local news	12	10	9
Editorials	40	17	18
Culture	32	19	12
Other	56	51	45
Average per respondent	3.3	2.6	2.3

The centripetal tendency of media behavior that we have observed throughout the Middle East is visible also in Iran. As the pro-Russians lead in radio-listening and newspaper-reading, so Table 20 shows that they lead in movie-going.

Table 20—Movie Attendance by Bipolarity

Prefer films from:	Pro-Russians	Pro-Americans	Neutrals
America	35%	57%	58%
Russia	43	19	19
Britain	4	19	19
Don't know	4	19	19

This distribution is noteworthy. A practically universal result obtained by polling, in most of the movie-going world, is the substantial preference for American films. Even the Neutrals in the Iranian sample, whose other media preferences were as dispersed as their political ideas, give American films a solid majority vote. So, too, the hardly less diffuse pro-Americans. The preference for Soviet films expressed by the pro-Russians is a rare case. The political bias of this choice is obvious, but its full meaning is better understood in the context of general attitudes toward the movies.

The pro-Americans go to the movies "to relax," (001) "to relax mentally," (056) "for pleasure," (011) "for pleasure and relaxation." (019) This shows in the sorts of films they prefer: "love and dance movies" (015); "comedies, historical and technicolor movies" (019); "musical pictures with an interesting story" (024); "love, fighting and detective movies." (056) Aesthetic and technical categories prevail among the reasons given for preferring American films: "the staging and acting," (019) "clarity of lighting," (021) "diversity of films and beautiful actresses," (024) "skillful actors," (067) "the technicolor." (075) An unusually large number mention "the beautiful sceneries"—since, for inhabitants of the severe Iranian plateau, the sight of rolling country and greenery is a feast for the eyes. These clearly apolitical tastes sometimes become vigorously antipolitical. One pro-American moviegoer, who prefers "love and detective stories and sometimes sports," exploded: "I hate the political pictures. It is better to let the movies free from politics." (021)

The context of movie-going is rather different among the pro-Russians. They go for "the real meaning of life," (096) "moral purposes," (100) "educational purposes," (184) "scientific and ethical advantages." (188) Those who go for pleasure do not "let themselves go" completely without a higher purpose: "to pass time and learn things," (144) "for pleasure and to get their moral points," (193) "to enjoy music and learn something." (068) They prefer Russian movies, not for trivia of technique and aesthetic, but for reasons consonant with these high purposes. They have "more ethics than in any other country's productions" (188); they are "more realistic and more moralistic." There is little talk of "beautiful sceneries" here. The nuance is rather from the ethical to the ideological: "I go to the movies because they are the most powerful instruments to influence one's ideas." (148) Good ideas should be shared and good ideologies propagated, hence Russian movies are best because they "teach lessons to the masses of people." (196) What do they teach? They "illustrate human struggle for peace and demonstrate equality for all mankind." (096) No apolitical nonsense here; art and life march forward together. A pro-Russian speaks of his recent favorites:

The Real Man was a masterpiece of perseverance, chivalry, self-sacrifice and all other good qualities which a real man should possess. In *The War of Stalingrad,* it was shown how the heroes of the Soviet Union cut the egoistic hands of Hitlerists. The result is this: that a nation with a strong theory and a doctrine of "the people" (everything for the people) shall never die. In that movie, we saw how Hitler was driven back to non-existence from behind the gates of Moscow. (147)

Style and Stakes: Feelings about the media often exhibit very profoundly a person's general view of life, for the world is represented to him by the media—with the greatest naturalism and impact by the movies. His responses often express the interplay of reality and revery in his personal style. More than political partisanship, as we understand it in the pluralist West, is implicated in the divergent media tastes just reviewed.

There are important personality differences between those who regularly shun political in favor of "lighter" films (which they admire for aesthetic reasons) and others who regularly prefer "serious" films heavily freighted with useful lessons of morality and ideology. The ones are using the media as sublimational channels for vicarious experience of the lives of others. This is what Aristotle called the cathartic function of art—a highly civilized behavioral sequence. The others, meanwhile, are using the media as a preparative rather than purgative—a more pragmatic behavioral sequence akin to the war paint and dances by which certain tribes prepare warriors for battle. These different modes of handling aesthetic experience produce different results. The sublimational mode leads to contented quietism; the inspirational mode elicits agitational activism.

When these divergent modes are regularly found among two distinct groups of people, then we are dealing with a psychic gap of social consequence. Among groups which exhibit uniform sociological characteristics, they spell class cleavage. When this is the most advanced class, such a split elite tends to render the whole body politic schismatic. Wrapped in contrary ideologies and political organizations, the schismatic groups become competing counter-elites. When affiliated to the rival poles of a bipolar world arena, these competing elites tend to bipolarize the structure of internal politics as well. The strategic model of the two-player, zero-sum game supplies the rules—no shifting coalitions, no mixed strategies, and winner take all! Postwar Iran has moved in this sequence. Two extremist groups, splitting away from their elite origins, have armed themselves with contrary ideologies that instigate divergent behavioral styles leading to incompatible lifeways. Incorporating these ideologies into conflicting political movements, they have associated themselves with the rivalrous American and Russian poles of the bipolar world. Thereby they began to reshape Iran internally in the bipolar mold. But the internal bipolarization will not be completed until one of the players acquires the trump card—the Iranian mass.

The politically-relevant segment of the masses is the big stake in the current phase of the game. Once it is clearly won by either side, the final coalitions will be fixed and the winner will take all. At the moment, the Moderates control the mass after surviving two major postwar crises over Azerbaijan and AIOC. Each of these was accompanied by a series of domestic crises—mass demonstrations in the streets, arrests and assassinations, interruption of parliamentary governance, flight of the Shah, overthrowing of governments. Recurrent crisis is a sign of sickness in any society; frequent and protracted crisis can be fatal. The Iranian elite survived its postwar crises at a heavy cost, including alienation of potential recruits into both extremes of the political continuum. These counter-elites made important gains by effective manipulation of the personal insecurities which breed and multiply during public crises —manipulation accomplished through their influential positions in the national communication network.

Leftist success, in this phase of the struggle for mass support, is due to several factors:

(1) They are *sociologically* better equipped for effective mass communication—i.e., they are better educated, better informed, younger, and more active among those segments of the Iranian population that are ready to be politicized.

(2) They are *psychologically* better equipped to incorporate propaganda successes in the recruitment and organization of a counter-elite—i.e., whereas the Rightist ideology obliges people to judge issues one at a time, the Leftist ideology is a comprehensive way of life embodied in a Movement. Also, Leftist directives, cumulating in a "line" consistent with its own organizational growth, are administered by Extremists. The Rightists are restricted by the preponderance of Moderates on their side.

(3) They are *politically* better equipped to exploit the limited margins of action permitted by the world bipolarity—i.e., whereas ambivalence toward the West (Anglophobia plus apolitical pro-Americanism) among moderate Rightists weakens the bonds with their "natural pole" in the bipolar world and makes their public policy oscillate from one crisis to another, Leftist leadership, more homogeneous with respect to the Soviet center, maintains clear and consistent lines of communication between local operations and world communism in critical situations.

Under these conditions, new political energies tend to flow Leftward. The comprehensive ideology provides clear and simple solutions that attract restless souls; the monolithic organization channels their activity into a common program. Given the moderate character of the Rightist posture, extremist temperaments of variant persuasion find more outlets for vigorous action (oratory, assassination, mass demonstration, mob violence) on the Left.

The oil crisis was a case. While Right Extremists grew impatient with the moderate measures and compromise solutions sought by the governing group, the vigorous young propagandists on the Left were making their own nationalistic symbols resound and organizing the populace around themselves. The techniques of *shuluq* (commotion) and *tamasha* (show) were clearly paying off on the Left. Some Right extremists, unable to restrain themselves, carried their colors into the rival camp and there made what seemed to be a common cause.

This *ad hoc* "united front" was finally routed (with a little Rightist *shuluq* led by Shaaban the Brainless) but the Left registered a significant gain. Not all the Rightists who had coalesced with the Left remained in the Leftist camp—but a substantial number doubtless did. More important, their defections deprived the Right of its own most vigorous and action-oriented elements. Rightist attrition while the Left consolidated meant that, in the next crisis, the extremist Left would be relatively and absolutely stronger. The symbol of this process was Dr. Mohammed Mossadegh.

5. The Meaning of Mossadegh

The political posture of Mossadegh derived from a combination of elements which, account taken of differences in their personal and national situations, we have described earlier as the "Nasser Syndrome." This difficult posture seeks to ride tandem on the two great currents of radical change surging through the Middle East —national independence and social democracy. The balance is delicate because the rider cannot control the velocity of the winds nor the height of the waves, but can only seek a steady course between these ungoverned elements. Mossadegh rode high to a fall; Nasser may do the same. Other riders will try the course after them. Each such player breaks the rules of the world political game by, more or less deliberately, overbidding his hand. This introduces a special type of chaos into the game.

Who was this aged Iranian that, for two long years, focused world attention upon his every word and deed? There is no mystery about the personality, for he gave ample public evidence of the self-dramatizing flair which identifies the propagandist-agitator type.[23] The fainting and weeping spells of "Mossy" were known throughout the newspaper-reading world, which was also permitted to share his active life in pajamas—his flight into hiding (before global cameras) from alleged assassins, his protest strikes against wicked adversaries at home and abroad. The vanity associated with such exhibitionism was manifested by Mossadegh's celebration of his 69th birthday over five successive years; retirement from the Majlis being mandatory at 70 gave these demonstrations a simultaneous practical aspect.[24]

Mossadegh was prepared for his climactic years by the entire course of his career. Born 1881 into the highest level of Iranian society, the world was his oyster. His father was a Minister of the Court, his maternal uncle a prince. After taking his diploma at the Ecole des Sciences Politiques in Paris, he was engaged at about age 17 in the Ministry of Finance, where he remained ten years. In good elite fashion, he then returned to Europe for advanced studies; first at the University of Liège in Belgium, then at the University of Neuchâtel in Switzerland. Equipped with a Doctorate of Jurisprudence, he returned to a brilliant political career at home, climbing rapidly up the ladder of power:

1915-1917: Finance Committee, Third Majlis
1918-1919: Deputy Finance Minister, then Chief of General Accounts Department, then Minister of Justice (at 38)

1920:   Governor-General, Province of Fars
1921:   Minister of Finance (first year of Reza Shah regime)
1922:   Governor-General, Province of Azerbaijan
1923:   Minister of Foreign Affairs

From this height, at 42 head of Reza Shah's foreign ministry, Dr. Mossadegh suddenly toppled. During 1924-28, as a simple member of the Majlis, he opposed the chief of state at every turn. According to one observer: "Dr. Mossadegh never supported anyone in the Majlis except himself and he never ceased to inveigh against foreign influence."[25] By 1928, Reza Shah had had enough. Mossadegh was imprisoned and finally banished from the capital to pastoral exile in Ahmadabad.[26]

The details of his fall from grace are obscure, for Iranian statesmen publish no memoirs.[27] But one root of the conflict was Mossadegh's oppositionism to the Shah's internationalizing-modernizing policies. Like many a young man before and since him, Mossadegh had returned from his European studies to a sense of shame about the dismal state of his homeland. (Recall the prominence of "shame" in the memoirs of both Naguib and Nasser.) His first book reformulated Muslim law according to the Shi'ite sect, using his advanced training in Western law for comparative purposes. Comparisons between Western and Iranian ways preoccupied much of his life; comparative studies of constitutional law, financial legislation, principles of finance came from his pen. He confronted the problem directly in *Iran and Capitulations,* and by a curious skirting maneuver in *The Principle of Non-Extradition for Political Crimes.*

Nationalism took on a xenophobic character when Mossadegh, throwing his fantasies in the face of facts, declared that Iran needed no financial assistance from abroad. He opposed American aid in any form and attacked, with equal bitterness, the Irano-Soviet commercial treaty. Mossadegh, some said, was one of the rare Iranians who had never asked a foreigner for a favor. This private and public style was destined for popularity. When Reza Shah was forced into exile, Mossadegh—remembered as the man who had dared to say "no" to the Shah— promptly resumed his political career. Elected deputy from Tehran in 1944, he soon sponsored a measure prohibiting further oil concessions to foil Russian designs against the subsoil of northern Iran. Six years later, he began his campaign against AIOC by drafting the nationalization law which precipitated the great oil crisis. This shook the world and split the Iranian ruling class that had nurtured him.

Dr. Mossadegh's deviation from the elite was primarily temperamental, not ideological. Rather Rightist than Leftist in his doctrines, he deviated by excessive zeal in seeking to activate these beliefs. The moderate ruling group sought to further the national interest by playing carefully with both poles of the world arena. The extremist Mossadegh would play with neither. Instead he aimed at driving them both from the native soil, though geopolitical destiny made this an all-but-impossible mission. Rebuffed by the practical men of his class, who gave higher priority to the effectiveness of their means than the sanctity of their ends, the agitational Dr. Mossadegh turned elsewhere for support. And with him, Iranian society took a turn.

For Dr. Mossadegh's illicit relationship with the left restored the banned *Tudeh* Party to a position of public prominence, while splitting his own Rightist constituency at a vital point (by alienating the solid Moderates). This was a dangerous game in which, given the circumstances, Dr. Mossadegh could hardly win and the Leftists (whom he thought to use) could hardly lose. The ironic outcome was that this outraged product of the West nearly ceded Iran to the East, this extreme Nationalist made common cause that served the Communists. Never, according to informed consensus, was Iran pushed so close to the Iron Curtain.

The Mossadegh movement was stopped, but others will come to try again the hazardous course he designed. For the meaning of Mossadegh lies in the *style* of his politics. His daring effort to slip between the horns of bipolar dilemmas is bound to attract new impatient, extremist young men whose aspirations must find outlets in ·action. Mossadegh failed as a politician because his calculus of power was faulty—in a bipolar world one does not maximize gains by shouting "a plague on both your houses." Hence his place in history is likely to be small, for conventional history is not written in terms of political failure. But in any history of the mass media as an agency of social change in Iran, his place must be large. For Dr. Mossadegh, the political failure, was a magnificent success as a propagandist. He spoke with the weight of the ancient learned and mighty to the hearts of the newly aspiring. Hear the testimony of a minor government employee about the radio: "If there is Dr. Mossadegh . . . everybody will remain silent and listen. But there is no attention for others' speeches." (134)

What Mossadegh did was to bring the mass media and their audiences into the arena of political conflict. Once there, they are a potential reserve of political activism which no future spokesman of extremist temperament is likely to overlook. The significance of this transformation in Iranian society—the initiation of the politically-relevant mass into the bipolar game—was lost upon most reporters, caught up in the daily flow of events, but noted by one astute editorialist of *The New York Times*. Wrote Clifton Daniel, in an article headlined "Mossadegh Career Unique in Iran":

> Dr. Mossadegh was one of the first to discover that, after generations of illiteracy and political inertia, something like an informed public opinion is beginning to emerge in Iran, and he has made great use of it. It has been his custom, whenever he has any obstacle to surmount or new policy to propose, to speak to the people by radio and ask for their support.[28]

Small wonder that the first target in the *coup d'état* whereby General Zahedi overthrew Mossadegh, was Radio Tehran. "Without a microphone," said a learned Iranian observer, "Mossadegh was impotent." How, one may ask, in a land so inadequately equipped with mass media or mass audience, had Mossadegh applied so effectively the modern technique of governance through public opinion? What had changed in Iran by reason of the Mossadegh style?

6. Epilogue: The Future of Media and Mass

In the spring of 1954, four years after the original survey, I returned to Iran with these questions in mind: What heritage of the Mossadegh method was still visible? How were his successors coping with this heritage? I interviewed leading Iranians at the Court, the Ministries, the Majlis; also key Americans—the Ambassador, the head of Point Four, the chief of military mission, and specialists on their staffs. On the Mossadegh heritage these men, who had watched his operations from strategic observatories, were substantially agreed. On what to do about it, there was less clarity and less unanimity. I visited the modern media—radio stations, newspaper offices, cinemas. Also bazaars and teahouses—where messages are relayed into the mainstream of oral communication —in middle-sized towns and ancient villages. In a land where systematic social research is non-existent and statistics are treacherous, one sees what one can. I gained the impression that Iran today is balancing between two perspectives of governance. These were expressed in interviews with two responsible directors of Press and Propaganda—one before, the other after, Mossadegh.

General Farzanagan: "The People Need a Normal Quiet Life." "What Mossadegh neglected to tell the people is that the world is larger than the city of Tehran. He encouraged people to believe they could decide issues that are beyond their real competence." So spoke General Farzanagan, director of Propaganda and Government Spokesman under Mossadegh's successor, General Zahedi. Intense, soft-spoken, obviously intelligent, Farzanagan is a modern type of military man. He received a complete civil education in the U. S.—from private schools through Harvard—and his two sons are now following the same course. No militarist or mandarin, Farzanagan prescribed social justice to cure social unrest. The Mossadegh technique, he said, was spurious: instead of solutions he offered excitement. To unleash popular hatred of foreigners does not improve the well-being of Iranians and, deep down, people are aware of this. But the crowd enjoyed watching an Iranian leader who, instead of "negotiating endlessly" with foreigners, just "slapped them down."

"The Communists learned from Mossadegh, after having taught him, how to use these techniques of falsification, how to build true stones into a false mosaic. They raise constantly the same question: Is there social justice? Do people earn a fair living? Every one of us knows that the answer is 'No,' just as all of us know that the little peasant (*za'im*) really has no chance in the courts against his village-owner (*malik*). Over and over they ask: Is there not corruption in government? All of us know the answer to each question is 'yes.' But do the questions go together? The falsity lies in stringing together true statements in a spurious syllogism, which leads to the false conclusion that Communism is the only and inevitable way out.

"These techniques have worked because there is a vacuum in the minds of the people, into which our enemy can pour what he wishes to be believed. The *Tudeh* preaches equality; Mossadegh preached nationalism. Both are fine ideals. What is false is that neither has any practice for his preachments. Meanwhile, by inciting people through hatred, they prepare them only for destruction and not construction. Under Mossadegh 'the sense of discipline was broken and irresponsible license was allowed to rule.' Of course our definition of 'the people' has to be different in this country: 17 of our 18 million people have not been involved in these excitements."

The mischief has been done among the other million, which is composed of three main groups. First, the intellectuals:

In the poisoned atmosphere of our universities, people who should know better accept the Communist propaganda because it soothes some of their pains. This is to be expected when there are so few appropriate jobs for so many teachers, students, aspirants, and when those with jobs get such miserable wages. What would people in your university [M.I.T.] think of paying engineers $35 a month?

Second, the opportunists. "Their loyalties are for hire and they find ways to benefit from any disturbance. They helped Mossadegh and the *Tudeh* to create mass hysteria, which is not the same as an informed public opinion. The third and largest group were exploited by the first two—e.g., shopkeepers and artisans, unhappy with the way things are, and ready to believe what they are told and repeat it to others." These people have now recovered from the Mossadegh mischief. "The shopkeeper now tends his shop instead of spending his time orating in public."

The other 17 million are "nice, decent, kindly people who have been fooled too long by too many promises." The Mossadegh style of creating public clamor can be contained. What they need is deeds not words. "The people now must be *shown,* not simply told, the virtues of a normal quiet life."

"How are we going about this? Well, there is a National Orientation Committee whose mission is to tame people and to give them hope. Depolitizing the media is one technique: we now have a radio station broadcasting *only* music from 11 A.M. to 11 P.M. (an idea pretty popular in the States and very appreciated here). At the same time, we just signed a contract with the Varga firm in Sweden for delivery of radios, starting with 2,000 and gradually increasing to 5,000 per month, at one-third of their current price in Iran."

We left General Farzanagan wondering whether he could succeed in welding his two objectives—"to tame people" and "to give them hope"—into a single policy.

Professor Issa Sadiq: "Literacy Can Be Dangerous." Professor Sadiq, now a member of the Senate, as Minister of Education under Reza Shah had created a department of Press and Propaganda in 1940-41. A thoughtful elder statesman, whose book *Modern Persia and Her Educational System* was published a quarter-century ago, he had long pondered the traditional structure of his society and its capacity for change. His evident interest in technical details, media relays, political relevance was located in a large context. The Iranian plateau, he pointed out, was an excellent receiving area for short-wave signals. The Russians used this condition to beam three powerful transmitters—from Moscow, Baku, and a secret place in South Caucasus—that are heard better in much of Iran than Radio Tehran. These are fully effective in jamming VOA and, somewhat less, BBC. Radio-listening, he continued, serves various purposes. Whereas Customs inspection estimated 350,000 receivers in Iran, Sadiq's independent estimate was closer to 500,000. Said he:

Radios come in through other channels than Customs and often less as tax-evasion than as a military secret. I have never heard of a tribal chieftain without a radio. This is his surest means of always knowing the whereabouts of the Shah and the Chief of Staff, which at times is for him an important item of military intelligence.

His estimate of Mossadegh was qualified—an "expert publicist," certainly not a "great strategist." It seems difficult for Iranians to perceive, said Sadiq, that radio is not a national policy but one among several instruments of policy. The Zahedi government, being military men, are even less than Mossadegh used to thinking of "words and deeds as an ensemble." Mossadegh overvalued words; soldiers overvalue deeds. But since they are inevitably associated in daily life, "the political art consists in making them go together in the direction one has chosen."

Take the problem of illiteracy, said Sadiq. Teaching people to read and write is surely an admirable goal. But without a comprehensive social policy, literacy can be dangerous. My village (which Sadiq owns) became largely literate as the result of a school I created there years ago. But I left it at that. Result: Over 1,600 pamphlets in Persian, but printed in Russia, have been distributed by the *Tudeh* in my village. They have attacked every government in its turn, twisted the thinking of people without other sources of information, recruited supporters. How can they know that what is described to them as a great Peoples' Democracy is rather the blackest tyranny? How, having so little to lose themselves, shall they resist the idea that they could only gain by making others lose all? He who reads must run. "Without relation to earning a living, understanding the life of their society, and being prepared for citizenship, you see, literacy can be dangerous!"

Postscript: Returning from Iran by way of London, in May 1954, I consulted the files of letters from Iranian listeners in the BBC archives. One dated September 16, 1953, from a small town on the Persian Gulf, asked:

Why is it that all the great capitalist countries, including Britain and the USA, are so afraid of the *Tudeh* Party and try to stop its growth with the most modern weapons? Is this party harmful to society?

This is a faithful Communist representation of the world, on the simple level of popular communication, and one may doubt that this writer is quite as naive as his questions are designed to suggest. But in scattered places around the vast Iranian area, people are asking similar questions, rhetorical in some measure, in these "loaded" formulae. And such spurious questions lead, as General Farzanagan pointed out, to a false choice.

For, in the curiously ahistorical process of social change now operating throughout the Middle East, psychic "participation" through opinion is spreading before genuine political and economic participation. People acquire a voice and even a vote before they acquire a "stake." They are stimulated to have opinions before achieving the lifeways historically regarded as requisite for people with opinions. This problem of timing underlies General Farzanagan's concern with the Communist techniques of deception and Professor Sadiq's caution that "literacy can be dangerous." Both are men of liberal stamp, but both confront a society still reeling from the impact of forces let loose by Dr. Mossadegh. Farzanagan wants social justice evolved within a "normal quiet life"; he wants "to tame people" while giving them hope. Sadiq, too, wants rising literacy but he has become wary of imbalanced social change—of spreading opinions without providing the context in which public opinion works efficiently.

The mark of Mossadegh is upon such men in Iran, as everywhere in the Middle East. How to develop a participant public without unleashing an unruly mob? Nasser has raised this problem in Egypt as have the extremist leaders in Syria and Jordan. A young Iranian professional man put it cogently: "There is no such thing as public opinion in Iran, there is only public emotion."[29] But public emotion has, since Mossadegh, been certified as an agency of social change.

XI.

Retrospect and Prospect

WE HAVE traversed a long and varied route through many lands, many lives. The personal meaning of modernization in the Middle East cannot, we have seen, be reduced to a simple formula. Yet, there are important regularities. To stress these where we find them does not "dehumanize" the persons to whom they apply. It does not lessen the dignity of an individual's dilemmas, his hurts and exhilirations, to note that these are shared by many other individuals caught up in the modernizing process. To see the common human situation of diverse people, localizing in their own time and place a process that is global in scope, can be humanizing in the measure that enlightenment leads to betterment. The perception of regularities may, in this sense, be the main gift of social research to social policy.

We have not "proved" our theory of modernization; we have only explained and exemplified the regularities it posits. These regularities are now, by scientific canons, only more plausible hypotheses than they were before. But those who must deal with the issues of modernization in the world today may, in the absence of rigorous proofs, find these propositions more useful than speculations which have not been disciplined by data.

A starting point, for this retrospective glance, is the remarkable finding on unhappiness (chapter III, table 10). Whatever merit the conventional dichotomy of urban anomie *versus* rural stability may have possessed once upon a time somewhere, in the Middle East today people talk as if they never heard such nonsense. In every country, the rural villagers declare themselves the most unhappy fellows. In every country, the modernizing individuals are considerably less unhappy—and the more rapidly the society around them is modernized the happier they are. Only where the mobile individuals have overrun the capacity of existing social institutions, as in Egypt and Syria, are they about as unhappy as their village brethren. Traditional society is passing from the Middle East because relatively few Middle Easterners still want to live by its rules.

As the traditional rules crumble, some of the basic relationships among human beings undergo transformation. The ancient power of the village elders declines to respectful deference while real influence goes elsewhere. The Traditional rule that *age brings wisdom* probably worked well in immobile isolate villages, where change was slow and experience was the only teacher. The longer one lived, the more experience he gained and the greater his title to wisdom. Now the young men no longer await their patrimony. They go off to the cities, take jobs under the modern discipline, learn from newspapers and movies. On many matters they are better informed—perhaps "wiser," perhaps not—than the old timers. As these are the matters of current interest, others (including their elders) turn to the young men for opinions and advice. The structure of influence thus changes in the community and in the family.

As the patriarchal family loses command, other ancient behavioral routines are opened to question. The Traditional rule that *woman is inferior by nature,* for example, worked well so long as she was given no opportunities for trying alternatives to her assigned sex- and work-roles. But as the men move out of the lifeways of rural subsistence agriculture, the women are no longer counted as essential units of the family's total labor force. The housewife often remains a conservative influence, but the daughter takes advantage of her new opportunities for a little education, a little adventure, a little excitement. As the boy is no longer his father's shadow, the girl is no longer her mother's replica. Thus mobility liberates the newer generations, of both sexes, and the foundations of Traditional society are undermined.

The male vanity culture which underlay Traditional institutions has proved relatively defenseless against the inroads of the mass media, particularly the movies. Among the more Traditional elements, such as the Beduin of the Jordan desert, the males still put up a stiff defense. Said one Transjordanian: "Movies spoil men. . . . Those who go get a very bad character and are no more men." But they have not yet been brought under steady attack. Where the impact of movies has been massive and sustained, as in modern Lebanon, the results are highly visible. Says Hourani: "The process of change is being speeded by one manifestation of Western civilization above all: the film which expresses a conception of the relations between man and woman which are far from those prevalent in the Islamic world."

The younger people acknowledge the impact of the media, but in quite another tone of voice. The "progressive" young Syrian bureaucrat echoed dozens of respondents in all countries: "When we see the lives of people in the West, and then compare it with our own lives, we find that we still have a long way to go before attaining their levels. The movies are . . . like a teacher to us, who tells us what to do and what not."

What do the movies teach? Where does the "long way to go" lead? Here is the nub of the process by which personality is being reshaped in the Middle East. The media teach new desires and new satisfactions. They depict situations in which the "good things" of life—of which most Middle Easterners never dreamed before—are taken for granted. They portray roles in which these richer lives are lived, and provide clues as to how these roles can be enacted by others.

Even a little such fantasy, in the Middle East, goes a long way. For the mechanism of empathy is thereby engaged. Operating at the level of a person's identity, empathy alters the basic self-imagery by which a person defines what he is and what he may become. To alter this self-imagery requires comprehensive re-arrangements of the self-system, that system which locates all elements of a person's environment in their proper place. The young ex-villager, when he has learned to read and earn his living in the city, sees his family, community, religion, class, nation in different relationship to himself than he used to do. His new view certainly differs from what his father's used to be. A whole new style of life is involved.

The Balgat Grocer's specific ambition was modest; he wanted to own a larger grocery store in nearby Ankara. But this so transformed his array of self-images— his necktie, his desire for "nice civilian clothes," his "eye at the higher places"—as to cleave him from his fellow villagers. "I am not like the others here. They don't know any better," said the Grocer. He is an "infidel, ungrateful for what Allah has given," responded the Balgati.

The Grocer's empathy went unrewarded as, in his own judgment, it was destined to do: "I have not the possibility *in myself* to get the things I want. They only bother me." This was the resignation of an older man, aware that the limits imposed by reality include one's own capacities. Among younger Transitionals new desires, once stirred, are not so stoically quieted. The younger man is more likely to *develop* the capacity within himself to achieve his desires and then *demand* opportunities from his environment. Where the increase of desirous individuals and the growth of opportunities are in balance, there the psychosocial conditions for stable growth are good. Where personal desires greatly exceed institutional capacities, there the prospects are for instability of a sort which impedes rational and cumulative modernization.

Our analysis of statistical data on 73 countries around the world confirmed this view of modernization as a "systemic" process. The demographic, economic, political, communication and cultural "sectors" of a modernizing society grow together, and this joint growth occurs in regular phases. One can even fix "critical ratios" between the sectors that indicate the limits within which balanced growth is likely to occur in each phase. Chapter II presented the case for the global validity of these views. Chapter III showed their applicability to the different levels of modernization achieved by the six Middle East countries we have surveyed.

In the case studies, we differentiated the countries where a balanced process of modernization is under way (Turkey and Lebanon); those where social change is seriously out of phase (Egypt and Syria); those where, for different reasons, a modernizing process was barely visible at the time of the 1950-1951 survey (Jordan and Iran).

These studies highlighted the radical role assigned to politics in countries where modernization is out of phase. A result of unphased growth, in our terms, is the "over-production" of Transitionals along the continuum of psychocultural modernization. These individuals are equipped with new desires and new skills; but their demographic and economic institutions are less well equipped to provide opportunities and satisfactions. This imbalance is a basic

problem which some Middle East countries, lacking more appropriate resources, are trying to solve by political means.

The growing class of Transitionals throughout the Middle East
focuses its problems and shapes its prospects. Having acquired a
taste for a better style of life, they now seek ways to achieve it.
But the traditional settings in which they live have been routinized,
even rigidified, by centuries of past practice. The newly-mobile
men and women, liberated by their imagination of better things
from reverence toward what *is*, become frustrated and depressed,
or antagonistic and aggressive, when their social institutions provide inadequate opportunities for mobility. They move toward
the extremes of political action, attracted toward the instruments
of propaganda, agitation and violence, by which they hope to disrupt the settled order and to speed their way toward a more satisfying way of life. Their image of a more satisfactory society, usually vague and diffuse, is provided by the mass media—originally
from the West and now increasingly from indigenous sources. In
the developing attitudes of these Transitionals, and in the growth
of mass media as a shaping influence, is contained a key to the
Middle Eastern future. What are the problems and prospects?

There is, first of all, the political problem of governance: who
shall govern, and in the name of what? The quest for a usable
identity is a major theme of current political activity throughout
the area. Political leadership everywhere justifies itself in the
name of the "public good"; but how shall the "public good" be
defined in Middle Eastern politics? Shall leaders act in the name
of nations—Egypt, Jordan, Syria, Iran? Shall they seek some larger
constituency—an "Arab nation" or an "Islamic unity"? The attraction of larger units for politicians operates in all times and places,
for in greater unity there is greater strength. But how to achieve
such unity? The sophisticates of Cairo will not yoke their tastes
and interests with the desert Wahhabis of Saudi Arabia simply
because they are both nominally Arab and Islamic peoples. Nor,
for the sake of a purely formal symbolism of unity, will King
Sa'ud or his competitive younger brother compromise their income
from the West in order to pursue some grander aspirations for
those who lead Egypt. Throughout the area the claims of regional,
religious and racial unity are continuously compromised by the
demands of nationalism and the interests of ruling elites.

But those who rule today may not survive the deep-seated conflicts of loyalty that rock the area. In many places, the traditional elite is gone or is going. Competition is fierce for larger shares in the new distribution of power. The Army and the bureaucracy, the landed gentry and the new capitalists, the secular intelligentsia and the urban proletariat—all these have staked out their claims. Many of these new aspirants to power will make their way into the new elites, whether by peaceful incorporation or violent subversion of the old elites. Before cohesion and direction can be achieved, however, they will have to provide a convincing symbolism of the "public good" around which a widespread consensus can be formed. Private and public identities must come into a stable relationship.

But the articulation of a stable identity is particularly difficult for individuals in the Middle East today, because the great current drama of the area as a whole is precisely its quest for a suitable collective identity. Consider the several phrases which have tongue-tied recent efforts to speak, in a single name, of the lands which reach from North Africa to the Indian subcontinent: Arab World, Muslim World, Fertile Crescent, Arab League, Northern Tier. Consider the very term "Middle East," a Western invention which has been taken up by native politicians. In their quest for a usable identity, the politicians naturally respond with misleading grace to such simplified nomenclature, which imputes to their area a homogeneity that corresponds to no observable reality. Here, as ever, it better suits politicians to speak in the name of a *unity* of some sort—and rather a larger than a smaller unity. No harm is done by this conventional manipulation of the symbols of identity, so long as claims by the desirous are not mistaken as descriptions by the innocent. No sober scholar would permit the homogeneity imputed by the phrase to obscure the actual heterogeneity of its object. Any accurate Middle East landscape will depict the political ties that bind in pale pastels over a distant horizon; the bold primary colors in the foreground will represent multiplicity and diversity.

For the term "Middle East" is devoid of affect, and even of specific reference, among the general population of the area. The terms in which leaders speak of a larger unity—if they speak at all on such matters—are the *Arab* or *Muslim* symbols of identity. These conceptions of the self are indigenous, but even the indigenous symbols have only agitated the quest for a collective identity without resolving it. The attempt to establish the Arab-Muslim syndrome as the symbolic base of a functioning polity is likely to fail on empirical grounds.

There are in the world approximately 350,000,000 Muslims, who form a population belt stretching from Morocco to Indonesia, extending north into Siberia and south to Zanzibar. This belt wanders through a galaxy of climes and times that have in common only the slightest thread of history, outlook and aspiration. There are, for example, more Muslims in the USSR than in any single country of the Middle East. There are more Muslims in the Far East than in all the Middle Eastern lands combined. Indeed there are more Muslims in Indonesia alone than in all Arab countries together. To speak of this enormous population spread over the earth's surface as a unified "Muslim world" is, on practically any issue of current world politics, simply wishful.

Even within the Arab area proper, there is no recent tradition of a politically-usable "unity of all Islam." The historic cleavage between Sunni and Shi'a Muslims corresponds roughly to the partition of Christendom between Greek and Roman Catholic versions of the apostolic succession. The majority Sunni branch itself contains an array of hostile sects whose impact is divisive upon the concept of a "Muslim world." From relatively small differences over dogma (originally involving major differences of political jurisdiction) there developed among Sunni Muslims a psychic gap of the same order as exists between fundamentalist Baptists and high-church Episcopalians. This has been exacerbated by the accretion of competing political and economic interests to the rival sects. Iraq and Iran, where Shi'ites prevail, are joined with Turkey, where Islam has been disestablished, in the Baghdad Pact. Jordan is linked to Iraq by the Hashemite dynasty and to Cairo by its Sunni majority; the split between these competing claims is intensified by the irredentist voices of the Palestine refugees.

The Cold War has only sharpened differences which seemed to matter less before "Arab-Muslim unity" became a key symbol of political effort. But these differences run deep and cannot simply be cancelled by fiat of current ideologies. Thus, the prevailing sect of Saudi Arabia is the fundamentalist and revivalist Wahhabism (although many Shi'a inhabit the al-Haba oases and most Dawasir people are Malikis). Their conception of the Koran, as a practical handbook of rules for daily life, is feasible for people who still live in a Beduin desert setting much like that to which Muhammad addressed his vivid message of Allah. The Yemen rivals Wahhabism in fanatic orthodoxy, but under the title of Zaidism, a Shi'a sect.

Under altered conditions, as in the Fertile Crescent or in cosmopolitan Cairo, Wahhabism and Zaidism often become the object of ideological recrimination or (perhaps more serious) of mockery and ridicule. Hence, even those Muslim Arabs who yearn for a common identity are often torn between the ritual pull of Mecca and the political tug of Cairo. But many Arabs feel no such yearning at all. In Egypt the Copts constitute a durable Christian minority. In Lebanon and Syria a small but potent sect of Druzes have, in the course of centuries, so far detached themselves that they hardly qualify as Muslims (indeed their ritual service is secret). Throughout the Arab area the Imami (Twelvers), by declaring their recognition of the first twelve Imams, separate themselves from the Ismailis (Seveners) who owe their special allegiance to the Aga Khan of Pakistan. Finally, two states in the area do not officially adhere to Islam at all—Lebanon, governed by an official Christian majority; and Israel, a Hebrew nation.

The pivotal roles in Middle Eastern communication filled by these non-Muslim, minority Muslim, dissident Muslim and marginal groups was shown in the case studies. The historic development of public communication has been largely the work of groups excluded from, or marginal to, the majority Arab-Muslim syndrome. The foregoing indications of diversity suggest that a collective identity symbolized by Pan-Islam may hardly be viable in the living Middle East. Indeed, such sentimental sorties into the symbolism of a majestic past have mainly obscured the conditions of genuine area unity in the future. The key is modernization. The top policy problem, for three generations of Middle Eastern leaders, has been whether one must choose between "Mecca or mechanization" or whether one can make them compatible.

The crux of the matter has been, not whether, but *how* one should move from traditional ways toward modern life-styles. The symbols of race and ritual fade into irrelevance when they impede living desires for bread and enlightenment. The evidence of our survey is clear that Middle Easterners have themselves identified poverty and ignorance as their twin curse. The values of modernity have infused into the area a new perception of a desirable future; the conflict now turns upon *power*. The question is *who* shall control the direction and tempo of modernization and under what banners? The elites have been riven internally by this, to them, paramount political question. It is only Western indifference that portrays the struggle between Nasser and Naguib in Egypt, the rise and fall of Mossadegh in Iran, the career of Shishakli in Syria as comic-opera. These "episodes" have a common mechanism and a common portent. Although played by rules different from our own, the Middle Eastern political game is deadly earnest and the stakes are the future of the area.

For the stakes are nothing less than the meaning of Islam itself. Both modernizers and traditionalists wish to reorganize secular life within Islam. The question is: *which* Islam? The rational code of Muhammad Iqbal portrays a very different Islam from the illiterate society ruled by King Sa'ud. As subversive doctrine, indeed, President Nasser's proposal to exploit the *Hajj* for current political advantage is no less secularizing than Khalid M. Khalid's argument from Koranic communalism to modern socialism. But these conflicting appeals to Islamic doctrine could make sense only in two radically different real worlds of feeling and behavior. The Middle East may choose either world, but not both together. The choice will follow those spokesmen of the New Feeling who show how Islam's most cherished symbols can be made compatible with the secular requirements of new lifeways. This is why Nasser defines the "role in search of a hero" as that of Spokesman—the clarifier of "who we are and what our role is to be." The Middle East today is at that critical juncture of need, in Max Weber's phrase, for "great rational prophecy."

Until the conflict is reduced to less crucial terms, to problems of technique rather than basic perspective, the quest for a satisfying identity will continue. Those who gain power to shape the future will name the future, and by this name those who are shaped will come to know themselves. Conversely, the ideological issue will not be resolved until the sociological issue is more clearly defined. Those who gain power will speak with the voice of, or at least in the name of, a dominant segment of the society as a whole. Who are to be this segment and who their spokesmen?

To cast the *dramatis personae*, the spokesmen and responsive chorus of Middle East transition, it is useful to identify the central characters who activate change and embody its meaning. Most scholars agree on the importance of "the innovator," but his specific role varies with the interests of the observer. Westerners concerned with economic development seek "the entrepreneur"—the innovating agent in their own social system and, possibly, an indispensable figure in any modernizing system. Students of communication seek "the Spokesman." His particular traits vary in different societies—in the American-style system of mass consumption he may be "the publicist," in the Soviet-style system of mass activism he may be "the agitator." But he fills the same essential function in all modernizing societies as innovator, in the symbolic realm, of the words by which men live.

"The Spokesman" is he who defines new identities for changing persons, reshapes old expectancies and formulates new demands to fit their new lifeways. Martin Luther played this crucial role, as Erik H. Erikson has shown us, in guiding Western man through the complex modernization of psyche called The Reformation. It is the Spokesman who unlocks chambers of the mind, releases the wellsprings of desire, opens new relationships between Self and Society.[1] He discovers for men-on-the-move, in Nasser's phrase, "who we are and what our role is to be." Every revolutionary movement of this century has been led, through the critical seizure of power, by its Spokesmen. Only later, in the "consolidation" phase, were they replaced by the Administrators: the loquacious Lenin by the silent Stalin, the articulate Atatürk by the managerial Menderes. Throughout the Middle East today, the continuing quest for a usable identity seeks its authentic Spokesmen. Where will they come from? How will they operate?

This is the problem of recruiting a functional new elite, and no problem is more critical in a modernizing society.[2] Traditional dynasties have toppled; elites formed under their reign seem incapable of governing without first reconstituting themselves. Their plight is illuminated by a series of expert "sector analyses"—Khadduri on The Army Officer, Issawi on The Entrepreneur, Franck on The Economic Planners, Shafaq on The Clergy, W. C. Smith on The Intellectuals.[3] While each sector exhibits widespread frustration, in none is this feeling more potent than among the intellectuals—for no other sector is called upon to perform a function so crucial in the present phase of transition. To the intellectuals others look for clarification of the New Way. What can entrepreneurs do when their plans for industrial expansion, as the Egyptian Chambers of Industries complained in 1951, are dismissed

by the demi-intelligentsia who run the government departments as
"*établissements nuisibles*"? What, in turn, can the government undertake when "the masses of the people still seem to be dominated
by a passive contempt, if not active animosity, toward the state"?[4]

The modernist intellectuals of Islam uneasily acknowledge their
obligation to devise and diffuse the new articles of faith that will
unify the elites and enlist the masses. But they have as yet found
no satisfying symbolism to subsume the rivalrous loyalties which
divide their cohorts and themselves. Against the symbols of modernism are raised the voices of tradition; against the symbols of
Arab-Muslim unity are counterposed the demands of Class and
Nation. Among the intellectuals these are often inner voices and
the debate is conducted internally by opposing selves. A process
of affective displacement is at work in the area, making its intellectuals into psychic D.P.'s. As Hourani phrased it: "To be a Levantine is to live in two worlds at once, without belonging to either."

Throughout the Middle East, modernist intellectuals were
shaped in the Western system of thought and valuation. Very
many of them went to school in the West, whether abroad or in
western universities located between Cairo and Istanbul. They
look and act—and were trained to think—like modern men. Gibb
has shown how integral the Western exposure has become:

> It is at the present time impossible to produce an adequate Arabic
> translation of any advanced work of modern science or philosophy. Even
> if the effort were made, the result would be unintelligible except to
> those readers who could mentally retranslate it into the Western terms.[5]

Their categories of thought are those of the modern West. But
their modes of feeling are more equivocal, more accessible to solici-
tation from different sides.

The sharp rise of xenophobia in public emotion has made it
hard for intellectuals to establish the crucial but subtle point that
the Western genesis of their modern perspectives is, so to speak,
an historical accident; that thoughtways, once acquired, develop
an autonomous status; that the appropriate criteria for evaluating
modernism are not its antecedents but its consequences. Without
the historic rights of asylum provided by these propositions for
intellectuals in the West, many Middle Eastern intellectuals now
feel obliged to drift with the swelling tide of Islamic self-glori-
fication. Some become ashamed of their modernism and try to
hide it. Some, tormented by the sense that they have sinned,

seek moral atonement through intellectual humiliation. Expiation has taken one form in the voluminous outpouring of Islamic apologetics, another through the self-immolating act (for a modernist intellectual) of adherence to the *Ikhwan*. Professor Smith sees in this "the intellectuals' intellect quite sold out to the blind emotional fury of a nostalgic mob."[6] Professor von Grunebaum warns that the further this *trahison des clercs* goes in the Middle East, "the more will [Islam] be forced to build a 'modern' house on fictitious traditionalist foundations."[7]

The failure to create an appropriate new symbolism, in a rapidly changing society, produces an historical deformity—a psychocultural gap between words and deeds that widens through time and develops, ultimately, an explosive charge. If the new words are missing that efficiently relate changing lifeways to changing values, then events tend to take their meaning from traditional symbolism—and from the stock of available attitudes which are sustained by these symbols. What people say tends to become incongruent with what they do. Under these conditions, as many Middle Easterners complain, "hypocrisy" becomes a public style and anxiety increases. The more attitudes and actions get out of phase, the more radical becomes the treatment required to restore equilibrium.

As the intellectual effort to reformulate Islam in a manner more suitable to modernizing society became inhibited, a psychic gap of serious proportions opened in the Middle East. In some lands, aphasia has gone further than in others. Egypt, to take an extreme case, seems increasingly the captive of a false position. Seeking hegemony over the Arab area and primacy among Muslims everywhere, Egypt has sought to erect a unifying symbolism on the majority Arab-Muslim syndrome. But this corresponds poorly to observable reality and provides no guidance for those men-in-motion who most need new words to match their new ways. Current Egyptian effort has done poorly by its Transitionals.

Turkey, the area's bright model of successful transition, met new wants with candor. Favored by an early start under conditions advantageous to rapid modernization, which included the splendid clarity and courage of its leadership under Atatürk, Turkey has maintained a remarkable equilibrium of words and ways. Its "communication revolution" shaped those new thoughts which enabled the New Turks to maintain stability while rapidly acquiring mobility. Thus Professor Smith:

. . . what most distinguishes the Turks in the Islamic world of the twentieth century is intellectual honesty. Nor does Turkey's dynamic advance leave undemonstrated the practical value of theoretical insight, since they constitute the only people in contemporary Islam who have really known what it is that they want.[8]

What this has meant to living persons is what we sought to convey in our parable of The Grocer, The Chief, and the sons of The Chief in Balgat.

The parable is valid only insofar as the hypothesis that the Middle East transition hinges upon its Transitionals is true. The failure of existing elites to name and shape the newly-mobile men, to incorporate their aspirations, has encouraged them to seek new channels of their own design. To link the future with the Transitionals' acquisition of modernity is not to ignore those who already are Moderns. One will look long in the West to find the intellectual peers of individual Moderns now living in each Middle East land. But one will look longer to find anything resembling the passive, destitute, illiterate and altogether "submerged" mass which looms so large in its sociological landscape. Not the quality of modernism, but its quantity, is inadequate. The aim of modernization is precisely to narrow the gap between bottom and top, to create a substantial "middle" sector—to increase the number of Transitionals who compose the living reality of transition. Along with this goes the need for a top-to-bottom consensus.

In the working out of such a consensus, the political problem intermeshes with the sociological problem: how can these traditional agrarian societies be reshaped in a manner more suitable for modern lifeways? For conceptions of the public good must conform to the characteristics of the public involved. As an astute observer of current Egyptian politics has remarked: "The military regime, it might be more accurate to say, has really been seeking to create a class to represent."[9] Creating a class to represent requires the creation of conditions in which new styles of life can be rewarding for people willing to try them. If the goal is a modern society, as most Middle East spokesmen today claim, then some of the major conditions are quite clear. Required are a balanced growth of urbanism, a program of industrialization (shifting surplus labor off the land into productive employment), education in the skills required for modern urban industrial living.

Cash is an essential solvent in modern life and the achievement of rising per capita income distribution is a major objective of modern societies. Here the political and sociological problems of the Middle East become intertwined with its economic problems. Economies long caught in the vicious circle of poverty cannot easily break through into the modern industrial system of expanding production of goods and services. This reflects no inherent and inevitable distaste for the good things of life among Middle Eastern peoples. It reflects rather the difficult process—which in the West occurred over several centuries—of stimulating desires and providing means for satisfying them where neither desires nor facilities have previously existed. Westerners engaged in Middle East economic development problems long ago recognized that, once a start is made, the reciprocity between desires and facilities tends to operate in the Middle East as elsewhere.[10]

The problem of stimulating productivity, many economists and other professional observers agree, is basically "psychological."[11] In the West, the problem turns upon "motivation": one is motivated to increase one's skill and output by the prospect of material reward. Incentive systems throughout modern society are a response to this psychological proposition. More recently, in the West, the idea has gained currency that *satisfaction* with one's work situation is also a motivation that leads to increasing efficiency—a proposition which underlies much of current "human relations" activity in industrial management.

In the Middle East the psychological problem is much more rudimentary, perhaps more fundamental. What is required there to "motivate" the isolated and illiterate peasants and tribesmen who compose the bulk of the area's population is to provide them with clues as to what the better things of life might be. Needed there is a massive growth of *imaginativeness* about alternatives to their present lifeways, and a simultaneous growth of institutional means for handling these alternative lifeways. There is no suggestion here that all Middle Easterners should learn to admire precisely the same things as people in the Western society. It is suggested, much more simply, that before any enduring transformation of the vicious circle of poverty can be started in the Middle East, people there will have to learn about the lifeways evolved in other societies. What they subsequently accept, adapt or reject is a matter which each man will, in due course, decide for himself.

The issue, in fact, was joined several decades ago. There is a large and growing preoccupation with modern lifeways and major efforts to adapt them to the Middle Eastern situation. Atatürk was the conspicuous model in the first half of this century. Others who followed his lead, like Reza Shah in Iran, effected less comprehensive and enduring transformations, but they left their marks. The "rising tide of expectation" has been clearly visible in the Middle East since World War I. In the present decade, the area's position as a major counter in the Cold War has complicated the "natural" process of social change. Other slogans and other policies have gained prominence. But the underlying requirement remains the same—the need of every Spokesman for an audience to rally and a constituency to represent.

Audiences and constituencies are composed of participant individuals. People "participate" in the public life of their country mainly by having opinions about many matters which, in the isolation of traditional society, did not concern them. Participant persons have opinions on a variety of issues and situations which they may never have experienced directly—such as what the government should do about irrigation, how the Algerian revolt could be settled, whether money should be sent to Jordan or armies to Israel, and so forth. By having and expressing opinions on such matters a person participates in the network of public communication.

The media teach people participation of this sort by depicting for them new and strange situations and by familiarizing them with a range of opinions among which they can choose. Some people learn better than others, the variation reflecting their differential skill in empathy. For empathy, in the several aspects illustrated throughout this book, is the basic communication skill required of modern men. Empathy endows a person with the capacity to imagine himself as proprietor of a bigger grocery store in a city, to wear nice clothes and live in a nice house, to be interested in "what is going on in the world" and to "get out of his hole." With the spread of curiosity and imagination among a previously quietistic population come the human skills needed for social growth and economic development. On this psychological fulcrum—involving nothing less than a characterological transformation throughout the area—hinge the problems of the Middle East. On the institutional capacity to provide this new style of life hinge its prospects.

Appendices

Appendix A
The Questionnaire

Revision VI   December 1950

Date of Interview_____
No. of Interviewer_____   Control No._____

Do you ever go to movies?   _____Yes_____No
Do you ever read a newspaper?   _____Yes_____No
Do you ever listen to the radio? _____Yes_____No

1. In general, how do you feel about the movies?

2. a. About how often do you go?
   _____   Once or more a week? (If more, how often?)
   _____   Once or twice a month?
   _____   Three or four times a year?
   _____   Less than three times a year?
                   (*If less than once or twice a month, ask question
                   b. If more often, ask c.*)
   b. Why don't you go more often?
   c. (*If more often, ask:*) In general, why do you go to the movies?

3. What sort of movies do you like best?

4. a. Which country makes this kind of movies best?
   b. What is it about their movies that is better than others?
      (*Probe for names of other countries whose films respondent is
      comparing.*)
   c. Do you remember a particular movie that is a good example of
      what you have just mentioned?

5. What influence do you think the movies have on people who see
   them?

6. Is there any place around here where movies are shown?

_____Yes_____No

(*If yes, ask:*) Why is it that you don't go?

7. a. Did you ever see a movie? _____Yes_____No
   (*If yes, ask:* When was the last time?*)
   b. Why haven't you gone since then?

8. What do you think you miss by not going to the movies?

9. How do you think people who go to the movies differ from those who don't?

10. In general, how do you feel about the newspapers?
    a. Do you read any newspaper? _____Yes_____No
    (*If no, ask:*)
    b. Do other people read the
       newspaper to you? _____Yes_____No
    (*If no to this, skip to question 13*)
    (*If yes, modify questions that follow to suit person who gets paper read to him.*)

11. How often do you read a newspaper?

_____Every day.

_____Several days a week.

_____Once a week.

_____Less than once a week.

(*If read once a week or less, ask:*)

Why don't you read a newspaper more often?

12. If the United Nations would publish a daily newspaper in each country, do you think you would be interested in reading it?
    _____Yes_____No   Why do you feel this way?

13. What newspaper do you read now? (*Name and place of publication.*)
    (*If only one, ask:*) Why?
    (*If more than one, ask:*) Which of these do you prefer? Why?
    (*Probe here.*)

14. What parts of the newspapers do you usually read? (*Read the following list out loud, beginning one time with "Foreign News" and the next time with "Letters from Readers." End by asking: ANY OTHER?*)

_____Foreign News

_____Domestic News

_____Sports

_____Socials
_____Main Editorials
_____Small Editorials
_____Shipping News
_____Translations (features)
_____Lottery Results
_____Art News and Reviews
_____Cartoons
_____Police Reports
_____Movie Announcement Reviews
_____Theatrical News and Reviews
_____Financial
_____Advertisements
_____Novels
_____Radio Program List
_____Cross Word Puzzle
_____Almanac
_____Poems
_____Letters from Readers
_____Other (specify)

15. a. Which parts interest you most? (*Respondent should name at least two.*)
    b. (*Refer to first two parts just mentioned and for each ask:*)
    What is it about _____ you especially like?

16. a. What parts of the newspaper interest you least?
    b. (*Refer to the first two parts just mentioned and for each ask:*)
    Why is it that you do not care for: _____?

17. What kind of people read _____?
    (*Insert name of newspaper respondent prefers*)

    _____

    Why?

18. What newspaper do you like least?
    What kind of people read it?
    Why?

19. What influence do newspapers have on the people who read them?

20. If you were made editor of a newspaper what kind of a paper would you run?

21. What other opinion do you have concerning newspapers you would like to mention?

(*Questions 22 through 26 to be asked only of non-newspaper readers*)

22. a. Have you ever read a newspaper or had one read to you?

_____Yes_____No (*If yes, ask:*) Which (alternative)?

b. (*If yes, ask:*) When was the last time?

c. Why is it that you don't do that any more?

23. What do you think you miss by not knowing what the newspapers have to say?

24. How do you think people who read newspapers differ from those who don't?

25. a. In general, are you interested in news about:

_____Foreign affairs

_____What the government is doing

_____What is going on in your own community

_____Sports

_____Cultural affairs

_____Social affairs

_____Editorials

_____Anything else

b. Which types of news (mentioned as being interested in) would you say you are most interested in?
Why?

c. How do you get this news?

d. Which news are you least interested in?
Why?

26. What other opinions about newspapers would you like to mention?

27. In general, how do you feel about the radio?

28. Do you ever listen to the radio?   _____Yes_____No
(*If yes, continue to question 29*)
(*If no, skip to question 44*)

29. What stations are heard best?
(*Specify:*)_____

30. How often do you listen to the radio?

_____Almost every day.

_____Two or three days a week.

_____One day a week.

_____Less than one day a week.

(*If less than one day a week, ask:*)

Why is it that you do not listen more often?

(The following program questions are designed to measure competence to judge on the basis of familiarity with radio schedules for individual programs, so we do not press for information as to hours, days, etc. We are not so much interested in such information as in seeing simply whether the respondent knows.)

31. a. Which radio program do you like best? What time is it on? What day? What station? How often do you listen to it? (*If no specific program known, say:*) What kind of things do you like to hear on the radio? (*Put answers in space 1 below.*)
    b. Which radio program do you like next best? What time is it on? What day? What station? How often do you listen?

Title of program	Time	Day	Station	How often listen
1. _____	_____	_____	_____	_____
2. _____	_____	_____	_____	_____

32. Can you describe program 1 to me? What is it like? Program 2?

33. Just what is it about program 1 that you like so well? About program 2? (*Probe here. If necessary reword this question to avoid getting the answer already given above. If previous question was probed extensively, then skip this question.*)

34. a. (*If favorite programs are foreign, ask:*) What do you think of the programs broadcast on local stations here?
    b. (*If news not mentioned as favorite, ask:*) How often do you listen to news on the radio? (*If relatively seldom, ask:*) How is it you do not listen to news more often?

35. Do you think any of the people who talk regularly on the radio and present programs should give their own names so you would get to know them?

    _____Yes_____No_____Don't care

    (*If yes, ask:*)   Which ones?_____

    Why?

36. a. Where are you when you usually listen?
    b. Is there any place else that you sometimes listen?

	Usually	Sometimes
At home.	_____	_____
At a friend's home.	_____	_____
At a coffee house.	_____	_____
At a school-house.	_____	_____
At a store.	_____	_____
Anywhere else.	_____	_____
(*Here specify.*)		

37. In general, do you usually plan ahead of time what you listen to on the radio or do you usually just listen at random?
_____Plan ahead_____Listen at random
Why is this?

38. Who usually decides what programs you listen to at:
_____:
How about at:_____:

39. What kind of people do you think listen to: _____
    (*Insert name or type of program respondent chose as No. 1*)

40. a. What type of programs don't you like to listen to?
    b. What is it about (the type of program mentioned) that you dislike? (*Do not ask this about more than two types.*)
    c. (*If radio plays not discussed along these lines earlier, ask:*)
       What do you think about the plays on the radio? How do they make you feel?

41. Are there some days during the week that you are more likely to listen than others?
_____Yes_____No
(*If yes, ask:*) Which days?
Why these?

42. If you were put in charge of a radio station, what kinds of programs would you like to put on? (*Probe here.*)

43. What other opinion do you have about radio that you would like to mention?

(*Questions 44 through 52 to be asked only of non-radio listeners*)

44. Do you know if there are any radio sets around here?
_____Yes_____No
(*If yes, ask:*) Where?
Why don't you ever listen there?

45. Have you ever heard the radio?
_____Yes_____No
(*If yes, ask:*) When was the last time?
Why haven't you listened since?

46. Have you ever been in a group that gathered together for the purpose of listening to a specific program?
_____Yes_____No
(*If yes, ask:*) The last time this happened, what was the occasion?

47. What do you think you miss by not listening to the radio?

48. Do you know anybody who does listen to the radio?
_____Yes_____No
(*If yes, ask:*) What do you think he (or they) get out of listening?

49. How do you think people who listen to the radio are different from those who do not listen?

50. What would have to happen for you to listen to the radio?

51. If you had access to a radio, what type of programs would you especially like to listen to? What is it about these that you like? (*for each*).

52. What other opinion do you have about radio that you would like to mention?

(*The following will help indicate which respondents know what they're talking about when we ask some of them for mental images of foreign radio later.*)

(*Questions 1, 2 and 3 to be asked of all respondents, and answers noted on check list below using numbers to show order of mention.*)

53. 1. Do you know what foreign countries make broadcasts that can be heard here? (*any language*)
2. Do you know which of these foreign countries send broadcasts in the Arabic language for us to listen to?
3. Which of the foreign countries get their programs rebroadcast by local stations? (In what language?)

(*Do not read following list to respondents. Merely check whichever they remember.*)

	1 Can be heard	2 Arabic language	3 Rebroadcast by local stations	Language of program re-broadcast
America				
Egypt				
France				
Germany				
Great Britain				
Greece				
Italy				
Pakistan				
Romania				
Russia				

Switzerland _____   _____   _____   _____
Turkey   _____   _____   _____   _____
Others: _____   _____   _____   _____

_____   _____   _____   _____   _____

(The following question deals directly with official foreign channels of communication. Some interesting psychological data related to the phenomenon of "selective perception" should result if this is properly probed. Consequently, it should be asked of everybody. Refer to column 2 in the previous question. If the large powers were mentioned, U.S.A., Great Britain or Russia, ask about each named. If not, ask about other countries. Ask about three countries, not just one, provided three are mentioned. Do not ask about more than three. Please write answers in spaces below.)

54. Why do you think _____ broadcasts in Arabic?

_____
    (country)

_____
    (country)

(The following question serves to separate those who listen to foreign broadcasts from those who do not.)

55. a. Do you ever listen to broadcasts direct from foreign countries?
    _____Yes_____No
    b. Do you ever listen to rebroadcasts here on local stations of foreign programs?
    _____Yes_____No
    (If no to both questions a *and* b, *ask:)*

56. Do you think you miss anything by not hearing programs broadcast from other countries?
    _____Yes_____No
    (If yes to question 56, ask:) What?
    (If no to question 56, ask:) Why not?
    (If no to both 55a and b, skip to questions about newsreels, unless respondent is a non-movie-goer. If respondent is a non-movie-goer, then skip to media comparison questions.)
(The following questions deal with listeners to foreign radio programs. Always remember that we do not want more than a few of such people in our total sample.)

57. How often do you listen to broadcasts from foreign countries?
    _____Almost every day.
    _____2 or 3 days a week.
    _____1 day a week.

_____1 or 2 days a month.

_____Less than once a month.

58. In the last month, which countries have you definitely heard broadcasting? (*Write answers in spaces below.*) How do you usually find out what programs will be broadcast by each of these?

Names of countries   Usually find out what programs broadcast by:

_____   _____

_____   _____

_____   _____

_____   _____

(*If respondent does not find out, ask*:) Is there any place you could find out for (each) _____? Do you care? _____

59. a. Which one of these foreign countries that you heard during the last month did you hear most often?
    b. Did you hear it direct or rebroadcast? _____
       (*Skip if not applicable.*)
    c. How is it that you heard this country most often?

60. a. Which country did you hear next most often?
    b. Did you hear it direct or rebroadcast? _____
       (*Skip if not applicable.*)

61. a. Which one of those heard did you listen to least?
    b. Did you hear it direct or rebroadcast? _____
       (*Skip if not applicable.*)

62. Which is your favorite country for listening to?
    Why?

(*If two favorite programs given earlier were foreign, skip to question 66a below. If only one of two favorite programs given earlier was foreign, then refer to this earlier discussion and ask if there is another foreign program, a second one, which respondent likes to hear.*)

63. a. Which foreign program (not station) do you like best?
    b. What other foreign program you like next best?

Name of program	Station	Day	Time	How often listen
a. _____	_____	_____	_____	_____
b. _____	_____	_____	_____	_____

    c. Can you describe these programs to me? What are they like?

64. What about program (a) makes you like it so well? program (b)?

(Ask question 65 about the 2 foreign programs mentioned, whether under Question 31, page 5 or above.) *

65. Do you remember where you first heard about program (a)? About program (b)?

66. a. Are there any foreign broadcasts that you would especially like to listen to but cannot?

    _____Yes_____No

    b. Why is it you cannot hear them?

    c. What have you heard about this (these) stations that makes you want to listen?

67. a. What foreign programs have you heard, either direct or on the local station, that you particularly disliked?

    b. What country(s) did they come from?

    c. What was it about them that you disliked?

68. a. With regard to news about the war, which foreign country would you say gives the most reliable and accurate information in its news broadcasts?

    b. What makes you think that broadcasts from (this country) are more reliable than the broadcasts from other countries?

69. What country do you suppose gives the least accurate information about the Korean war?

70. a. Which foreign country do you think broadcasts the best entertainment programs?

    b. Can you give an example?

    c. What makes you think the entertainment programs from (this country) are better than those from other countries?

71. Which country gives the least entertaining programs, according to your personal taste?

72. Which foreign country do you think tries to give the most accurate picture in its broadcasts of its own way of life? (*Probe for competence to judge, examples, etc.*)

73. a. From what you have heard people say, what country do you think makes the most radio propaganda?

    b. Have you heard an example of the way they go about this?

74. Referring now again to the radio programs broadcast at different times of day on foreign stations, or rebroadcast on the local stations,

---

* Refers to political propaganda, as more relevant to these days.

have you ever heard any you thought worth talking about with other people?

_____Yes_____No

(*If yes*) Which program(s)?

Whom did you talk about it with? (*Age and occupation*)

What made you want to tell him (her)? (for each)

Did he (she) listen because you talked about the program?

_____Yes_____No_____Don't know

(*If no, ask:*) Why not?

75. What other things would you like to say about foreign radio?

76. a. Which country makes the newsreels you like best?
    b. What is it about them that is better than the newsreels from other countries?
    c. How often do you see newsreels when you go to movies?
    every time_____   _____hardly ever
    sometimes_____   _____never

77. Is there any difference in the truthfulness of newsreel news and radio news?

    _____Yes_____No

    (*If yes, ask:*) What is the difference?

78. What other ideas about movies or newsreels would you like to mention?

(*In the following question, be sure respondent understands what a Documentary Film is.*)

79. a. Have you ever seen any foreign documentary films?
    _____Yes_____No
    (*If no, skip to media comparison questions*)
    b. Do you remember one that you particularly liked?
    _____Yes_____No
    c. (*If yes, ask:*) Where did you see it?
    d. What was it about it you particularly liked?
    _____Title
    e. What country made it?
    f. Do you remember one that you disliked?
    _____Yes_____No
    g. (*If yes, ask:*) Where did you see it?
    h. What country had made it?
    i. What was it about it that you particularly disliked?
    _____Title

80. Would you like to see more of them?
_____Yes_____No
(*If yes, ask:*) On what subject?

Media Comparison

81. The last time you got news (meaning today or yesterday) how did you get it—by radio, newspaper or did somebody else tell you?
_____Radio domestic.
_____Radio foreign.
_____Newspaper.
_____Word of mouth (Who told you?) (*Get age and occupation.*)
When?

82. a. Do you remember two pieces of news that you learned at that time?
_____Yes_____No
(*If yes, ask:*) What were they about?
1. _____
2. _____
b. How did you feel when you heard about (1)?
c. Did you happen to mention this to anybody?
_____Yes_____No
(*If yes, ask:*) Tell me something about the person you talked to. (*Age, occupation, social status*) What was said?
d. How did you feel when you learned about (2)?
(*If no to question* (c), *ask:*)
What about the second?
(*Only ask question* (e) *if no news remembered on Questions 81 and 82.*)
e. Many people have difficulty remembering news they hear the same day. Why do you suppose this is so?

83. Where do you usually get your news?

84. Of all the interest you have in doing things like reading newspapers, listening to radio, and going to movies—those three—what part of that interest, what percentage of it, what fraction, would you assign to newspaper reading compared to radio and to movies?
_____*Per cent* Interest in newspapers
_____*Per cent* Interest in radio
_____*Per cent* Interest in movies
100 Per cent Total interest in such activities
(*If not apparent from earlier answers, ask:*) How is it you have a greater interest in:

85. Do you remember hearing a discussion lately between people about something in the news?

_____Yes_____No

(*If yes, probe for what kinds of persons and what all about.*)

86. If for some reason we had to close down all of our radio stations or all of our newspapers, which would you rather see happen? Why?

87. Thinking of radio and newspapers: (*Check answers on chart below.*)
   a. Which do you think generally gives the news about foreign affairs first? How about news about domestic politics?
   b. Which do you think gives the most complete news about foreign affairs? How about news about domestic politics?
   c. Which do you think gives the most truthful news about foreign affairs?

	Foreign Affairs			Domestic Relations		
	Radio	Newspapers	No diff.	Radio	Newspapers	No diff.
First	_____	_____	_____	_____	_____	_____
Most complete	_____	_____	_____	_____	_____	_____
Most truthful	_____	_____	_____	_____	_____	_____

   d. What makes you think _____ is more truthful than the other on foreign affairs? On domestic politics?
   (*Probe for reasons where differences in attitude on domestic and foreign news.*)

Mental Images and Stereotypes

(*The next section is designed to get the mental images of respondents towards the world. We shall see whether people who are psychologically indifferent have the same general mental picture as those who are greatly concerned. We shall also try to measure competence to judge.*)

88. a. Do you understand any foreign language?

_____Yes_____No

   b. (*If yes, ask:*) Which ones?
   (*Interviewer should test his knowledge a little if possible and mark down how well he speaks.*)

   c. Do you read any newspapers or magazines published in this (these) language(s)?

_____Yes_____No

   d. (*If yes, ask:*) Which ones?

   e. How do the contents differ from newspapers (magazines) which are published in our country?

89. a. In the last four years, about how many foreigners have you had the occasion to know and talk with? (*Write approximate number.*)

    b. What nationalities? (*Mark answer on list below.*)

    _____French   Others (*Specify*)

    _____Italian   _____

    _____American   _____

    _____British   _____

90. Have you ever visited any foreign countries?

    _____Yes_____No

    Which ones?_____   When_____

    _____   _____

    _____   _____

91. From what you know or have been told about other countries, what two words can you think of that best describe the people who live in each of the following countries? I do not want to know whether the country is rich or poor, but what kind of people live in these countries.

    a. In general, the French are:

    _____&_____

    (*Where a blank is inserted in asking a question, fill it with reference to the country in which the interview is being made.*)

    b. In general, the _____ are:

    _____&_____

    c. In general, the Americans are:

    _____&_____

    d. In general, the English are:

    _____&_____

    e. In general, the Russians are:

    _____&_____

92. If for some reason, you could not live in our country, what other country would you choose to live in?

    Why?

    (*Take criterion given by respondent as reason for living there, and ask how he feels about the same point in discussing the other countries under Question 94.*)

93. Suppose that I could tell you anything you wanted to know about (country mentioned as most want to live in). What two questions would you be most interested in asking? (*Do not probe.*)

    1.

    2.

94. (*If not mentioned*) How about Great Britain—how would you feel about living there? Why?
Russia?
United States?
(*If U.S.A. not mentioned as country respondent would choose to live in, ask:*)
Suppose that I could tell you anything you wanted to know about U.S.A., what two questions would you be most interested in asking?

95. a. Do you know what U.N. is? (*get definition*).
b. Where is the United Nations meeting now?
c. Do you remember who is the Secretary General?

96. a. How do you feel about the behavior of the United States in world affairs? How about its behavior towards our country? (*Among other things, probe for past changes in opinion which might be psychologically revealing.*)
How long have you felt that way?
b. Have you, yourself, seen any specific examples of this behavior? (Have you changed your attitude about U.S.A. recently?)
c. What part, what proportion, of the information you get about that country comes from newspapers, what part from movies, what part from radio, and what part from other peoples?

         _____Per cent Newspapers
         _____Per cent Movies
         _____Per cent Radio
         _____Per cent Other people
         100 Per cent Total

97. a. How do you feel about the behavior of Russia in world affairs? How about its behavior towards our country? (*Probe also for changes.*)
How long have you felt that way?
b. Have you yourself seen any specific examples of this behavior? (Have you changed your attitude about Russia recently?)
c. Where do you hear most about what Russia is doing . . . newspapers, newsreels, radio, or from what people say?

         _____Per cent Newspapers
         _____Per cent Newsreels
         _____Per cent Radio
         _____Per cent What people say
         100 Per cent Total

98. a. What about the behavior of Great Britain in world affairs? Towards us? (*Probe, also, for changes.*)

How long have you felt that way?

b. Have you, yourself, seen any specific examples of this behavior? (Have you changed your attitude about Britain recently?)

c. Where do you hear most about what Great Britain is doing? Newspapers, newsreels, radio, or what people say?

   _____Per cent Newspapers

   _____Per cent Newsreels

   _____Per cent Radio

   _____Per cent What people say

   100 Per cent Total

Psychological Characteristics

99. a. In general, how do you feel about your life . . . are you happy with the way things have turned out for you, or not? Which of the following best describes how you feel?

   _____Very happy.   _____Fairly unhappy.

   _____Fairly happy.   _____Very unhappy.

b. What in particular makes you feel this way?

100. a. What is the biggest problem that people in the same circumstances as yourself face in life?

b. Is there anything that you as an individual can do to solve this problem? (*If no, ask:*) Why not?

101. a. What would you say is the biggest problem that our country as a nation faces today?

b. Generally would you say that the problem is very difficult, fairly difficult, or fairly easy to solve?

   _____Very difficult

   _____Fairly difficult

   _____Fairly easy

c. What do you think people in the same circumstances as yourself can do to help solve this problem?

102. Suppose that you were made head of the government. What are some of the things you would do?

(*If no answer, say:*)

Many people have difficulty trying to answer this question. Why do you suppose that is?

103. How do you feel about the possibility of another world war starting within the next two years? (*Read the following to respondent:*)

   _____Very sure there will be a world war within two years.

_____Fairly sure there will be.

_____Fairly doubtful there will be.

_____Definitely do not think there will be a world war within the next two years.

Background Characteristics

Now tell me something about yourself.

104. What is your occupation?

105. How do you like your work?
 _____Very much.
 _____Fairly much.
 _____Only a little.

106. a. What are some of the things you like to do in your spare time?
 b. Which of these things do you like to do best? (*Mark* "1"). Which next best? (*Mark* "2".) Which least?
 c. Which do you spend the most time doing? The least?

Activity	Like Most	Like Least	Most Time	Least Time
_____	_____	_____	_____	_____
_____	_____	_____	_____	_____
_____	_____	_____	_____	_____
_____	_____	_____	_____	_____

107. Which would you prefer . . . would you rather have a great number of friends whom you know fairly well or only a few friends whom you know very well?
 _____Very many friends: know fairly well.
 _____Only a few friends: know very well.

108. Do you think that the people who are successful achieve their success mainly because of the friends that they have who help them along or mainly because of their own skill and knowledge?
 _____Mainly because of friends.
 _____Mainly because of own skill and knowledge.

109. Has anyone come to you for advice recently? If so, what in general was it about and who was the person? (*Age, occupation, social status, and relationship.*)
 _____Yes_____No
 Why do you think he came to you for advice?

110. Have you, yourself, gone to anyone for advice recently? If so, what

was it about, and who was the person? (*Ask about relationship, age, occupation, and social standing.*)
Why did you go to him for advice?

111. a. How often do you go to your place of religious worship?
  b. In guiding your actions every day, do you personally find that your religious beliefs are very important, fairly important, a little important, or not important at all.

  _____Very important.
  _____Fairly important.
  _____A little important.
  _____Not important at all.

112. *Respondent's Personal Characteristics*:
  (Do Not Ask These Questions If You Already See The Answers)
  _____Age_____Sex _____Religion
  (Please write exact religious sect.)
  _____No. of Children _____Age of Eldest Child
  _____Age of Youngest Child

Marital status:	*Education:*
_____Single	_____Almost none
_____Married	_____Elementary
_____Divorced	_____High school
_____Separated	_____College or Univ.
_____Widowed	_____Professional School
	(Law, Medicine, etc.)
	_____Technical School

Literacy:
_____Illiterate
_____Can read but not write
_____Can read and write
_____Place of birth

In what place did you spend most of your life before the age of 20?
Present residence_____
Housing conditions _____

Socioeconomic Status:

Relative to neighborhood	Relative to fixed standard
_____	_____Destitute
_____	_____Poor
_____	_____Modest
_____	_____Well-off
_____	_____Rich

If respondent owns radio:

_____Make of Radio

Type	Condition
_____Crystal Set	_____Good Working Order
_____Battery Set	_____Works Poorly
_____Regular Set	_____Broken

Can Hear: Long Wave: Medium: Short:

_____   _____   _____

113. Language in which interview conducted: _____

114. How much interest did respondent show in knowing which universities are cooperating in this psychological study?

115. a. What clubs or similar organizations do you belong to?
b. How much time do you spend in these activities?

116. What did you think of this interview?

117. Please write your own psychological description of respondent, including short physical description, mention of occupation and social role, type of neighborhood, type of personality, and his psychological attitude during interview, plus any other useful observations.

Appendix B
Replication of the Empathy Index

SEVERAL YEARS after the original typology had been developed and applied to the Turkish data, a graduate thesis replicated its test of empathy on the Syrian respondents.* The report on Turkey had shown that urbanism, education, age and socioeconomic status (SES) were associated with media behavior; but predictions based on these factors alone failed to account for known regularities of media participation. There were too many deviant cases, particularly on the lower sociological levels, where people of similar background were found to differ in exposure and response to the media. Mr. Marsh cross-tabulated the apposite data on empathic, semi-empathic, non-empathic respondents (See Table). He then adapted the original Empathy Index to the Syrian interviews, with results leading to these conclusions:

"Analysis has demonstrated that the association between empathy and the following items of media behavior persists, and is therefore relatively autonomous, at the .05 level of significance or higher, with respect to the following homogeneous educational, SES, and age groups:

"1. With respect to low education, in accounting for dependence upon word-of-mouth sources of news.

"2. With respect to high education and younger age in accounting for preference for Western music radio programs.

"3. With respect to low education in accounting for preference for Arab League countries' radio stations.

"4. With respect to low education and middle SES in accounting for preference for foreign news in newspapers.

"5. With respect to low education and middle and low SES, in

---

* This is a condensation of conclusions in R. M. Marsh, "Marginal Projectivity and Communication Behavior in Modern Syria" (M.A. Thesis, Columbia University, 1953). The term "projectivity," which was used in the original Turkish report, has been conformed to the term "empathy" used in this book.

accounting for preference for domestic-national news in newspapers.

"6. With respect to low education and middle SES, in accounting for preference for the Syria national radio.

"7. With respect to low education and middle and low SES, in accounting for high frequency newspaper reading.

"In all these designated respects, empathy continues to manifest a degree of autonomy which is significant at the .05 level or higher. But the full value of the concept is not exhausted at this statistical level; rather, this statistical support for the hypotheses of the study enables us to impute even greater stability to the underlying pattern whose emergence has been noted above. This pattern can now be described in the following way: The Index of Empathy is more sensitive to the demographic and media behavior characteristic of the low educated and the low (and sometimes middle) SES groups than to the high educated and high SES groups.

"This pattern first became evident in the discussion of the demographic profile of the empathy types. There, it was observed that there was not so high an association between various demographic indices and the high empathy group as there was between the demographic indices and the low empathy group. In concrete terms, such background factors as high formal education, elite occupations, urban residence, and particular religious affiliation—the very factors which might be expected to differentiate the empathic people from the less empathic people— these factors are not associated markedly with empathy. On the basis of this sample and the Index constructed, such 'empathy-stimulating' factors as high education, elite occupation, etc., do not give rise to the characteristic ability to identify with an enlarged and unfamiliar sphere of human activity. Instead of this, these factors appear to result in a *fairly even distribution* of Empathy Index types.

"In the discussion of the demographic profile of the empathy types, it was not until such background factors as low education, low occupational stratum, housewife status, low SES, rural residence, and religious affiliation *per se* were taken into consideration that an association of some significance was observed. For the resultant of these background factors was not a more or less equal distribution among all the empathy types, but a clear clustering in the non-empathic type.

"Therefore, the first general aspect of this pattern is that while high education, elite occupation, urban residence, and particular religious affiliation do not definitely lead to the ability and willingness to identify with a larger and unfamiliar sphere of human activity, the converse factors (low education, low occupational stratum, etc.) do lead rather definitely to the inability and unwillingness to identify with a larger and unfamiliar sphere of human activity, as measured by the Empathy Index.

"Since the Index permitted a more clear location and a more specific definition of the non-empathic type than of the other types, it followed that the operation of empathy would be most significant with respect to the groups homogeneous as to low education and middle and low SES, in this case. This is the second general aspect of the configuration which emerges from this analysis.

"Both of the major hypotheses of this study have been verified, at least partially. That is, the construction of the Index of Empathy has enabled a prediction of media behavior. The people with high empathy scores tended to be more highly exposed to the mass media, minimally exposed to word-of-mouth communication of news, and critical in their preferences for different types of media. And in several important 'cases,' these findings were not simply a spurious association, with education or SES being the real determinant, but were, in fact, genuine determinants of media behavior. In lieu of the introduction of further 'inde-

Syrian Correlates of Empathy

	N	Empathic	Semi-Empathic	Non-Empathic
N	249*	55	94	100
Sex				
Male	200	25%	35%	40%
Female	49	10	39	51
Age				
30 and under	109	28%	39%	33%
31-40	52	25	35	40
41-50	46	15	37	48
51 and over	39	11	38	51
Education				
Illiterate	62	5%	21%	74%
Elementary or less	84	14	45	41
Secondary or more	102	39	42	19
SES				
Destitute, poor	91	12%	34%	54%
Modest	91	22	40	38
Well-off, rich	65	34	41	25
Occupational Class†				
Elite	73	41%	41%	18%
Middle	79	23	39	38
Lower	68	9	29	62
Housewives	26	—	46	54

* Where N is less than 249, the difference represents cases lacking usable data.

†*Elite* includes nobility, landlords, professionals, students; *Middle* includes entrepreneurs, technicians and the semi-skilled; *Lower* includes farmers, laborers, and the unskilled.

pendent variables,' the conclusion must be that the Index of Empathy has not simply gotten at a duplication of formal education or SES. It has elicited from the respondents an orientation to larger and unfamiliar world perspectives which, in the foregoing designated respects, is relatively independent of education and SES in accounting for various facets of mass communications media behavior in modern Syria."

The thesis went on to suggest further uses for the Empathy Index as follows:

"The hypothesis for future research is that the Index of Empathy will uncover systematic variations which we have termed 'covert' aspects of mass media behavior—variations which cannot be accounted for on the basis of the factors of education, SES, and so forth. To cite an example, all people with elementary education might have a similar *amount of exposure* to the media, but not a similar type of 'quality' of exposure. The people with high empathy scores in this homogeneous group might, more often than those with lower empathy scores, *go beyond* the stimuli of the media to construct imaginative sequels, criticisms, and alternatives."

Mr. Marsh then concluded:

"It is hoped that this cursory review will suggest that the notion of world-mindedness, or empathy, is of more than academic importance. It has relevance for a wide range of social phenomena, especially problems of social change, communications behavior, and political sociology."

Appendix C
The Latent Structure Analysis*

A CENTRAL PURPOSE of this book has been to analyze modernization as a process with some distinctive *quality* of its own, which would explain why modernity is felt as a *consistent whole* among people who live by its rules. We know that urbanization, industrialization, secularization, democratization, education, media participation do not occur in haphazard and unrelated fashion even though we often are obliged to study them singly. Our multiple correlations (chapter II) showed them to be so highly associated as to raise the question whether some are genuinely independent factors at all—suggesting that perhaps they went together so regularly because, in some historical sense, they *had to* go together.

What we needed was a unifying factor of response made by people living in a modernizing environment. This unifying factor, or key variable, we identified as "style of life." The evidence of our interviews in country after country showed that, if one could classify a person as Modern or Transitional or Traditional, then one could regularly predict many other things about him. How, then, do modernization of a society and changing lifestyles among its people go together? This is the familiar quest of the social scientist for reciprocity between his models of individual and institutional behavior.

The method we adopted was Latent Structure Analysis (LSA), developed by Paul F. Lazarsfeld, to test rigorously whether a variety of particular opinions contains some single more general attitude. The mathematical and technical complexities are such that we must refer the reader interested in methodology to Lazarsfeld's own exposition, contenting ourselves here with a summary statement of the conception underlying what we did and why. The fundamental concept of LSA

---

* I wish to thank P. L. Berkman for "processing" my typology through the complex computations of latent structure analysis and R. H. Somers for expert advice on this report.

is Freud's proposition that the varied overt activities of an individual—his "manifest behavior"—can be correlated with, and hence predicted from, the latent structure of his attitudes. A person's attitudes form a "latent structure" when, underlying their apparent diversity, some common element can be identified which renders them compatible and consistent with a personality trait of the individual in question. Such structures are "latent" because they are not overtly expressed in particular actions; in fact, said Freud, manifest activities are more or less deliberately designed to obscure the latent structure, which is the individual's personality—his secret. The latent structure can only be inferred from repeated observation of varied actions by the same individual. Accordingly, the Freudian concept was applied for many decades only in clinical analysis of individual cases, often pathological cases.

Lazarsfeld provided a method by which a latent structure could be inferred from an individual's responses to a questionnaire—his expressed opinions constituting, in this case, his manifest behavior. By this method, behavioral characteristics can properly be inferred from the *frequency* of expressed opinions among many individuals; hence the derivation of latent structures can be extended from clinical cases to sample surveys. For our purpose we adapted LSA, which is a brilliant innovation in factorial analysis, to a special type of factorial problem.

Our typology classified individuals according to "sociological" (rather than attitudinal) factors—e.g., urbanism, literacy, socioeconomic status, media participation. The statistical studies reported in chapter II showed that a matrix of these factors, around the world, consistently differentiated Modern from Traditional *countries*. The application to our Middle Eastern data, in chapter III, showed that *individuals* could also be differentiated by a personality mechanism called *empathy*. The underlying theoretical hypothesis holds that empathy is more *functional* in Modern than in Traditional society. The next question was whether empathic personality and modern sociological attributes occur together so regularly in the same individuals as to justify the assumption of some more fundamental or latent attribute underlying both. LSA did verify the existence of the latent attribute which we call "style of life"; and it permitted the identification of three rank orders—Traditional, Transitional, Modern—along a single basic scale composed of all five factors in our typology.

The data subjected to LSA came from the total of 1,357 interviews in hand when the test was taken.* The two-class model of LSA was used. Here the procedure is to dichotomize the data on each item in

---

* Distributed as follows: Turkey 257, Lebanon 262, Egypt, 259, Syria 200, Jordan 263, Iran 116.

the test. Positive (+) and negative (−) are terms without intrinsic meaning and are used merely to identify the high and low scorers on each item. This procedure later tests empirically its own initial assumption that the sample population *can* be accounted for by two latent classes (such as Modern and Traditional). It does so by determining the most probable item-patterns of each class; in so doing the latent parameters generate data which identify the "refruitment base" for each item-pattern. This surplus information enabled us, in the present test, to derive from the two-class model our three-class typology.

We have already explained the theoretical grounds for our selection of urbanization, literacy, SES, media exposure and empathy in chapter II. For the LSA, variant definitions were used to dichotomize (+ or −) each item and the scoring procedure may be recapitulated as follows:

Table 1—LSA Dichotomous Scoring Procedure

Item	+	−
Urbanism	communities over 2,000	communities under 2,000
Literacy	secondary or higher education	elementary or less education
SES	high-status occupations	low-status occupations
Media Exposure	scored 7-12 on media index	scored 0-6 on media index
Empathy	scored 3-6 on projective questions	scored 0-2 on projective questions

Naturally, as in any dichotomous scoring procedure, the line that divides + from − is arbitrary. On the SES and literacy items, our division seems generally acceptable: several area experts agreed that our classification of "high" and "low" occupations would be adhered to rather widely throughout the area. On the media exposure and empathy items, the boundary between + and − was limited by the wording of our questionnaire and there was no viable alternative. On urbanism, for which we have used 20,000 and 50,000 as our usual boundaries in this book, we took account of the objections made by several experts that these were too high. They argued that, in the Middle East setting, individuals living in communities over 2,000 are already "townspeople" with many characteristics of urbanites. This did not square with our own impressions, but the weight of expert testimony was conceded. Using these dichotomies, the item-by-item results are shown in Table 2. The first row gives the probability that a *literate* respondent will come from either of the latent classes (I or II), the second row gives these figures for an *urban* respondent, and the three next rows for respondents scoring *high* on SES, Media Exposure, Empathy.

There is a clear and consistent division between the classes on all items. The smallest difference is on the urbanism item. This indicates that towns of 2,000 do not adequately differentiate urban from rural.

Had we kept the urbanism boundary at our higher 50,000 figure, the differential in row 2 would have increased considerably. Also, had we fixed the empathy boundary a notch higher, a larger differential would have appeared in row 5. But as the differences shown below were wide enough on all items to test our types, the complete LSA distribution was made on this basis—as shown in Table 3.

Table 2—Latent Classes by Items

	LATENT CLASS	
	I	II
Item	Modern	Traditional
1) Literate	.85	.00
2) Urban (community over 2,000)	.91	.56
3) High SES	.84	.13
4) High Media Exposure	.93	.28
5) High Empathy	.93	.56

When these five items were scored dichotomously, they produced 32 possible combinations. Each respondent was sorted into the item-pattern representing his sequence of answers to the interview questions. For example: the "pure" Modern who was literate, urban, and high on SES, Media Exposure, Empathy was scored as item-pattern (1) + + + + +; the "pure" Traditional who was illiterate, rural, and low on the other three items was scored as item-pattern (32) — — — — —. Between these extremes thirty variations occurred. This raised the question: at what point do item-patterns stop being Modern and become Traditional? This was handled empirically, by fixing the boundary between classes where the individual respondents formed substantial groups.

Since a two-class LSA model makes obvious only the location of the "pure" item-patterns at both extremes, how can an intermediate class be identified? On this point the method, again, is reassuringly empirical. By his answers to questions (the manifest data) each individual supplied his own item-pattern. By applying the latent parameters to all item-patterns, we learned the "recruitment cluster" for any group of item-patterns—i.e., the probability that any individual showing a particular item-pattern will come from one of the hypothesized latent classes rather than the other. The rank ordering and magnitudes enable us to decide which variations in item-patterns are likely to be of small predictive significance. We can therefore assign each individual (despite variations) to his modal class—the class from which the majority of respondents with item-patterns *like* his are more likely to come. When a certain variant in the scale of item-patterns acquires numerous recruits, then we infer that we may have a significant sub-class, which in due course may become a distinct intermediate class.

Table 3—Complete Latent Structure of Item Patterns

(Col. 1) Recruitment Cluster	(Col. 2) Item Pattern					(Col. 3) COMPOSITION OF Latent Class I (Modern)	(Col. 4) Latent Class II (Traditional)	(Col. 5) PERCENTAGE RECRUITED FROM: Latent Class I	(Col. 6) Latent Class II	TOTAL
	1 Literate	2 Urban	3 SES	4 Media	5 Empathy	(%)	(%)	(%)	(%)	(%)
A (Modern) (1)	+	+	+	+	+	56.5	0.0	100.0	0.0	100
(2)	+	+	+	+	−	4.4	0.0	100.0	0.0	100
(3)	+	+	+	−	+	4.1	0.0	100.0	0.0	100
(4)	+	+	−	+	+	10.7	0.0	100.0	0.0	100
(5)	+	−	+	+	+	5.6	0.0	100.0	0.0	100
(6)	+	+	+	−	−	.7	0.0	100.0	0.0	100
(7)	+	+	−	+	−	.8	0.0	100.0	0.0	100
(8)	+	+	−	−	+	.4	0.0	100.0	0.0	100
(9)	+	−	+	+	−	1.1	0.0	100.0	0.0	100
(10)	+	−	+	−	+	.4	0.0	100.0	0.0	100
(11)	+	−	−	+	+	.4	0.0	100.0	0.0	100
(12)	+	+	−	−	−	.1	0.0	100.0	0.0	100
(13)	+	−	+	−	−	.1	0.0	100.0	0.0	100
(14)	+	−	−	+	−	.1	0.0	100.0	0.0	100
(15)	+	−	−	−	+	.03	0.0	100.0	0.0	100
(16)	+	−	−	−	−	.005	0.0	100.0	0.0	100

Item						Col. 3	Col. 4	Col. 5	Col. 6	
B (Transitional)										
(17)	+	+	+	+	−	1.1	10.2	10.0	90.0	100
(18)	+	+	+	−	−	.9	1.0	47.0	53.0	100
(19)	−	+	+	+	−	.9	.7	56.0	44.0	100
(20)	+	+	−	+	−	7.7	1.9	80.0	20.0	100
(21)	+	−	+	+	−	2.9	.7	81.0	19.0	100
C (Traditional)										
(22)	−	+	+	−	−	.7	.07	91.0	9.0	100
(23)	+	−	+	−	−	2.3	.07	97.0	3.0	100
(24)	+	+	−	−	−	6.1	.2	97.0	3.0	100
(25)	−	−	+	+	−	2.3	.05	98.0	2.0	100
(26)	−	+	−	+	−	6.0	.1	98.0	2.0	100
(27)	−	−	+	−	−	1.8	.01	99.4	.6	100
(28)	−	−	−	+	−	19.7	.1	99.5	.5	100
(29)	+	+	−	−	−	4.7	.01	99.8	.2	100
(30)	−	−	−	+	−	15.4	.01	99.94	.06	100
(31)	−	−	−	−	−	15.5	.01	99.94	.06	100
(32)	+	−	−	−	−	12.1	.001	99.992	.008	100
TOTAL						100.0*	100.0*			

Col. 5 = Col. 3 ÷ (Col. 3 + Col. 4)
Col. 6 = Col. 4 ÷ (Col. 3 + Col. 4)

* Because of rounding, the column does not total exactly 100%.

Table 3 shows how this procedure arranged our Middle East respondents. Column 2 includes all of the 32 item-patterns produced by our five dichotomous items. Column 3 gives the probability with which individuals exhibiting each of these item-patterns can be expected to fall into Latent Class I; or, conversely, the relative proportion of individuals in Latent Class I that can be expected to exhibit each of the possible item-patterns. Column 4 provides the same information for Latent Class II. Columns 5 and 6 show, in rank order, the probable percentage of individuals with a *given item-pattern* who can be expected to be recruited from Latent Classes I and II respectively. Column 1 identifies the "recruitment clusters" into which the item-patterns have been arranged on the basis of their ranking in Columns 5 and 6.

The result is clearest with the two most extreme patterns. LSA predicts, in probability terms, that all respondents with pattern (1) + + + + + will come from Latent Class I; it predicts, further, that virtually all of the respondents displaying pattern (32) − − − − − will come from Latent Class II. The probabilities for the remaining item-patterns identify two "sets" which are associated with the respective extremes. These can be grouped in the classes postulated by the two-class model, for the high probability coefficients predict that virtually every correspondingly-patterned individual will be assigned to one of these classes. Table 3 shows that 100 per cent of the individuals exhibiting any of the 16 item-patterns identified as Recruitment Cluster A can be expected to be recruited from Latent Class I; the probabilities are very high, though not so uniform, for individuals exhibiting the 11 item-patterns identified as Recruitment Cluster C.

This leaves the five item-patterns (17 through 21) which we have grouped as Recruitment Cluster B. Here some ambiguity does exist. Adhering strictly to the modal-class rule, one would assign pattern (17) − + + + + to Recruitment Cluster A, but this would introduce a measure of heterogeneity into a group of patterns *otherwise homogeneous* in terms of their probable recruitment from Latent Class I. Similarly with patterns (20) − + − + + and (21) − + + − +, whose assignment to Recruitment Cluster C would disorder its homogeneity. As these patterns show a drop of 10 per cent from the lower limit (91.0) of recruitment from Latent Class II into Cluster C, there is evidently a "natural boundary" here. A similar drop of 10 per cent separated pattern (16) from (17) in recruitment of Latent Class I into Cluster A. As for patterns (18) − − + + + and (19) − + + + −, which are recruited bimodally (i.e., approximately equal proportions from both Latent Classes), it is evident that assignment to either I or II would automatically misclassify about half of the individuals exhibiting each item-pattern.

Consequently—and in line with our initial hypothesis about the existence of Modern, Traditional, *and* Transitional styles of life in the Middle East—we introduced a third intermediate group, to which the relatively ambiguous item-patterns of Recruitment Cluster B were assigned. This group comprises individuals whose style of life is neither clearly Modern nor Traditional; it mixes principal components of both lifestyles into a distinct and different style which we call Transitional. While this Transitional group is not *necessarily* a Class in the latent-class sense, its use as a distinctive type introduces additional control and discrimination into the analysis of several relevant dependent variables, as was shown in the case studies.

We now have, therefore, three Recruitment Clusters—which we have called "types" to avoid confusion with the LSA term Class. The Modern Type (total 605) is represented by all individuals recruited exclusively from Latent Class I. The Traditional Type (total 531) is represented by all individuals with item-patterns recruited to the extent of 91 per cent or more from Latent Class II. Between them is the Transitional Type (total 221), represented by all individuals with item-patterns recruited more evenly from both latent classes.

The controlling characteristics of these three types emerge more clearly when their respective item-patterns are considered in detail. We note, first, that literacy (Item 1) operates as the single most powerful discriminator between the types. All of the Modern item-patterns are "positive" on literacy; all those representing the Traditional Type are "negative" on this item. This reconfirms the critical function of education for modern and modernizing persons. But literacy is a necessary, not sufficient, condition of a Modern style of life. Among literate respondents there is still considerable variation in degree of Modernity. Some literates are far more Modern than others; some illiterates are far less Traditional than others.

The Transitionals, despite their illiteracy, are much closer to a Modern style of life than the equally illiterate Traditionals. As shown in Table 3, Traditionals are "positive" (+) on *two or less* of the five items, and Transitionals are "positive" on *at least three* items. This means that the illiterate individual becomes a Transitional type *only* if he exhibits one of the item-configurations shown in Table 4.

Table 4—The Transitional Patterns

Urban	— — — —	High Media Exposure	High Empathy
Urban	High SES	— — — —	High Empathy
Urban	High SES	High Media Exposure	— — — —
— — — —	High SES	High Media Exposure	High Empathy
Urban	High SES	High Media Exposure	High Empathy

As between two illiterates, the one who is urban shows himself more responsive to modernization than the one who is rural. Hence, urbanization reappears as a distinctive component of Transitionalism—whereas 4 of the 5 Transitional patterns score + on item 2, only 4 of 11 Traditional patterns do so. Moreover, every Transitional recruited from Latent Class I scores + on either media or empathy and the great majority (almost 3 to 1) score + on both these items. It would appear, then, not that these Transitionals were misclassified in Latent Class I, but that an empathic individual who participates in the media can (even without formal schooling) develop a pretty close approximation to a Modern style of life.

We note, finally, that the Transitionals differentiate themselves into three subgroups corresponding to:

> High Transitionals (pattern 17)
> Middle Transitionals (patterns 18-19)
> Low Transitionals (patterns 20-21)

The significance of these subgroups is illustrated throughout the case studies. What we stress here is that the Transitionals exhibit a *combination* of attributes ordinarily associated with a Modern style of life. They lack education but compensate for this by scoring heavily on other indices. It is particularly their use of empathic skills, to compensate for lack of formal education, which makes Transitionals men-in-motion and equips them to live in a modernizing world. And empathy, we have seen, flourishes best in an urban setting, with a cash nexus between desires and satisfactions, and with mass media to stimulate imagination and shape imagery.

Notes

INTRODUCTION

* I am indebted to the Foundations' Fund for Research in Psychiatry for an opportunity to work on the problems of interviewing discussed herein.

1. As so often happens, the poor held extravagant but not entirely mistaken suspicions, for American interest in the Middle East at this time did, *inter alia*, reflect the not entirely disinterested curiosities of the Cold War.

2. Unlike the Western experience, where women are often the pioneers of new levels of living, the women in the Muslim countries are being uprooted more slowly than the men. *Cf.* the discussion of sex differences in Hortense Powdermaker, "Social Change Through Imagery and Values of Teen-Age Africans in Northern Rhodesia," *American Anthropologist,* Vol. 58, 1956, pp. 783-813; among the Bemba-speaking young people studied by Dr. Powdermaker, the movies and radio had distributed images of European styles of life far beyond the orbits of personal contact. And see also the discussion of class and generational differences in the relative emancipation of Egyptian women in Morroe Berger, *The Middle Class in the Arab World* (privately printed by the Princeton University Conference, 1957), pp. 14-16.

3. I don't know if any full-scale study has been made of the impact of American immigration barriers on the origins of Fascism in the 1920's (through blocking Italian immigration) and on world chaos since; as long as the capable and energetic could "rise" to America, a global safety-valve existed quite like that provided by domestic social mobility. In Mr. Lerner's analysis there are many who would like to live in the United States or in Western Europe but who, aware that they cannot get a visa, can only turn against these countries of desire in ambivalent rejection—and, sometimes, in self-rejection too. See Patricia L. Kendall, "The Ambivalent Character of Nationalism Among Egyptian Professionals," *Public Opinion Quarterly,* Vol. 20, 1956, pp. 277-292.

4. A recent study of Algerians by Horace Miner indicates that urbanization does not reduce the suspicion with which men regard each other vis-à-vis their womenfolk; they can guard their women less in the city but are no less convinced that all other men are intriguing against them—a projection, it would seem, of their own required self-image as virile males. The appeal to hatred of the foreigner as social cement is always understandable among underdogs, especially when, as is so often the case, the underdogs mistrust each other.

5. This was in 1954, prior to the turn toward a heavier despotism of the Menderes regime, and prior to the current desperate inflation, which has been given added impetus by just such public works as the road to Balgat and the new powerful radio

transmitter in Istanbul.

6. Professor Lerner comments that a kind of literacy is required to read the labels on tin cans—one reason why it is difficult for a modernizing society, even with the aid of the movies, to skip print entirely.

7. See her book, *New Lives for Old* (1956).

Melville Herskovits and other anthropologists have forcefully argued against the term "preliterate" (preferring "nonliterate") as connoting an ethnocentric assumption of historical stages in which the preliterates will someday become, like us, literate. I believe that, whether we like it or not, they will, though the question remains what language or languages they will employ for dramatizing their past and their aspirations to themselves and communicating in private and in public, within an area and throughout the globe. Depending on accidents of history and geography, they may write in one tongue and listen to broadcasts in another. Cf., e.g., David Apter, *The Gold Coast in Transition* (Princeton: Princeton University, 1955).

8. Morris' discussion, and my own, are not of course meant to blur the many variants both of Christianity and of Islam, nor to overlook the many similarities of origin and creed.

9. I am indebted to Carter Zeleznik's observations on his experience in Ethiopia for a better understanding of this.

CHAPTER ONE

THE GROCER AND THE CHIEF: A PARABLE

1. Under the Ottoman Empire, a traditional Turkish phrase for referring to the glory of the Sultan was "master of the whole world." The shepherd, like his elders, apparently falls back on the old imagery in a moment of crisis.

2. Silence does not obviate desire. In Turkish villages it is customary for the head of household to bury his hoard of metal coins in a secret garden spot; when he dies there is a frenzied treasure hunt for the cache. Tabu on talk, as Freud suggested, is a way of inhibiting the passage from desires to deeds. Traditional men, like the wise monkeys, find it safer to see no evil, speak no evil, hear no evil. This particular custom has the practical merit of restricting plans for a treasure hunt while papa is still alive.

CHAPTER TWO

MODERNIZING STYLES OF LIFE: A THEORY

1. G. E. von Grunebaum (ed.), *Unity and Variety in Muslim Civilization* (1955), p. 3.

2. *Ibid.*, p. 12.

3. See autobiographical literature of human migration, especially W. I. Thomas and F. Znaniecki, *The Polish Peasant in Europe and America*, v. 5 (1927).

4. Robert Park, *Human Communities* (1952).

5. S. Ratner, *American Taxation, Its History As A Social Force in Democracy* (1942).

6. This formulation approaches the typology on American society developed by David Riesman in *The Lonely Crowd* (1950). Cf. my article "Comfort and Fun: Morality in a Nice Society," *The American Scholar* (Spring 1958).

7. Oscar Handlin, *The Uprooted* (1952).

8. W. H. Auden, *"Petition."*

9. J. W. Beach, *The Twentieth Century Novel* (1932).

10. P. F. Lazarsfeld and F. N. Stanton, *Radio Research, 1942-43* (1944).

11. Elihu Katz and P. F. Lazarsfeld, *Personal Influence* (1955).

12. A. Bergson (ed.), *Soviet Economic Growth* (1953).

13. Industrialization was measured by proportion of gainfully employed males in non-agricultural occupations. H. H. Golden, "Literacy and Social Change in Underdeveloped Countries,"*Rural Society* XX (1955), pp. 1-7. See also: UN Statistical Office, *National and Per Capita Income in 70 Countries* (1949).

14. W. W. Rostow, *The Process of Economic Growth* (1952), pp. 102-6; Colin Clark, *Conditions of Economic Progress* (1940), pp. 6-7.

15. C. L. Becker, *Progress and Power* (1936); H. A. Innis, *Empire and Communications* (1950), p. 11.

16. For an earlier report, see Lerner: "A Scale Pattern of Opinion Correlates," *Sociometry*, 16 (August 1953), pp. 266-71.

17. A Lazarsfeldian latent structure analysis of our data confirmed the hypothesis beyond expectation. This analysis, which involves complicated technical procedures, is being prepared for separate publication. A condensed version is presented in the Appendix.

18. D. Lerner and D. Riesman, "Self and Society," *Explorations* (June 1955).

19. W. E. Hocking, Foreword (p. vi) to *The Arab World* by N. Izzeddin (1953).

CHAPTER THREE

THE PASSING OF TRADITIONAL SOCIETY: A SURVEY

1. C. Y. Glock, "The Comparative Study of Communications and Opinion Formation," *Public Opinion Quarterly*, 16 (1952-53), pp. 512-523.

2. C. Y. Glock, personal letter.

3. Major BASR reports based on the preliminary analysis of each country are:

D. Lerner, G. K. Schueller and M. Stycos, "Mass Communication Audiences in Turkey"

J. M. Stycos, "Communication and Public Opinion in Jordan"

W. N. McPhee and R. B. Meyersohn, "The Radio Audience of Lebanon"

W. N. McPhee and R. B. Meyerohn, "Syrian Attitudes Towards America and Russia"

B. B. Ringer, "Partisanship and Communication Behavior in Iran"

B. B. Ringer and D. L. Sills, "The Political Extremes in Iran"

P. L. Kendall and B. B. Ringer, "Climates of Opinion in Egypt"

P. L. Kendall and Elihu Katz, "Communication Behavior and Political Attitudes in Four Arab Countries"

4. The following published articles were based on data in the BASR reports:

D. Lerner, "A Scale Pattern of Opinion Correlates," *Sociometry*, 16 (August 1953)

D. Lerner, "The Grocer and the Chief," *Harper's Magazine* (September 1955)

D. Lerner and D. Riesman, "Self and Society," *Explorations* (June 1955)

P. L. Kendall, "The Ambivalent Character of Nationalism Among Egyptian Professionals," *Public Opinion Quarterly*, 20 (1956), pp. 277-289

B. B. Ringer and D. L. Sills, "Political Extremists in Iran," *Public Opinion Quarterly*, 16 (1952-53), pp. 689-701

5. These studies can be identified by number, as BASR reports 24, 74, 75, 79, 94, 106, 108, 116, 117, 118, 119, 121, 122, 123, 126, 135, 147, 148, 149, 153, 158, 233, 234, 403, 412, 415, 417. See BASR *Twentieth Anniversary Report*.

CHAPTER FOUR

TURKEY: FROM THE PAST

1. M. W. Thornburg, *Turkey: An Economic Appraisal* (1949), p. vii.

2. *The Turkish Letters of Oghier Ghiselin de Busbecq* (1927), p. 135.

3. A. E. Yalman, "The Press," in E. G. Mears (ed.), *Modern Turkey* (1924).

4. Yalman, *The Development of Modern Turkey as Measured by Its Press* (1914). Also S. W. Baron, *The Jewish Community* (1942), p. 198.

5. Halil Inalcik (conversation).

6. Irfan Orga, *Portrait of a Turkish Family* (1950), p. 62.

7. Lucy Garnett, *The Women of Turkey and Their Folk Lore* (1891), v. II, p. 474.

8. Garnett, *Home Life in Turkey* (1909), p. 278.

9. Selma Ekrem, *Unveiled* (1931), p. 183.

10. Garnett, *Home Life in Turkey*, p. 181.

11. "On the day of the Last Judgment, when Mahomet summons the faithful to heaven from the purgatory where they are being punished for their sins, in order that they may partake of eternal bliss, the only path which they can tread will be a huge white-hot gridiron, over which they must pass with bare feet. . . . Then, wonderful to relate, all the paper which they have preserved from being trampled underfoot in the manner we have described will suddenly make its appearance and adhere to the soles of their feet and serve them well by preventing them from receiving any hurt from the hot iron. So great is the merit to be acquired for saving paper from ill treatment." de Busbecq, *op. cit.*, pp. 27-28.

12. Accounts vary slightly on the exact date and circumstances. Ubicini gives 1727, with the return of Saad from his father's Embassy in France, *Letters on Turkey* (1856), p. 236. Yalman gives 1728, dating from a *fetva* of the Sheikh el-Islam, *Develop-ment of Modern Turkey*, p. 20. D. W. Webster dates the first press and paper factory from 1728 and the first published book from 1729, but attributes them directly to the influence of Nevşehirli Damad Pasha who returned from Europe to serve as Grand Vezir for twelve years, *The Turkey of Ata-türk* (1939).

13. Ubicini, *op. cit.*, p. 237.

14. Yalman, *Development of Modern Turkey*, p. 20.

15. Ubicini, *op. cit.*, p. 235 (footnote).

16. S. W. Baron, *op. cit.*, v. I, p. 348.

17. Yalman, *op. cit.*, p. 24.

18. Sir Edward S. Creasy, *Turkey* (1906), p. 377. Note Ubicini's statement that the professional military class of *Janissaries* opposed these innovations as violently as the professional religious class of *'Ulema* opposed printing, *op. cit.*, p. 7.

19. Halide Edib, *Conflict of East and West in Turkey* (1935), p. 52.

20. Sir Mark Sykes, *The Caliph's Last Heritage* (1915).

21. Edib, *op. cit.*, p. 105. The corresponding figure of 20 per cent literacy among a 14 million population in 1918 is doubtful: the Young Turks did not accomplish nearly so much in one decade.

22. Full English text in Webster, *op. cit.* (1939), Appendix D.

23. République Turque . . . , *Annuaire Statistique* (1952), p. 79.

24. *Small Statistical Abstract*, 1947-1950 (Ankara, 1951), No. 330, p. 61.

25. *Annuaire Statistique* (1952), p. 57.

26. *Ibid.*, p. 79.

27. *Small Statistical Abstract*, No. 330, p. 68 (Adapted).

28. *Small Statistical Abstract* (Ankara, 1948), No. 291, p. 93.

29. *Annuaire Statistique* (1952), p. 102.

30. *Ibid.*, p. 102.

31. R. D. Robinson, Institute of Current World Affairs, Letter No. 43 (22 November 1949).

32. Webster, *op. cit.*, p. 205.

33. *Ibid.*, p. 314.

34. Eleanor Bisbee, *The New Turks* (1951), p. 85.

35. Webster, *op. cit.*, p. 144.

36. Cf.: Reşat Nuri Güntenkin, *The Autobiography of a Turkish Girl* (1949).

37. Cf.: Mahmut Makal, *A Village in Anatolia* (1954).

38. *Annuaire Statistique* (1952), p. 95.

39. Bisbee, *op. cit.*, p. 89.

40. United Nations, *Review of Economic Conditions in the Middle East* (1953), p. 80.

41. *Annuaire Statistique* (1952), p. 157.

42. *Ibid.*, p. 98.

43. UNESCO, *Progress of Literacy in Various Countries* (Paris 1953), p. 140.

44. *Annuaire Statistique* (1952), p. 102.

45. *Ibid.*, p. 194.

46. *Ibid.*, p. 191.

47. *Ibid.*, p. 192.

48. *Ibid.*, p. 305.

49. *Ibid.*, p. 528.

50. Turkish Information Office (New York), *News from Turkey*, v. VII, No. 10.

51. *Le Monde* (Paris), 7 December 1954.

52. *The New York Times*, 20 August 1954.

53. H. A. R. Gibb and H. Bowen, *Islamic Society and the West* (1950), v. 1, pt. 1, p. 244.

54. J. A. Morrison, *Alisar: A Unit of Land Occupance*, Ph.D. Thesis, Univ. of Chicago (1939).

55. Muzafer Sherif, *An Outline of Social Psychology* (1948), pp. 374-385.

56. J. G. Frazer, *Psyche's Task. Influence of Superstition on the Growth of Institutions* (1909), p. 82.

57. H. G. Dwight, *Stamboul Nights* (1917).

58. Bisbee, *op. cit.*, pp. 129, 162-67.

CHAPTER FIVE

TURKEY: TOWARD THE FUTURE

1. Paul Stirling, *The Social Structure of Turkish Peasant Communities*, Ph.D. Thesis, Oxford (1951), p. 91.

2. The fine phrase "sense of variousness and possibility" is used by Lionel Trilling to describe the "open" modern personality in *The Liberal Imagination* (1950).

3. See David Riesman (ed.), *American Journal of Sociology* (Sept. 1956), special interviewing issue.

4. See P. F. Lazarsfeld, "The Obligations of the 1950 Pollster to the 1984 Historian," *Public Opinion Quarterly* (Winter 1950-51).

5. W. Durant and H. Cantril, *How Nations See Each Other* (1953), especially Table 5, pp. 46-47.

6. On the distribution of values in modern society the works of H. D. Lasswell are indispensable. See especially: *Power and Personality* (1948), *Power and Society* (1950).

7. D. Riesman, *The Lonely Crowd* (1950).

8. On modern "propaganditis," see E. Kris and N. Leites, "Trends in 20th Century Propaganda," in D. Lerner (ed.), *Propaganda in War and Crisis* (1951).

9. C. I. Hovland *et al.*, *Communication and Persuasion* (1953), pp. 105-111.

10. Marcel Clerget, *La Turquie, Passé et Présent* (1947), pp. 197-200.

11. L. V. Thomas and R. N. Frye, *The U.S. and Turkey and Iran* (1951), p. 109.

CHAPTER SIX

LEBANON: TWO WORLDS IN SMALL COMPASS

1. The Lebanese population includes 25% urbanites (cities over 50,-000). Daily newspaper circulation is 81 per 1000: 36 radios per 1000: an-

nual film attendances 5 per capita. UNESCO, *World Communications* (1951). Among school-age children 73% were attending elementary school in 1942-1945, as compared with 42% average in other Arab countries. R. D. Matthews and M. Akrawi, *Education in the Arab Countries of the Near East* (1949), p. 544.

Two estimates of literacy: 60-65 per cent by J. Donato, "Lebanon and Its Labor Legislation," *International Labor Review*, LXV, 1. (January 1952) p. 71; 70 per cent by A. Tannous, "The Village in the National Life of Lebanon," *Middle East Journal*, Vol. III, No. 2 (April 1949), p. 162.

2. P. K. Hitti, *History of the Arabs* (1953), pp. 735-36.

3. Hitti, *History of Syria* (1951), p. 695.

4. G. E. von Grunebaum, *Islam* (1955), p. 224.

5. Hitti, *History of Syria*, p. 676.

6. Matthews and Akrawi, *op. cit.*, p. 503.

7. G. Antonius, *The Arab Awakening* (1938); A. Hourani, *Syria and Lebanon* (1947); G. Haddad, *Fifty Years of Modern Syria and Lebanon* (1950).

8. Matthews and Akrawi, *op. cit.*, pp. 422, 424.

9. E. Atiyah, *An Arab Tells His Story* (1946).

10. H. J. Liebesny, "Religious Law and Westernization in the Moslem Near East," *American Journal of Comparative Law* (Autumn 1953), p. 498.

11. C. Issawi, "Middle Eastern Entrepreneurs," S. N. Fisher (ed.), *Social Forces in the Middle East* (1955), pp. 119-21.

12. An extreme example: In the village of Bar Elias, 5,285 acres were divided into 32,643 plots. W. B. Fisher, *The Middle East* (1950), p. 182.

13. Land is utilized intensively—about 1½ acres available per head of farming population. D. Warriner, *Land and Poverty in the Middle East*, London (1948), p. 82. Annual population increase has been estimated at 2.2 per cent. (Tannous, *op. cit.*, p. 153.) According to some specialists the land can support only 300,000 farming persons—half the present population; cf. C. Issawi and C. Dabezies, "Population Movements and Population Pressure in Jordan, Lebanon, and Syria," *The Milbank Memorial Fund Quarterly*, Vol. XXIX, No. 4 (October 1951), pp. 389, 395-96.

14. Issawi, *op. cit.*, p. 120. More conservative estimates in Donato, *op. cit.*, p. 65, and Haddad, *op. cit.* (800,000 and 700,000 respectively).

15. One estimate locates 86 per cent of 1,12,000 overseas Lebanese in No. and So. America. G. Menassa, *Plan de reconstruction de l'économie Libanaise et de reforme de L'état* (1948), p. 384.

16. Issawi, *op. cit.*, pp. 120-21. Cf. R. Widmer, "Population," S. B. Himadeh, *Economic Organization of Syria* (1936), pp. 16-17.

17. Issawi and Dabezies, *op. cit.*, p. 395; Europa Publications, *The Middle East*, p. 209.

18. Postwar estimate: 77 passenger cars per 10,000 population in Lebanon, by far the highest rate in the Middle East. U.N., *Review of Economic Conditions in the Middle East, 1949-1950*, p. 66.

19. In al-Munsif, a Greek Orthodox village, only 55 per cent lived at home all year; 36 per cent regularly lived away and returned only occasionally; the remainder commuted on a daily or weekly basis. J. Gulick, "Conservatism and Change in a Lebanese Village," *Middle East Journal*, Vol. VIII, No. 3 (Summer 1954). In Bishmizzeen, about 14 per cent lived in Beirut or Tripoli nine months and summered in the village. A. Tannous, "Emigration, A Force of Social Change in an Arab Village," *Rural Sociology*, Vol. VII, No. 1 (March 1942). J. Gulick, *Social Structure and Culture Change in a Lebanese Village* (1955), p. 136.

20. Warriner, *op. cit.*, p. 90. Tan-

nous, "Emigration," *loc. cit.*, pp. 70-71.

21. UNESCO, *Report of the Commission on Technical Needs, Press Film, Radio* (1949), p. 225; A. Hillelson, "The BBC Arabic Broadcasts," *Royal Central Asian Journal,* Vol. XXVI, Part II (April 1939), pp. 261-64.

22. In al-Munsif, "traditional dances as the *dabki* are looked upon at best with sentimental attachment by most of the middle-aged people and with unfeigned derision by many, though not all, younger people . . . it is the samba, rumba, and tango which please the young people most." Gulick, *Social Structure* . . . , pp. 100-101.

23. P. F. Lazarsfeld and H. Field, *The People Look at Radio* (1946), p. 43.

24. Tannous, *Trends of Social and Cultural Change in Bishmizzeen, An Arab Village of North Lebanon,* Thesis, Cornell University (1940), p. 225.

25. A traditional villager said: "Most people here don't want to make a lot of money. All they really want is to make enough so they will not be hungry and without clothes." Gulick, *Social Structure* . . . , p. 139. The educated youth of al-Munsif, however, scorned manual labor and preferred urban amenities.

26. Matthews and Akrawi, *op. cit.,* p. 551.

27. Tannous, *Trends of Social and Cultural Change* . . . , p. 208. Similar results were obtained by Gulick in al-Munsif.

28. D. Potter, "The Bazaar," in S. N. Fisher, *Social Forces* . . . , p. 103.

29. UNESCO, *Report of the Commission on Technical Needs* . . . , p. 176.

30. *Ibid.*, p. 120.

31. A set cost $84 in 1949. *Ibid.*, p. 226. An unskilled worker earned between $1.40 and $1.80 daily. *Review of Economic Conditions* . . . , 1949-1950, p. 53.

32. Musa al-'Alami of Jordan concluded, after Arab defeat in Palestine, that "The woman must be equal to the man so that she may share in the formation of . . . a new Arab society." "The Lesson of Palestine," *Middle East Journal,* Vol. III, No. 4, p. 399. Lebanese reform party of Kemal Jumblat also advocates female emancipation.

33. Hourani, *op. cit.*, pp. 92-93.

34. H. Granqvist, *Birth and Childhood Among the Arabs* (1947), p. 155.

35. J. Van Ess, *Meet the Arab* (1943), p. 161.

36. C. S. Coon, *Caravan* (1951), p. 168.

37. Wm. Douglas, *Strange Lands and Friendly Peoples* (1951).

38. Gulick, *Social Structure and Culture Change* . . . , p. 61. Tannous, *Trends of Social and Cultural Change,* p. 232.

39. Matthews and Akrawi, *op. cit.,* p. 422.

40. Granqvist, *op. cit.*, pp. 153-54. See, for the historic span, E. W. Lane, *Manners and Customs of the Modern Egyptians* (1923).

41. H. Herzog, "On Borrowed Experience," *Studies in Philosophy and Social Science* (1944), p. 71.

42. H. Kohn, *Western Civilization in the Near East* (1936), p. 269.

43. Proportions of the sects in 1947 were estimated as: Maronites (29 per cent), Sunnis (21 per cent), Shi'ites (19 per cent), Greek Orthodox (10 per cent), Druzes (7 per cent), Greek Catholics (6 per cent), Armenian Orthodox (5 per cent). Hourani, *op. cit.*, p. 386.

44. Matthews and Akrawi, *op. cit.,* p. 416.

45. Hourani, *op. cit.*, p. 64.

46. Estimate of 28,000 organized among 150,000 potential trade unionists in 1952. G. E. K., "Some Aspects of Lebanese Trade Unionism," *The World Today,* Vol. IX, No. 9 (September 1953), p. 409. Estimate 14,000 in T. B. Stouffer, "Labor Unions in

the Arab States," *Middle East Journal*, Vol. VI, No. 1 (Winter 1952), pp. 84-85.

47. Issawi, "Foundations of Democracy in the Middle East," *International Affairs*, Vol. XXXII, No. 1, p. 40. P. Rondot, *Les Institutions Politiques du Liban* (1947), p. 126.

48. G. E. K., *op. cit.*, pp. 410-11.

49. Rondot, *op. cit.*, p. 95n.

50. Hourani, *op. cit.*, p. 62. See also pp. 184-85.

51. "Under the list system, 'the fiction of representation is reduced, in numerous cases, to the predominance of brutal force and the influence of bribes.'" Menassa, *op. cit.*, p. 387. See also C. G. Hess and H. L. Bodman, Jr., "Confessionalism and Feudality in Lebanese Politics," *Middle East Journal*, Vol. VII (Winter 1954), p. 16.

52. J. L., "Peaceful Change in Lebanon," *The World Today* (April 1953), pp. 162-73.

53. D. Riesman, *The Lonely Crowd* (1950), p. 196.

54. Issawi, "Foundations of Democracy in the Middle East," pp. 39-40. Cf. Britt, "Lebanon's Popular Revolution," *Middle East Journal*, Vol. VII, No. 1 (Winter 1953); J. L., *op. cit.*, pp. 163, 168.

55. Hess and Bodman, *op. cit.*; J. L., *op. cit.*, p. 172.

56. R. H. Nolte, "Lebanese Elections," Institute of Current World Affairs Newsletter RHN 48, Beirut (13 July 1953).

57. W. Z. Laqueur, *Communism and Nationalism in the Middle East* (1956), p. 162. Estimates C. P. membership at 8-10,000.

58. *Ibid.* Occupational breakdown of Chamber after elections listed 21 landowners, 17 lawyers, 2 doctors, 2 journalists, 2 merchants, and one engineer. Haydar, *The Lebanese State* (in Arabic), Beirut (1953), pp. 45-47. Cited in George Grassmuck, "Public Administration: Problems of Teaching and Research in the Middle East,"

Session on Comparative Administration, American Political Science Association Convention, Boulder, Colorado (1955). Of 42 elected members, 31 had served with one or more previous Parliaments. "Chronology," *Middle East Journal* (August 1953), p. 505.

59. U.N., *Economic Development in the Middle East, 1945-54*, pp. 151, 158, 170.

60. K. Mandelbaum, *The Industrialization of Backward Areas* (1955), p. xvi.

61. Donato, *op. cit.*, pp. 69-70. Menassa, *op. cit.*, p. 35.

62. *The New York Times* (18 January 1958), p. 3.

CHAPTER SEVEN

EGYPT: THE VICIOUS CIRCLE

1. Clare Hollingworth, *The Arabs and The West* (1952), p. 257.

2. Gamal Abdul Nasser, *Egypt's Liberation. The Philosophy of the Revolution* (1955), pp. 39-40.

3. 1947 Census: 19,088,839 people; 5,963,059 acres. Charles Issawi, *Egypt: An Economic and Social Analysis* (1947), pp. 44-45. C. V. Kiser, "Demographic Position of Egypt," in F. W. Notestein (ed.), *Demographic Studies of Selected Areas of Rapid Growth* (1944), pp. 117-18.

4. Ragnar Nurkse, *Problems of Capital Formation in Underdeveloped Countries* (1953), p. 4.

5. B. M. Mattison, "Rural Social Centers in Egypt," *Middle East Journal* (Autumn 1951), p. 463. See also Dr. Ahmed Hussein Pasha (former Minister of Social Affairs), paper prepared for Third Agricultural Conference in Cairo on March 26, 1949.

6. M. L. Cooke, *Nasser's High Aswan Dam—Panacea or Politics* (1956).

7. Kiser, *loc. cit.*, p. 103. République d'Egypte, Ministère des Finances et de l'Economie, Département de la Statistique et du Recensement, *An-*

nuaire Statistique (1953), pp. 22, 24. U.N., *Monthly Bulletin of Statistics* (April 1954), p. xx.

8. Royal Institute of International Affairs, *The Middle East* (1950), p. 142. Also: U.N., Department of Economic Affairs, Research Memorandum No. 11, *Middle East: Population* (March 1951), p. 10. Europa Publications, *The Middle East: 1953* (1953), 3rd ed., p. 82. Issawi, *op. cit.,* p. 48.

9. Issawi, *op. cit.,* pp. 51, 152. Egyptian Government, Ministry of Finance and Economy, *Statistical Pocket Year Book 1952* (1953), pp. 22-23. U.N., *Review of Economic Conditions in the Middle East,* Supplement to *World Economic Report* (1951), pp. 36, 44, 53.

10. Egyptian Government . . . , *Statistical Pocket Year Book* (1953), pp. 98-105.

11. Hans Kohn, *Western Civilization in the Near East* (1936), p. 289.

12. Issawi, *op. cit.,* pp. 54-55.

13. Nurkse, *op. cit.,* p. 9.

14. H. Habib-Ayrout, *The Fellaheen* (1942), pp. 21, 110.

15. See H. A. R. Gibb, *Modern Trends in Islam* (1945).

16. G. E. von Grunebaum, *Islam* (1955), chap. XI. See also W. C. Smith, "The Intellectuals" in S. N. Fisher (ed.), *Social Forces in the Middle East* (1955).

17. R. I. I. A., *The Middle East,* 2nd ed. (1954), p. 250.

18. Issawi, *op. cit.,* p. 261n. *Annuaire Statistique* (Annual). Official statistics are cited only in the absence of independent estimates and with the caution that even by Middle East standards Egyptian statistics are capricious.

19. Hollingworth, *op. cit.,* p. 229.

20. Morroe Berger, *Bureaucracy and Society in Modern Egypt: A Study of the Higher Civil Service* (1957).

21. *Annuaire Statistique* (1952), p. 296.

22. R. Matthews and M. Akrawi, *Education in the Arab Countries of the Near East* (1949), p. 84.

23. *Annuaire Statistique* (1952), p. 284.

24. Issawi, *op. cit.,* pp. 61-62.

25. Matthews and Akrawi, *op. cit.,* p. 84.

26. E. A. Speiser, *The U. S. and The Near East* (1947), p. 144.

27. Nasser, *op. cit.,* pp. 67-68. Further page references to this book are given after each quotation.

28. D. Warriner, *Land Reform and Development in the Middle East* (1957), p. 48.

29. Mohammed Naguib, *Egypt's Destiny* (1955), pp. 215-216. Further page references to this book are given after each quotation.

30. Text quoted from *Egyptian Mail* No. 10993-268 (February 27, 1954), pp. 1, 4.

31. The classic short essay and long bibliography is Robert Michel's article "Intellectuals" in the *Encyclopedia of the Social Sciences.* On Egypt see Smith, *op. cit.*

32. Majid Khadduri, "The Army Officer," in Fisher (ed.), *op. cit.,* p. 178. Also his "Role of the Military in Middle East Politics," *American Political Science Review,* XLVII, 2 (June 1953), pp. 511-524.

33. UNESCO, *World Communications* (1951), p. 142. A subsequent UNESCO report on *Progress of Literacy in Various Countries* (1953), p. 205, cited the 1937 census figure of 85.2% illiteracy in the population *over ten years old.* The differential is understandable since literacy is proportionately highest among the 7-12 year olds, the current school population. Within the next decade, in fact, many of these will have forgotten their rudimentary 3 R's through disuse. Comparisons with independent estimates suggest that great care is needed in dealing with official Egyptian figures on literacy and education, since these are presented to show the best possible picture. Even its brightest aspect, however, is dim.

34. Issawi, *op. cit.*, pp. 182-3.
35. *World Communications*, p. 37.
36. Europa Publications, *The Middle East* (1953), pp. 102, 107.
37. *World Communications*, pp. 38, 176, 196.
38. *Statistique Annuaire* (1953), p. 632.
39. Film Centre, *The Use of Mobile Cinema and Radio Vans* (UNESCO, 1949), p. 25.
40. *World Communications*, p. 61.
41. *Ibid.*, p. 62.
42. Osgood Carruthers, "Voice of Arabs Stirs Mideast," *New York Times* (January 15, 1956).
43. Edmond Taylor, *The Real Case Against Nasser* (1956), p. 26.
44. *Ibid.*, pp. 26-27.
45. Quoted in W. Z. Laqueur, *Nationalism and Communism in the Middle East* (1956).
46. Personal communication from an officer of the Egyptian Information Department (dated March 26, 1957).
47. G. E. von Grunebaum, *op. cit.*, p. 229.
48. Taylor, *op. cit.*, p. 34.
49. *Atlantic Monthly*, October 1956 (italics mine).

CHAPTER EIGHT

SYRIA: THE LURES OF EXTREMISM

1. All figures and quotations in this section, unless otherwise noted, are from these sources: *The Economic Development of Syria*, Report of a Mission Organized by the International Bank for Reconstruction and Development at the Request of the Government of Syria (1955), pp. 10-11, 18-26, 133-34, 369-74, 400, 453. U.N. *Review of Economic Conditions in the Middle East, 1951-1952* (1953), pp. 42, 64, 66. See also A. Farra, *L'Industrialisation en Syrie* (1950). The official labor force estimate is 70,000 but the U.N. estimate of 50,000 "excluded smaller business establishments, areas untouched by organized labour," apprentices and helpers, some 15,000 construction workers, and the craftsmen.
2. Estimated to be over $250 by C. Issawi, "Economic and Social Foundations of Democracy in the Middle East," *International Affairs*, XXXII (January 1, 1956), p. 40.
3. D. Warriner, *Land and Poverty in the Middle East* (1948), p. 88. N. Sayem-Addahr, "Agrarian Structure and Economic Development in Syria," Ph.D. dissertation, Columbia University (1952), pp. 132-33.
4. Issawi, *op. cit.*, pp. 31-33.
5. The media data are taken from: UNESCO, *Reports on the Facilities of Mass Communication* IV (1950), pp. 542-43.
6. *Ibid.*, p. 219.
7. U.N., *Preliminary Report on the World Social Situation* (1952), p. 62.
8. A. H. Hourani, *Syria and Lebanon*, pp. 199-206; R.I.I.A., *The Middle East* (1955), pp. 471-72; G. Antonius, *The Arab Awakening* (1938), pp. 381-82.
9. A. N. Poliak, *Feudalism in Egypt, Syria, Palestine and the Lebanon* (1939).
10. Warriner, *op. cit.*, pp. 93-94. Also A. Khuri, "Land Tenure," in S. B. Himadeh, *Economic Organization of Syria* (1936), p. 66.
11. *Ibid.*, p. 91. "Conditions of Work in Syria and the Lebanon Under French Mandate," ILO, XXXIX, 4 (April 1939), p. 526. République Française: Ministère des Affaires Etrangères, *Rapport à la Société des Nations sur la Situation de la Syrie et du Liban* (1938).
12. R.I.I.A., *op. cit.*, p. 468.
13. They numbered 360,000 in 1930, and today officially only 150,-000. R. Widmer, "Population," in S. B. Himadeh, *op. cit.*, p. 12.
14. V. Vacca, "Notizie Biografiche Su Uomini Politici Ministri e Deputati Siriani," *Oriente Moderno*, XVII (October 10, 1937), pp. 471-95.

15. M. Perlmann (Personal Letter).

16. R.I.I.A., *op. cit.*, p. 474.

17. H. H. Williams, *Foreign Study for Syrians*, Occasional Paper No. 4 (January 1953), Institute of International Education.

18. Antonius, *op. cit.*, p. 374.

19. R. D. Matthews and M. Akrawi, *Education in the Arab Countries of The Near East* (1949), p. 352. In 1951-52: in government schools, 237,775; in national elementary schools (the former private schools), 52,270; in foreign elementary schools, only 7,140. *Statistical Abstract of Syria*, 1951 and 1952, Damascus, p. 52.

20. P. K. Hitti, *History of Syria, including Lebanon and Palestine* (1951), p. 472.

21. R.I.I.A., *op. cit.*, p. 482.

22. M. Khadduri, "The Role of the Military in Middle East Politics," *The American Political Science Review*, XLVII (June 2, 1953), p. 517.

23. *Statistical Abstract of Syria*, 1950, p. 49; Williams, *op. cit.*, pp. 32, 50; *The Economic Development of Syria*, p. 156.

24. A. Hourani, *Minorities in the Arab World* (1947), p. 82.

25. G. M. Haddad, *Fifty Years of Modern Syria and Lebanon* (1950), pp. 183, 197-98.

26. T. C. Young, "The Social Support of Current Iranian Policy," *Middle East Journal*, VI, 2 (Spring 1952), p. 130.

27. *The Economic Development of Syria*, p. 196.

28. R. Levy, *Sociology of Islam* (1930-33).

29. Hitti, *op. cit.*, pp. 628-29.

30. D. Lerner, *The Nazi Elite* (1951), pp. 87-90.

31. For a summary of Mrs. Vatolina's views see "Communism: Prospects in the Middle East: A Soviet View," *Jewish Observer and Middle East Review*, IV, 50, pp. 11-12. For the U. S. estimate, see *The Strategy and Tactics of World Communism*, Report of Subcommittee No. 5 National and International Movements, Supplement IIIB, *Communism in the Near East*, U. S. Congress, House Committee on Foreign Affairs (1949), pp. 12-13.

32. Hourani, *Syria and Lebanon*, p. 91.

33. H. D. Lasswell, D. Lerner, and C. E. Rothwell, *The Comparative Study of Elites* (1952), p. 11.

34. International Press Institute, *News From the Middle East*, Geneva (1953).

35. D. Lerner, "The Strategy of Truth," in *Sykewar* (1949).

36. Khadduri, *op. cit.*, p. 518.

37. J. Kimche, *Seven Fallen Pillars* (1950), pp. 296, 299-300.

38. P. M. G., "President Shishakli and the Shaping of Syrian Policy," *The World Today*, IX (December 12, 1953), pp. 521-22; "Democracy Must Wait," *Time* (February 8, 1954), LVIII, 6, p. 33.

39. *Second Statement on Achievements of Syria's Government of the New Regime During the Last Three Months*, March-June 1952. Address by H. E. General Fawzi Selo, Chief of State, Prime Minister, to the Syrian People, Issued by the Directorate General of Information, Damascus, n.d.

40. R. Alan, "Palace Politics in the Damascus Oasis," *Commentary*, XV, 2 (February 1953), p. 155.

41. *The Economic Development of Syria*, p. 55.

42. *Second Statement on Achievements . . .* , pp. 7-8, 12, 19.

43. Khadduri, *op. cit.*, p. 523.

44. Chronology, *Middle East Journal*, VIII, 2 (Spring 1954), p. 185.

45. P. M. G., *op. cit.*, pp. 522-24.

46. Chronologies, *The Middle East Journal*, IV, V, VI, VII.

47. "Soviet is Pushing its Cause in Syria," *The New York Times* (March 19, 1956).

48. Mrs. L. N. Vatolina believes that chances for the spread of Communism are best in Syria and Lebanon; but in the latter "close collabora-

tion with one section is bound to antagonize other communities." (See note 31)

49. W. Z. Laqueur, *Communism and Nationalism in the Middle East* (1956), p. 161.

50. Khalid Bakdash, "For the Successful Struggle for Peace, National Independence, and Democracy We Must Resolutely Turn Toward the Workers and Peasants." Report to plenary session of the central command of the Communist Party in Syria and Lebanon held January 1951. Translated by Harold Glidden, *Middle East Journal*, VII, 2 (Winter 1953), pp. 206-16.

CHAPTER NINE

JORDAN: ONE STATE WITH TWO PEOPLES

1. R. Patai (ed.), *The Hashemite Kingdom of Jordan*, Human Relations Area Files (1956), p. 45.

2. P. K. Hitti, "Historical Setting," *Ibid.*, p. 35.

3. G. Antonius, *The Arab Awakening: The Story of the Arab National Movement* (1938), p. 357.

4. F. I. Qubain, "Literature" and T. Succar, "Music" in Patai, *op. cit.*

5. I. Chizik, "The Political Parties in Transjordania," *Royal Central Asian Journal*, XXII, Part I, 1935, pp. 96-99; A. Konikoff, *Transjordan: An Economic Survey*, 2nd Edition (1946), p. 24; Colonel F. G. Peake, "Transjordan," *Royal Central Asian Journal*, XXVI, Part III (1939), pp. 384, 391.

6. Konikoff, *op. cit.*, p. 18.

7. Patai, "Culture Groups," in Patai, *op. cit.*, p. 66; E. T. Mogannam, "Developments in the Legal System of Jordan," *Middle East Journal*, VI, 2 (Spring 1952), pp. 194-206.

8. W. Z. Laqueur, *Communism and Nationalism in the Middle East* (1956), pp. 124-25.

. 9. Royal Institute of International Affairs, *The Middle East: A Political and Economic Survey* (1954), p. 360.

10. R. Matthews and M. Akrawi, *Education in the Arab Countries of the Near East* (1949), p. 544; R.I.I.A., *op. cit.*, p. 560; Konikoff, *op. cit.*, p. 18.

11. R. Patai and F. Qubain, "The Town," in Patai, *op. cit.*, p. 268.

12. Report of the Director of the UNRWAPRNE, GAOR: Sixth Session, Supplement No. 16 (A/1905) (1951), p. 2.

13. K. Davis, "Population Analysis," and C. Issawi, "Agricultural Potential," in Patai, *op. cit.*, pp. 42, 572.

14. J. Baster: "The prospect of the Jordanian economy absorbing during the next ten years the present unemployed refugees plus the natural population increase of the refugees and their hosts . . . [is] remote, if the persons absorbed are required to be self-supporting and independent of further continuous aid from abroad." "The Economic Problems of Jordan," *International Affairs*, XXXI (January 1, 1955), p. 35.

15. Report of the Director of the UNRWAPRNE, *op. cit.*, p. 1.

16. Issawi, "Labor Relations and Organization," in Patai, *op. cit.*, p. 429.

17. U.N., Department of Economic Affairs, *Review of Economic Conditions in the Middle East, 1951-1952* (1953), p. 112.

18. Patai, *op. cit.*, pp. 421-23 and p. 45; R.I.I.A., p. 150, estimates 60% urbanization.

19. Europa Publications, *The Middle East: 1953* (1953), p. 189; Patai, *op. cit.*, p. 274.

20. School population also varies erratically. In 1951 about 115,000 students (already a threefold increase) enrolled in 451 State schools, 210 private schools (catering mostly to Christians) and 54 UNRWA schools for refugees. Two years later, there were 170,000 students in all types of schools. But few teachers had professional training, only 6% holding college diplomas, the majority being secondary school graduates. Over

three-fourths of elementary school pupils were in the first four grades, indicating a very high rate of attrition. Patai, *op. cit.*, pp. 286-87.

21. All media figures in this section are taken from UNESCO, *Report of the Commission on Technical Needs* (1950), pp. 208, 356-57, 531 and UNESCO, *World Communications* (1956), p. 160. See also J. C. Hurewitz and W. Sands, "Propaganda," in Patai, *op. cit.*, p. 548.

22. U. S. Information Agency, *Geographical Distribution of Radio Sets and Characteristics of Radio Owners in Countries of the World* (September 1954), p. 30.

23. Patai, *op. cit.*, p. 382.

24. Laqueur, *op. cit.*, pp. 124-25.

25. T. McFadden, *Daily Journalism in the Arab States* (1953), p. 43.

26. International Press Institute, *News From the Middle East* (1954), p. 24

27. E. Wright, "Abdullah's Jordan: 1947-1951," *Middle East Journal*, V. 4 (Autumn 1951), p. 454.

28. Peake, *op. cit.*, p. 391.

29. Wright, *op. cit.*, pp. 449, 457-58.

30. *The New York Times* (May 7, 1951), p. 12.

31. Hurewitz and Sands, "Political Dynamics," in Patai, *op. cit.*, p. 524.

32. *The New York Times* (July 28, 1956).

33. Glubb Pasha, *The New York Times* (March 16, 1956).

34. Laqueur, *op. cit.*, pp. 126, 132.

35. R.I.I.A., *op. cit.*, p. 350.

36. J. B. Glubb, *The Story of the Arab Legion* (1948), p. 195; Eliahu Epstein, "The Nomad Problem in Transjordan," *Palestine and Middle East Economic Magazine* (February 2, 1937), p. 87 f.; Konikoff, *op. cit.*, pp. 18, 47-48.

37. C. S. Coon, *Caravan: The Story of the Middle East* (1951), p. 201.

38. On the "two-step flow" see E. Katz and P. F. Lazarsfeld, *Personal Influence* (1955), chap. II.

39. A. Hourani, *Syria and Lebanon* (1946), p. 64; Glubb, "The Beduins of Northern Iraq," *Royal Central Asian Journal*, XXII, Part I (1935), pp. 18-19.

40. "Beduin of the Negeb: Sons and Fathers of the Desert," *Palestine and Middle East Economic Magazine*, II (November 1937), p. 526.

41. Wright, *op. cit.*, p. 458.

42. *Islamic Review*, XL (January 1, 1952), p. 3.

43. C. C. Adams, *Islam and Modernism in Egypt* (1933), p. 110.

CHAPTER TEN

IRAN: IN A BIPOLAR WORLD

1. H. L. Hoskins, *The Middle East* (1954), p. 166.

2. G. Lenczowski, *Russia and the West in Iran, 1918-48* (1949).

3. Hoskins, *op. cit.*, p. 13.

4. *Ibid.*, p. 190.

5. H. F. Grady, "How The Iranian Crisis Began," *The New Leader* (April 27, 1953), pp. 3-4.

6. Hoskins, *op. cit.*, pp. 173-74.

7. *Ibid.*, p. 171.

8. A. K. S. Lambton, *Landlord and Peasant in Persia* (1953), p. 393.

9. *Ibid.*, p. 395.

10. J. A. Hobson, *Imperialism* (1954), p. 134. See pp. 206-22 for fuller analysis of the relationship between imperialism and dupery.

11. Czeslaw Milosz, *The Captive Mind* (1953). Also review by D. Lerner in *American Sociological Review*, XIX (August 1954), pp. 488-89.

12. R. N. Frye in (with L. V. Thomas), *The United States and Turkey and Iran* (1951), p. 209.

13. See: J. Morier, *The Adventures of Hajji Baba of Ispahan* (1949).

14. Hoskins, *op. cit.*, p. 175.

15. Frye, *op. cit.*, pp. 183, 185.

16. Hoskins, *op. cit.*, p. 165.

17. As no census has ever been

taken, the following illustrates the range of authoritative estimates:

14-16,000,000—*Statesman's Yearbook,* (1955), p. 1289.

15,000,000—R. N. Frye, *op. cit.,* p. 7.

16,549,837—Overseas Economic Consultants, *Iran,* H.M.S.O. (1948), p. 49.

17,750,000—Overseas Consultants, Inc., *Report on the Seven Year Development Plan* . . . (1949) II, p. 5.

18,772,000—Europa Publications, Ltd., *The Middle East: 1953,* p. 249.

19,139,563—estimate by Iranian Ministry of Interior in 1951, cited in *Statesman's Yearbook* (1955), p. 1289.

19,798,000—U.N., *Population and Vital Statistics Reports* (January 1954) (official government estimate).

18. M. A. Djamalzadeh, "An Outline of the Social and Economic Structure of Iran," *International Labor Review,* LXIII (January 1951), p. 26.

19. On these demographic estimates, compare sources cited in Note 17. A high figure of 2% net natural increase is given by L. P. Elwell-Sutton (personal letter).

20. U.N. Research Memorandum No. 11, p. 10.

21. Overseas Consultants, Inc., *op. cit.,* II, p. 82 and Exhibit B-17.

22. For small variations in the sample bases of Tables 16-20, see the BASR report by Ringer and Sills.

23. For clinical analysis of this personality type see H. D. Lasswell, *Psychopathology and Politics* (1930). Also *Power and Personality* (1948) and *The Analysis of Political Behavior* (1948).

24. *The New York Times* (December 27, 1953).

25. M. Clarke, "New Iran Premier Foe of Foreigners," *The New York Times* (May 7, 1951), p. 11.

26. *Ibid.* (May 7, 1951), p. 11. Europa Publications, *op. cit.,* p. 405.

27. See R. N. Frye, *op. cit.*

28. C. Daniel, "Mossedegh Career Unique in Iran," *The New York Times* (March 1, 1953), IV, p. 5.

29. M. Panter-Downes, "Letter from Teheran," *The New Yorker* (April 21, 1956), p. 131.

CHAPTER ELEVEN

RETROSPECT AND PROSPECT

1. D. Lerner and D. Riesman, "Self and Society," *Explorations* (June 1955).

2. Cf. H. D. Lasswell, D. Lerner, C. E. Rothwell, *The Comparative Study of Elites* (1952).

3. S. N. Fisher (ed.), *Social Forces in the Middle East* (1955).

4. *Ibid.,* p. 152.

5. H. A. R. Gibb, *Modern Trends in Islam* (1947), p. 48.

6. Fisher, *op. cit.,* p. 200.

7. G. E. von Grunebaum, *Islam* (1955), p. 229.

8. Fisher, *op. cit.,* pp. 200-01.

9. M. Berger, *Bureaucracy and Society in Modern Egypt* (1957), p. 185.

10. J. W. Williamson, *In A Persian Oilfield* (1927), chaps. XI, XVII, XVIII.

11. See, especially, the work of E. E. Hagen and P. N. Rosenstein-Rodan.

Index

F
A